DATE DUE

JE 27 '95			
JE 17 '94			
DE 27 '94			
JY 27 '95			
MY 21 '97			
DE 9 '06			
OC 14 '09			

DEMCO 38-296

Speaking of Diversity

Speaking of Diversity

Language and Ethnicity in Twentieth-Century America

PHILIP GLEASON

THE JOHNS HOPKINS UNIVERSITY PRESS
BALTIMORE AND LONDON

This book has been brought to publication in part by support from the Institute for Scholarship in the Liberal Arts, College of Arts and Letters, University of Notre Dame.

The Johns Hopkins University Press
701 West 40th Street, Baltimore, Maryland 21211-2190
The Johns Hopkins Press Ltd., London

∞

The paper used in this book meets the minimum requirements of American National Standard for Information Sciences—Permanence of Paper for Printed Library Materials, ANSI Z39.48-1984.

LIBRARY OF CONGRESS CATALOGING-IN-PUBLICATION DATA

Gleason, Philip.
    Speaking of diversity : language and ethnicity in twentieth-century America / Philip Gleason.
        p.   cm.
    Includes bibliographical references and index.
    ISBN 0-8018-4295-6
    1. Ethnicity—United States. 2. United States—Ethnic relations. 3. Minorities—United   States.   4. United   States—Religion. 5. Catholics—United States.   I. Title.
E184.A1G563   1992
305.8′00973′09045—dc20   91-35706

Contents

Introduction

Arthur O. Lovejoy once remarked that despite a popular belief to the contrary, philosophers are "persons who suffer from a morbid solicitude to know what they are talking about." Although he put the point amusingly, Lovejoy meant it seriously. And since the passage occurs in one of his earliest and best-known essays in the history of ideas, "On the Discrimination of Romanticisms," we can safely assume that he thought this way of characterizing philosophers ought to apply to intellectual historians as well.[1] I think it also applies with special force to historians who deal with ethnic and religious issues. The essays collected in this book are intended to illustrate that conviction; but in keeping with the spirit of Lovejoy's remark, let us begin by inquiring just what he was talking about.

If knowing what one is talking about is taken to mean doing one's homework, performing the necessary research, or getting the facts straight, then historians surely have as good a claim to Lovejoy's quasi definition as philosophers. Indeed, most would probably feel they have a better claim, since they tend to regard philosophers as indisposed to research and only moderately interested in empirical evidence.

But simply doing one's homework was not what Lovejoy had in mind when he spoke of philosophers' morbid solicitude to know what they are talking about. The context of his remarks leaves no doubt that he was talking about conceptual clarity, about knowing what one means by the terms one uses. Relatively few historians—especially American historians—would claim that Lovejoy's witticism, thus understood, captures their essential professional concerns. True, there are occasional outstanding works, such as Daniel T. Rodgers's *Contested Truths*, which focus directly on how the meaning of key terms has shifted over time, and the so-called linguistic turn (i.e., the influence of postmodern literary and cultural theory) has alerted intellectual historians to the importance of "discourse." But "discourse" is less a clarifying concept than a candidate for clarification itself, and prominent intellectual historians such as Bruce

Kuklick and David Hollinger have criticized the hermetic quality of some of the work inspired by the "linguistic turn."[2] For these reasons, the recent talk about discourse cannot be taken as evidence that historians as a group have been converted from their relative indifference to terminological precision.

The difference between historians and philosophers in this regard reflects a fundamental difference in what we might call cognitive temperament. Historians and philosophers simply go at their intellectual tasks in different ways. And although I believe that historians ought to cultivate a greater sensitivity to terminology, the impatience with these matters they sometimes display is not the result of sheer perversity. At least three reasons for it can be suggested.

First, historians characteristically believe that immersion in empirical detail puts them in the most rewarding contact with what William James called the "rich thicket of reality." By contrast, they are apt to associate concern for definitional niceties with the ultra-abstractionist's preference for "skinny outlines" and barren generalizations.[3] Second, the social scientists and other conceptualizers who deal with historical data so often disagree among themselves on fundamental points that workaday historians can plausibly excuse themselves for bypassing definitional problems wherever possible. Finally, historians of ethnicity (among others) can argue that their highly informal approach to terminological issues is justified because the concepts that figure most prominently in their accounts—"nativism," "racism," "prejudice," "assimilation," and so on—long ago entered the realm of general public discourse, losing in the process whatever conceptual precision they may once have possessed.

Many objections might be made to this set of reasons, but let us assume for the sake of argument that they have some validity. Nothing further need be said about the first one, which philosophers might be disposed to regard as little more than an invidious restatement of the temperamental difference between practitioners of the two disciplines. Points 2 and 3, however, deserve a word of elaboration because, to the extent that what they assert is true, they should actually be understood as reasons for historians to be more, rather than less, sensitive to conceptual and linguistic issues.

With respect to point 2, the historian who deals with subjects on which conceptual disagreements exist, or where definitions of key terms vary, must be painstakingly attentive to these matters in order to avoid pitfalls of the apples-and-oranges variety. While this may require explicit discussion of theoretical points, it does not betoken abandoning history for speculation. On the contrary, it is entailed by a methodological principle that all historians accept: evidence must be handled carefully and critically.

The same consideration applies to the third point, for the widespread use of terms such as *racism, ethnicity,* and *pluralism* in popular discussion in itself constitutes an important kind of historical evidence. The meaning of these terms, when so used, is inevitably fuzzy, and their application correspondingly loose and overlapping. But that does not detract from their importance as evidence. Several other facts add materially to their evidentiary value: that their usage is often charged with passion; that the terms themselves take on heavy moral overtones, both positive (as in most usages of *pluralism*) and negative (as in virtually all usages of *prejudice*); that their salience in public discourse, and the connotations they bear, change over time; and above all, that the terms in which the discussion of ethnic and religious issues is carried on go a long way toward determining how those issues are understood and evaluated. All this makes the popular terminology of ethnicity historical evidence of the highest importance.

The essays that follow will, I hope, serve to illustrate and substantiate this highly compressed statement of the reasons that justify historical study of the terminology of diversity. It is perhaps pertinent to add here that my own convictions on this score derive from having carried out these investigations; they were not the precipitating cause for undertaking the research in the first place. In other words, I did not embark on the first of these studies out of any prior conviction that the semantic, or conceptual history, approach would be particularly rewarding. More on that in a moment, but before commenting on the background and genesis of the essays, I want to state explicitly what will soon become evident to the reader, namely, that they are not based on, nor do they intentionally incorporate, any systematically articulated theory of language, rhetoric, hermeneutics, or "discourse." Most of them were originally written before historians had heard much about the linguistic turn, and I have not attempted to revise them in the light of recent interest in these matters. Although they deal with matters that can legitimately be called linguistic, they are the product of the traditional, commonsense approach conventionally employed by historians. In other words, they reflect the characteristic methodological bias of the historian. But I am immodest enough to claim that they also illuminate important conceptual issues in ways that cannot be duplicated by any other method.

The focus on terminology is most consistently central in part 1, "Coming to Terms with Ethnicity." The first of these essays, on the melting pot as a symbol of ethnic interaction, was what got me started on this line of investigation. As I noted above, I did not undertake it from any particular sensitivity to the importance of language. I had recently completed a doctoral dissertation that involved issues of ethnicity and religion, and I was looking for a new project. An offhand comment by one of my professors in graduate school, Thomas N. Brown, had earlier alerted me to the variety of meanings that the melting pot had for different people. Sometime thereafter, I ran across Henry Pratt Fairchild's shocking suggestion that the village dog pound was a better symbol than the melting pot for what immigration was doing to American nationality and culture. That really caught my attention, and, after the dissertation was out of the way, I began collecting other specimens of melting pot usage. The myth-and-symbol approach to American studies, which was still in some vogue, no doubt helped convince me that the project was worth pursuing more systematically.

That, as nearly as I can reconstruct it, was the process that led to the original melting pot essay. Researching and writing it persuaded me that the semantic history approach was worthwhile, for it seemed quite clear that the ambiguities of usage of *melting pot* not only reflected but also contributed to conceptual confusion about the substantive issues that the melting pot somehow symbolized. This conclusion had purely historical interest when the article was published in 1964, for the melting pot had yet to make its comeback as part of the terminology of the ethnic revival. That happened with a vengeance over the next fifteen years, and the updating of *melting pot* usage that constitutes the second essay in this collection documents its undiminished capacity to confuse, along with a much enhanced power to evoke outrage on the part of many of those who use it.

Research for the second essay confirmed what was obvious to the casual observer, namely, that those who reject the melting pot typically champion "pluralism" as the preferred alternative. But it also revealed something not at all obvious: that in many contexts of usage, *pluralism* (or *cultural pluralism*) differs very little in meaning from certain versions of *melting pot*. This finding suggested the value of a more systematic historical comparison of "pluralism" and "assimilation," the concept conventionally symbolized by the melting pot. Chapter 3, which embodies the results of that investigation, shows that the concept of pluralism is at least as ambiguous as the symbol of the melting pot, has often blended with the latter, and has been equally productive of confusion.

Between the writing of the second and third essays, I undertook a more ambitious investigation of how ethnic factors figured in collective American self-understanding over the entire span of U.S. history from

independence to the present. The results were published under the title
"American Identity and Americanization" in the *Harvard Encyclopedia
of American Ethnic Groups* (1980). Although highly relevant to the
themes of the present volume, that essay is not reproduced here because
of its length, because it is already available in a paperback edition, and
because it would overlap too much with some of the other essays included
in the collection.[4] It deserves mention at this point, however, because it
reinforced my belief in the value of this historical approach, and because
it called my attention to, or deepened my understanding of, various issues
discussed in these pages, including the relationship between pluralism
and assimilation.

Chapter 4, "Minorities (Almost) All," is not so direct an offshoot of
the encyclopedia project as some of the other chapters, but I place it
next in order since, like the first three essays, it too deals with a term/
concept that applies to the group level of ethnic interaction. The importance of the minority concept and certain ambiguities in its usage first
attracted my attention while I was working on "Americans All" (chapter
5), which was originally published in 1981. Although the term is briefly
noted there, its historical evolution was first sketched out for a conference
on the life and work of Louis Adamic in 1981 and brought to its present
state of elaboration for another conference in 1989. Chapter 5 on *identity*
differs not only in focusing on a term rooted more in psychology than
sociology but also in that it derives directly from my assignment for the
ethnic encyclopedia. Since the editors insisted the article had to be about
"American identity," I had to establish what *identity* meant before I could
discuss it historically. Tracing its usage not only aided me in deciding
how to approach the larger subject but also persuaded me that the semantic history of the term was worth separate treatment. Chapter 5 is
the result.

Research for the encyclopedia entry made me realize for the first
time that World War II not only changed American thinking about the
role the nation should play on the world stage but also reshaped Americans' collective understanding of themselves as a people. This came
about because the wartime stress on the need for national unity based
on "the ideals America stands for" gave unprecedented salience to the
ideological dimension of American identity and caused ethnicity (not to
mention race) to be downplayed. These developments were obscured at
the time because of the emphasis placed on "tolerance for diversity" as
an element in the democratic ideology, which made it appear that "pluralism" was carrying everything before it, whereas the real imperative
was ideological unity. Besides furnishing a striking instance of how the

terms employed can baffle understanding of what is taking place, this paradoxical wartime development not only provided the matrix from which sprang the postwar campaigns against prejudice, discrimination, and segregation; it also paved the way for the repression of ideological dissent in the era of the Cold War. On another front, so to speak, the war also reawakened interest in the study of "national character," especially "the American character," and contributed mightily to the development of the new interdisciplinary discipline known as American studies.

These themes, which were adumbrated in my contribution to the *Harvard Encyclopedia of American Ethnic Groups*, recur in various contexts in the essays collected here. But the subject is so important, and so little studied, that it deserves to be highlighted by placing together as part 2, "World War II and American Identity," the three essays most directly relevant to the topic. Chapter 6, "Americans All," provides an overview of the subject, while chapter 7 shows how the great democratic revival of the late 1930s and early 1940s fed into the development of American studies and reshaped national self-understanding in a more general way. Chapter 8 explores the interreligious tensions that pitted Catholics against Protestants and secular liberals in the immediate postwar years. Although this essay might with equal justification be placed in part 3, it fits here because the controversies—in which the basic charge against Catholics was that their church was un-American—dramatized the tensions latent in the ideological revival and exposed some of the ambiguities of pluralism.

The story of Protestant/Catholic/secularist tensions provides a transition to part 3, "Religion and American Diversity," by reminding us that religion figured much more prominently as an element in intergroup relations at midcentury than it does today. Analytically, "religion" has been so undervalued in recent times that it comes as a shock to discover that in the fifties and early sixties, social scientists regarded the main confessional groupings (Protestant, Catholic, and Jewish) as very important categories of social analysis. Given everything that has happened on the racial, ethnic, and gender fronts since the 1960s, religion's decline as an interpretive principle is historically understandable. But if historians wish to do justice to the realities of an earlier time—even a time as recent as the first half of the twentieth century—they will have to develop a greater sensitivity to religion as an analytical category and as a factor in the intellectual and emotional lives of the people they are studying.

So much for exhortation. I hope the essays in part 3 will lend substance to the message. Chapter 9 offers evidence for the contention that religion was a key social category at midcentury by showing that Marcus L. Hansen's famous principle of third-generation interest ("what the son wants to forget the grandson wants to remember") attracted no notice at all until it was taken up by students of American Jewish life in the early 1950s. Will Herberg really put "Hansen's law" into circulation, but a number of other commentators interpreted the contemporary Jewish religious revival in similar terms. The essay also suggests several reasons why Jewishness was in those days interpreted in religious rather than ethnic terms, a phenomenon closely linked to World War II.

Chapter 10 is a more broad-ranging review of the way historians have dealt with the relationship of religion to immigration and American group life, paying particular attention to the role of education and to the elusive notion of "civil religion." The last of the essays applies to the particular case of American Catholics the conceptual history approach employed earlier in studying ethnic interaction in general. In tracing the usage by American Catholics of the terms *Americanism* and *Americanization* from their introduction in the 1850s to the present time, it reveals significant shifts in the way Catholics have conceptualized their relationship, and that of their church, to American culture and institutions. This essay has been extensively revised from a version published in 1973. The others are, except for minor editorial changes, republished here in their original form.

NOTES

1. Arthur O. Lovejoy, *Essays in the History of Ideas* (Baltimore, 1948), 232.

2. Daniel T. Rodgers, *Contested Truths: Keywords in American Politics since Independence* (New York, 1987); Bruce Kuklick, "New Directions in European Intellectual History," *Intellectual History Newsletter*, 9 (Spring 1984), 24–28; David A. Hollinger, "The Return of the Prodigal: The Persistence of Historical Knowing," *American Historical Review*, 94 (June 1989), 610–21. See also James T. Kloppenberg, "Deconstruction and Hermeneutic Strategies in "Intellectual History," *Intellectual History Newsletter*, 9 (April 1987), 3–22; and for an advocate's view, Peter Schöttler, "Historians and Discourse Analysis," *History Workshop*, no. 27 (Spring 1989), 37–65.

3. William James, "What Pragmatism Means," as reprinted in Perry Miller, ed., *American Thought* (New York, 1954), 176.

4. Philip Gleason, "American Identity and Americanization," in Stephan Thernstrom, Ann Orlov, and Oscar Handlin, eds., *Harvard Encyclopedia of American Ethnic Groups* (Cambridge, Mass., 1980), 31–58; reprinted in William Petersen, Michael Novak, and Philip Gleason, *Concepts of Ethnicity* (Cambridge, Mass., 1982), 57–149.

Part One

Coming to Terms
with Ethnicity

|| 1 ||

The Melting Pot: Symbol of Fusion or Confusion?

The background of this essay, insofar as I can reconstruct it, is described in the Introduction. This investigation convinced me that historical study of the terminology of ethnicity is a worthwhile and rewarding line of inquiry. Working through the materials discussed here persuaded me that the ambiguities of melting pot symbolism both reflected and contributed to confusion in the public mind about the processes of ethnic interaction actually taking place in American society. That is an unambiguous drawback to melting pot usage. But could it have been avoided? Not, in my opinion, by adopting any of the metaphoric alternatives reviewed in the essay—*stew, salad bowl, mosaic,* and so on. The problem, as I argue in the conclusion of this essay, is that none of these alternatives—and none of more recent vintage, for that matter—conveys as effectively as the melting pot the idea of ever-changing process, a crucial element in the process of ethnic interaction which any adequate symbol for it must somehow embody. As the concluding comments about cultural pluralism indicate, this project also alerted me to other terms and concepts that were candidates for historical analysis.

Most of this research on melting pot usage was done in 1962; the results were presented in abbreviated form at a meeting of the Ohio-Indiana American Studies Group, which took place at Case–Western Reserve University in May 1963, and the article was originally published the following year in *American Quarterly*. Hence when I say that the melting pot "is currently recovering a good deal of its respectability," the reader should keep in mind that I am referring to a time before the ethnic revival of the late sixties and early seventies. How that development affected melting pot usage is the subject of the second chapter.

Readers of the *Republic* will recall that after Socrates has outlined the structure of his ideal city, he devises a mythological explanation of its origin in order to furnish a symbolic representation and justification

3

for the distinctions that exist between Guardians, Auxiliaries, and the mass of the people. According to the "myth of the metals," the governing classes spring from races with gold or silver souls, while the ordinary citizens are members of a humbler iron-souled race. In the present century, a different sort of myth of the metals has flourished among Americans who would reject the Platonic variety. Our myth of the metals, compressed into one key image, is the melting pot. Unlike Plato's, it was not deliberately contrived to provide a supernatural sanction for the existing social order, but it is intimately related to the origins and nature of American society; and at a time when students of American civilization are absorbed in the scrutiny of images, myths, and symbols, it is appropriate to take a look also at the melting pot.

Hans Kohn regards the notion of the melting pot as "a fundamental trait of American nationalism,"[1] and few symbols associated with American nationality have entered more deeply into the language. References to the melting pot appear not only in formal studies of ethnic adjustment in the United States, but the expression is also used by foreign observers, and it crops up frequently in the press as well. A Chicago newspaper, for example, editorially commended the selection of Miss Hawaii to represent the United States in the 1962 Miss Universe contest because she was the "typical child" of "a true American-style 'melting pot' "; and before the 1962 election, Joseph Alsop surveyed a neighborhood in San Francisco where various ethnic elements "coexisted in an amiable melting-pot style." Television and the advertising industry also made use of the symbol. A national network's musical salute to the diverse elements in the American population was called "The Melting Pot"; and an advertisement for a recent book on cities asks, "Cities and suburbs—melting pots or trouble spots?"[2]

Melting pot, then, is both widely current and used by a variety of writers with the evident expectation that its meaning will be clear; there is much evidence to support the assertion that the "melting pot concept is stubbornly entrenched in our national subconscious" and that it is "part of the American official mythology."[3] On the other hand, there has been widespread disagreement about what the melting pot symbolizes, and many people have for differing reasons explicitly repudiated the symbol, believing that it distorts American experience or betrays American ideals. Is the melting pot even a symbol? The tendency to place the expression within quotation marks indicates that it is a somewhat self-conscious symbol, but at the same time it differs from such deliberately chosen national symbols as the flag; nor is it a specific real object, like the Liberty Bell, which is elevated to the level of a symbol because of some historical association. Still less does the melting pot resemble a symbolic document such as the Constitution or our national heroes who have taken on symbolic stature. And, indeed, the melting pot is often referred to as a "concept" or a "theory" rather than a symbol.

In the following pages I propose to trace some of the ways in which the term *melting pot* has been understood and used and to evaluate it as a symbol. To forestall as much confusion of terminology as possible, it would be well to make clear at the outset that the term can be used as a simile (America is like a melting pot), a metaphor (America is a melting pot) or a symbol (Millions of immigrants came tumbling into the melting pot). What distinguishes the symbol from the simile or metaphor is the absence of any overt comparison between two things that are understood to bear an analogical relationship to each other. The symbol is, as it were, cut loose freely from the thing symbolized and enjoys a separate existence of its own, while at the same time it is recognized as a metaphor, half of which is left unstated.[4] The melting pot is perhaps used with equal frequency as a metaphor and as a symbol, as these levels of figurative language are distinguished here; but since it has become so conventionally understood as representing the process of ethnic interaction, and since it has taken on such a vivid life of its own, the melting pot will, for the most part, be referred to here as a symbol.

The use of the melting pot as a symbol for the process whereby immigrants are absorbed into American society and somehow changed into Americans dates from 1908 when Israel Zangwill's play, *The Melting-Pot*, was first presented. The group of ideas and attitudes which the term is usually thought of as representing did not, however, originate with Zangwill but was much older. In general, that cluster of ideas included the belief that a new nation, a new national character, and a new nationality were forming in the United States and that the most heterogeneous human materials could be taken in and absorbed into this nationality. It was frequently maintained as a corollary that the "new man" who was to be produced by the cross-fertilization of various strains in America would be superior to any the world had previously seen; intermarriage between the different elements often figured as the chief agency in the formation of the new composite American.

The outstanding early statement of these notions was Crèvecoeur's celebrated answer to the question, "What then is the American, this new man?" Crèvecoeur's discussion in his *Letters from an American Farmer* (1782) developed or implied all of the themes listed above; moreover, he used the word *melt* to describe the process of forming a new nationality.

"Here," he wrote, "individuals of all nations are melted into a new race of men." As a result of his use of the word, and his treatment of the general theme, Crèvecoeur has been called the originator of the melting pot symbol.[5] This is incorrect. Crèvecoeur did not use the symbol of a melting pot at all, although he did give forceful expression to the ideas that it is often understood to symbolize. After Crèvecoeur, DeWitt Clinton used the key word *melt* in commenting on how the English tongue was "melting us down into one people," and in the 1840s a nativistic congressman recalled an earlier day when immigrants "*melted* into the mass of American population" instead of clannishly preserving their own identity.[6] But if anyone used the expression *melting pot*, it attracted no attention and did not enter into general usage. Emerson seems to have come closest to the symbol when he wrote in his journal that the energies of the various nationalities in America would "construct a new race, a new religion, a new state, a new literature," which would be as vigorous "as the new Europe which came out of the smelting-pot of the Dark Ages." It seems, however, that no particular attention was drawn to Emerson's metaphor until 1921.[7] Frederick Jackson Turner referred to the "composite nationality" of the American people in his famous address on the significance of the frontier in 1893; he described the frontier as a "crucible" where "the immigrants were Americanized, liberated, and fused into a mixed race, English in neither nationality nor characteristics."[8] Turner thus anticipated the use of a term that Zangwill used interchangeably with the *melting pot* in his drama.

No doubt there were others in the nineteenth century who used similar terms, or even *melting pot* itself; it remains true, nevertheless, that the melting pot symbol did not go into general usage until the presentation of Zangwill's play. An article entitled "Are We a People?" which was reported in July 1908, in the *Literary Digest* furnishes a suggestive bit of negative evidence. This discussion by Franklin H. Giddings, the Columbia sociologist, concerned itself with immigrant assimilation and American nationality and employed a number of figurative expressions such as *blending, fusing, melting, smelting process*, and *amalgam*. But it did not contain the expression *melting pot*.[9] It seems unlikely that this article would have contained no reference to the melting pot if it had appeared a year or so later.

A consideration of several background factors helps explain why *The Melting-Pot* had such impact and why the symbol passed into general use so rapidly. First, there was the tremendous immigration of the period. Between 1900 and the outbreak of World War I, an average of about one million immigrants a year entered the United States. Predominantly "new

immigrants" from Southern and Eastern Europe who gathered in con-
spicuous enclaves in the great cities, these millions attracted much public
attention, and the "immigration problem," which a governmental commission investigated to the tune of forty-one volumes, became involved
in practically all the political and social issues of the Progressive Period.
Public attitudes were shifting and uncertain in these years, which John
Higham calls the most obscure in the whole history of American nativism.[10] There were strong currents of opinion unfriendly to free immigration and fearful of the nation's ability to absorb the newcomers. But
the return of prosperity and the military and imperial feats at the turn
of the century engendered a surge of nationalistic self-confidence
strongly reinforcing the traditional view that America could welcome and
assimilate all who came to her shores. Zangwill's play thus appeared at
a time when there were millions of immigrants in the country who were
themselves immediately concerned with the matter of assimilation, and
when the American people at large were troubled and uncertain about
the question. The play was popular, the title was known to hundreds of
thousands who never saw it performed, the times required discussion of
immigration, and there was need for a handy and generally accepted
symbol for the whole complicated business—more favorable circumstances for launching the new symbol could hardly be imagined.[11]

The Melting-Pot opened in Washington on October 5, 1908. Theodore Roosevelt was among the first-nighters and later referred to it as
an "extraordinarily able and powerful play." "I do not know when I have
seen a play that stirred me as much," he wrote to Zangwill. Roosevelt
and Oscar Straus, secretary of commerce and labor, were both quoted
in subsequent advertising as saying, "It is a great play," but Roosevelt
probably attracted more attention to it by criticizing some lines that
portrayed Americans as taking a lighthearted view of divorce and public
corruption.[12] The passage was rewritten by Zangwill, and the play moved
to Chicago, where it played for one week and a short time later returned
for a longer run. By September 6, 1909, when it opened in New York,
The Melting-Pot had already been mentioned by Jane Addams as a play
whose title could furnish the theme for an important sociological treatise,
and the Literary Digest referred to it as a "much-discuss drama."[13]

Although the New York critics were unenthusiastic, The Melting-
Pot played 136 times and "the public crowd[ed] the performances," according to one reviewer, who explained its popularity by saying, "It is a
play of the people, touched with the fire of democracy, and lighted ra-
diantly with the national vision."[14] Oddly enough, it was an English Jew
who was said to have captured the American spirit and who gave the

nation a new symbol for itself. Israel Zangwill had already established himself as a novelist and dramatist, especially by his *Children of the Ghetto*, and he was also the leading promoter of a modified Zionist program, being the founder of the Jewish Territorial Organization. His work in assisting Jewish emigrants familiarized Zangwill with the immigration situation in the United States, and it is a mistake to assert, as some critics of the melting pot have done, that he was simply naive and uninformed about the state of affairs in America. Furthermore, Zangwill's essay *The Principle of Nationalities* indicates that he had pondered long on themes related to nationalism and the interaction of different national groups in the same state; several of the ideas that are presented dramatically in *The Melting-Pot* are restated in more systematic fashion in this study, published in 1917.[15] A decade earlier, however, Zangwill had declared that *The Melting-Pot* was a *"Tendenz-Schauspiel"* in the sense that it dramatized a problem rather than trying to provide an answer to it.[16]

The principal "problem" that Zangwill dealt with in *The Melting-Pot* concerned the situation of the Jews in the United States. This, of course, reflected his overriding preoccupation with the destiny of the Jews in the modern world and his conviction that for Jews it was a question of "renationalization or denationalization." To Zangwill, this set of alternatives meant that Jews should either acquire a homeland and develop their own nationality in their own nation, or they should become really and inwardly part of the nation in which they found themselves, thus "denationalizing" themselves as a distinct people.[17] The notion of the United States as a melting pot—a place where Old World nationality drops away and various elements fuse into a new nationality—operates in the play as a general framework within which the drama of the Jewish protagonist is enacted.

The protagonist, whose speeches launched the melting pot as *the* symbol for the American assimilative process, is David Quixano, a young Jewish immigrant whose family has been murdered in the Kishineff pogrom; he is a composer who is at work on a great "American symphony" that will capture in music the vast racial and ethnic harmony gradually coming into being in America. David meets and falls in love with Vera, a settlement house worker who is also an immigrant from Russia. Vera is a Christian, but the lovers resolve to marry in spite of the religious difference, following David's conviction that in America immigrants are to cast off their inherited attitudes, loyalties, and prejudices. Then David learns that Vera's father is the Russian officer who directed the Kishineff massacre and whose face haunts David's memory of that terror. In his revulsion, he abruptly breaks off the romance with Vera, thus betraying in his own mind the ideal of the melting pot, which he interprets to mean that the European past is to have no hold at all upon the immigrant in America. After suffering remorse for this lapse from his principles, added to the customary agonies of a lover, David is reunited with Vera in the last scene, immediately after the triumphant performance of his American symphony. The play ends with a paean of praise and hope for the melting pot as David and Vera stand on the roof of the settlement house transfixed by the vision of the Statue of Liberty gilded in the distant sunset.

David is "prophetically exalted" by this vision and delivers the following speech, which deserves quotation as the play's fullest description of the working of the melting pot:

> It is the fires of God round His Crucible. There she lies, the great Melting-Pot—listen! Can't you hear the roaring and the bubbling? There gapes her mouth—the harbour where a thousand mammoth feeders come from the ends of the world to pour in their human freight. Ah, what a stirring and a seething! Celt and Latin, Slav and Teuton, Greek and Syrian,—black and yellow—
>
> [Vera] Jew and Gentile—
>
> Yes, East and West, and North and South, . . . how the great Alchemist melts and fuses them with his purging flame! Here shall they all unite to build the Republic of Man and the Kingdom of God. Ah, Vera, what is the glory of Rome and Jerusalem where all nations and races come to worship and look back, compared with the glory of America, where all races and nations come to labour and look forward!
>
> Peace, peace, to all ye unborn millions, fated to fill this giant continent—the God of our *children* give you Peace.[18]

In an earlier speech, which was used in advertising the play, David spoke of America as "God's Crucible, the great Melting-Pot where all the races of Europe are melting and re-forming"; he also asserted that "the real American"—the fusion of all races, the coming superman"—had not yet made his appearance, but was "only in the Crucible."[19]

These "incidental dithyrambs on the 'crucible' theme," as one reviewer called them,[20] do not constitute a very detailed theory of ethnic adjustment in the United States, but insofar as it specifically concerned the Jews in America, *The Melting-Pot* seemed clearly to preach the doctrine of complete assimilation. Jews who did not wish to forget their distinctive identity, it was suggested in one passage, should "work for a Jewish land" instead of emigrating to America. The emphasis on assimilation was not well received by many American Jews. An editorial in the *American Hebrew* called it a "counsel of despair" that could not be taken seriously, and several years later a Jewish writer declared that the Jews had no intention of denying their heritage for the contents of any pot—even though it be the Melting-Pot."[21]

Aside from the Jewish question, *The Melting-Pot* seems to imply that immigrants should actively will their own assimilation; but since the process is portrayed as automatic, it probably makes no difference whether they do or not. It is God's melting pot; He is the Alchemist who presides over it, and presumably the process can go forward without conscious human collaboration. The play clearly indicates that the processes of the melting pot are unfinished; the product will be novel, but it has not yet come out of the crucible. This means that all that goes into the pot contributes to the "real American," the coming superman who is to make his appearance in the future. The whole vision is oriented toward the future—"the ideals of the fathers shall not be foisted on the children." Not only the immigrants but America as a whole is seen in the process of becoming. To a character who is a caricature of the idle-rich American, David prophesies: "There shall come a fire round the Crucible that will melt you and your breed like wax in a blowpipe— . . . America *shall* make good!"[22]

A reviewer in the *Forum* took issue with the assumption that immigration was still forming America. Speaking for the "traditional Americans to whom Mr. Zangwill would deny the national name," he showed concern over the "indiscriminate commingling of alien races on our soil" and flatly denied that "the scum and dregs of Europe" could enrich America. On the other hand, many immigrant spokesmen have found the melting pot equally unacceptable because it seemed to require too great a degree of assimilation. According to a very nationalistic German-American writer, *The Melting-Pot* was "simply a mixture of insipid phrases and unhistorical thinking" and represented "just the contrary of that toward which we strive." He warned that any attempt to "do away with our German cultural type . . . in the smudge kitchen of a national melting pot" would come to naught. In addition to Jews and Germans, spokesmen for the Norwegian and the Slavic immigrants have been critical of the notion of the melting pot.[23]

These immigrant critics obviously understand the melting pot differently from the *Forum* reviewer: the complaint of the former is that it means too much conformity to America as it already exists, while the latter is fearful that America itself is to be transformed. This ambiguity in the meaning or "theory" of the melting pot was present at the beginning and was to persist. But before considering the "theoretical" aspects of the subject, we should examine the use of the melting pot as a symbol, because the theoretical ambiguity has not lessened the use of the symbol, and the popularity of the symbol has perpetuated and aggravated the ambiguities of meaning.

The melting pot symbol was introduced at a propitious moment, achieved almost instant popularity, and has been employed by countless writers with every imaginable embellishment and variation. Two magazines have used *The Melting Pot* as their title; a novel called *On the Way to the Melting Pot* was published in Norwegian; and a study of immigration was entitled *The Melting-Pot Mistake*. Librarians frequently arrange immigrant stories under some such rubric as "Out of the Melting Pot," and the field of immigrant fiction was surveyed by Carl Wittke in an article entitled "Melting Pot Literature." Dumas Malone summarized the information about immigrants who were included in the *Dictionary of American Biography* in an article on our "Intellectual Melting Pot."[24] We have also had linguistic, rural, frontier, urban, and civil rights melting pots, as well as "melting pot wards."[25] The United States is usually thought of as *the* melting pot, but smaller units also claim the title: Puritan Boston was called a melting pot in the twentieth century; a very old state, Pennsylvania, and the newest one, Hawaii, share the same honor; and now the nation of Israel threatens to usurp America's place as the modern melting pot.[26]

"What's in the Melting Pot?" asked the *Survey* in 1912, but not until 1922 did the House of Representatives furnish an "Expert Analysis of the Metal and Dross in America's Modern Melting Pot."[27] "The Pot's Constituents" have usually been found to be various immigrant groups, but foreign bodies of a different sort are also spoken of as being in the crucible. W. F. Adams handled the symbol very straightforwardly when he said that "solid groups of Irish of the lowest class were thrown as cohesive masses into the melting pot"; but for some reason, it is the small Czech group whose career in the melting pot has been most closely scrutinized. Thomas Capek traced their passage "Through Intermarriage into the Melting-Pot," another writer focused on the Czechs in the microcosmic melting pot of Colfax County, Nebraska, and a third had written more generally of the Czech "ingredient."[28]

The ordinary immigrants have sometimes had rather strange companions in the pot. Carl Russell Fish did not hesitate to bring the Pilgrim

Fathers perilously close to a dunking, and he declared that their story survived as a "vital spirit sweetening the melting pot." Both labor and religion have been in the pot, but one hopes that these inoffensive abstractions were not part of the "slag" that George Creel complained of in 1922. It is perhaps poetic justice that Israel Zangwill was deposited in his own pot, but the reader is brought up short at seeing the following heading in an index: "Melting pot: children in."[20] It was suggested as early as 1912 that the universally held conceit of national superiority be cast into the melting pot, and in 1916 President Woodrow Wilson called for the enlargement of the melting pot to include the whole world; therefore, it is not surprising that Sisley Huddleston found "Europe in the Melting Pot" in 1922.[30] But however much the melting pot might be internationalized, it still concerned Americans primarily as it related to this country and its history. Looking into our past, Americans could see the melting pot beginning to simmer in colonial Pennsylvania; it was still "simmering gently" at the end of the War of 1812, but by the election of Andrew Jackson in 1828 it had come to "full boil." A century later the restrictive laws of the 1920s were said to bring the "America of the Melting Pot" to an end, and Henry Pratt Fairchild predicted with no regret that the symbol was so battered that it would not be called into service by subsequent writers.[31]

One of the principal reasons for the durable popularity of the melting pot is that it brings before the mind's eye a vivid picture, and one is almost irresistibly impelled to describe what one sees happening in and around the pot. Once a person writes—or even thinks—*melting pot*, one is caught. Only the strongest can resist the temptation to embellish the image, and there are few phenomena of nature which have been more comprehensively reported than the workings of the melting pot. It is, for instance, obvious that a melting pot requires a fire; but what kind of fire? In the play, David Quixano called it a "purging flame," and Zangwill later spoke of the melting pot burning off at the top while new material was added at the bottom. Woodrow Wilson saw the need for a "fire of pure passion" around the crucible, while Max Farrand pointed out that it worked best when the fires were kept at "forced draught"; a reviewer of a recent book on Polish-Americans declared, however, that the fire could be cooled by "the winds of action of . . . patriotic immigrant societies."[32]

Even greater efforts of the literary imagination have been expended in describing the action and contents of the melting pot. David Quixano contributed a number of images: he described the pot as roaring, bubbling, stirring, seething, melting, and fusing. Although this might seem to furnish an adequate picture, it proved quite superficial. Other writers have shown that the pot also simmers, boils, ferments, devours, curdles, and coagulates. Furthermore, a critical West Coast observer was able to penetrate the vapors of the melting pot to see the "yellow froth" that defiled it; and, unhappily, the pot was not without both "scum" and "dross."[33]

Confronting the image of a great melting pot, one could appropriately take a variety of actions. One could, for example, keep watch over it, become concerned about its capacity, or draw lessons from it. For the person who desired a more active role, it was possible to stir the pot; but this had to be done cautiously since there was the danger of overtaxing it, and cracks had been detected. Some observers spoke of the need to make sure that the melting pot really melted its contents, especially when the cold draughts of World War I blew across the Atlantic and caused the contents of the pot to recrystallize, with dangerous lines of fracture appearing between ethnic masses.[34] Occasionally a writer would call attention to the need for forms into which the molten contents might be poured, but unfortunately a good deal of vagueness enveloped the subject of what was to come from the melting pot. David Quixano foresaw a superman emerging from the crucible, while President Wilson would settle for "the fine gold of untainted Americanism" as a product; a hostile critic feared that a new language was supposed to "steam forth" from the pot. Many more, of course, were uneasily aware that the melting pot could fail completely; some even claimed that it did not exist.[35]

The fact that the melting pot symbol has been used so often and in so many ways does not mean that it has won universal acceptance as the most satisfactory symbol for the process of ethnic adjustment and interaction in America. Indeed, it has been called a "startlingly bad" symbol,[36] and a great number of alternatives have been suggested, many of them consciously offered as replacements for the melting pot. In the play, Zangwill used the term *crucible* as a synonym for *melting pot*, but it has never led an independent life as a symbol—it remains merely a synonym. George R. Stewart suggested the term *transmuting pot* as a clarifying replacement for *melting pot*; he feels that *transmuting pot* is better because it specifies that the immigrants are on the whole changed into traditional Americans instead of producing a new and exotic national type.[37] Other alternatives to the melting pot can be grouped in five rough classifications:

1. *Culinary*. It is probably indicative of something about our national character that culinary symbolism supplies more replacements for the melting pot than any other source. In one of the more graphic examples,

Karl E. Meyer likens America to a pressure cooker rather than a melting pot, and other writers have suggested stew, soup, salad or salad bowl, and mixing bowl as alternatives.[38]

2. *Color.* Other images suggest light or color in some way. America has been compared to a flower garden containing various blossoms (ethnic groups) of different color, size, fragrance, and so on. The country has also been called a mosaic, a kaleidoscope, and a cultural rainbow. Emily Green Balch, a respected student of immigration, suggested the metaphor of irradiation to describe the way in which various ethnic groups interact with each other and their American surroundings.[39]

3. *Musical.* Two metaphors relate to music. In advocating his "federation of nationalities" ideas, Horace Kallen suggested visualizing America as an orchestra rather than as a melting pot because in an orchestra individuals and small groups work together to produce a harmony of sound from a variety of different instruments. Another writer described America as containing a host of different nationalities who were engaged in a stately and formal dance: America was "The Choir Dance of the Nations."[40]

4. *Mechanical.* For a gadget-minded people, we have been quite unimaginative in suggesting mechanical metaphors for the nation and what is going on in it. The most explicitly mechanistic symbol is that of a weaving machine that combines different elements into one fabric. This metaphor was mentioned by Fairchild in 1926 with the note that probably no one had ever heard of it. Denis Brogan has much more recently suggested that America resembles a pipeline where a number of different elements are all racing along in the same direction, but with little interaction between them.[41]

5. *Derogatory.* At least four alternative symbols are unmistakably insulting to the immigrants who came to America and are in the process of assimilation. In 1921, George Creel asked whether *dumping ground* was not a more fitting metaphor than the melting pot, and five years later Henry Pratt Fairchild declared flatly that "if we must have a symbol for race mixture, much more accurate than the figure of the melting pot is the figure of the village pound." Fairchild later added two other symbols to the derogatory category when he compared America to a catch basin and a cul-de-sac for immigrants.[42]

If we turn from the symbolic to the theoretical melting pot we encounter more disagreement; indeed, it would be more correct to speak of theories of the melting pot because there are almost as many versions of the theory as there are embellishments of the symbol. The main difficulty in pinning down the theory is that many writers simply refer to "the melting pot theory" as though the figure of speech itself conveyed a clear and univocally understandable concept that requires no further definition; the symbol, in other words, is assumed to be a theory. The melting pot may be an example of "concrete symbolism," as Zangwill put it,[43] but it is hardly precise enough to constitute a theory; a theory of the melting pot should spell out just what is meant by the melting of various elements together and how it takes place. Unfortunately, few who speak of the melting pot theory do this; usually one must infer what the theory is thought to be from the way the symbol is handled.

The most fundamental ambiguity in the melting pot as a symbol and the point of greatest confusion in the theory is whether only the immigrant is changed or whether America, the host society, is also changed by the processes of the melting pot. Does the theory imply that the entire make-up of American life is inevitably changed exactly in proportion to the quantity of the various immigrant ingredients thrown into the pot, as George R. Stewart seems to believe; or is Lawrence Frank Pisani correct in thinking that only the immigrants, the ingredients in the pot, are affected by the melting process? A closely related and equally basic question is, Does the melting pot receive immigrants, strip them of their cultural heritage, and make old-style, Anglo-Saxon Americans of them? or, Does it combine the immigrants with the native-born Americans in a new amalgam embodying the best qualities of both elements? Here again one can find diametrically opposed answers; in at least one case the contradictory versions were both advanced in the same book.[44]

There are several other points of confusion about the melting pot theory. Does it refer to biological "blending," that is, intermarriage, or does it refer to cultural assimilation? Is the theory to be understood as descriptive or prescriptive: does it show us how a process is taking place or tell us how to further the action of that process? There is also disagreement about the relationship of the melting pot theory to the Americanization movement of the World War I period: one writer asserts that the Americanization movement was an outgrowth of "the philosophy underlying the melting pot theory," but another claims that it was a repudiation of the laissez-faire approach of the "melting-pot idea." It is suggestive of the confusion surrounding the melting pot as a theory that Horace Kallen, who devoted much energy to attacking the melting pot, has recently been hailed for his vision in discerning what "so many others of us refused to see and to feel, . . . that our country is a true melting-pot."[45]

There are two general considerations that help to account for the confusion that arose about the meaning of the expression *the melting pot*: the first of these concerns the play by Zangwill; the other, the subsequent use of the expression by persons who interpreted it in different ways.

Because the expression is so closely connected with Zangwill's play, one looks to *The Melting-Pot* to discover the theory of immigrant assimilation which is dramatized there. It is, as we have seen, possible to draw some inferences about Zangwill's ideas on immigrant assimilation from the play; nevertheless, that it was criticized by native-born American and immigrant spokesmen for opposite reasons indicates that a dramatic presentation is not a satisfactory method of conveying in unequivocal terms and adequate detail a theory about so complex a process as immigrant assimilation. Furthermore, Zangwill was primarily concerned in the play with Jewish assimilation in America, and his treatment therefore concentrates on this one relatively small, and particularly complicated, aspect of the larger problem, thus introducing other elements of uncertainty. In short, Zangwill's play did not provide a comprehensive statement of any theory of immigrant adjustment, and it was natural that such "theory" as was presented there should be interpreted differently by different persons.

What Zangwill did was to restate dramatically many of the imprecise traditional notions about America's absorptive power and supply a new symbol that soon gained widespread popularity. As a symbol, the melting pot could be freighted with any one of a number of meanings depending upon the view of immigration and assimilation held by those who used it. Those favorably disposed toward free immigration and confident of America's assimilative power might interpret the melting pot to mean that the nation could continue to receive immigrants, absorb them in some unspecified fashion, and profit from the diverse cultural traits that they added to the national composite. To those less favorably disposed and less confident the melting pot could symbolize a more purposeful process of purging away the inherited culture of the immigrant and remolding him into an old-line, Anglo-Saxon American with all the approved habits, attitudes, and beliefs.

An example of the former attitude is Percy Stickney Grant's article on "American Ideals and Race Mixture," which appeared in the *North American Review* in 1912 in answer to an alarmist view of "The Future of American Ideals" by the restrictionist, Prescott F. Hall.[46] Grant argued that "fusion is the law of progress" and that America would be strengthened by the acceptance and assimilation of new and vigorous strains in the national mixture. He was sympathetic to the immigrant throughout and concluded his discussion by quoting approvingly the "familiar words of Israel Zangwill" on the virtues of "the great Melting Pot." Within a few years, however, the outbreak of the war in Europe and its reverberations in this country caused attitudes toward the melting pot to shift drastically. The tolerant and optimistic view that it was automatically working to produce a new and better American declined sharply, and the conviction grew that it was the function of the melting pot to make immigrants into patriotic Americans after the pattern of the Americans who got here first.

The return to Europe of thousands of immigrants who were reservists in the armies of the belligerents, the burst of war enthusiasm on the part of those who remained, and the growing bitterness of various ethnic groups shocked many Americans by revealing the strength of the ties that bound the immigrants to their homelands. Most of the anxiety was centered on the German-Americans, but there was a more generalized suspicion that the nation could not count on the undivided loyalty of the entire immigrant population. In these circumstances, the movement to Americanize the immigrant which had gotten under way before the war was given a powerful new impetus, and there was much talk of heating the melting pot, stirring it, and "our bounden duty to keep our eye" on it.[47] "Put baldly," wrote a contemporary student, the devotees of the crude, current notion of the 'melting pot,' bid America take the immigrant, . . . strip him of his cultural heritage, throw him into the great cauldron, stir the pot vigorously, speak the magic word 'Americanization' and through the mystic vapors would rise the newly created 'American.' "[48]

As American nationalism mounted during the war and the immediate postwar period, this view of the melting pot became almost unalterably fixed, and the American whom the pot was supposed to produce conformed more and more to the stereotype of the "hundred-percent American." In 1919 two critics of this attitude satirized it by imagining a "keeper of the melting pot" who addresses the immigrants as follows: "Jump into the caldron, and behold! You emerge new creatures, up-to-date, with new customs, habits, traditions and ideals. Immediately you will become like us; the taint will disappear. . . . You will become full-fledged Americans. The magic process is certain."[49] This, to be sure, is exaggerated, but consideration of the melting pot pageant of the Ford Motor Company's school for its immigrant employees suggests that the keeper's speech did not fundamentally misrepresent the expectations of some Americans. In one version, the pageant features a "Ford English School Melting Pot" perhaps seven to eight feet in height and ten to twelve in diameter; the legend *E Pluribus Unum* appears above the bail of the pot. A number of immigrants, dressed in native costume and carrying placards showing their country of origin, descend into the center of the pot from the rear; the transmogrified "new Americans" appear in two lines on the steps leading up and over the rim on either side. Gone now are the beards and kerchiefs! All are dressed stiffly in business suits and bear in one hand a scroll—presumably their naturalization papers—and in the other a small American flag. According to some reports, the Americanized immigrants sang the national anthem as they left the pot, and one observer suspected that each carried an Eversharp pencil in his pocket.[50]

As a result of identification with such activities, the melting pot came to be looked upon as almost exclusively a purger of "foreign dross" and "impurities"; the melting pot "theory" tended to lose all association with the idea that immigrants could make valuable contributions to a yet unfinished American culture. Consequently those who were repelled by the narrowness of the more extreme Americanizers tended also to reject the melting pot, which stood, in their minds, for enforced conformity to a repugnant version of Americanism. The melting pot acquired in World War I a bad reputation with liberals which it has not yet fully lived down. The critics of that era who did most to fix liberals' distaste for the melting pot were Horace M. Kallen and Randolph S. Bourne.

Kallen's first discussion of the subject appeared early in 1915 in a lengthy two-part article in the *Nation*, "Democracy *versus* the Melting-Pot," which was reprinted in 1924 with very minor changes in a volume containing other essays by Kallen on ethnic adjustment in America. He attacked the melting pot, not only because he found the hundred-percentism of the Americanization program abhorrent, but also because he did not want immigrants to be "melted" at all: he was convinced that they neither could nor should divest themselves of their ethnic identity.

> What is inalienable in the life of mankind is its intrinsic positive quality—its psycho-physical inheritance. Men may change their clothes, their politics, their wives, their religions, their philosophies, to a greater or lesser extent; they cannot change their grandfathers. Jews or Poles or Anglo-Saxons, in order to cease being Jews or Poles or Anglo-Saxons, would have to cease to be, while they could cease to be citizens or church members or carpenters or lawyers without ceasing to be. The selfhood which is inalienable in them, and for the realization of which they require 'inalienable' liberty is ancestrally determined, and the hap-

piness which they pursue has its form implied in ancestral en-
dowments.[51]

Not only the exaggerated form of the melting pot was wrong, according to Kallen, but any kind of policy which had as its goal assimilation
of the immigrant. Instead of assimilation, Kallen proposed as the correct
policy the recognition and deliberate fostering of the enduring quality of
ethnic differences; the goal, properly envisaged, was that America should
bécome a federation of distinct nationalities using English as "the language of its great tradition," but preserving for the "emotional and in-
voluntary life" of each nationality "its own peculiar dialect or speech, its
own individual and inevitable esthetic and intellectual forms."

> Thus "American civilization" may come to mean the perfection
> of the coöperative harmonies of "European civilization"—the
> waste, the squalor and the distress of Europe being elimi-
> nated—a multiplicity in a unity, an orchestration of mankind.
> As in an orchestra every type of instrument has its specific
> *timbre* and *tonality*, founded in its substance and form; . . . so
> in society, each ethnic group may be the natural instrument, its
> temper and culture may be its theme and melody and the har-
> mony and dissonances and discords of them all may make the
> symphony of civilization.[52]

When he restated his position in 1924, Kallen rejected—without changing his fundamental point—the criticism that his ancestrally endowed,
inalienable psycho-physical ethnic identities were based on a faulty theory of race. At the same time he coined the term *cultural pluralism* to
describe his approach.[53]

Kallen, who was German born, Jewish, and a supporter of Zionism,
had a personal emotional involvement in the preservation of ethnic distinctiveness, but Randolph Bourne, who came from old American stock,
also advocated roughly the same policy. He and John Dewey, who held
similar views, represented American cultural nationalists, who, disgusted
by the extremes of the Americanizers, nevertheless firmly believed in
the necessity to work purposefully for a genuine American nationality
and culture. The nationalism they wanted, however, would be truly democratic and international, and they allowed for the active partnership of
the immigrant in the creation and life of the American national culture.
Bourne's position was outlined in an article entitled "Trans-National
America," which appeared about a year after Kallen's essay was first

published. He referred critically to the melting pot a dozen times, de-
claring among other things that it had never existed and that as long as
Americans had thought in melting pot terms, they were looking to the
past instead of the future. While denying the existence of the melting
pot, Bourne paradoxically attacked the Americanized second-generation
immigrants who were products of the melting process; indeed, he quite
forgot his democratic tolerance in describing the "tame flabbiness" of
the "cultural half-breeds" who were unlucky enough to have lost their
"foreign savor."[54]

Bourne's ideal was a cosmopolitan dual nationality that would permit
one to be fully American and at the same time fully Italian, Polish, and
so on. John Dewey had the same thing in mind when he asserted that
the true American is "not American plus Pole or Germans. But the American is himself Pole-German-English-French-Spanish-Italian-Greek-
Irish-Scandinavian-Bohemian-Jew-and so on."[55] Dewey's remarks were
addressed to educators, and he saw the schools as a key agency in ac-
tualizing his rather baffling prescription for nationality. A few years later
some sort of high point was reached in the proposals for systematically
inculcating cosmopolitan nationalism in the American people: a series
of articles in the *Survey* which began by criticizing the Americanizers'
view of the melting pot ended with the suggestion that a cabinet-level
department of "Nation Building" be established in Washington.[56]

Another hostile critic of the melting pot was Horace J. Bridges, who
included in his essays *On Becoming an American* an analysis of "The
Fallacy of the Melting-Pot." Bridges' quarrel was really only with that
version of the melting pot which conceived it as a device for reducing
everyone to a predetermined homogeneity. In his positive prescription
for cultural cross-fertilization, Bridges did not differ too widely from the
interpretation of the melting pot as a blender of diverse cultural heritages,
and he explicitly rejected the view that foreign nationalities should be
preserved intact.[57] There was, however, one student of ethnic adjustment
who saw clearly that the melting pot could be interpreted in tolerant and
liberal fashion. Isaac B. Berkson's *Theories of Americanization* contained
a perceptive analysis of the "melting pot theory" which commended its
hospitality to the contributions of all groups and characterized it as pervaded by "a spirit of humane toleration, and a notion of the dynamic
nature of society." But, in the end, Berkson also rejected the melting pot
because it required that the unique identity of each ethnic group be
"annihilated" as the price of that group's adding its bit to the composite
American culture.[58]

By the early 1920s, hostility to the melting pot "theory" probably prevailed among the majority of those who held liberal views on immigration and ethnic adjustment; most—but not all—of this hostility stemmed from the belief that the theory required the stripping away of inherited cultures and the imposition of Anglo-Saxonism by indoctrination. At the same time, many of those who *did* feel that such was the proper function of the melting pot had become disillusioned by its failure to operate in the desired fashion. Immigrant resistance to Americanization programs, the bickering of nationalities over the provisions of the Versailles treaty, and the spread of "bolshevik" tendencies all contributed to the conviction that the melting pot had failed. The suspicion that the "dross" outweighed the "metal" was reinforced by the "expert analysis of the melting-pot" of the eugenicist H. H. Laughlin whose report to the House Committee on Immigration and Naturalization dealt with the proportion of the "socially inadequate" in the immigrant population.[59] To those who stressed racial considerations, the melting pot was wrong, not so much because it had failed, but because the notion of race mixing was itself misguided; race mixing meant mongrelization, not the production of a superior nationality. The most important frontal attack was Henry Pratt Fairchild's *Melting-Pot Mistake* (1926), which criticized the melting pot for encouraging racial amalgamation, although admitting it was a fairly good symbol for the process. However, Fairchild found the melting pot as a symbol for cultural assimilation "pitiably inadequate" because cultural heritages could not be melted together and because it focused on the process of interaction rather than the result.[60]

Even those who disagreed with Fairchild on many points might concur in calling the melting pot a mistake, and since both friends of immigration and restrictionists were critical of the symbol, he seemed quite justified in predicting "that it is not likely ever to be dragged into service again."[61] For at least two reasons, this turned out to be another "melting pot mistake": the first reason is that the symbol had already become firmly embedded in American speech; the second, which is perhaps hardly to be distinguished from the first, is that in spite of its theoretical vagueness, the melting pot continued to find occasional employment by students of society as a conceptual tool.

All through his career Frederick Jackson Turner looked upon the frontier as a melting pot in which the distinctive American nationality was forged. Edward N. Saveth says that for Turner "the melting pot becomes an important institutional determinant" and that the "concept" is recurrent in his writings; Merle Curti refers to the melting pot in his recent case study of the validity of certain aspects of the Turnerian approach.[62] Another student of society who used the melting pot as a conceptual tool was Bessie Bloom Wessel, who formally defined it to refer to the amalgamation of different stocks through intermarriage in her *Ethnic Survey of Woonsocket, Rhode Island.* This examination of the "melting" process was endorsed, as to both method and results, in a Foreword by the noted anthropologist Clark Wissler. On the whole, however, sociologists regarded the "melting pot theory" as outmoded or unsophisticated; even so, they usually mentioned it as a primitive earlier approach.[63] The study that undoubtedly gave the greatest impetus to the use of the melting pot as a conceptual tool was Ruby Jo Reeves Kennedy's survey of the patterns of mate selection in New Haven from 1870 to 1940. Her article, "Single or Triple Melting-Pot" (1944), introduced the multiple, or compartmentalized, melting pot. Since her research showed that marriages between different nationalities were increasing but still tended to take place within the confines of the three major religious divisions, Kennedy concluded that immigrant assimilation took place within the "triple-melting-pots" of Protestantism, Catholicism and Judaism. Kennedy's triple-melting-pot thesis was given popular currency and applied much more broadly to religious sociology in Will Herberg's widely read and influential study, *Protestant-Catholic-Jew.*[64]

Because of the sociologists' discovery of the multiple melting pot, or perhaps because of the mounting evidence that some sort of "melting" has indeed occurred in the American population since 1900, the melting pot is currently recovering a good deal of its respectability. There are still those whose distaste for the term has not abated: Horace Kallen remains unconverted, in spite of admirers who would credit him with the discovery of the melting pot, and Carl N. Degler, Karl E. Meyer, Amitai Etzioni, and Franklin D. Scott have all lately found fault with it, while a recent writer in the *American Journal of Psychiatry* criticized the melting pot with racial arguments reminiscent of the 1920s.[65] On the other hand, Arthur M. Schlesinger, Sr., included the melting pot, "in the best sense of the term," among America's ten greatest contributions to civilization; an editor of the *New Republic* associated prejudice and narrow provincialism with cultural pluralism and seemed more favorably inclined toward the melting pot; David Riesman found that the early melting pot had some attractive features, and Theodore H. White, Louis B. Wright, and the authors of a recent college text in American history have also spoken positively of it within the last few years.[66] Hans Kohn, along with Herberg, feels that those who saw America as a melting pot early in this century were more accurate observers than those who held that ethnic identity would persist indefinitely.[67]

Resisting the temptation to ask what the melting pot boils down to, we may now attempt to draw some conclusions. We should note, first of all, that it is the melting pot as symbol rather than as theory which is of primary importance; the difficulty in framing an adequate theory of immigrant adjustment was, in fact, one of the principal reasons for the popularity of the symbol. As a symbol, the melting pot stands in some fashion for the process of interaction of different ethnic groups and for the society in which the process is taking place. At the time the symbol came into general usage, this process was not understood in any clear and comprehensive way, yet it was of great public importance and was much discussed. Theoretical concepts such as "assimilation" were employed in this discussion, and so were popular figurative terms like *mixing, melting, blending,* and *fusing.* The melting pot provided a large symbol, a comprehensive figurative framework, which subsumed into itself many metaphoric terms already in common use; it seemed to conform in some way to the process that was going on, and it lent itself to picturesque elaboration that made it ideal for colorful use by journalists. Consequently, the symbol became extremely popular and entered deeply into the whole thought process respecting immigration; for many people, no doubt, it was the basic piece of intellectual equipment where immigration was concerned. But considering the lack of precise understanding of the subject and the very loose use of the symbol, it was bound to be ambiguous; it could not convey anything univocal because what it stood for was neither clearly nor univocally understood.

If we concede that the ambiguities of the melting pot symbol *reflected* the confusion existing in the public mind about the processes of immigrant adjustment, the next question is, Did the symbol of the melting pot *add* to that confusion? The answer is that it did. All of us, as George Eliot observed, "get our thoughts entangled in metaphors";[68] we tend to equate literally the symbol with the thing symbolized. In this particular instance, the substitution in thought and discussion of a very concrete symbol (melting pot) for a very subtle and complex thing symbolized (ethnic interaction) was almost bound to result in added confusion. The very effectiveness of the symbol tended to focus undue attention upon it rather than transferring attention to the thing symbolized, and all too frequently discussion of immigration was cast into the wrong terms. Human beings are not metals; they do not literally "melt"; they do not "fuse"; groups of human beings are not really "alloys." Everyone, of course, "knew" this—but to talk continually in terms of the melting pot, employing the vocabulary of metallurgy, tended inevitably to color the general public understanding of immigration and ethnic adjustment. Unconsciously, one suspects, many people came to feel that there was something wrong with immigrants if they did not visibly start "blending." Furthermore, the elaboration of the symbol proceeded, quite naturally, along lines proper to the operation of a melting pot. But were all these elaborations appropriate to the processes that were supposed to be symbolized? Does it not seem likely that figures such as *heating up the pot* or *pouring into molds* suggested ideas respecting immigration that might not otherwise have been thought of at all? At the very least, these figures of speech lent a spurious plausibility to certain ideas simply because they fitted in so nicely with the symbolism of the melting pot, not necessarily because they were appropriate to the reality of ethnic interaction.

Perhaps the most serious distortion of understanding that the melting pot symbolism entailed was the notion of uniformity of product. We think of what comes out of a melting pot as uniform in color, consistency, texture, and other qualities; the repeated use of melting pot symbolism reinforced, if it did not generate, the expectation that the result of ethnic interaction should also be absolutely uniform. It is this emphasis on uniformity which more than anything else has caused liberals to condemn the melting pot "theory."

But granting all its confusions and even the particularly unfortunate connotation of uniformity—which can be mitigated by interpretation[69]— the melting pot remains the best symbol that has been devised for ethnic interaction in America. It is by far the most popular symbol, and its very ambiguity allows its use by those who disagree about what it means, but these are not the chief reasons for calling it the best symbol. It is the unique merit of the melting pot that the element of ever changing process is intrinsic to the symbol itself and that what is symbolized, ethnic interaction, is above all an ever changing dynamic process. There are two other distinctive merits of the melting pot symbol: first, the strong implication that the interaction of the various elements proceeds according to its own inner laws in the general direction of reducing the most glaring differences and is subject to human manipulation to only a limited degree; and, second, the suggestion that the final result of the interaction cannot with certainty be known beforehand.

If we compare the melting pot with some of the alternative symbols mentioned earlier, its superiority is, I believe, clear. If the melting pot can be validly criticized because it suggests too strongly uniformity of product, this is surely even more true of George R. Stewart's "transmuting pot"; what this verbal change in fact does is specify one version of the melting pot—the version in which immigrants are to be changed into something that is predetermined. Unless one thinks that the element of predetermination is present to a greater degree than can be implied by melting pot, it is hard to see why *transmuting pot* should be preferred. The alternative symbols of soup, stew and the like certainly have nothing to recommend them on aesthetic grounds and are usually justified by arguments exactly the opposite of Stewart's: they are urged as substitutes because the melting pot is alleged to imply too strongly that the distinctive ethnic identities disappear, while in a stew, carrots, for example, do remain somehow carrots even after an indefinite period of stewing. Here the matter resolves itself into the question of whether one would agree that a third-generation Irish-American is to an immigrant Irishman as a carrot-in-the-pot-nine-days-old is to a raw carrot. Furthermore, these symbols do not convey as forcefully as the melting pot the sense of ever changing process, and they suggest a chef more strongly than the melting pot suggests a directive human manipulator. Practically all the other alternative symbols surveyed—salad, mosaic, flower garden, and so on— are fundamentally defective in that they are essentially static; they do not convey the notion that the materials involved are in a process of transformation. Even those that seem to involve action (e.g., weaving machine, orchestra) fall down here since the constitutive elements are themselves unchanging. Furthermore, a weaving machine implies a weaver, and an orchestra requires a conductor. Perhaps something could be done with irradiation, but it hardly seems worthwhile to take up all the others from choir dance to dog pound.

As a symbol the melting pot seems to me superior to these, and it certainly has in its favor the weight of popular usage. Among intellectuals the real challenger of the melting pot symbol is not another symbol but rather the concept of cultural pluralism. This concept, which is almost as old as the melting pot, and whose history is equally involved, cannot be discussed here. It is pertinent to note, however, that although it is an abstract concept, "cultural pluralism" has accumulated an emotional charge equal to that carried by any symbol; moreover, it is not without a few ambiguities of its own and has perhaps even generated a little confusion. In the form first proposed by Kallen, cultural pluralism amounted to a kind of "ethnic predestination,"[70] and it did not prove to be an accurate prognosis of the future development of immigrant groups in the United States. It is now much modified and amounts, on the whole, to tolerance of as much cultural diversity as is compatible with the minimum essential national unity. Every idea—even cultural plu-ralism—can be interpreted in narrow and dogmatic fashion, and it is worth pointing out to the cultural pluralist critics of the melting pot that

that much abused symbol has represented, for many Americans, aspirations and values that resemble those cherished by pluralists—openness toward the future; receptiveness to immigrants and the cultural values they bring; and the gradual and harmonious integration of these immigrants and their descendants into the ever evolving life of the nation.

NOTES

Source: American Quarterly, 16 (Spring 1964), 20–46. Reprinted by permission of the publisher.

1. Hans Kohn, American Nationalism: An Interpretative Essay (New York, 1961), 172.

2. Chicago Sun-Times, July 14, October 6, 1962; South Bend Tribune, television supplement for July 29–August 4, 1962; New York Times Book Review, November 18, 1962, 17. Cf. Edward W. Chester, Europe Views America: A Critical Evaluation (Washington, D.C., 1962), chap. 2. Although obviously relevant to the theme, Nathan Glazer and Daniel P. Moynihan's Beyond the Melting Pot (Cambridge, Mass., 1963), appeared too late to be considered here.

3. Andrew M. Greeley, "Areas of Research on Religion and Social Organization," American Catholic Sociological Review, 23 (Summer 1962), 111.

4. C. S. Lewis, "Bluspels and Flalansferes," 36–50, and Owen Barfield, "Poetic Diction and Legal Fiction," both in Max Black, ed., The Importance of Language (Englewood Cliffs, N.J., 1962) are especially helpful on metaphoric language.

5. J. Hector St. John de Crèvecoeur, Letters from an American Farmer (New York, 1957), 39; Louis B. Wright, The Cultural Life of the American Colonies, 1607–1763 (New York, 1957), 45; Joseph Leftwich, Israel Zangwill (New York, 1957), 251.

6. Merle Curti, The Roots of American Loyalty (New York, 1946), 74; Edith Abbott, ed., Historical Aspects of the Immigration Problem. Select Documents (Chicago, 1926), 755.

7. Emerson's remarks were first published in 1912 in Journals of Ralph Waldo Emerson with Annotations, 10 vols., ed. Edward Waldo Emerson and Waldo Emerson Forbes (Boston, 1909–14), 7:116. Stuart P. Sherman drew particular attention to this "notable passage" in his Introduction to Essays and Poems of Emerson (New York, 1921), xxxiv.

8. Frontier and Section. Selected Essays of Frederick Jackson Turner, with an Introduction by Ray Allen Billington (Englewood Cliffs, N.J., 1961), 51.

9. Franklin H. Giddings, "Are We a People?" Literary Digest, 37 (July 11, 1908), 37–38.

10. John Higham, Strangers in the Land: Patterns of American Nativism, 1860–1925 (New Brunswick, N.J., 1955), 158 and chaps. 5–7.

11. Compare Eric F. Goldman, Rendezvous with Destiny. A History of Modern American Reform, rev. ed. (New York, 1956), 61.

12. Washington Evening Star, October 6, 1908; Roosevelt to Zangwill, October 15, 1908, in The Letters of Theodore Roosevelt, 8 vols., ed. Elting E. Morison et al. (Cambridge, Mass., 1951–54), 6:1288–89; Chicago Inter Ocean, October 25, 1908, magazine section, 10; New York Times, September 5, 1909; Current Literature, 45 (December 1908), 671; Leftwich, Zangwill, 251–59 discusses the play.

13. Literary Digest, 38 (April 24, 1909), 691; 39 (September 18, 1909), 440.

14. *Survey*, 23 (November 6, 1909), 168.

15. Israel Zangwill, *The Principle of Nationalities* (New York, 1917). Annamarie Peterson, "Israel Zangwill (1864–1926): A Selected Bibliography," *Bulletin of Bibliography and Magazine Notes*, 23 (September–December 1961), 136–40 lists Zangwill's writings. Mrs. Peterson kindly informed me that she knows of no serious study of Zangwill's sociological views. Letter to the author, January 12, 1963. Leftwich, *Zangwill*, is a topically organized biography.

16. Israel Zangwill, "America—'The Melting Pot,' " *Chicago Inter Ocean*, December 6, 1908, magazine section, 10.

17. Ibid.

18. Israel Zangwill, *The Melting-Pot. A Drama in Four Acts* (New York, 1909), 198–99.

19. Ibid., 37–38. Cf. Zangwill, "America—'The Melting Pot.' "

20. *Chicago Inter Ocean*, October 22, 1908.

21. Zangwill, *Melting-Pot*, 47; *American Hebrew*, quoted in *Current Literature*, 45 (December 1908), 672; Rabbi Joel Blau, quoted in Henry Pratt Fairchild, *Race and Nationality as Factors in American Life* (New York, 1947), 144. For other Jewish reactions, see *Literary Digest*, 37 (October 31, 1908), 628–29; Leftwich, *Zangwill*, 252ff.

22. Zangwill, *Melting-Pot*, 157, 92.

23. *Forum*, 42 (November 1909), 434–35; Julius Goebel, quoted in Robert E. Park, *The Immigrant Press and Its Control* (New York, 1922), 61–62; Einar Haugen, "The Struggle over Norwegian," *Norwegian-American Studies*, 17 (Northfield, Minn., 1952), 23; Joseph A. Wytrwal, *America's Polish Heritage. A Social History of the Poles in America* (Detroit, 1961), 244ff.; Louis Adamic, *From Many Lands* (New York, 1940), 301, 303.

24. *Union List of Serials in Libraries of the United States and Canada*, 2d ed., ed. Winifred Gregory (New York, 1948), 1706; Einar Haugen, *The Norwegian Language in America. A Study of Bilingual Behavior*, 2 vols. (Philadelphia, 1953), 1:152; Henry Pratt Fairchild, *The Melting-Pot Mistake* (Boston, 1926); Theodore Blegen, *Grass Roots History* (Minneapolis, 1947), 19; Carl Wittke, "Melting Pot Literature," *College English*, 7 (1946), 189–97; Dumas Malone, "Intellectual Melting Pot," *American Scholar*, 4 (1935), 444–59. Cf. also Mircea Vasiliu, *Which Way to the Melting Pot?* (New York, 1963).

25. Albert H. Marckwardt, *American English* (New York, 1958), 57–58; Douglas G. Marshall, "Nationality and the Emerging Culture," *Rural Sociology*, 13 (1948); 42; Edward N. Saveth, *American Historians and European Immigrants, 1875–1925* (New York, 1948), chap. 5; Samuel Lubell, *The Future of American Politics*, 2d ed. (Garden City, N.Y., 1956), chap. 5; J. Joseph Huthmacher, "Urban Liberalism and the Age of Reform," *Mississippi Valley Historical Review*, 49 (September 1962), 234.

26. "Boston's Melting Pot," *Literary Digest*, 54 (April 14, 1917), 1063; Ralph Wood, ed., *The Pennsylvania Germans* (Princeton, N.J., 1942), 3; Gerrit P. Judd IV, *Hawaii, An Informal History* (New York, 1961), chap. 13; J. Isaac, "Israel—A New Melting Pot?" in W. D. Borrie, ed., *The Cultural Integration of Immigrants* ([Paris], 1959), 234–66.

27. *Survey*, 28 (April 27, 1912), 161–62; *Analysis of America's Modern Melting Pot*. Hearings before the Committee on Immigration and Naturalization, House of Representatives, 68th Cong., 3d sess., November 21, 1922. Serial 7-C. Statement by Harry H. Laughlin (Washington, D.C., 1923), 729, 760.

28. W. F. Adams, quoted in Carl Wittke, *We Who Built America. The Saga of the*

Immigrant (New York, 1939), 131; Thomas Capek, *The Cechs (Bohemians) in America.
A Study of Their National, Cultural, Political, Social, Economic, and Religious Life*
(Boston, 1920), chap. 7; John S. Hejhal, "The Czechs in the Melting Pot: American-
ization in Colfax County, Nebraska, 1869–1959" (Master's thesis, University of Wy-
oming, 1959); Joseph Martinek, "Czechoslovakian Ingredient in the Melting Pot,"
American Czechoslovak Flashes, October 15, 1917, cited in R. A. Schermerhorn, *These
Our People. Minorities in American Culture* (Boston, 1949), 620.

29. Carl Russell Fish, "The Pilgrim and the Melting Pot," *Mississippi Valley
Historical Review*, 7 (December 1920), 187–205; Roger Butterfield, *The American
Past* (New York, 1947), 228; Margaret Mead, "How Religion Has Fared in the Melting
Pot," in C. Kluckhohn et al., *Religion and Our Racial Tensions* (Cambridge 1945),
chap. 4; George Creel, quoted in Higham, *Strangers in the Land*, 277; *Zangwill in
the Melting-Pot. Selections from the Works of the Author*, ed. Elsie E. Morton (London,
n.d.); Bessie Bloom Wessel, *An Ethnic Survey of Woonsocket, Rhode Island* (Chicago,
1931), 289.

30. Percy S. Grant, "American Ideals and Race Mixture," *North American Review*,
195 (April 1912), 514; *The New Democracy. Presidential Messages, Addresses, and
Other Papers (1913–1917)*, vol. 4 of *The Public Papers of Woodrow Wilson*, 6 vols.,
ed. Ray Stannard Baker and William E. Dodd (New York, 1925–27), 180–81; Sisley
Huddleston, "Europe in the Melting Pot," *Atlantic Monthly*, 130 (1922), 414–20.

31. Wood, *Pennsylvania Germans*, 17; Hansen, *The Atlantic Migration,
1607–1860.* (New York, 1961), 72; Russel B. Nye, *The Cultural Life of the New Nation,
1776–1830* (New York, 1960), 123; David A. Reed, "America of the Melting Pot Comes
to an End," *New York Times*, April 27, 1924; Fairchild, *Melting-Pot Mistake*, 11.

32. Zangwill, *Melting-Pot*, 199; *Literary Digest*, 48 (February 28, 1914), 425;
Public Papers of Woodrow Wilson, 4:180; Max Farrand, "Assimilation," *New Republic*,
9 (December 23, 1916), 209–10; review by Stanley R. Pliska, in *Journal of Southern
History*, 28 (February 1962), 110.

33. Zangwill, *Melting-Pot*, 198–99; Hansen, *Atlantic Migration*, 72; Nye. *Cultural Life of the New Nation*, 123; Saveth, *American Historians and European Immigrants*, 146; Fish, "The Pilgrim in the Melting Pot," 190; Cushing Strout, *The
American Image of the Old World* (New York, 1963), 135; Wood, *Pennsylvania Germans*, 17; "Yellow Froth on the Melting Pot," *Sunset, The Pacific Monthly*, 35 (May
1916), 36; Edwin E. Grant, "Scum from the Melting-Pot," *American Journal of Sociology*, 30 (May 1925), 643; *Analysis of America's Modern Melting Pot*, 725, 729,
760.

34. J. B. Murphy, "What America Means and How to Americanize the Immigrant," *Immigrants in America Review*, 1 (September 1915), 92; editorial, "The Ca-
pacity of the Melting Pot," ibid., 2 (April 1916), 14; Max Henrici, "The Lesson of the
Melting Pot," *American Leader*, 9 (March 9, 1916), 277–79; Henry Berman, "Stirring
the Melting Pot," *Jewish Immigration Bulletin*, 4 (September 1914), 2–4; James D.
Whelpley, "The Overtaxed Melting Pot," *Living Age*, 63 (April 11, 1914), 67–72; Simon
J. Lubin and Christina Krysto, "The Strength of America; I, Cracks in the Melting
Pot," *Survey*, 43 (December 20, 1919), 258–59; Gerald C. Treacy, "The American
Melting Pot," *America*, 23 (July 17, 1920), 295; Walter V. Woehlke, "Confessions of a
Hyphenate," *Century Magazine*, 93 (1916), 930.

35. Fairchild, *Melting-Pot Mistake*, 120; Zangwill, *Melting-Pot*, 37–38; *Public
Papers of Woodrow Wilson*, 4:180; *Forum*, 42 (November 1909), 435; An Unassimi-
lated Foreigner, "The Failure of the Melting Pot," *Nation*, 110 (January 24, 1920),
100–102; Randolph S. Bourne, "Trans-National America," *Atlantic Monthly*, 118 (July
1916), 89; "The 'Melting Pot' a Myth," *Journal of Heredity*, 8 (March 1917), 99–105.

36. George R. Stewart, *American Ways of Life* (New York, 1954), 23.

37. Ibid., 23–24. Cf. also W. Lloyd Warner and Leo Srole, *The Social Systems of American Ethnic Groups* (New Haven, Conn., 1945), 155.

38. Karl E. Meyer, *The New America. Politics and Culture in the Age of the Smooth Deal* (New York, 1961), chap. 9; Wytrwal, *America's Polish Heritage*, 119; Francis J. Brown and Joseph S. Roucek, eds., *One America. The History, Contributions, and Present Problems of Our Racial and National Minorities*, 3d ed. (New York, 1952), 518; Carl N. Degler, *Out of Our Past. The Forces that Shaped Modern America* (New York, 1959), 290, 296; Frederick Jackson Turner, *The United States 1830–1850. The Nation and Its Sections* (New York, 1935), 55, 286.

39. Wytrwal, *America's Polish Heritage*, 245; Horace M. Kallen, *Culture and Democracy in the United States.* (New York, 1924), 58–59; Stephen Graham, *With Poor Immigrants to America* (New York, 1914), 287–88; Richard M. Dorson, *Bloodstoppers and Bearwalkers. Folk Traditions of the Upper Peninsula* (Cambridge, Mass.: 1952), 10; Barbara Miller Solomon, *Ancestors and Immigrants. A Changing New England Tradition* (Cambridge, Mass.: 1956), 193.

40. Kallen, *Culture and Democracy*, 124–25; Graham, *With Poor Immigrants*, chap. 16.

41. Fairchild, *Melting-Pot Mistake*, 151–52; D. W. Brogan, *The American Character* (1944; New York, 1956), 119–20.

42. George Creel, "Melting Pot or Dumping Ground?" *Collier's*, 68 (September 3, 1921), 9–10; Fairchild, *Melting-Pot Mistake*, 125; Fairchild, *Race and Nationality*, 117. The inevitable comparison of the melting pot to a "witches' " cauldron" also implied derogation of the immigrants. Cf. William W. Cook, *American Institutions and Their Preservation*, 2d ed. 2 vols. (New York, 1929), 2:578. Madison Grant said New York was becoming a "*cloaca gentium.*" Quoted in Oscar Handlin, ed., *Immigration as a Factor in American History* (Englewood Cliffs, N.J., 1959), 185.

43. Zangwill, "America—'The Melting Pot.' "

44. Stewart, *American Ways of Life*, 23–24; Lawrence Frank Pisani, *The Italian in America. A Social Study and History* (New York, 1957), 255; Edgar T. Thompson, ed., *Race Relations and the Race Problem* (Durham, N.C., 1939), 250, 284.

45. Clyde V. Kiser, "Cultural Pluralism," *Annals*, 262 (March 1949), 128; Ellen Terry Bremer, "Development of Private Social Work with the Foreign Born," ibid., 143; comment by Stanley H. Chapman in Horace M. Kallen, *Cultural Pluralism and the American Idea* (Philadelphia, 1956), 109.

46. Percy Stickney Grant, "American Ideals and Race Mixture," *North American Review*, 195 (April 1912), 513–25.

47. See, for example, *Immigrants in America Review*, 1 (September 1915), 3, 23, 92. On Americanization, see Edward George Hartmann, *The Movement to Americanize the Immigrant* (New York, 1948).

48. Julius Drachsler, *Democracy and Assimilation. The Blending of Immigrant Heritages in America* (New York, 1920), 233.

49. Lubin and Krysto, "Strength of America," 258.

50. See photograph in *Outlook*, 114 (1916), 197; Walter Lippmann, *Public Opinion* (New York, 1922), 86–87; Ray Allen Billington, "Cultural Contribution versus Cultural Assimilation," in Caroline F. Ware, ed., *The Cultural Approach to History* (New York, 1940), 79–80; Fairchild, *Race and Nationality*, 129; Higham, *Strangers in the Land*, 248.

51. Horace M. Kallen, "Democracy *versus* the Melting-Pot," *Nation*, 100 (February 18, 1915), 190–94; ibid. (February 25, 1915), 217–20; quoted from Kallen, *Culture and Democracy*, 122–23.

52. Kallen, *Culture and Democracy*, 124–25.

53. Ibid., 155ff., 43.

54. Randolph Bourne, "Trans-National America," 86–97; reprinted in Bourne, *History of a Literary Radical and Other Essays*, ed. Van Wyck Brooks (New York, 1920), 266–99.

55. John Dewey, "Nationalizing Education," in National Education Association of the United States, *Addresses and Proceedings of the Fifty-Fourth Annual Meeting*, 54 (1916), 183–89.

56. Lubin and Krysto, "Strength of America," esp. 258–59, 690ff.

57. Horace J. Bridges, *On Becoming an American. Some Meditations of a Newly Naturalized Immigrant* (Boston, 1919), chaps. 8–10; see also the review of this book quoted in Handlin, *Immigration as a Factor*, 156–58.

58. Isaac B. Berkson, *Theories of Americanization. A Critical Study with Special Reference to the Jewish Group* (New York, 1920), 73–78.

59. *Analysis of America's Modern Melting Pot*, passim; Roy L. Garis, *Immigration Restriction. A Study of the Opposition to and Regulation of Immigration into the United States* (New York, 1927), 239ff.; Robert A. Divine, *American Immigration Policy, 1924–1952* (New Haven, Conn., 1957), 7, 12–14.

60. Fairchild, *Melting-Pot Mistake*, esp. 119–20.

61. Ibid., 11.

62. Saveth, *American Historians and European Immigrants*, 122ff.; Merle Curti et al., *The Making of an American Community. A Case Study of Democracy in a Frontier County* (Stanford, Calif., 1959), 61, 105, 297.

63. Wessel, *Ethnic Survey*, 23, vii; Christine Avghi Galitzi, *A Study of Assimilation among the Roumanians in the United States* (New York, 1929), 157–58; William C. Smith, *Americans in the Making. The Natural History of the Assimilation of Immigrants* (New York, 1939), 114.

64. Ruby Jo Reeves Kennedy, "Single or Triple Melting-Pot," *American Journal of Sociology*, 49 (January 1944), 331–39; Will Herberg, *Protestant-Catholic-Jew: An Essay in American Religious Sociology*, rev. ed. (Garden City, N.Y., 1960), chaps. 2, 3.

65. Kallen, *Cultural Pluralism and the American Idea*, 197–98; Degler, *Out of Our Past*, 295–96; Meyer, *New America*, chap. 9; Amitai Etzioni, "The Ghetto—A Reevaluation," *Social Forces*, 37 (1958–59), 260; Franklin D. Scott in Henry Steele Commager, ed., *Immigration and American History: Essays in Honor of Theodore C. Blegen* (Minneapolis, 1961), 123; J. M. Radzinski, "The American Melting Pot: Its Meaning for Us," *American Journal of Psychiatry*, 115 (April 1959), 873–86.

66. Arthur M. Schlesinger, Sr., "America's Influence: Our Ten Contributions to Civilization," *Atlantic Monthly*, 203 (March 1959), 67; Christopher Jencks, "The Next Thirty Years in Our Colleges," *Harper's Magazine*, 223 (October 1961), 126–27; David Riesman, *Individualism Reconsidered* (Garden City, N.Y., 1955), 54–55; Theodore H. White, *The Making of the President 1960* (New York, 1961), 267ff.; Louis B. Wright, *Cultural Life of the American Colonies*, 45; Harry J. Carman, Harold C. Syrett, and Bernard W. Wishy, *A History of the American People*, 2d ed., 2 vols. (New York, 1961), 2:796–97.

67. Kohn, *American Nationalism*, 155, 171; Herberg, *Protestant-Catholic-Jew*, 20.

68. Quoted as epigraph in Black, *The Importance of Language*.

69. The stress on uniformity is largely obviated by thinking of the melting pot as an unfinished process, where there is no "drawing off" of the product. If we picture

a pot without a tap, in continuous interaction, would it not conform to the reality to suppose that if one dipped into the contents in 1960 one would find the specimen one took considerably more "melted" than it might have been in 1930 or 1900? Still, this would not imply absolute homogeneity of contents throughout in 1960 any more than in 1900.

70. Berkson, *Theories of Americanization*, 87. Cf. Sidney Ratner, ed., *Vision and Action. Essays in Honor of Horace M. Kallen on His 70th Birthday* (New Brunswick, N.J., 1953), 106.

|| 2 ||

Confusion Compounded:
A Melting Pot Update

The racial crisis of the 1960s and the broader ethnic revival it set off catapulted the melting pot once more into prominence, but with more negative connotations than ever. Its becoming almost exclusively a term of abuse did not, however, clear up all the ambiguities attending its use, even though *melting pot* was conventionally cast as the evil twin, with *pluralism* being the good twin. On the contrary, confusion was compounded by the widespread resort to terms that, as I put it in this essay, "impose upon the phenomena a conceptual framework that is at the same time murkily vacuous yet rigid and highly judgmental."

The update on melting pot usage that follows here was written when the ethnic revival was at its height. The paper itself was, like the original melting pot essay, presented at a meeting of the Ohio–Indiana American Studies Group, held this time at Bowling Green State University in May 1976. It did not find its way into print until 1979, by which time the ethnic revival was nearly over. That fact was far less clear than it is in retrospect, but several major critiques of the revival had already been published and others were soon to appear.[a] Even if these writers also found fault with the melting pot—as, for example, Orlando Patterson did—their works helped to correct the rhetorical imbalance created by the excesses of the revivalists.[b] Others discussed the melting pot in more frankly sympathetic terms. Justice William O. Douglas did so in his opinion in the DeFunis case; so did Ralph Ellison, who noted, among other things, that "the melting-pot concept was never so simplistic or abstract as current arguments would have it."[c] David Hollinger's reflections on its relation to democracy were published under the title "Two Cheers for the Melting Pot"; and Werner Sollors wrote several pieces defending the melting pot, vindicating it, and revealing its hitherto unrecognized symbolic associations, from the sexual to the alchemical.[d]

I have not made a systematic review of the relevant literature, but my impression is that usage of the term continued to be preponderantly negative in the eighties, though not nearly so much so as in the preceding

decade. According to Richard Alba, the "simplistic dualism between melting pot and cultural pluralism no longer dominates debate about ethnicity," and other sociological studies of assimilation refer to the melting
pot in a relatively positive manner.[e] It is still unusual to encounter out-
rightly favorable employment of the symbol in what might be called
policy-related contexts, but Arthur M. Schlesinger, Jr., has done so in
discussing multiculturalism, and a nationally syndicated cartoonist did
portray Mr. and Mrs. Average Citizen gazing in bewilderment at a huge
pile of cooking pans, each with a separate ethnic label, and asking,
"Whatever happened to that big melting pot?"[f] And the rhetorical climate
has cooled sufficiently to permit increased employment of the term in
descriptive contexts—including nonethnic ones such as a newspaper
column by the "Cultivated Gardener" headed "All-American Garden a
Melting Pot."[g] But another recent example breathes a very different
spirit—a tee shirt reading "America is like a melting pot: the people at
the bottom get burned and the scum floats to the top."[h] With that we
are ready to reenter the passionate rhetorical world of the ethnic revival
at its height.

A number of years ago I contributed to the *American Quarterly* an article
entitled "The Melting Pot: Symbol of Fusion or Confusion?" (see above,
chap. 1). It was not a particularly "relevant" piece when it appeared,
since the ethnic revival was still several years in the future. Although
Glazer and Moynihan's *Beyond the Melting Pot* had just appeared, that
work was not what prompted the investigation. Rather, what piqued my
curiosity about the melting pot was the remark made by Henry Pratt
Fairchild in 1926 that the village dog pound was a better symbol than
the melting pot for "race mixture" in America. I came across this striking
substitution of metaphors in the late 1950s. In the context of the then
current preoccupation with myths, symbols, and national character, the
melting pot seemed a promising subject to research. In the decade that
has passed since the article appeared, the situation has changed markedly. Our interest in symbols and myths has abated, but the melting pot
is referred to more frequently in public discussion than at any time since
World War I. In view of these shifts, it will be worthwhile to update the
melting pot analysis by reviewing the way the expression has been used
in the past dozen years. As the present title suggests, I believe recent
usage confirms the conclusions I arrived at in 1964, so let me begin by
recapitulating several of the main points made in the original article.[1]

    1. The melting pot as a symbol for ethnic interaction entered the

language in 1908 as a direct result of the presentation of Israel Zangwill's play *The Melting-Pot*. The word *melt* had been used in connection with immigrant assimilation as far back as Crèvecoeur, and the metaphor of a crucible had been used a number of times before 1908. But neither of these expressions calls up quite the same thing—*melting process*, for instance, differs considerably from *melting pot*, and no one expected Arthur Miller's play *The Crucible* to deal with immigration.

2. The image of the melting pot almost irresistably invites elaboration. Those who use it soon find themselves talking about purging fires, simmering contents, scum on the top, dross, fumes, ladles, molds, and on and on. Largely because of its vividness and aptness for journalistic embellishment, the melting pot caught on, becoming incomparably the most popular metaphor for the process of ethnic interaction. And as a result of its widespread use, it became a basic piece of intellectual equipment in discussions of immigration and assimilation.

3. Although *melting pot* has been indispensable to public discussion of these issues since 1908, its meaning is so ambiguous that it never furnished a satisfactory tool of analysis. Some people interpreted the function of the melting pot as that of purging away the cultural impurities of immigrant groups and transforming them into hundred-percent Americans according to the Anglo-Saxon model. Others, however, saw the whole society as in the melting pot and anticipated that it would produce in the end a new culture, blended from the elements of all. They looked toward a new American, a new national character. Attitudes toward the melting pot were as diverse as the several versions of what it meant. The man who wrote the play, Israel Zangwill, was an English Jew who considered the melting pot an admirable ideal, but other Jews rejected it as a mess of pottage that demanded as its price the surrender of their birthright. The same division of opinion occurred among other immigrant groups, and among older Americans as well.

4. The melting pot acquired a bad reputation with liberals at the time of World War I which it has never been able to throw off. Horace Kallen attacked it as a betrayal of true Americanism in 1915, and most other progressives agreed that what Kallen called cultural pluralism offered a much more attractive model. They objected to the hundred-percent Americanization version of the melting pot; but in the 1920s Fairchild and other conservatives (such as Hiram Evans of the KKK) turned against the melting pot precisely because it failed to purge away the foreignness of immigrants in the manner prescribed by that version of melting pot theory. Despite its falling into disfavor among both liberals and conservatives, however, *melting pot* continued in use in later decades

because the symbol and all its contradictory meanings had become so deeply enmeshed in the language.

Thus far the melting pot analysis of 1964. Something I have learned since then about how British writers use the term should be added before we review more recent usage. The point is important because if Zangwill had been an American rather than an English writer, it is most unlikely he would have used the symbol at all—and our subsequent thinking about ethnic interaction would thereby have been changed. The melting pot has had a very different metaphoric career in Britain from what it has had in America. British writers before and after Zangwill use the expression as a generic metaphor for any process involving basic change. In the United States, however, there is no evidence it was used metaphorically at all before 1908, and since then it has been strictly limited to the process of ethnic and cultural blending. Thus the *Oxford English Dictionary* notes that *melting pot* is "often *fig.* with reference to thorough remodeling of institutions, etc." and gives an example from 1877 in which John Morley advised against sending the British constitution to the melting pot. On the American side, Craigie and Hulbert make no mention of metaphoric usage in their *Dictionary of American English on Historical Principles*, but the recent *Random House Dictionary of the English Language* (college ed., 1968) gives the following as the first definition of *melting pot*: "a country, locality, or situation in which a blending of races and cultures is taking place."

Herbert Butterfield is a good example of a contemporary British writer who is fond of the melting pot as a generic metaphor for change— he has spoken at various times of the British constitution, scientific ideas, and systems of historical interpretation as being in the melting pot.[2] Another English writer, H. G. Schenk, describes the romantic period as one in which all ideas and ideals were in the melting pot; E. E. Y. Hales said the future of the Italian states was in the melting pot in 1848; and twenty years ago R. R. Bolgar found the discipline of classical studies "tremb[ling] on the edge of the melting pot." So frequently is the melting pot used as a generic metaphor by British writers that George Orwell treated it as showpiece of hackneyed terminology in his essay "Politics and the English Language." In complaining of mixed journalistic metaphors, Orwell gave this egregious example: "the jackboot is thrown into the melting pot."[3]

Americans never use the melting pot in this generalized sense, but a recent article on school counseling programs demonstrates that we can mix metaphors quite handily in discussing the strictly ethnic vessel: the article is entitled "Gatekeeping and the Melting Pot."[4] What is most remarkable about recent usage, however, is that the melting pot is repeatedly invoked by those who reject what they think it stands for and that the image is lavishly embellished by people who deny that the melting pot ever existed.

Glazer and Moynihan's widely noted *Beyond the Melting Pot*, which was published in 1963, set the tone for much recent usage in asserting that "the point about the melting pot is that it did not happen."[5] Although the two authors concede that "the specifically *national* aspect" of ethnicity generally disappears in three generations, most later commentators assume that Glazer and Moynihan have completely discredited what one reviewer called the "fearful and contemptuous" theory of the melting pot.[6] In 1965 sociologist William Petersen referred to the melting pot as a "gruesome metaphor" that was misleading in its implications, a view evidently shared by the reader of a liberal Catholic journal who objected to a columnist's "resurrecting the corpse of the melting pot theory" and who went on to assert that it "produce[d] a poisonous brew out of sweet intentions."[7] Equally gruesome is the view ascribed to revisionist historians of American education who are said to regard the melting pot as "some sort of waspish cauldron, which cannibalistically devoured the immigrant's past and his ethnic identity." After these extremes, it is a relief to find the melting pot characterized merely as a "transparent fiction" or a theory that won't hold water.[8]

Considering the prevailing standards of public discourse, one would have to say that the scatological possibilities of the melting pot have been surprisingly neglected. But thanks to Geno Baroni's reminder that in the past Americans were expected to "melt or get off the pot," they have not been entirely overlooked.[9]

According to the colonial historian Michael Kammen, the melting pot is an inept metaphor, but it did work for the blacks in the sense that it turned many different kinds of Africans into one kind of African-American. After making this straightforward point, Kammen falls victim to the overpowering urge to embroider the imagery. "Thus," he adds cutely, "the only American melting pot has perhaps always been a black one, though in this case the putative pot has been reluctant to call the kettle black."[10]

Black writers, so far as I have seen, have not decoded this utterance, but they have had a good deal to say about the melting pot. A dialogue between Rev. Jesse Jackson and Dr. Alvin Poussaint provides a vivid example of how melting pot imagery entraps even those who ostensibly reject the symbol. After saying that the melting pot doesn't work and that the "melting pot concept of equality" was designed to cover up the murder of the Indians and the theft of their land, Rev. Jackson goes on to state his preference for the soup bowl as a symbol of ethnic interaction. But that substitution does not seem to solve the problem, for although each group "has poured in a bit of their blood, sweat and tears," "blacks have been pushed to the bottom of the soup bowl and are the last to be recognized and the first to be scorched." Warming now to his subject, Rev. Jackson warns that "it's either you let my people go and recognize me or we're gonna blow a hole in the bottom of this thing and let every-body go down the drain. Or we're gonna turn over the whole bowl so some rearrangements can be made." At this point, Dr. Poussaint observes that blacks "have the basic strengths to rearrange the soup," but he wonders how many believe that the way to survival is "to leave the whole bowl of soup—get out of the melting pot." To this, Jackson responds: "Of course, sometimes blacks get to thinking they can just sneak into a corner of this bowl and stay there, oblivious to the other forces going on in the bowl and some try to make a decision to escape the bowl. The fact is . . . we've put too much in this bowl to all of a sudden give it up."[11]

Jesse Jackson is by no means the only one to treat the supposedly alternative symbol of the soup bowl as though it were interchangeable with the melting pot. Michael Novak, the best-known prophet of white ethnicity, pointed out in a newspaper column that the standardizing pressures of American life were "driving out diversity and praising (um, um, good!) the homogenized soup of the melting pot," and in his *Rise of the Unmeltable Ethnics* (1972) he flatly states, "The melting pot is a kind of homogenized soup."[12]

The title of Novak's book is derived from melting pot symbolism, and the work itself is a priceless cabinet of metaphoric curiosities. Novak maintains, of course, that there never really was a melting pot. Thus he writes that immigrants "gambled a great deal on the melting pot. It did not exist." They found American life "not a melting pot [but] a jungle!" Yet the myth of the melting pot was very real. According to Novak, it "has dominated the social sciences for three decades," and he suggests that "melting-pot ideology" may have been devised as a means of re-ducing the "political and economic power" of immigrant groups.[13]

But while explicitly rejecting the metaphor and what it stands for, Novak cannot free himself from the imagery it provides for discussion of ethnic interaction. Indeed, he revels in melting pot imagery. We have already seen that he equates melting pot and soup, and in endorsing the statement that "America is a sizzling cauldron for the ethnic American," he accepts an obvious variant of the melting pot. The symbol itself he uses with little regard for theoretical or metaphoric consistency. In one place, Novak reports that Norman Mailer "tried to embrace the melting pot," but further on he contradicts himself by citing Mailer as evidence for the statement that "good writing in America is inherently subversive of 'the melting pot.' " Elsewhere he claims that although we "did not have one before, . . . now national television is our melting pot." The rhetoric of Spiro Agnew ("one of the most meltable of ethnics") is a product of the melting pot: "Crackling phrases had been simmering in the melting pot for generations and his speechwriters pulled them out molten." In an apocalyptic figure, Novak associates the melting pot with the agony in southeast Asia: "We had set out to pour the acids of our melting pot over Vietnam."[14]

This sampler of metaphoric usage could be extended, but it should suffice to confirm the point that the image of the melting pot still exerts a powerful hold on the imagination of those who write on ethnic matters and that it is used with great figurative abandon in the most diverse contexts and with every conceivable embellishment. This rank luxuriance of metaphoric usage of course magnifies the problem of conceptual ambiguity, for if it was never very clear just what the melting pot "meant," its meaning becomes even more elusive when it is employed with such wild imprecision. Even a sober academic comparison, "The Melting Pot in Canada and the United States," used the metaphor in a wide variety of senses—in some places it meant simply the environment; elsewhere, "the idea and process of ethnic interaction" and the society in which it goes on; but it also seemed to be equated with "achievement orientation applied to entire groups," with equality of opportunity, and with "the culture of all those . . . whose credo was the American idea."[15] And what are we to make of an inquiry into the nature of the new ethnicity that talks about "the consequences of a melting pot theory which in theory has included all but in reality left out the unmeltables and created a generation from melted parents who search for an identity not found in the melting pot"?[16]

But despite the lack of clarity in specific cases, several generalizations may be ventured concerning the overall situation today.

1. First, those who refer to the melting pot nearly always regard it quite negatively. Occasionally one comes upon a writer who defends the melting pot as an ideal or argues that the process it symbolizes did take place,[17] but the predominant attitude is definitely hostile.

2. Two assumptions account for most of this hostility. The first is the belief that the melting pot holds up complete homogenization as the ideal; the second, and very closely related, belief is that the melting pot actually amounts to forced Americanization. Fused together, these two

assumptions lead to the conclusion that the melting pot is designed to turn all immigrants and their descendants into reproductions of white Anglo-Saxon Protestant Americans.

3. Third, not only do most writers reject this melting pot with vehemence, but they go on to deny that it ever had any reality. The conventional wisdom is thus twofold: as an ideal or goal the melting pot is reprehensible, but in the practical order (fortunately, one presumes) it didn't exist, never happened, failed to melt, and is a myth.

4. Finally, one may conventionally expect to find a rejection of the "melting pot" coupled with an endorsement of "pluralism." This is, of course, a convenience in distinguishing the children of light from children of darkness, but it is not otherwise very informative. For, aside from being vaguely associated with the notion that diversity is a good thing, "pluralism" is pretty much a conceptual black box—it can mean almost anything.

Melting pot is thus not the only obscure and confusing term in vogue in discussions of this sort, and we must glance ever so briefly at the interlinked ambiguities of *pluralism* and *ethnicity*.

John Higham has recently made a monumental contribution by tracing the tortuous complications of "Ethnic Pluralism in Modern American Thought." Here he shows that Kallen's original formulation stressed the value of preserving consciously held cultural features (such as language); with Robert E. Park, however, cultural pluralism had become merely the first stage of the assimilation cycle. Since Park's time, pluralism has been variously interpreted as referring primarily to religious differences, as a form of veto group politics, and as describing a particular pattern of social interaction. Most recently, Higham argues, pluralism has ceased to be a policy of intergroup relations and has given way to "a new particularism, which encourages a heightened solidarity within any segment of the population that can define itself as somehow distinct."[18]

Another way of illustrating the slipperiness of pluralism as a concept is to ask what kind of differences between groups constitute the grounds on which they may be said to be pluralized. For Kallen, the differences were quite tangible: an ensemble of consciously prized social and cultural features such as language, press, theater, ethnic societies, etcetera. But as these aspects of ethnic culture have been eroded by assimilation, the grounds of pluralism have become progressively more elusive. Thus Milton Gordon argues that structural pluralism succeeds cultural pluralism, by which he means roughly that people still sort themselves out ethnically for purposes of informal socialization, even though, outwardly, they may all seem alike. For the ethnocultural analysts of political behavior, it is collective voting patterns that demonstrate the reality of pluralism. And Michael Novak has pushed pluralism to a new level of etherialization by grounding it in such matters as distinctive reactions to pain among persons of different ethnic backgrounds, and more generally upon "emotions, instincts, memory, imagination, passions, and ways of perceiving [which] are passed on to us in ways that we do not choose, and in ways so thick with life that they lie far beyond the power of consciousness (let alone analytic and verbal reason) thoroughly to master, totally to alter."[19]

Perhaps the most important point made in Higham's superb analysis is his insistence that the doctrine of pluralism "has unconsciously relied on the assimilative process which it seemed to repudiate."[20] For what is it but assimilation to a common core of universalistic norms (such as tolerance and justice) that prevents the stress on group solidarity and pride from expressing itself in hostility to outsiders, in prejudiced attitudes and discriminatory behavior? Anthropologists report that what are called plural societies elsewhere in the world are generally either "tyrannies ruled by one of the constituent groups" or are societies "disrupted by open conflict and plagued by instability." They express doubt that democracy can work in a society deeply divided by intense and conflicting ethnic loyalties. For this reason Higham concludes that pluralism is workable only if based on "an underlying consensus about basic values, . . . a unifying ideology, faith, or myth."[21]

To the degree that ethnic spokesmen advert to such considerations, they usually do so merely to assert that pluralism is not the same as polarization, that it somehow means unity rather than division. The rhapsodic Mr. Novak, for example, proclaims that "we will find greater unity in those depths in which unity irradiates diversity than we will by attempting, through the artifices of the American 'melting pot' . . . to become what we are not."[22] "The new ethnicity does not stand for the Balkanization of America," he assures us:

> It stands for a true, real, multicultural cosmopolitanism. It
> points toward a common culture truly altered by each new infu-
> sion of diversity. Until now . . . the melting pot has had only a
> single recipe. That is why at present the common culture seems
> to have become discredited, shattered, unenforceable. Its co-
> coon has broken. Struggling to be born is a creature of multi-
> cultural beauty, dazzling, free, a higher and richer form of life.
> It was fashioned in the painful darkness of the melting pot and
> now, at the appointed time, it awakens.[23]

Here the foremost critic of the melting pot proposes a classical melting pot ideal in visualizing the creation of a new common culture out of
multicultural materials, yet it seems likely that Novak considers this a
departure from melting pot thinking. It is a perfect illustration of the
way confusion has been compounded in discussions of this sort. But note
also that Novak does not explain *why* the new ethnicity will work out in
such a benign and harmonious way; he simply asserts that it will. Surely
this is an instance of Higham's point that pluralism "has unconsciously
relied on the assimilative process which it seemed to repudiate"—a reliance that in this case is unconsciously betrayed by the very language
involved.

Without entering further into the problem of what ethnicity means—
or the even murkier terrain of "new ethnicity"[24]—the evidence already
presented seems to me to establish the point that the terminology employed in such discussions confuses rather than clarifies our efforts to
understand the situation and to identify policy issues. But, one might
object, what is being talked about is a confusing business—a tangle of
diffuse feelings, ill-defined identities, impalpable hopes, obscure resentments, vague social goals, and crosscutting interests. In dealing with
these matters, we must learn to tolerate ambiguities because there is no
way to reduce the swirl of reality to neat conceptual categories.

This objection has great force—except that it is not really an objection to my position. For my complaint is not that the reality is complex
and elusive; nor is it that terms such as *melting pot, pluralism,* and
ethnicity are ambiguous. My complaint rather is that these ambiguous
terms are handled as though they had one univocal meaning, which
everyone understood and to which everyone attached the same positive
or negative significance. I complain further that prevailing usage encourages us to think that by invoking these terms as incantations we
have gotten a useful handle on the phenomena, that we know something
about the situation we didn't know before, that we are in a better position
to judge what action should be taken, what policy should be supported.
What we are dealing with here are terms that have been reified. But they
have been reified on such a low level of conceptual clarity that, when
applied in discussions of group life and social policy, they *prevent* us
from grasping complexities or appreciating ambiguities. For what this
terminology actually does is impose upon the phenomena a conceptual
framework that is at the same time murkily vacuous yet rigid and highly
judgmental.

Perhaps the most unfortunate aspect of the terminological situation
is the impression that the melting pot and pluralism are absolutely di-

chotomous—that they rule each other out, that to espouse pluralism is to condemn the melting pot, or that to defend the melting pot is to wage war on all forms of diversity. This view, I would say, is simply wrong. Both terms are figurative, rich and complex in implication; they can be interpreted in many different ways and can cover a wide range of social phenomena or policy options. In short, they are not mutually exclusive; rather, they overlap and merge into each other. The reason they overlap is that each was intended by its originator to comprehend the full spectrum of tendencies in American society—the impulse to unity *and* the tendency toward multiplicity, the elements shared universally *as well as* the features that set people apart. The melting pot, to be sure, lays greater stress on *unum* than on *pluribus*, while pluralism reverses the emphasis; but both terms implicitly comprehend both ends of the polarity. The difference between them is really a matter of differential emphasis.

But, to repeat, contemporary usage treats *melting pot* and *pluralism* as mutually exclusive and associates *pluralism* with everything good in social policy and *melting pot* with everything bad. The consequence of this oversimplified dualism is to keep people from recognizing what their agreements and disagreements actually are. Because pluralists must reject the melting pot, they find it difficult to recognize the essential role played in their own ideology by reliance on "an underlying consensus about basic values." Because it was introduced with noisy anti–melting pot fanfare, the proponents of the "Ethnic Heritages" program for the schools seem not to realize that their goal—which is to bring about through better intergroup understanding "a more harmonious, patriotic, and committed populace"[25]—is in the classical melting pot tradition both in its aims and in seeking to realize those aims through the educational system. And in denigrating Americanization and the inculcation of universal values, proponents of the new pluralism forget that they too have a stake in the American rules of the game whereby all of us try to recognize the claims of justice and to resolve our conflicts by reason and by mutual give and take.

Perhaps the spokesmen for various ethnic interest groups cannot be expected to be fastidious in their use of language. They are interested not primarily in understanding what is going on but in getting something for their constituents. It is to their advantage to denigrate the melting pot and to identify their own particular interests with the universal claims of justice and with the true meaning of Americanism. But the sort of confusion this tactic reinforces is not healthy for the polity as a whole. Government by discussion is hopeless if it is impossible to determine what is being discussed, and the resolution of disputes is frustrated if people cannot tell what is really at issue. For this reason, those of us who deal in words and are dedicated to ideas have an obligation to do what we can to clarify the situation. Scholars of immigration and ethnicity, in particular, must take care not to legitimatize oversimplifications by their own carelessness.

NOTES

Source: "Confusion Compounded: The Melting Pot in the 1960s and 1970s," *Ethnicity,* 6 (1979), 10–20. Copyright by the Academic Press; reprinted by permission.

a. Orlando Patterson, *Ethnic Chauvinism: The Reactionary Impulse* (New York, 1977); Howard F. Hill and Robert F. Stein, *The Ethnic Imperative* (University Park, Pa., 1977); Richard N. Current, *Unity, Ethnicity, and Abraham Lincoln* (Fort Wayne, Ind., 1978), a lecture reprinted in Current, *Arguing with Historians: Essays on the Historical and the Unhistorical* (Middletown, Conn., 1987), chap. 11; Arthur Mann, *The One and the Many: Reflections on the American Identity* (Chicago, 1979); Stephen Steinberg, *The Ethnic Myth: Race, Ethnicity, and Class in America* (New York, 1981).

b. Patterson, *Ethnic Chauvinism,* 148–51; Patterson did not, however, criticize the melting pot in his earlier article, "On Guilt, Relativism, and Black-White Relations," *American Scholar,* 43 (Winter 1973–74), 122–32. Mann's *One and Many,* a model of balance and good sense, includes denunciation of the melting pot among the "excesses" of the revivalists (43). See also Mann, "The Melting Pot," in Richard L. Bushman et al., eds., *Uprooted Americans: Essays to Honor Oscar Handlin* (Boston, 1979), 291–318.

c. "The melting pot," Douglas wrote, "is not designed to homogenize people, making them uniform in consistency. . . . It is a figure of speech that depicts the wide diversities tolerated by the First Amendment under one flag." Quoted from DeFunis v. Odegaard, 416 U.S. 312 (1974), p. 344, in Kevin M. Fong, "Comment: Cultural Pluralism," *Harvard Civil Rights–Civil Liberties Law Review,* 13 (1978), 135; Ralph Ellison, "The Little Man at Chehaw Station," *American Scholar,* 47 (Winter 1977–78), 39–40. Neil Larry Shumsky, "Zangwill's *The Melting Pot*: Ethnic Tensions on the Stage," *American Quarterly,* 27 (March 1975), 29–41 argues that Zangwill's play is more complex than usually thought.

d. David Hollinger, "Two Cheers for the Melting Pot," *Democracy,* 2 (1982), 89–97; reprinted as "Democracy and the Melting Pot Reconsidered," in Hollinger, *In the American Province: Studies in the History and Historiography of Ideas* (Bloomington, Ind., 1985), 92–102; Werner Sollors, "A Defence of the Melting Pot," in Rob Kroes, ed., *The American Identity: Fusion and Fragmentation* (Amsterdam, 1980), 181–214; Sollors, "The Rebirth of All Americans in the Great American Melting Pot: Notes Toward the Vindication of a Rejected Popular Symbol," *Prospects,* 5 (1980), 79–110; Sollors, *Beyond Ethnicity: Consent and Descent in American Culture* (New York, 1986), chap. 3.

e. Richard D. Alba, *Ethnic Identity: The Transformation of White America* (New Haven, Conn., 1990), 3. For other studies see Richard M. Bernard, *The Melting Pot and the Altar: Marital Assimilation in Early Twentieth-Century Wisconsin* (Minneapolis, Minn., 1980); William L. Burton, *Melting Pot Soldiers: The Union's Ethnic Regiments* (Ames, Iowa, 1988); Alan Wolfe, "The Return of the Melting Pot," *New Republic,* 203 (December 13, 1990), 27–34; David Reimers, "Assimilation versus Pluralism," paper presented at American Studies Association convention, New Orleans, November 1990. Charles Hirschman, "America's Melting Pot Reconsidered," *Annual Review of Sociology*, 9 (1983), 397–423 surveys studies of assimilation, observing among other things that "the melting pot image is typically only used as a straw man."

f. Arthur Schlesinger, Jr., referred positively to the melting pot in his critique of a multicultural curriculum proposed in New York. See Schlesinger, "When Ethnic Studies Are Un-American," *Wall Street Journal*, April 23, 1990; Schlesinger, *The Disuniting of America: Reflections on a Multicultural Society* (Knoxville, Tenn., 1991); Engelhardt cartoon, *Chicago Sun-Times*, June 11, 1984.

g. *Chicago Tribune*, September 10, 1989. Along the same lines, a YMCA official was paraphrased as saying, "To some, the YMCA is a health-oriented melting pot offered to the community at a nominal fee." *South Bend Tribune*, January 3, 1985.

h. Reported in Mike Royko's column, *Chicago Tribune*, November 27, 1990.

1. See above, chap. 1. Henry Pratt Fairchild's comment is from his *Melting-Pot Mistake* (Boston, 1926), 125.

2. Herbert Butterfield, *The Englishman and His History* (Cambridge, 1945), 70; Butterfield, *The Origins of Modern Science* (New York, 1951), 71; Butterfield, *History and Human Relations* (London, 1951), 67.

3. H. G. Schenk, *The Mind of the European Romantics* (London, 1966), 50; E. E. Y. Hales, *Pio Nono* (Cambridge, 1962), 90; R. R. Bolgar, *The Classical Heritage* (Cambridge, 1958), 2; George Orwell, "Politics and the English Language," in his *Shooting an Elephant* (London, 1953), 94. Owen Barfield, "Poetic Diction and Legal Fiction," in M. Black, ed., *The Importance of Language* (Englewood Cliffs, N.J., 1962), 70, writes that "the whole theory of human society is in the melting-pot." Thor Heyerdahl, a Norwegian whose English was learned in Europe, writes that objections to various hypotheses about the origins of the Pacific islanders "put the whole problem into the melting pot again." *Kon Tiki* (New York, 1950), 20. C. N. Cochrane is an English writer who used the melting pot in something like its American sense in his *Christianity and Classical Culture* (New York, 1944), 147n.; In a curious, quasi-generic usage of the term, an American undergraduate described a recording as follows: "The style of *America* can be vaguely described as a melting pot of the Moody Blues, without the syrupy synthetic strings, and Crosby, Stills, Nash, and Young, without the virtuosity." See Notre Dame *Scholastic*, 113 (May 5, 1972), 43.

4. F. Erickson, "Gatekeeping and the Melting Pot: Interaction in Counseling Encounters," *Harvard Educational Review*, 65 (February 1975), 44–70.

5. Nathan Glazer and Daniel P. Moynihan, *Beyond the Melting Pot*, 2d ed. (Cambridge, Mass., 1970), xcvii, 290.

6. Review of *Beyond the Melting Pot* by G. Paulding, *Reporter*, 29 (October 10, 1963), 59.

7. William Petersen, *The Politics of Population* (Garden City, N.Y., 1964), 211–12; letter of J. Feinstein in *National Catholic Reporter*, January 14, 1972.

8. Patricia Rooke, "From Pollyanna to Jeremiah—Recent Interpretations of American Educational History," *Journal of Educational Thought*, 9 (April 1975), 24; Rudolph J. Vecoli is quoted in *Jednota Annual, 1973*, 12 (Middletown, Pa., 1973), 107, as using "transparent fiction"; "theory-that-won't-hold-water" comes from a student's examination paper, spring, 1973.

9. *National Catholic Reporter*, May 6, 1977.

10. Michael Kammen, *People of Paradox* (New York, 1972), 82.

11. "A dialogue on separatism," *Ebony*, 25 (August 1970), 62ff. Rev. Jackson referred to overturning the bowl and blacks' being scorched a year before the *Ebony* dialogue was published. Cf. *Chicago Sun-Times*, March 19, 1969. See another reference to Jackson's analysis of the melting pot in M. Dickeman, "Teaching Cultural Pluralism," in *Teaching Ethnic Studies: Concepts and Strategies. Forty-third Yearbook, National Council for the Social Studies* (Washington, D.C., 1973), 12.

12. Michael Novak, *National Catholic Reporter*, December 12, 1971; Novak, *Rise of the Unmeltable Ethnics* (New York, 1972), 60. Cf. also 141. Bayard Rustin also equated soup and melting pot. "We have consistently fallen for the old melting pot concepts," he wrote. "But there *never* was a melting pot; there is not *now* a melting pot; there never will be a melting pot; and if there ever were, it would be such a tasteless soup that we would have to go back and start all over!" Rustin, "Coalition," *Journal of Current Social Issues*, 10 (Summer 1972), 25.

13. Novak, *Unmeltable Ethnics*, 257, 72, 138, 229.

14. Ibid., 38, 52, 170, 129, 118, 123, 278.

15. Marian C. McKenna, "The Melting Pot in Canada and the United States: Some Comparative Views," paper delivered to the convention of the Organization of American Historians, Dallas, Texas, 1968. A revised version was published as "The Melting Pot: Comparative Observations in the United States and Canada," *Sociology and Social Research*, 53 (July 1969), 433–447.

16. Otto Feinstein, "Why Ethnicity?" in issue devoted to "Immigrants and Migrants: The Detroit Ethnic Experience," *Journal of University Studies*, 10 (Fall 1974), 5.

17. Among those who take such views are William V. Shannon, "The Irish," *American Jewish Historical Quarterly*, 55 (September 1965), 30–31; and Mark M. Krug, "Teaching the Experience of White Ethnic Groups," in *Teaching Ethnic Studies*, 256–72. Colin Greer, who attacked the "myth" of the melting pot some years back (*Saturday Review*, November 15, 1969, 84ff.), has more recently observed that, ethnic diversity notwithstanding, "the melting pot did melt." In this latter work, however, Greer is interested mainly in pushing a class analysis. See Greer, *Divided Society: The Ethnic Experience in America* (New York, 1974), 19, 25ff.

18. John Higham, *Send These to Me: Jews and Other Immigrants in Urban America* (New York, 1975), 196–230; quotation from 229. The last essay in this collection, "Another American Dilemma," 231–46, is also extremely valuable. Cf. also James H. Powell, "The Concept of Cultural Pluralism in American Social Thought, 1915–1965" (Ph.D. diss., University of Notre Dame, 1971).

19. Novak, *Unmeltable Ethnics*, xvi, 38ff., and passim, Cf. Milton M. Gordon, *Assimilation of American Life* (New York, 1964), esp. 159, 235–41. Robert P. Swierenga, "Ethnocultural Political Analysis: A New Approach to American Ethnic Studies," *Journal of American Studies*, 5 (April 1971), 59–79, is a good introduction to this approach and review of the literature of the 1960s.

20. Higham, *Send These To Me*, 198.

21. Ibid., 229–30.

22. Novak, *Unmeltable Ethnics*, 71.

23. Novak, "The New Ethnicity," *Center Magazine*, July–August 1974, 25.

24. For the "new ethnicity," besides Novak's *Unmeltable Ethnics*, see Michael Wenk, Silvano M. Tomasi, and Geno Baroni, eds., *Pieces of a Dream: The Ethnic Worker's Crisis with America* (New York, 1972); Perry L. Weed, *The White Ethnic Movement and Ethnic Politics* (New York, 1973); Andrew M. Greeley, *Ethnicity in*

the United States: A Preliminary Reconnaissance (New York, 1974); Nathan Glazer and Daniel P. Moynihan, eds., *Ethnicity: Theory and Practice* (Cambridge, Mass., 1975); Richard Krickus, *Pursuing the American Dream; White Ethnics and the New Populism* (New York, 1976).

25. This language is taken from the legislation, as quoted in "Guidelines for Application" September 1975, sent out by the Office of Education for applications under the Ethnic Heritages Studies Program.

|| 3 ||

The Odd Couple:
Pluralism and Assimilation

This chapter, originally written five years after "Confusion Compounded," explores a problem noted toward the end of that essay, namely, the problematic relationship between assimilation, which the melting pot is understood to symbolize, and pluralism, which has historically been contrasted to both assimilation and the melting pot. This discussion focuses more directly on conceptual content than did the two surveys of melting pot usage. But conceptual content is inseparable from the terminology in which it is embedded, and the essay reprinted here will show that the concept of pluralism is at least as complex and ambiguous as the symbol of the melting pot.

A shorter version of this essay was presented at a conference, "Language Problems and Public Policy," which was sponsored by the Forum for Interdisciplinary Research in December 1981. John Edwards, a psycholinguist at Saint Francis Xavier University, Antigonish, Nova Scotia, invited me to take part in the conference, and the expanded version of my paper first appeared in a collection he edited under the title *Linguistic Minorities: Policies and Pluralism* (1984).

Nothing that has transpired since 1984 seems to me to require modification of the historical review up to that point. Four works published since then demonstrate that scholars of ethnicity continue to interpret pluralism in different ways. According to Rivka Shpak Lissak's understanding, cultural pluralism requires "the perpetuation of ethnic-cultural uniqueness and the cultivation of distinct immigrant cultures through cultural institutions" purposefully maintained by self-conscious *groups*.[a] By contrast, Mary C. Waters sees the "ultimate goal of a pluralist society" as a situation of "symbolic ethnicity" in which every individual is free to identify, or not identify, with elements of his or her ethnic-cultural heritage on a strictly voluntaristic basis.[b] For Gary Gerstle, the currently normative sense of *cultural pluralism* is a universalistic "belief in the right of every individual, in the United States and around the world, to life, liberty, and the pursuit of happiness, irrespective of creed, color, or nationality."ᶜ Lawrence H. Fuchs deals with the problem of multiple meanings by introducing a whole range of subspecies—voluntary pluralism, coercive pluralism, predatory pluralism, sojourner pluralism, tribal pluralism, caste pluralism, and racial pluralism. His own position, however, is quite clear: the normative version of American pluralism recognizes and celebrates individual rights, not group rights.ᵈ

The resurgence of racialist thinking and its association with a "strong" version of cultural pluralism, both of which are noted at the end of this essay, have continued since 1984. A new development along these lines, which can only be mentioned here (although it deserves extended treatment in its own right), is the recent emergence of "multiculturalism" as a public issue. Earlier associated primarily with Canada, where it was adopted as official policy in 1971, *multiculturalism* seems to have gained its first foothold in this country among educators, who used the term more or less synonymously with *cultural pluralism*. In 1990, it burst upon the general public when a "multicultural" curriculum was proposed for the New York schools which its critics regarded as embodying objectionably racialist features.ᵉ

By that time, another stream of influence—that represented by the new "cultural studies"—merged with and reinforced the educationists' multiculturalism at a higher level of abstraction.ᶠ This movement, which is championed principally by academics in the fields of language, literature, and women's studies, derives from European theorists such as Michel Foucault and Jacques Derrida, whose work is said to "legitimize diversity" and "empower" resistance to "Eurocentric domination." The 1987–88 curricular battle at Stanford University dramatized the programmatic possibilities of ideas that obviously lend themselves to application in racial, ethnic, and gender studies. According to one of its Latino proponents, the "multiculturalism" that draws on these sources was, by 1990, fast becoming "the new common sense" in artistic and literary circles."ᵍ

All this unquestionably complicates matters, especially since there are various kinds of multiculturalism, some of which (according to champions of other versions) amount to nothing more than "warmed over cultural pluralism."ʰ But it is quite clear that the demands of the more extreme multiculturalists have aroused a strong reaction and that this reaction includes a vigorous reaffirmation of the universalistic values embodied in liberal assimilationism. Indeed, Arthur Schlesinger, Jr., opened his critique of multiculturalism with a genuflection toward the melting pot.ⁱ Thus, though the terms of the debate are murkier than

ever, the contrasting positions are still fundamentally the same as those
described at the end of "The Odd Couple."

Students of ethnicity in the United States are agreed that the terms
pluralism and *assimilation* designate two quite different concepts.
Pluralism, generally speaking, affirms the existence and persistence of
diversity and prescribes its preservation. Assimilation is associated with
unity; it concerns itself with and generally approves of the processes by
which various elements have been blended into the overall national culture.

I would not deny the broad differences between pluralism and assimilation, but I believe they have been greatly exaggerated and handled
much too rigidly. The tendency to dichotomize the two viewpoints includes the moral aspect as well as the theoretical; in many discussions
of the so-called new ethnicity, they were treated as mutually exclusive
categories, and pluralism was associated with everything good in social
policy and assimilation with everything bad. This is unfortunate from
the viewpoint of theoretical understanding because the two concepts, as
they have been used historically, overlap and relate to each other in a
dialectical manner. The failure to appreciate this fact confuses matters
grievously, especially with respect to policy debate, because it beclouds
the issues and prevents people from recognizing what their agreements
and disagreements actually are.

In the pages that follow I will sketch the way these two concepts
have been used in twentieth century discussions of American ethnic
affairs. This review will show that at the very beginning of its theoretical
career, and in the last few years, pluralism was strongly antiassimilationist; from the late 1930s through the 1960s, however, pluralism resembled assimilation much more closely.

Assimilation was the first of the two terms to come into general use.
It emerged around 1900 in the context of concern over the nation's
capacity to absorb the millions of immigrants who were pouring into the
country and referred in the broadest sense to the blending of different
elements into one people. *Assimilation* was used interchangeably with
Americanization, and the production in 1908 of Israel Zangwill's drama
The Melting-Pot introduced a vivid image that gained immediate and
widespread popularity as a symbol for the process of assimilation. Intermarriage was often linked with assimilation, but it was usually distin-

guished from "amalgamation," or biological mixing. As one writer put it, the end product of assimilation was nationality, and that implied not "unity of blood," but "unity of institutions and social habits."[1]

But while assimilation was an elastic term that could accommodate a wide variation of interpretations, it became more closely identified with a narrow nativistic insistence that immigrants had to conform themselves closely to the prevailing American norms before they could be considered satisfactorily assimilated. This development is reflected in Henry Pratt Fairchild's *Immigration* (1913), a work by a leading sociologist of old American stock who accepted the prevailing scientific racialism of the day and was deeply troubled about the implications of immigration for the national culture. Basing his discussion on the "physiological analogy" of the digestion of food by the body, which he believed underlay the concept of assimilation as a social process, Fairchild said that "true and complete assimilation of the foreign elements in the United States involves such a complete transformation and unification of the new constituents that all sense of difference between the new and the old completely disappears." Fairchild added that assimilation presupposed the existence of a national type that the immigrant was to conform to, and the "native American" was that national type.[2]

This version of assimilation not only was offensively ethnocentric; it also proposed a standard impossible to meet in practice. First-generation immigrants simply could not make themselves over so completely, even if they had been willing to do so (which most of them were not), and even if the receiving society had been willing to regard them as unqualified Americans after they had done so (which it was not). It was therefore natural that spokespersons for immigrant groups would reject assimilation altogether if this was what it meant. The work that prompted their boldest champion to step forth was not Fairchild's book, but Edward A. Ross's *Old World in the New* (1914), a veritable diatribe against the new immigrants. Ross, a progressive sociologist at the University of Wisconsin, did not discuss assimilation systematically, but his disbelief that immigrants could come up to American standards was patent throughout, and in the chapter entitled "American Blood and Immigrant Blood" he really let himself go. Even the physical appearance of the newer immigrants betrayed them as a "sub-common" people of obviously low mentality who really belonged in animal skins, beside wattled huts, at the end of the great ice age. Ross was appalled by their "sugar-loaf heads, moon-faces, slit mouths, lantern jaws, and goose-bill noses." Jews he singled out as puny and sissified, the saddest possible contrast to the type of the American pioneer.[3]

This was too much for Horace M. Kallen, a German-born Jew, a Zionist, a Harvard Ph.D., and a colleague of Ross's at the University of Wisconsin. The appearance of *The Old World in the New* prompted him to set forth a radically antiassimilationist interpretation of American nationality in an article entitled "Democracy *versus* the Melting Pot." Originally published in the *Nation* in February 1915, this essay was reprinted with very minor changes in 1924, at which time Kallen gave the name "cultural pluralism" to his position.[4] Since he was reacting to extreme hundred-percent Americanism, it is perhaps understandable that Kallen went to the opposite extreme in his formulation of cultural pluralism. His statement was long and diffuse, downright obscure in places, but the overall argument may be summarized as follows.

First, Kallen denied that there was an American nationality as such, a generic national identity defining the whole people considered as a collectivity, to which the immigrants could be assimilated. Such a generic national culture had at one time existed, he stated, but it had been dissipated by the great waves of immigration. As a result, the United States in the twentieth century was not really a nation but a political state within the borders of which dwelt a number of distinct nationalities.

Second, Kallen assumed that these distinct nationalities would perpetuate themselves indefinitely. Although the language here was vague, his thinking was clearly rooted in a romantic kind of racialism. "Like-mindedness" was the key to nationality, and it was "inward, corporate and inevitable" because it sprang from "a homogeneity of heritage, mentality and interest." Members of an ethnic group shared a "prevailing intrinsic similarity" that Kallen seemed to regard as forever fixed. "What is inalienable in the life of mankind," he declared, "is its intrinsic positive quality—its psycho-physical inheritance." Because a person "cannot change his grandfather," ethnic nationalities were destined to perdure indefinitely through a kind of biological determinism.

The third feature of Kallen's thinking brings us to the policy question. Given the existence of many nationalities in the same country and the prospect of their remaining permanently distinctive, what should be done? Kallen saw two alternatives, which he designated the options of "unison" and "harmony." By *unison* he meant the effort to make everyone conform to a common pattern—essentially the hundred-percent Americanization policy. By *harmony* he meant the glad embrace of the existing multiplicity. Kallen opted decisively for harmony; indeed, he affirmed that it was the truly American and democratic policy, whereas the effort to enforce conformity to a common pattern actually violated democratic ideals and the spirit of American institutions.

Kallen had turned the tables on the Americanizers very neatly, but as a policy prescription his cultural pluralism amounted to little more than a lyrical vision. The following rhapsodic passage is the closest he ever came to describing how cultural pluralism would be put into operation, how his "great and truly democratic commonwealth" would function in practice:

> Its form would be that of the federal republic; its substance a democracy of nationalities, cooperating voluntarily and autonomously through common institutions in the enterprise of self-realization through the perfection of men according to their kind. The common language of the commonwealth . . . would be English, but each nationality would have for its emotional and involuntary life its own peculiar dialect or speech, its own individual and inevitable esthetic and intellectual forms. The political and economic life of the commonwealth is a single unit and serves as the foundation and background for the realization of the distinctive individuality of each *natio* that composes it and of the pooling of these in a harmony above them all. Thus "American civilization" may come to mean the perfection of the cooperative harmonies of "European civilization"—the waste, the squalor and the distress of Europe being eliminated—a multiplicity in a unity, an orchestration of mankind.[5]

As this passage reveals, the assumption of automatic harmony among a multiplicity of permanently distinct ethnic nationalities should be added as the fourth feature of Kallen's original formulation of cultural pluralism. It was, in fact, precisely this assumption that permitted Kallen to disregard entirely the need for assimilation to American ways that other commentators stressed so heavily. For although he denied the existence of American nationality as such and repudiated the Americanization programs of the day, Kallen silently included assimilation in his theory by postulating a degree of consensus adequate to assure cooperation and harmony among all elements in his contemplated federation of nationalities. Kallen thus made tacit provision for the *unum* of the national motto, although his rhetorical stress was altogether on *pluribus* and his theoretical assumptions seemed to rule out any kind of fundamental merging-into-one of the many immigrant nationalities that made up the American people.

The publication of Kallen's article in 1915 attracted the attention of a few intellectuals, but its republication and the introduction of the term *cultural pluralism* in 1924 passed almost completely without notice. No doubt the principal reason for this neglect was that the passage in 1924 of a stringent immigration restriction law removed ethnic concerns from the forefront of public discussion. More than a decade passed before the expression *cultural pluralism* entered into circulation, even in the limited universe of scholarly observers of intergroup relations.

Before examining the way cultural pluralism was understood in the late thirties, however, we must pause to catch up on what was happening to the concept of assimilation. As the examples of Fairchild and Ross attest, cultural anxieties on the part of old-line Americans caused them to formulate the concept in a narrow and nativistic way even before the outbreak of World War I intensified the atmosphere of social and cultural crisis. The outburst of ethnic nationalism and the manifestations of immigrant loyalty to Old World homelands that marked the neutrality years (1914–17) convinced many more Americans that "hyphenation" was a danger and lent greater urgency to programs of Americanization. But as these efforts at forced assimilation took on a chauvinistic character that bordered on the hysterical, a reaction against them set in. Not only were liberal intellectuals put off by their hypernationalism; thoughtful observers also recognized that they were counterproductive—rather than facilitating the integration of immigrants into American life, forced Americanization programs left them more alienated than ever. In these circumstances, a more liberal version of Americanization was set forth.

Its most impressive embodiment was the series of "Americanization Studies" sponsored by the Carnegie Corporation and published by Harper Brothers in the immediate postwar years.[6] According to this interpretation, Americanization did not mean forcing immigrants into a predetermined "old American" mold. Rather, they were to be assisted toward full partnership in the national life by means of "a mutual giving and taking of contributions from both newer and older Americans in the interest of the common weal." Far from demanding the suppression of immigrant languages and societies, the liberal Americanizers looked upon these elements of the immigrants' heritage as the vehicles that made it possible for them to play a role in society. Though outwardly "foreign," ethnic newspapers and organizations brought them into contact with their new homeland in countless ways and thus acted as agencies of Americanization in spite of themselves. In time, the immigrants (or their children) would be fully incorporated into the national life, which was, by definition, assimilation. The process was "as inevitable as it is desirable"—inevitable because it was the natural outcome of ongoing social interaction; desirable because by its workings immigrants eventually became full participants in a democratic social order.[7]

This understanding of assimilation was quite in line with the most authoritative sociological thinking of the day. The congruence was natural since Robert E. Park of the University of Chicago was a major participant in the "Americanization Studies" project *and* the principal author of the standard treatise on sociology in the period between the two world wars. This was the famous *Introduction to the Science of Sociology* (1921) by Park and E. W. Burgess that served as "the green bible" for generations of graduate students as sociology came of age in the American university.

Assimilation figured here as the culminating phase of "the four great types of [social] interaction," which were competition, conflict, accommodation, and assimilation. This sequence in slightly modified form was soon christened "the race-relations cycle" and took on special importance for students of intergroup relations in the United States. Park did not restrict his focus to this country, however; rather, he regarded assimilation as "central in the historical and cultural process" on the broadest scale.[8] But while he and Burgess gave great prominence to assimilation, their discussion left certain ambiguities as to the meaning of the concept.

They defined assimilation as "a process of interpenetration and fusion in which persons and groups acquire the memories, sentiments, and attitudes of other persons and groups, and, by sharing their experience and history, are incorporated with them in a common cultural life." This definition, and the preponderance of the discussion in the 1921 volume, seemed to make assimilation primarily a psychological and cultural process, a matter of the subjective consciousness of people who come to think of themselves differently from the way they had before the process began.[9] Yet the authors played down the degree to which "like-mindedness" was required for assimilation, indicated that it might leave fundamental cultural patterns or racial characteristics unchanged, and talked in one place as though assimilation was more a matter of interdependence in social relationships than of subjective disposition or cultural orientation.[10] This left the degree of cultural cohesion required for assimilation quite indeterminate; yet being "incorporated in a common cultural life" was central to the definition.

Park continued to grapple with the problem, and by the time he wrote the entry on "Assimilation, Social" for the *Encyclopaedia of the Social Sciences* (1930) he had grown definitely skeptical about cultural cohesion as a defining feature of assimilation. In fact, he began his "most concentrated theoretical discussion of assimilation" by saying that it was more a political than a cultural concept. It was simply the name of the process by which people of diverse backgrounds who occupied a common territory "achieve[d] a cultural solidarity sufficient at least to sustain a national existence." Culturally speaking, the process was to be understood in minimalist terms. "The common sense view of the matter," Park reported approvingly, "is that an immigrant is assimilated as soon as he has shown that he can 'get on in the country.' " Indeed, he added, it was questionable whether culture as anthropologists conceived it could be said to exist at all in a complex modern society with its highly refined division of labor, specialization of roles, and so on. In these circumstances, assimilation did not mean close conformity to a definite cultural pattern but merely the acceptance of "those ideas, practices and aspirations which are national . . . the generally accepted social customs and political ideas and loyalties of a community or country."[11]

This loose and largely political interpretation of assimilation left much room for diversity among the subgroups of a population all of whose constituent elements accepted a minimum of general norms that enabled them to get along together, to undertake essential collective tasks, and to discuss their differences in a free and open manner. Indeed, this was a version of assimilation that could be understood "pluralistically."

More detailed research would be required to establish in detail just how the concept of assimilation was used by social scientists and commentators on intergroup relations in the 1930s, but it is safe to say that it had become somewhat problematic.[12] On the one hand, assimilation was regarded in the abstract as a very significant process; it was also believed to be proceeding inevitably in American society, and with generally beneficent results since it operated to reduce the likelihood of intergroup conflicts and to facilitate the participation of minorities in American society. At the same time, however, assimilation still carried nativist overtones as a result of its association with chauvinistic hundred-percent Americanism and the racial xenophobia of the early 1920s. Virtually all informed commentators in the 1930s deprecated efforts at forced Americanization, and increasing attention was being paid to the costs of assimilation considered as a natural social process. The "marginal" situation of the second generation, for example, was thought to exact a heavy psychological toll, and there were also more generalized murmurs of regret at the decline of diversity in American culture.

Complicating the picture further was the enhanced cognitive authority of the anthropological concept of culture, which was rapidly coming to be regarded as "the foundation stone of the social sciences,"[13] One result of this development was that the term *acculturation* was often used more or less interchangeably with *assimilation*; but it was not clear whether the two terms meant precisely the same thing or, if not, wherein they differed. Park, as we have seen, was moving toward a differentiation of assimilation from cultural incorporation, but the preponderance of usage was in the other direction, and two of Park's students later remarked that *assimilation* and *acculturation* illustrated the way in which the terminologies of sociology and anthropology "half-blended in a grand confusion."[14]

The growing prestige of the anthropological concept of culture had two other notable effects: it discredited the idea that differences in group ways of life were explainable in racial terms; and it inculcated the ethical imperative of tolerance for diversity, which was assumed to follow as a corollary from the empirical finding that cultural values and norms differed from group to group. The latter point was often spoken of as "cultural relativism," and it had a good deal more in common with cultural pluralism than mere verbal similarity.[15] But both developments, along with the general influence of the anthropological outlook, were important background factors in the reintroduction of the expression *cultural pluralism* in the late 1930s and its popularization in the next decade. And if acculturation stood in a somewhat ambiguous relation to assimilation, the status of cultural pluralism was considerably more paradoxical, for it was no longer posited as an alternative to assimilation; rather, it was usually presented as an enlightened and liberal means of achieving the goal of assimilation, a harmoniously united society.

The 1937 volume *Our Racial and National Minorities*, edited by Francis J. Brown and Joseph S. Roucek, was the earliest major landmark in the reintroduction of the term *cultural pluralism*. The evidence it provides indicates clearly that Kallen was not the source from which the new version stemmed, although he was the one who put the expression into circulation in the first place. Part 4 of this compendium of specialized studies by different authors was entitled "The Trend toward Cultural Pluralism," but not one of the contributors to this part referred to Kallen, and his name was missing from the sixty-six-page bibliography of the book. The chapters included in part 4 emphasized the positive contributions to American life made by Indians, Negroes, and immigrants and urged preservation of "the best that each group has brought." But while it was portrayed as desirable to preserve "the fundamentals of [group] heritages . . . for generations,"[16] the writer who discussed these matters most explicitly denied flatly that *cultural pluralism* meant "the ultimate preservation of different cultural streams in our civilization." E. George Payne, a prominent educational theorist at New York University, did not regard such an eventuality as harmful; it was simply that inevitable acculturation ruled it out and pointed toward the emergence of "a new and superior culture." Cultural pluralism, Payne explained, "does not imply that the special cultures will continue unchanged for all time. The theory involves essentially a technique of social adjustment which will make possible the preservation of the best of all cultures."[17]

This version of cultural pluralism differed sharply from Kallen's original formulation since he did assume that distinct ethnic cultures would perdure indefinitely, not as contributors to a common American culture but as equal participants in a federation of nationalities. Despite his use of the same term, Payne's cultural pluralism was actually a liberal variation of assimilation theory much like that of the post–World War I Americanization Studies. As such it strongly resembled the approach that many earlier commentators had associated with the melting pot, although Kallen wrote his piece as a corrective to melting pot thinking.

Brown and Roucek's volume (of which two later editions were published) opened the era in which *cultural pluralism* entered into general usage and eventually became a conventional touchstone of liberal enlightenment among commentators on American society. The most thorough investigation of the subject, done by James H. Powell, identifies some sixty-four persons who wrote about cultural pluralism between 1940 and 1955.[18] Powell distinguishes three versions of cultural pluralism in that era: Kallen's original federation-of-nationalities type; the liberal Americanization version; and a third alternative that combined elements of the other two in envisioning the retention of ethnic cultures as supplements to, rather than as substitutes for, an overall American culture.[19] The third type, which was sometimes called "cultural democracy," differed from the second only hazily in stressing diversity within unity as a permanent rather than a temporary condition. Both of these versions made explicit provision for assimilation while simultaneously calling for toleration of diversity; the federation-of-nationalities type, however, was strongly antiassimilationist. But according to Powell, no one who interpreted cultural pluralism in the federation-of-nationalities sense applied the concept to American society; rather, it was used exclusively in reference to the "minorities problem" of Eastern Europe.[20] This is a most important finding because it means that when *cultural pluralism* attained popularity in commentary on the American scene, it designated a variety (or two varieties) of assimilationist theory rather than constituting a significant alternative to assimilationism.

Even more striking is that by midcentury Horace Kallen himself had abandoned the federation-of-nationalities version of cultural pluralism. Although he touched on related matters in the forties, Kallen's first major statement on the subject in three decades was *Cultural Pluralism and the American Idea* (1956), a volume consisting of three essays by Kallen and responses to his ideas (overwhelmingly favorable) by nine other scholars. He was still glowingly committed to cultural pluralism, but it was a very different thing from what he had outlined in 1915 and 1924. All hint of racialism was, of course, gone; and there was no suggestion that immigrant nationalities would perpetuate themselves indefinitely. Indeed, pluralism was no longer specifically related to ethnicity at all. It embraced the "diverse utterance of diversities—regional, local, religious, ethnic, esthetic, industrial, sporting, and political."[21]

Kallen had also enlarged his terminology: besides cultural pluralism he spoke now of "the philosophy of Cultural Pluralism" and of philosophical pluralism more generally; of spontaneous pluralism, of fluid, relational pluralism, of the actual pluralism of experience; and, with very negative overtones, of absolutist pluralism and isolationist pluralism.[22] The relationship between pluralism and Americanization had also changed. In the twenties, Kallen attacked Americanization vehemently; but now he spoke approvingly of an "Americanization, supporting, cultivating a cultural pluralism, grounded on and consummated in the American Idea."[23] *American Idea* was appropriately capitalized, since Kallen regarded it with religious awe and declared that it represented "that apprehension of human nature and human relations" to which all must be converted if they were to live together peaceably.[24] But despite elevating Americanism into a civil religion, Kallen still thought he was opposed to assimilation. When an admiring commentator hailed him for discerning "that our country is a true melting-pot," he indignantly disavowed all sympathy for the melting pot.[25]

As Kallen's performance suggests, the concept of cultural pluralism had by the mid fifties become highly elusive and contradictory, not to say hopelessly muddled. The most important factors in bringing this situation about were the great revival of the democratic ideology in World War II, the postwar critique of conformity, and the popularization of pluralism as an interpretation of American politics.

The war of course created an urgent need for national unity.[26] Since assimilation is associated with unity, while pluralism implies differentiation, one would naturally expect the war to generate a strong push for assimilation. That did happen, although it seemed that just the opposite was going on. What obscured matters was that the demand for unity was usually couched in the language of pluralism and diversity instead of being talked about in terms of assimilation or Americanization. The explanation for this seemingly paradoxical state of affairs was that unity was sought on the common ground of ideological consensus, and the principle of tolerance for diversity was heavily stressed as a key element in the democratic ideology behind which all were supposed to rally in the wartime crisis.

Unity was sought on the basis of ideological consensus because, as Gunnar Myrdal insisted at the time, "this War is an ideological war fought in defense of democracy."[27] It pitted the United States against totalitarian regimes that denied the premise of human equality and perverted the ideals of freedom and self-determination beyond recognition. Confronted by the monstrous contrast of Nazism, it was quite understandable that Americans were galvanized to a deeper appreciation of democracy and that their leaders should reaffirm the nation's collective commitment to freedom, equality, and respect for human dignity. To be an American was to identify oneself with these values. Race, religion, or ethnic background were secondary issues; true Americanism was defined by ideological commitment.

But if ideological consensus was to serve as an effective basis for national unity, Americans would have to do more than profess democratic principles—they would have to live up to them, which was something they were notoriously *not* doing in the area of race relations. This was the reason that tolerance for diversity came to be regarded as so vital an element of the democratic creed. It was bad enough that racial prejudice and discrimination were embarrassing inconsistencies that invited exploitation by enemy propagandists; even more distressing was that intergroup hostilities weakened national unity and thus hampered the war effort. The need for mutual tolerance and good will among all segments of the population was recognized even before the United States became involved in the fighting. But the outburst in 1943 of race riots in Detroit and mob violence against Mexican-Americans in Los Angeles lent much greater urgency to the task of reducing intergroup tensions. According to one count, there were no fewer than 123 national organizations working for better intergroup relations by the end of the war.[28] This sort of "action for unity," as one study called it, carried over into the postwar era. At the same time, programs of "intercultural education" were widely adopted in the schools, and the study of race and minority problems became major specialties among social scientists.[29]

Cultural pluralism and *cultural democracy* became part of the standard terminology of this broad movement to improve intergroup relations, but its goals were social harmony and national unity, not heightened consciousness of the differences among cultural groups in the population. On the contrary, differences among population groups were precisely the problem, and the real message of many of the preachments about diversity was that fundamentally people were more alike than different and that the failure to be guided by recognition of that fact was what constituted prejudice.[30]

The word *assimilation* was not generally used in discussions of race relations—no doubt because it was too closely associated with the sensitive issue of intermarriage—but the goals of the struggle for civil rights and integration were, as Lewis M. Killian puts it, "fundamentally and unrelentingly assimilationist."[31] In these circumstances, the original antiassimilationist version of cultural pluralism, vaguely racial in its assumptions and open to a segregationist interpretation, simply could not be admitted.[32] But as it gained currency in the loose tolerance-for-diversity sense, the concept of cultural pluralism became quite blurry and moved in the direction of self-contradiction. Verbally it seemed to celebrate differences between groups; actually it rested on the assumptions that basic consensus made Americans one people in essentials, that the differences between groups were relatively superficial, and that toleration of those differences was required by the value system on which consensus was grounded.

But while assimilationist assumptions and goals were thus fundamental to the campaign for better intergroup relations, those who were committed to the good cause did not think of themselves as assimilationists. On the contrary, the word *assimilation* had a disreputable air about it. Those concerned with the most serious problem, race relations, had good reason to avoid using the term. In the area where it had been traditionally used—discussions of immigrant adjustment—the conventional wisdom of the day held that assimilation had done its work, and perhaps overdone it. Immigration had been virtually cut off for a generation, and it was widely held that the children and grandchildren of the earlier immigrants were becoming completely Americanized. Hence assimilation was no longer a problem: Americans could relax on that score. And being able to relax, a good many felt embarrassed about the extremes to which assimilationist efforts had sometimes been carried. Awakening to the realization that our minorities were vanishing, social commentators in the postwar years were clearly uncomfortable with the concept of assimilation.[33] Cultural pluralism was much more attractive. It took unity for granted—and why not, if assimilation was an accomplished fact?—and combined with it an appealing invocation of diversity.

Rising postwar concern over the evils of "mass society" highlighted certain negative consequences of assimilation and, by doing so, reinforced the appeal of cultural pluralism.[34] The critics of mass society were, after all, champions of diversity; they bemoaned its decline and the concomitant homogenizing of society into a bland, standardized sameness. Assimilation was clearly one of the main culprits here; it was hardly more than another name for homogenization.

Even more troubling, however, was the linkage between immigrant assimilation and a constellation of socio-psychological morbidities that the critics discerned in mass society—alienation, anxiety, anomie, overconformity, ethnocentrism, and, most ominously, authoritarianism. It was a commonplace in those days that immigrants and their children were to some extent "marginalized" by the process of assimilation and plunged as a result into a kind of "psychological civil war." The bearing of this phenomenon on the symptomology of mass society was not developed in a systematic way, but there is evidence that it was perceived by observers at midcentury. Erik H. Erikson, for example, mentioned immigration in connection with identity problems, and other influential writers portrayed immigrants as archetypically American in their being uprooted and cut off from the past.[35] Being rootless, ethnic Americans were vulnerable to status anxieties; they might easily become ethnocentric, and they were almost bound to be conformists. In short, they were prime candidates for recruitment into irrational, authoritarian social movements, and their support for McCarthyism was interpreted by several commentators along the lines suggested by this sort of mass society analysis.[36]

No one argued that immigrant assimilation was primarily responsible for the evils of mass society. But given the linkages just outlined, it was obviously part of the problem rather than being a solution to it. The antidote for tendencies toward massification was diversity; hence pluralism was bound to be stressed. And that is what happened: a group of political analysts emerged in the 1950s who offered "pluralism" as an interpretation of the American system and as a preventive for the dangers of extremism inherent in the politics of a mass society.[37] These writers drew on an intellectual tradition different from that of students of intergroup relations; they seldom, if ever, referred to cultural pluralism as such, and the focus of their interest was different. Yet their approach was compatible with the midcentury versions of cultural pluralism, and since that had become extremely vague anyhow, the newer political pluralism merged with the existing tradition of usage to make *pluralism* more diffuse and generalized than ever.

Pluralism, in the new sense, designated a theory of interest group politics. It portrayed the American system as an interplay between different groups—labor unions, business associations, religious bodies, professional societies, and so on—which mobilized their resources to influence political decision making by means of publicity, lobbying, and other forms of pressure. Alliances were forged and dissolved according to the changing needs of the groups involved. Political parties functioned as coalitions of interest groups. Since they were naturally desirous of attracting as much support as possible, parties inclined toward comprehensiveness; this made them reluctant to embrace rigid ideological positions or to identify themselves with extremist solutions to problems. That interest groups (sometimes called "veto groups") often nullified each other also worked against domination of the system by extremist elements. Moreover, the individual citizen belonged to a variety of different interest groups, and the "crosscutting pressures" set up by multiple group loyalties likewise militated against all-out commitment to an overriding ideological goal.

According to the pluralists' interpretation, the diffusion of power and influence among a multitude of shifting groups thus forestalled many of the dangers of a mass society in which atomized individuals were apt to be swept up in irrational movements that promised a totally new order. But their theory also excluded totalitarian extremism by definition—that is, they insisted that for pluralism to work, all the groups involved had to exercise moderation, had to abide by the rules of the game. This meant, in general, accepting the constitutional framework, following agreed-upon democratic procedures, and being guided by the conventions of civility and basic decency in the political struggle. Without this kind of democratic consensus, pluralism would imply not an acceptable and indeed healthy "limited warfare" but a brutal contest in which naked force would quickly dominate political life and democratic government would be impossible.[38]

Ethnic groups did not have a distinctive place in this theory, as they had with respect to cultural pluralism. Yet it certainly covered the case of ethnic groups along with all others that opted to participate in the political process. And we have already seen that Horace Kallen had by 1956 vastly extended what he still called cultural pluralism to embrace a whole range of diversities besides those of ethnic origin. These points of contact make it understandable that the two versions of pluralism blended together. Yet there was another similarity between them that is even more significant from our perspective. *Each was predicated on consensus around the American value system despite seeming to place a premium verbally on diversity.*

The consequence of this double dose of pluralism, as we might call it, was that Americans tended to mislead themselves as to how deeply they were committed to diversity. In discussions of the political system and of the key social issue of intergroup relations, pluralism and diversity were endlessly extolled. Indeed, pluralism was made virtually synonymous with the democratic social and political order.[39] This inevitably gave rise to confusion as to the relation of cart and horse because it obscured the point that pluralism and toleration for diversity did not define democracy but were corollaries that flowed from the prior acceptance of democratic values as the basis of national unity. For, in spite of all the celebration of diversity, it was not pluralism as such that constituted the American identity; rather, it was ideological consensus, a common commitment to the ideals of freedom, equality, and democratic self-government.

All of this was clear enough in the realm of ideology as such. It was notorious that "un-American" ideas, movements, and organizations were beyond the pale of tolerable diversity. In the era of the Cold War there was no question of applying to Communists the principle of pluralistic acceptance: they were a part of a totalitarian movement that was excluded by virtue of its self-definition and its intrinsic nature. But there was another group, bitterly opposed to Communists but sometimes likened to them anyhow, whose situation was more ambiguous—American Catholics. As a religious minority they presumably belonged in the pluralistic picture. But their Americanism seemed very questionable to some influential observers (including, incidentally, Horace Kallen).[40] The controversies that arose between Catholics and elements of the Protestant, Jewish, and liberal communities often featured charges of "divisiveness" and are highly revealing of the complexities of pluralism and assimilation in the 1950s. This whole area takes on added importance because cultural pluralism seemed to be resolving itself into religious pluralism. We must therefore look briefly into the relation of pluralism to American Catholicism, despite the complications it entails.

The case for regarding Catholics as full partners in the pluralistic experiment was strong. They had been in the land since early colonial days; freedom of religion was a basic American postulate; religion itself was a key element in the culture of many ethnic groups; and the American Catholic community was made up of a large number of ethnic subgroups. Besides these important points, Catholics had often been victims of nativist hostility, which gave added force to their claim for tolerance as fully accredited actors on the pluralistic scene.

At the same time, the Americanism of Catholics seemed doubtful to many, just as it had in the past. Uneasiness at midcentury revolved primarily around the church's internal organization and discipline, which was hierarchical and authoritarian; her teachings on the union of church and state and various moral issues such as divorce and birth control, which were conservative if not reactionary; and her doctrinal dogmatism and generally absolutist intellectual stance.[41] In view of these characteristics, many American liberals (Protestant, Jewish, and secular) found Catholic professions of commitment to American principles unconvincing. The Catholic church was too undemocratic to be trusted; according to her severest critics, she was too close to being totalitarian to merit unqualified admission to the theater of American pluralism.

These doubts were brought into focus in the late 1940s and early 1950s as sharp religious controversy broke out, pitting Catholics against libertarians (religious and nonreligious), the latter being supported by others who entertained a more generalized religious suspicion of Catholics.[42] A number of factors were involved, but the most important and enduring source of friction centered on the question of public support for religious education and particularly the use of public funds for Catholic parochial schools. It was in this context that the issue of divisiveness was raised.

The term had been used earlier, but it was given special prominence when the president of Harvard University, James B. Conant, warned in 1952 against the dangers to democratic unity posed by a "dual system" of public *and* private schools. Affirming his commitment to the "fundamental belief in tolerance for diversity so basic to our society," and denying that he advocated suppressing private schools, Conant nevertheless contended that the public schools should serve "all creeds and economic groups within a given geographic area," and he pointed out that many foreign observers had commented on the function of public schools in "assimilat[ing] so rapidly the different cultures which came to North America in the nineteenth century." Then Conant added two sentences that attracted wide attention: "The greater the proportion of our youth who fail to attend our public schools and who receive their education elsewhere, the greater the threat to our democratic unity. To use taxpayers' money to assist private schools is to suggest that American society use its own hands to destroy itself."[43]

Catholics naturally resented the implication of divisiveness; and they made the point that it was the very existence of Catholic schools, not just public support for them, that Conant branded as a threat to democratic unity.[44] From their viewpoint, the maintenance of a separate school system reflecting their distinctive religious and moral values was a legitimate expression of pluralism, thoroughly in line with American principles, and in no way a threat to democratic unity. On the contrary, they interpreted the exclusive equation of democratic education with the public schools as evidence of a "statist" or even totalitarian tendency in American life. As one of the most respected Catholic spokesmen put it, "the notion of 'public education' as meaning a unitary and monolithic school system which singly and alone is entitled to public support has rightly been called . . . 'an aberration in the general picture of our society, which is pluralistic.' "[45]

The pertinent question for us is not whose interpretation here was correct; it is, rather, What distinguishes the "divisive" from the "pluralistic"? The two terms are practically interchangeable in denotation, for that which is divided has thereby been made plural, and if something is pluralized it must necessarily have been somehow divided.

Perhaps there were attempts to draw analytical distinctions; if so, they did not attract widespread notice, to say nothing of gaining general acceptance. The real difference between divisiveness and pluralism as it comes through in the literature is strictly connotative, rather than denotative; that is, *divisiveness* was an invidious term for forms of social differentiation one disapproved of, while *pluralism* was a positive label for differences one found acceptable or good. The tacit criterion for distinguishing good from bad forms of social differentiation was presumably the democratic ideology or, more precisely, whether the difference in question was or was not compatible with the democratic value system. Catholics and their antagonists differed on this basic question, and that was why institutions that were "pluralistic" to the former were "divisive" to the latter. But the terminology in which the controversy was carried on tended to conceal rather than clarify what was really at issue, namely, differing interpretations of democracy and what it permitted or required in the sphere of education. Discussions carried on in this fashion, as John Courtney Murray once observed, seldom reached the arduously attained level of clearcut disagreement. Instead they floundered in confusion.[46]

On rare occasions pluralism as such was evaluated negatively in connection with the Catholic threat. In June 1951 the *Christian Century* ran a lengthy report on what was perceived as an effort to mobilize Catholics in Buffalo into religiously segregated associations with the goal in mind of "mak[ing] this a Roman Catholic city." Accompanying this alarmist account was an editorial headed "Pluralism—National Menace," which began by warning that Buffalo was not the only city "facing the threat of a plural society based on religious differences." The idea of a plural society," the editors continued, "is so new to Americans that many will not even understand the term." They might have added that those familiar with current thinking on cultural pluralism would have been the most shocked of all, for what the *Christian Century* was talking about differed radically from the benign versions of pluralism to be found in the American literature. This species was described in unrelievedly negative terms. It applied to a situation in which different elements existed side by side in the same polity without mingling, each pursuing its own group interests as far as it could. A pluralistic society of this sort had no national will; anarchy, instability, or the domination of one element by another was to be expected; and materialistic economic considerations were exalted above all else because nothing of a more elevated nature united the various groups of the society.[47]

This version of pluralism derived from the writings of J. S. Furnivall, the earliest of the "plural society" theorists, a group whose work did not become generally known, even to American social scientists, until the 1960s. The work of these scholars dealt with colonial and newly postcolonial lands and was quite negative in assessing the social costs of internal cleavages deriving from differences in race, language, religion, and so on. It was a kind of nightmare vision of Kallen's original federation-of-nationalities pluralism gone sour, and its application to the American scene was anomalous in the extreme. What the episode indicates is the degree to which growing Catholic strength and assertiveness disturbed spokesmen for Protestantism. Confronting this kind of pluralism, the editors of *Christian Century* felt no embarrassment in calling universal public education "the *sine qua non* of a homogeneous society" and in urging "straightforward, uncompromising resistance to any efforts by any group to subvert the traditional American way of life."[48]

Although the *Christian Century*'s editorial attracted much attention among observers of the religious scene, interreligious feeling mellowed in the mid-fifties, and the fearsome variety of pluralism it presented left no trace on subsequent usage. In January 1958, *School and Society* even ran an article entitled "Subsidized Pluralism," which argued that the time had come to provide public funding for private schools that were set up to meet special group needs not adequately provided for by the public schools. The author, Robert F. Creegan, was affiliated with a state teachers college in New York; he regarded pluralism as "a philosophy of freedom" that merited public support, and he felt that a way could be found to provide it without contravening constitutional prohibitions in respect to church/state and desegregation.[49]

This proposal caught the attention of Joshua A. Fishman, then at the University of Pennsylvania, who arranged a symposium on the topic at the 1958 meeting of the American Psychological Association.[50] The preponderance of opinion there was unsympathetic. Marshall Sklare of the American Jewish Committee seemed bemused that the topic was being discussed at all, and he suggested that it might be more timely to think about moderating pluralism rather than strengthening it. Subsidized pluralism would deepen "divisiveness" and would cause concern among Jews because "greater support for parochialism" might increase the dangers of authoritarianism and anti-Semitism.[51] Other black and Jewish participants were firmly opposed to the idea, alluding to the evils of segregation, apartheid, and "cultural *parallelism*." It was even suggested that by expanding the welfare state, Creegan's proposal would reinforce tendencies toward totalitarianism and thus imperil genuine diversity and freedom.[52] Only Charles Donahue, a Catholic professor from Fordham University, argued that the proposal was justifiable in terms of the nation's tradition of religious pluralism.[53]

In reviewing the discussion, Fishman brought out several points highly relevant to the relation of pluralism and assimilation. Despite verbal adherence to cultural pluralism, he observed, Americans were not really in agreement about what groupings in society were viable candidates for permanent survival and merited public support along the lines visualized by Creegan's proposal. Racial and religious groupings seemed permanent but were ineligible for public support on account of constitutional prohibitions; immigrant ethnic groups were eligible, in Fishman's view, but assimilation worked against the likelihood of their survival, and they were "not popularly defined (or even self-defined) as meriting permanent existence in American society." The latter groups were thus too far gone along the road to assimilation to make group maintenance feasible; and, leaving the constitutional issue aside, Americans did not want to encourage religious diversity because it might cut too deeply, upsetting the existing modus vivendi. For although they had learned to live with diversity, Americans were not really committed to promoting it. "The kind of diversity we have come to respect," Fishman wrote, " . . . [and] to proclaim via brotherhood weeks, interrelations committees, assembly programs for school children, and hollywoodized fiction is a respectable, westernized, protestantized diversity—a diversity of agreeable sorts and proportions. Above all, it is a participationist diversity and not a separatist diversity."[54]

The tone of Fishman's analysis left some doubt as to whether he approved or disapproved of the national taste in diversity, but he had put his finger on the underlying paradox of pluralist thinking in the 1950s, that is, its assimilationist substructure. Almost equally striking is the

aptness of the labels *participationist* and *separatist* for designating the
divergence that developed among American Catholics themselves in reference to pluralism.

Catholics were virtually at one in regarding religious differences as
the key differentiating elements in a pluralistic society. By religious differences they understood "divergent and incompatible views" with respect to basic questions such as the existence and nature of God, the
ontological order of reality, the nature and destiny of man, and the sources
of moral obligation. Because it involved differences so fundamental, pluralism necessarily implied "disagreement and dissension within the community"; but it also implied "a community within which there must be
agreement and consensus." This, as Murray observed laconically, constituted "no small political problem," for some way had to be found
whereby all religious groups could participate in the oneness of the community, despite their dissensions; yet the common principles of participation could not be such as to interfere with the maintenance by each
group of its distinctive religious identity.[55]

With this formulation of the pluralistic problem nearly all Catholics
would have agreed. Where they differed among themselves was in their
assessment of the relative importance of these dialectical contraries and
in the inferences they drew as to policies to be followed in the practical
order.[56] The traditional and still predominant approach in the 1950s can
be called "separatist" in that it gave priority to preserving the religious
identity of Catholics by means of Catholic schools and other religiously
based associations that performed a boundary-maintaining function.
Such an approach was, in the minds of its supporters, required by the
facts of the pluralistic situation and justified by American pluralistic
principles.

The contrasting "participationist" interpretation of pluralism rose to
prominence in the 1950s when it won the support of the liberal Catholic
intelligentsia, whose principal organ was the weekly journal *Commonweal*. The great concern of these *Commonweal* Catholics, as they were
sometimes called, was to bring the church out of its "Catholic ghetto"
and into the "mainstream" of American life. From their standpoint, separatism was precisely what was wrong with American Catholicism; they
were therefore highly critical of "ghetto organizations" that sealed Catholics off from interaction with their fellow citizens of other (or no) religious background. According to their understanding, American society
was pluralistic because it consisted of persons and groups of diverse origin
and character, all of whom worked together in the common enterprise
of national life. The appropriate response to this situation was for Cath-

olics, *as individuals,* to involve themselves in "pluralistic" activities, that is, organizations, causes, and movements in which Catholics took their places alongside Protestants, Jews, and secular liberals in working for goals that would advance the common good of society.

The assimilationist tendency of this approach is obvious. It was further reflected in the sympathetic interest shown by Catholic liberals of the fifties in the historical tradition of ecclesiastical "Americanism," which was recovered by a great outpouring of scholarship in the postwar era. But the term *assimilation* was never used in reference to the participationist strategy—at least not with positive connotations. Rather, it was simply called "pluralism."

American Catholics thus collectively espoused two sharply contrasting versions of pluralism—one that justified the self-segregation of Catholics in denominationally based social and cultural associations and another that justified the mixing together of Catholics and non-Catholics in every sort of social context except those relating directly to worship. This naturally gave rise to confusion. And as pluralism came to be closely identified with democracy in general American usage, Catholic confusion took on a more impassioned polemical quality because spokesmen for both versions interpreted pluralism as a normative concept, one that should guide behavior. In other words, the separatist and the participationist versions—each simply described as "pluralistic"—were offered as *the* democratic prescription for how Catholics should respond to the conditions of American life. It was difficult at best for Catholics to decide how they should respond to American life; by using the same equivocal term to designate opposite strategies, they made it an almost insoluble problem.

As Catholics thrashed about in this semantic muddle, their situation vis-à-vis pluralism was becoming a matter of more general theoretical interest. Will Herberg's *Protestant-Catholic-Jew* (1955) was the first major landmark in this development. Glazer and Moynihan's *Beyond the Melting Pot* (1963) and Milton Gordon's *Assimilation in American Life* (1964) continued to emphasize the importance of religion as a key element in pluralism, but the appearance of these books presaged an era in which race and ethnicity came to dominate the consciousness of those who talked and wrote about pluralism.

Herberg's brilliantly provocative analysis of the postwar "revival of religion" gave the factor of religion unprecedented salience as the key element in American cultural diversity. Yet if Herberg articulated a new form of pluralism, as Powell maintains, he did so largely in the process of tracing the workings of assimilation, and the moral he drew from his investigation was that religion itself was in danger of being assimilated to the "American Way of Life."[57] He was a determined religious pluralist in resisting such an eventuality, but he clearly regarded assimilationist forces as much stronger in American society than those tending to preserve cultural or religious diversity.

Assimilation figured in Herberg's argument in at least three ways, which are distinguishable but closely related. The problem he set out to explain was how it could be that American society was experiencing a great revival of religion, while in every other respect it seemed to be growing more secularized than ever. To solve this paradox he turned to the social psychology of an immigrant-derived people. The religious revival, he suggested, was their response to the psychic malaise induced by contemporary mass society. People felt rootless and alone in mass society; religion gave them a sense of where they belonged by providing a link of continuity with the past and a meaningful location in the world of the present. Religion was the only viable linkage with the past because assimilation had eroded all the other elements of immigrant culture. In identifying themselves with organized Protestantism, Catholicism, and Judaism, persons of immigrant background were therefore giving expression to their residual ethnic loyalties and at the same time protecting themselves from anomie, alienation, and the other ills of mass society.[58]

Its role in leaching away the nonreligious elements of immigrant heritages (language, societies, etc.) is the first way in which assimilation figures in Herberg's analysis. The second relates to the Americanization of immigrant religious heritages, for, while they survived, they did not survive unchanged by assimilation. Herberg devotes separate chapters to the history of Protestantism, Catholicism, and Judaism showing how each tradition was modified in interaction with New World circumstances, the last two being most clearly Americanized as they moved toward equal standing as "the three great faiths of democracy."[59]

The mention of democracy brings us to the third dimension of assimilation in Herberg's interpretation, and the only one toward which he adopted a definitely critical stance. The democratic ideology, or what he called the "American Way of Life," was, in Herberg's judgment, the *real* religion of Americans, and he thought they prized traditional organized religion because it was functionally useful in buttressing the national ideology. Protestantism, Catholicism, and Judaism, in other words, enjoyed public approbation because they provided three equally acceptable ways for the individual to manifest his or her commitment to the "spiritual values" underlying the "American Way of Life," not because they were looked upon as embodiments of autonomous religious truth. Herberg had great admiration for democracy as a socio-political ideology, but he resolutely opposed the tendency to erect it into a civil religion. His conviction that such a tendency existed and that it threatened to denature the true religious quality of the "three great faiths of democracy" is a measure of the degree to which he believed assimilation was carrying everything before it.[60]

Herberg's analysis of religious pluralism thus testified to the pervasive influence of assimilation. In the racial sphere, the assimilationist-oriented drive for integration and civil rights assumed new importance after the mid-fifties and soon demanded equal time with religion from those who discussed the sources of diversity in American life. In 1963 Glazer and Moynihan's *Beyond the Melting Pot* brought the convergence of these elements into full articulation by proposing that religion and race were the two most important organizing principles in American society. In the nation's great cities, they said, "four major groups emerge: Catholics, Jews, white Protestants, and Negroes, each making up the city in different proportions." Looking into the future, they ventured the prediction that religion and race would "define the next stage in the evolution of the American peoples."[61]

This forecast was based on a study of New York City which had shown that group identity among Negroes, Puerto Ricans, Jews, Italians, and Irish was a powerful force in shaping the social and political life of the metropolis. Only the racial half of the prediction was borne out by events, but the book has been so closely linked to the great upsurge of racial and ethnic consciousness that followed its publication that the reader today is startled by the importance attached by the authors to religion. The same linkage with the new ethnicity has probably misled those only casually acquainted with the book into thinking that it provides an unqualified confirmation of the cultural pluralist interpretation of American society. The position taken by the authors is considerably more complex, although it is pluralist in a general sense.

Glazer and Moynihan invited an oversimplified reading by the title they chose and by the statement, made twice, that "the point about the melting pot is that it did not happen."[62] For, despite this seemingly categorical assertion, they did not deny the reality of assimilation. On the contrary, they regarded assimilation as a powerful solvent that washed out immigrant languages, customs, and "the specifically *national* aspect" of ethnic cultures in two or three generations. For that reason they looked upon "the dream of 'cultural pluralism' " as no more realistic than "the hope of a 'melting pot.' "[63] Glazer and Moynihan might therefore have said with equal justice that cultural pluralism "did not happen" either; what their analysis actually suggested was that the processes designated by both terms had really taken place, although neither had worked out as people seemed to expect. The melting pot did change immigrants and their descendants quite profoundly; yet ethnicity persisted in American society despite the transformation wrought by assimilation. Pluralism did exist and was based on ethnicity; but ethnicity itself had been reshaped by the assimilative forces of American society and no longer constituted itself clearly around identifiable cultural traits or foreign nationality. Thus the ethnic group was "not a survival from the age of mass immigration but a new social form" produced by the interaction of group heritage and American conditions.[64]

This subtle analysis underscored the dialectical relationship of assimilation and pluralism, but it was usually portrayed by later spokesmen for the new ethnicity as having completely discredited the "fearful and contempuous" theory of melting pot assimilation.[65] Something of the same sort happened to Milton Gordon's *Assimilation in American Life*, which appeared the year after Glazer and Moynihan's book and presented an interpretation congruent with theirs in certain respects.

Gordon's work was the most ambitious theoretical study till then undertaken of the role played in American society by ethnicity, assimilation, and pluralism, and any attempt to capture its main points in a few words runs the risk of distortion. Nevertheless, we must confine ourselves to three aspects of the book: the salience it accords to race and religion; the treatment of assimilation and pluralism as such; and the nature of its contribution to later thinking about these matters. The first point will not detain us long, but it is important to note that, like Glazer and Moynihan, Gordon treated religion and race as the main sources of diversity in American life. He also referred to *Protestant-Catholic-Jew*, and in one place made use of Herberg's image of multiple melting pots, the most important of which had religious or racial labels. And a long chapter entitled "The Subsociety and the Subculture in America" is divided into subsections devoted to Negroes, Jews, Catholics, white Protestants, and intellectuals (whom Gordon considered a kind of incipient ethnic group).[66]

Gordon began his treatment of assimilation proper with an informative review of the way social scientists had defined it and related concepts such as acculturation and amalgamation. On the basis of this review and his earlier discussion of social structure and culture, he then elaborated a seven-stage model of the assimilation process.[67] The crucial distinction was between the first stage, "cultural or behavioral assimilation," and the second, "structural assimilation." The former, which Gordon equated with acculturation, referred to the adoption by those undergoing assimilation of the cultural patterns of the host society. He left the meaning of *cultural patterns* vague, but in general cultural assimilation meant adopting the English language and conforming to other visible, external features of American culture. Structural assimilation, on the other hand, meant large-scale entry into the "cliques, clubs, and institutions of [the] host society" on the level of primary-group relationships. In other words, structural assimilation was not a matter of how one acted but of who one interacted with.

The remaining stages involved in the process Gordon listed as follows: marital assimilation, marked by large-scale intermarriage; identificational assimilation, marked by the development of a sense of peoplehood based exclusively on the host society; attitude receptional assimilation, which referred to the absence of prejudice against the group being assimilated; behavior receptional assimilation, referring to the absence of discrimination against those being assimilated; and civic assimilation, meaning that there were no political differences concerning issues of power and values between the group being assimilated and the host society.

Gordon referred variously to this scheme as an ideal type, an analytical model, and an array of assimilation variables,[68] but the reader could hardly be blamed for assuming that it was being presented as a description of social reality. For by applying the model to American society, Gordon was able to elicit facts that led him to conclude that cultural assimilation was the first to take place, but its taking place did not necessarily mean that structural assimilation would follow. These conclusions were said to be borne out by the history of immigration, from which one would infer that social reality did conform to the model.[69] Moreover, the variables were interrelated causally from structural assimilation on down. For although cultural assimilation did not necessarily bring structural assimilation in its wake (and had not done so historically, according to Gordon), structural assimilation *was* indissolubly linked to marital assimilation, which led in turn to identificational assimilation, and so on down the line, "like a row of tenpins bowled over in rapid succession by a well placed strike." This insight led to a formulation that sounded as much like a fact of nature as an analytical relationship: "Structural assimilation, then, rather than acculturation, is seen to be the keystone of the arch of assimilation."[70]

By analogy to the distinction between cultural and structural assimilation, Gordon also distinguished between cultural and structural pluralism. *Cultural pluralism* was the appropriate term to use before cultural assimilation took place, when the intergroup situation was characterized by diversity of languages, customs, and other visible manifestations of cultural differences. *Structural pluralism*, however, was the proper designation after the various groups involved had undergone acculturation but were not yet structurally assimilated. Readers who followed all this could hardly have been surprised by Gordon's assertion that structural pluralism was "the major key to the understanding of the ethnic makeup of American society." And they certainly would have been justified in assuming Gordon was making a statement about social reality when he said that *structural pluralism* was "a more accurate term for the American situation . . . than cultural pluralism, although some of the latter also remains."[71]

Whatever he may have intended, and despite language suggesting here and there that his conceptual scheme was a purely theoretical construct not meant to be taken as a description of social reality, Gordon's analysis implied that such assimilation as had actually taken place was shallow and superficial—being largely confined to the first of seven possible stages—and that pluralism was a much deeper and more meaningful reality in American society than assimilation. This brings us to the influence the book had on subsequent thinking about pluralism and ethnicity. I have not systematically surveyed the literature with that question in mind, but, as one professionally interested in ethnicity during the entire period since the book was published, my impression is that Gordon's work was, like Glazer and Moynihan's, generally regarded as having discredited the "assimilationist myth." His distinction between cultural and structural pluralism, although noted by serious students of ethnicity, had no impact on popular usage, an area where the ethnic revival was soon to make "cultural pluralism" more of a shibboleth than ever. By offering scholarly confirmation of the persistence of some sort of pluralism based on ethnicity, Gordon's work doubtless reinforced this outcome, despite its argument that cultural pluralism was passing from the scene as a result of cultural assimilation.

Writing in 1972, Micahel Passi touched on this matter in professing puzzlement at what he deemed Gordon's inconsistency. He could not understand how Gordon could perceive the reality of pluralism as fully as he did and still maintain that cultural assimilation had actually taken place on a large scale. In Passi's view, cultural pluralism was as much a continuing fact as structural pluralism, and he interpreted Gordon's obtuseness on this point as evidence of the "transitional nature" of his book.[72] Passi wrote as an advocate of the new ethnicity, and he was certainly correct that thinking on pluralism and assimilation had changed drastically in the years since Gordon's book had appeared.

The transition toward which *Beyond the Melting Pot* and *Assimilation in American Life* pointed was the great upsurge of ethnic feeling that arose as an aspect of the radical social and cultural changes of the late 1960s. These developments are too complex to enter into; and what was variously called the ethnic revival, the new ethnicity, or the new pluralism produced a literature too extensive to review.[73] All we can do here is highlight a few of the issues most directly related to assimilation-pluralism polarity.

The assertion of ethnic claims in many parts of the world suggests the inadequacy of a strictly national explanation, but in this country the most important single factor in the ethnic revival was the new spirit of group-centered militance shown by American blacks. The mid-sixties shift from the assimilationist-oriented drive for integration and civil rights to a more aggressively particularistic emphasis on black power, black pride, and black culture legitimized *ethnicity*—a word that came into widespread use only in the late 1960s as the designation for the kind of "we-group" feeling that would have been branded in the 1940s or 1950s as ethnocentrism. After it was legitimized by blacks, ethnicity was quickly taken up by other groups in American society.

The rapid emergence of red power, brown power, and white ethnic movements underscores another important point about the assertion of ethnicity, namely that it served group interests. Ethnicity became a means for mobilizing group energies to enforce group demands, and it was generally associated with a claim on public authorities for the redress of wrongs or some other kind of action designed to benefit the group in question. Glazer and Moynihan pointed out in 1963 that ethnic groups were also interest groups, and as national policy moved toward affirmative action, the significance of the group interest dimension of ethnicity stood forth more clearly than ever. Students of the "plural society" type of pluralism, whose work was becoming more widely known in the 1970s, also stressed the group interest angle, some even portraying it as the basic element in the whole phenomenon of ethnicity and pluralism.[74]

The persistence of ethnicity (as qualified by Glazer and Moynihan and Gordon), the influence of the black example, and the group interest angle all figure as positive factors in the enhanced salience of pluralism that marked the revival of ethnicity. But there was an equally important negative factor: the discrediting of assimilation that was an inevitable by-product of the revulsion from traditional Americanism brought on by the racial upheaval and the Vietnam War. The crisis engendered by these and related developments (e.g., urban riots and campus disruptions) severely shook the confidence of Americans in their national values and institutions. Few, it is true, accepted the extreme view that "AmeriKKKa" was fundamentally vicious and oppressive, but the damage to collective self-esteem was sufficient to discredit assimilation because assimilation means identification with national values, ideals, and institutions.[75] In the distemper of the sixties, "Americanization" became a term of abuse, and the melting pot was held up to scorn as a hateful symbol for a contemptible goal, which had, however, not been realized because of the enduring ethnicity of our pluralistic population.

The new ethnicity thus accentuated the ostensible contrast between pluralism and assimilation; and by associating the former with admirable social goals and the latter with disreputable goals it made the terminology more value laden and rigidly judgmental. This aggravated the semantic obscurities of the past and generated some new ones as pluralism was ritualistically invoked in the support of the most diverse positions. Critics of the new ethnicity soon appeared, and the picture grew more complicated in the mid-1970s.[76] From the vantage point of the early 1980s, the most significant development appears to be the emergence of a radically "separatist" interpretation of pluralism, which is associated with a revival of racialist thinking, and which is likely to arouse a reaffirmation of assimilation as a respectable social policy.

In the early stages of the ethnic revival, most people seemed to have a participationist version of pluralism in mind when they used the term. *Participationist* here means the kind of pluralism that embodies a healthy chunk of assimilation without labeling it as such. It envisages loosely defined groups interacting on a basis of consensus about basic social values, showing mutual respect and tolerance, each conceding the right of others to be different, but none in fact differing significantly enough to constitute a "divisive" element in the overall harmony of society. This was the kind of pluralism promoted by the American Jewish Committee, the most influential single force in the white ethnic movement. Its National Project on Ethnic America was intended to ease the confrontation between blacks and working-class whites and thereby to "help polarization dissolve into pluralism."[77] The leaders of this "depolarization project" were alert to the dangers of ethnocentrism and destructive separatism and sensitive to the "difficulty of going beyond fragmentation toward a genuine pluralism." The same notes are sounded repeatedly in the hearings on a 1970 bill to establish "ethnic heritage studies centers." The sponsor, Congressman Roman C. Pucinski of Illinois, disavowed any intention of promoting separatist ethnic consciousness. "The main thrust of this legislation," he declared, "is to try to eliminate the differences [between people] by letting people know about each other and recognizing their differences."[78] A book review in a Sunday newspaper supplement suggests the bland and innocuous manner in which this participationist version of pluralism came across to the general reading public: "Cultural pluralism means that each culture within a country will have its respected place, and every individual will be free to choose the elements he may find attractive in another life style."[79]

Pluralism meant more than that to many spokesmen for ethnic groups, and the rise of black nationalism in the late sixties legitimized demands for "militant pluralism" all along the line. This term was used by Nathan Hare, the embattled organizer of a black studies program at San Francisco State University, who defined it as "the right [of a group] to exist as an equal, akin to parity, as a distinct category." Paralleling the rhetoric of black separatism, if not directly inspired by it, was the call for "community control" of institutions, such as schools, which served a black clientele.[80] Chicano separatists envisaged a "Plan of Aztlan" whereby all the territories ceded by Mexico to the United States in 1848 would be restored to Chicano control.[81] Separatism and tribal autonomy had always figured prominently in the relationship of American Indians to the national society, and as the new ethnicity gathered momentum, Vine Deloria proposed that tribalism be applied across the board to guarantee "the basic sovereignty of the minority group," strengthen its bargaining position, and guard against the dangers of "co-optation." The contrast between this approach and the participationist vision of individuals freely choosing elements of other life styles was brought out starkly in Deloria's comment that, in the arrangement he urged, everyone would have his or her special enclave, and "alienation would be confined to those times that people stray from their own neighborhood into the world of other peoples."[82]

Ethnic activists pioneered in separatist pluralism, but it eventually affected academic studies too. Among scholars, the tendency toward a more militant pluralism first took the form of increasingly strident rejection of "assimilationist values, with their connotations of elitism and a monocultural society" and an insistence on the perduring quality of ethnicity.[83] These were the main themes of Michael Passi's historical critique of academic studies of ethnicity, and the cultural pluralists were his heroes. However, James Powell's dissertation, written in the same year (1971), showed that most advocates of cultural pluralism had really been liberal assimilationists or, at best, advocates of unity-cum-diversity. Powell reported this finding with detachment; by the late 1970s others were reacting more indignantly. Nicholas Montalto, for example, branded the cultural pluralism of many involved in the intercultural education movement of the 1940s as "almost hypocritical"; theirs was a "pluralism of deception." Another historian charged that those seeking reform in Indian educational policy in the 1930s were not real cultural pluralists because they did not believe "in the indefinite preservation of cultural qualities requiring political self-determination or permanent self-sepa-ration." Their thinking was "flawed or insidious," and the cultural de-mocracy they offered was merely a "softer version" of "crass assimila-tionism."[84]

Writers of this persuasion tend to be highly critical of the liberal democratic assumptions of the earlier cultural pluralists. In this respect their outlook reflects the alienation from national values and institutions that pervaded social commentary in the late sixties and early seventies. Nicholas Montalto brings out the connection in a frank avowal of the "biases which may have shaped his perceptions" of the issues involved in intercultural education and pluralism. "I believe that the disorders of our society, the spiritual unrest, the materialism that provides the only confirmation of self-worth, the loss of creativity and freedom, are con-sequences of an out-moded social system, which attempted to suppress those centers of valuation and opinion in conflict with the 'core culture.' In its uncorrupted form," he continues (without elaborating on corrupted forms), "the revival of ethnic consciousness is but one aspect of a larger movement for social change, a movement to protect the environment, to adapt technology to human needs, to find satisfaction in work, to regain power over our lives, to eliminate racism, and to reorder relations among the nations."[85]

Montalto included the elimination of racism among the goals asso-ciated with the ethnic revival, but the new pluralism has in fact been accompanied by a strong resurgence of racial thinking. *Racial thinking* as used here does not mean holding that one race is inherently superior or inferior to another. It refers rather to the outlook that regards race as a valid social category, that accepts the classification of individuals into racial categories on the basis of ancestry or the "rule of descent," and that justifies differential treatment of individuals according to their racial classifications. The development of this sort of racialism has been closely linked to affirmative action and other forms of "benign quotas" that are predicated on the assumptions spelled out above.[86] It is thus to be under-stood primarily as the unanticipated by-product of policies intended to overcome the effects of America's historic racism. But there were also more positive factors in the development of racial thinking. One was the heavy emphasis by black nationalists and their counterparts in other groups on the distinctive racial qualities, "soul," or consciousness of *la raza*, that marks the group in question. Another was the insistence of the new pluralists that ethnicity is a "primordial" quality that deserves more adequate recognition in the institutional arrangements of society.[87] In thus harking back to something like Kallen's original federation-of-nationalities pluralism, the new pluralists found themselves being led almost irresistably to the vaguely racialist interpretation of ethnicity that Kallen himself entertained in the teens and early twenties.

In view of the extent to which racialist assumptions have been tacitly accepted in practice, it is not surprising that one can now discern the beginnings of a new theoretical interest in the subject which treats seriously the possibility that genetically determined factors in social life are real and demand scientific attention. Pierre L. van den Berghe's *Ethnic Phenomenon* (1981) is the most explicit manifestation of this tendency and the most fully elaborated. Van den Berghe grounds his interpretation in socio-biological theory, arguing that "ethnic and racial sentiments are [an] extension of kinship sentiments. Ethnocentrism and racism are thus extended forms of nepotism—the [genetically based] propensity to favor kin over nonkin." From this it follows that "ethnocentrism and racism, too, are deeply rooted in our biology and can be expected to persist even in industrial societies, whether capitalist or socialist."[88] Van den Berghe is well aware that this view is flagrantly at odds with both liberal and radical ideologies, and well as with the scholarly consensus on race that has prevailed for a half-century, and he is at pains to make clear that he does not *approve* of ethnocentrism and racism. His position, rather, is that to be able to deal with these unattractive aspects of our nature, we must understand how deeply they are embedded in our evolutionary history.[89]

Van den Berghe is "adamantly universalist" in ideological orientation and has written critically of the American revival of ethnicity,[90] but another writer sympathetic to the new ethnicity hints at a somewhat similar biologically linked racialism. This is Fred Wacker, who seems to regard the abandonment of Larmarckian racialism not as a clear scientific advance but as a problem requiring explanation. He interprets the shift away from Lamarckianism (by which is meant the belief that the cultural traits of a people are transmitted by hereditary mechanisms) as resulting from two kinds of factor: ideological considerations, such as a commitment to democratic reform and the elimination of prejudice; and changes in scientific assumptions, specifically "a movement toward a stronger and more dogmatic environmentalism." Wacker takes explicit note of Kallen's racialism but does not treat it as a scientific error or a faulty basis on which to erect a theory of cultural pluralism. He is, however, sufficiently embarrassed by Kallen's sharing the same assumptions as the nativist racists of the day to add: "One can argue . . . that it makes an important and even vital difference whether a person looks at racial or group stereotypes as positive heritages or marks of backwardness."[91]

Wacker's writings illustrate how the logic of the new ethnicity leads its proponents toward a scientific rehabilitation of racialism. But they are not the only ones tending that way. Certain critics of "the myth of ethnicity" start from the other side of the street, so to speak, but they contribute to the same result by drawing so sharp a distinction between race and other heritage-related social groupings as to make the conclusion inevitable that only race is real and deserving of recognition. They sometimes, but not invariably, add the allegation that the revival of ethnicity is merely a cover for white racist backlash against affirmative action.[92]

A recent and authoritative example of this general line of interpretation is provided by M. G. Smith, a West Indian scholar prominent in the study of plural societies. Although he does not accuse the editors of the *Harvard Encyclopedia of American Ethnic Groups* of being motivated by backlash, he regards their having subsumed race under the more general heading of ethnicity as a "monumental confusion" that vitiates the conceptual foundation of their whole undertaking. According to Smith, race is a reality in nature; it has social consequences; and to disregard these facts, no matter how high-minded the reasons, makes it impossible to understand "those fundamental differences within America between its major racial stocks on the one hand and the multitude of ethnic groups on the other which have exercised and continue to exercise such profound influences on the development and structure of the society from its earliest beginnings."[93]

As a result of the practical and theoretical revival of racialism—in addition to the affirmation of "unmeltable" ethnicity and the discrediting of traditional Americanism—a drastically "separatist" variety of pluralism has developed in the past ten years or so. It resembles Kallen's 1915 version of cultural pluralism but differs fundamentally from the cultural pluralism that has predominated since the late 1930s and that Kallen himself championed in the 1950s. Not everyone who speaks of pluralism today has this militantly separatist variety in mind, for the term is still used in a participationist sense and invoked to celebrate the blandest sort of diversity. This circumstance, coupled with the vagueness that has always surrounded the expression and its use for so long without acknowledgement of the assimilationist substructure it tacitly embodied, tended to mask what was happening for some time. But the recognition that something significant was afoot has gradually dawned, and in 1981 Milton Gordon illuminated the topic brilliantly in an important article entitled "Models of Pluralism: The New American Dilemma."[94]

As the subtitle indicates, Gordon believes the nation now confronts a situation comparable in importance to that addressed in Gunnar Myrdal's classic work, *An American Dilemma* (1944). For Myrdal, the dilemma had to do with the unwillingness of Americans to live up to the requirements of the democratic ideology in their actual treatment of blacks. He did not regard the ideology itself as problematic; nor did he find it difficult to specify what "the American Creed," as he called it, actually required in the way of equal treatment of blacks. Today, however, it is precisely these matters that have become problematic: the liberal democratic consensus has been challenged, and Americans disagree among themselves about what would constitute equal treatment and how it should be realized.

The traditional position Gordon designates *liberal pluralism*. This corresponds to the participationist pluralism that flourished in the forties and fifties. Premised on democratic individualism, it envisages ethnic and racial relations as falling outside the scope of legal coercion or direct governmental control, except that the state is supposed to prevent discrimination. Racial and ethnic groups have no juridical standing in the polity and no legal rights as entities in themselves; individuals are free to associate themselves with such groups as they see fit, but their doing so, or not doing so, has no bearing on their status in law or their entitlement to the benefits of citizenship. Equality is understood in terms of equal opportunity for individuals, regardless of racial or ethnic background, not in terms of equality of outcomes for groups considered collectively. Officially, liberal pluralism prescribes tolerance and a laissez-faire policy with respect to the perpetuation of structural differentiation and cultural distinctiveness among the groups composing the population. In fact, however, its universalistic premises run contrary to the logic of particularistic distinctiveness, and liberal pluralism deprecates differentiation that tends to become "divisive."

Against the traditional position, Gordon contrasts the newer *corporate pluralism*. This approach corresponds to what I have called the militantly separatist version, but Gordon develops its implications more systematically. It envisages formal standing before the law for ethnic and racial groups; recognizes group rights in the political and economic spheres; and makes the enjoyment of rights by individuals conditional, to some extent, on whether they belong to specified groups. With respect to equality, corporate pluralism would require proportionally equal outcomes for groups rather than equality of opportunity for individuals. And without explicitly rejecting the need for national unity, it would officially foster structural separatism and cultural and linguistic differentiation among the constituent groups in society. Corporate pluralism would not require what Gordon calls "area exclusivism," or the establishing of territorial enclaves, but it would find such a development acceptable, even though it might result in limitations on the rights of outsiders to travel through or reside in the areas in question.

Although he lays out the two positions in an abstract, "ideal typical" manner, Gordon is convinced that they correspond to real differences in outlook and policy that now confront the American people and demand a choice. Moreover, he insists that the choice is not between unrelated alternatives in discrete areas of concern; rather, "there is an inherent logic in the relationship of the various positions on these public issues which makes the choice one between two patterns—two overall types of racial and ethnic pluralism each with distinctly different implications for the American way of life."[95]

Gordon is correct on these points, in my opinion; and I would add that his spelling out so clearly the contrasting meanings of *pluralism* is a major contribution toward raising the discussion from the morass of semantic confusion to the hard-won level where clearcut disagreement becomes possible. My own belief is that as more people come to realize what the corporate version of pluralism actually implies, there will be a strong reaffirmation of the traditional values of democratic universalism and a frank espousal of assimilation understood as a social policy promoting identification with those democratic values by all Americans, regardless of ethnic or racial background. The beginnings of such a reaffirmation are already discernible;[96] as the illiberal—indeed, anti-liberal—implications of corporate pluralism come to be appreciated for what they are, the reaffirmation will gain in strength.

Until Gordon's analysis appeared, proponents of corporate pluralism could draw on the moral capital accumulated by a whole generation's uncritical celebration of liberal pluralism despite the fact that it (corporate pluralism) rested on diametrically opposed theoretical foundations and prescribed quite different social policies. Now it should be clear to those committed to the traditional values of liberal democracy that they can no longer endorse any and every call for "cultural pluralism." In the past, the great majority of those who championed cultural pluralism were far more deeply committed to assimilation understood as ideological consensus on democratic values than they seemed to realize. Now it is the democratic consensus itself that is at issue—what it consists in and what it implies for government action in the area of racial and ethnic relations. Pluralists may have thought they could take all that for granted, but they cannot. They cannot even begin to discuss these fundamental questions constructively until the terminology of pluralism is demystified and people realize that it usually confuses rather than clarifies what is really at issue.

NOTES

Source: John Edwards, ed., *Linguistic Minorities: Policies and Pluralism* (London, 1984), 221–57. Copyright by the Academic Press; reprinted by permission.

a. Rivka Shpak Lissak, *Pluralism and Progressives: Hull House and the New Immigrants, 1890–1919* (Chicago, 1989), esp. 8–9 (for quotation), 27, 147–56, 173, 182–84. See also Michael R. Olneck, "The Recurring Dream: Symbolism and Ideology in Intercultural and Multicultural Education," *American Journal of Education*, 98 (February 1990), 147–74.

b. Mary C. Waters, *Ethnic Options: Choosing Identities in America* (Berkeley, Calif., 1990), esp. 7–8, 167.

c. Gary Gerstle, *Working-Class Americanism: The Politics of Labor in a Textile City, 1914–1960* (Cambridge, 1989), 289ff. Gerstle points out that this understanding of *cultural pluralism* emerged in the 1940s and is not what Horace Kallen had in mind when he introduced the term.

d. Lawrence H. Fuchs, *The American Kaleidoscope: Race, Ethnicity, and the Civic Culture* (Middletown, Conn., 1990). Fuchs rejects Kallen's original federation-of-nationalities pluralism and equates what he (Fuchs) calls "voluntary pluralism" with Kallen's later assimilationist-oriented version of cultural pluralism (74). He states, "When Americans celebrated diversity, often calling it pluralism, they were really celebrating individual rights" (561, n. 1).

e. *New York Times*, February 7, 1990; and, for critical discussion, Diane Ravitch, "Multiculturalism: E Pluribus Plures," *American Scholar*, 59 (Summer 1990), 337–54. For earlier educational developments, see Olneck, "Recurring Dream"; Christine E. Sleeter and Carl A. Grant, "An Analysis of Multicultural Education in the United States," *Harvard Educational Review*, 57 (November 1987), 421–44. Scott McConnell and Eric Breindel, "Head to Come," *New Republic*, 202 (January 8–15, 1990), 18–21 links the New York case with the earlier battle at Stanford University over Eurocentrism in the curriculum.

f. A key "text" in popularizing the term is Rick Simonson and Scott Walker, eds., *The Graywolf Annual Five: Multi-Cultural Literacy* (St. Paul, Minn., 1988). Although it contains little theorizing of the rarefied European sort, this "diversity" anthology provides materials suitable for college use. The title was adopted in reaction to E. D. Hirsch's *Cultural Literacy*, but *multicultural(ism)* was so new a term that it is not used prominently (if at all) by any of the contributors. Even Ishmael Reed, who does use *monocultural*, entitles his piece "America: The Multinational Society." Nor is the new term included in the list of words and expressions the editors drew up as a supplement to Hirsch's list, although *multilingual* and *multinational* are there. (I am grateful to Werner Sollors for calling my attention to this work and noting several of the points made here.)

g. George Yudice, "Latino Identity and the Reconceptualization of 'America' as a Multicultural Society," paper presented at the American Studies Association convention, New Orleans, November 1990.

h. Ibid. In another piece, Yudice and a coauthor refer also to "hegemonic pluralism" and "ersatz pluralism." See Juan Flores and George Yudice, "Living Borders/ Buscando America: Languages of Latino Self-Formation," *Social Text*, 8, no. 2 (1990), 62, 66.

i. Arthur Schlesinger, Jr., When Ethnic Studies Are Un-American," *Wall Street Journal*, April 23, 1990. Ravitch, "Multiculturalism," advocates "pluralism," understood in a liberal assimilationist sense, as opposed to the "particularism" of the extreme multiculturalists. For a critique by the former prophet of the ethnic revival, see Michael Novak, "A Call for Disunity," *Forbes*, 146 (July 9, 1990), 65; see also John Leo, "A Fringe History of the World," *U.S. News & World Report*, 109 (November 12, 1990), 25–26; and Fred Siegel, "The Cult of Multiculturalism," *New Republic* 204 (February 18, 1991), 34–40.

1. Richard Mayo-Smith, quoted in Robert E. Park and Ernest W. Burgess, *Introduction to the Science of Sociology*, 3d ed., rev. (Chicago, 1969 [orig. ed. 1921]), 741. Cf. also Sarah E. Simons, "Social Assimilation," *American Journal of Sociology*, 6 (1900–1901), 790–822; John R. Commons, *Races and Immigrants in America* (1907; New York, 1920), 209. On the melting pot, see above, chap. 1.

2. Henry Pratt Fairchild, *Immigration* (New York, 1913), 398–99.

3. E. A. Ross, *The Old World in the New* (New York, 1914), 282–304.

4. Horace M. Kallen, "Democracy *versus* the Melting Pot," *Nation*, 100 (February 18, 25, 1915), 190–94, 217–20; reprinted in Kallen, *Culture and Democracy in the United States* (New York, 1924), 67–125. John Higham, *Send These to Me: Jews and Other Immigrants in Urban America* (1975; Baltimore, 1984), 198–232, is a splendid analysis of ethnic pluralism in modern American thought. For other perspectives, see Milton M. Gordon, *Assimilation in American Life* (New York, 1964), chap. 6; Milton R. Konvitz, "Horace Meyer Kallen (1882–1974): Philosopher of the Hebraic-American Idea," in *American Jewish Year Book, 1974–1975* (New York, 1974), 55–80; Moses Rischin, "The Jews and Pluralism: Toward an American Freedom Symphony," mimeo, available from American Jewish Committee Project on Group Life and Ethnic America; Arthur Mann, *The One and the Many: Reflections on the American Identity* (Chicago, 1979), 136–48.

5. Kallen, *Culture and Democracy*, 124. For a fuller analysis of Kallen's position, see Philip Gleason, "American Identity and Americanization," in Stephen Thernstrom, Ann Orlov, and Oscar Handlin, eds., *Harvard Encyclopedia of American Ethnic Groups* (Cambridge, Mass., 1980), 43–45.

6. This 10-volume series was republished in 1971 with new introductions by contemporary scholars. For background on the original series and a general review of its findings, see William S. Bernard, "General Introduction to the Republished Studies," in Frank V. Thompson, *Schooling of the Immigrant* (1920; Montclair, N.J., 1971), vii–xliii.

7. Park and Burgess, *Science of Sociology*, 773; William I. Thomas, Robert E. Park, and Herbert A. Miller, *Old World Traits Transplanted* (1921; Montclair N.J., 1971), esp. chap. 9. Thomas's name was not included among the authors when the book was originally published for reasons explained in Donald R. Young's introduction to the reprint. Young also observes that the book "supports a pluralistic policy" in

general, although it "recognized that immigrant groups and their original heritages cannot survive indefinitely" (xiv). Thomas, Park, and Miller dealt critically with the Kallenesque type of pluralism (229ff.). Kallen, *Culture and Democracy* (150–65, 169–70) returned the compliment with a negative assessment of *Old World Traits*, although he had earlier (155) alluded to the "brilliant work" of W. I. Thomas on *The Polish Peasant*. He was presumably unaware that Thomas had any part in *Old World Traits*.

8. Park and Burgess, *Science of Sociology*, 506, 735–36. Fred H. Matthews, *Quest for an American Sociology: Robert E. Park and the Chicago School* (Montreal, 1977) is the best study of Park and his influence.

9. Park and Burgess, *Science of Sociology*, 735–36, 506, 510, 665.

10. Ibid., 737, 756, 758–60.

11. Edwin R. A. Seligman and Alvin Johnson, eds., *Encyclopaedia of the Social Sciences*, 15 vols. (New York, 1930–35), 2:281–83. Cf. Matthews, *Quest for an American Sociology*, 167–69.

12. The matters touched upon in this paragraph and the two following are dealt with at greater length in chap. 6.

13. Stuart Chase, *The Proper Study of Mankind* (New York, 1948), 59.

14. Everett C. Hughes and Helen M. Hughes, *Where Peoples Meet* (Glencoe, Ill., 1952), 30–31. About the same time another scholar wrote, "The relationship between assimilation and such other terms as 'diffusion,' 'accommodation,' 'culture contact,' and 'transculturation' remains rather vague even at this date." *Social Behavior and Personality. Contributions of W. I. Thomas to Theory and Social Research*, ed. Edmund H. Volkart (New York, 1951), 260–61n. Gordon, *Assimilation in American Life*, which is discussed in a later section of this chapter, makes a helpful distinction between cultural and structural assimilation and equates cultural assimilation with acculturation.

15. Illustrative of the affinity between the two concepts is that a volume of essays by Melville J. Herskovits (published posthumously and edited by his wife, Frances Herskovits), is entitled *Cultural Relativism; Perspectives in Cultural Pluralism* (New York, 1972).

16. Francis J. Brown and Joseph S. Roucek, eds., *Our Racial and National Minorities* (1937; New York, 1939), 762.

17. Ibid., 763.

18. James H. Powell, "The Concept of Cultural Pluralism in American Social Thought, 1915–1965" (Ph.D. diss., University of Notre Dame, 1971), 169–70. Largely ignored earlier, says Powell, cultural pluralism "had, as it were, arrived" (173–74).

19. Ibid., 128ff.

20. Ibid., 129. Actually, Powell covers one work that does discuss the federation-of-nationalities version as applicable to American society, *but only to reject it* with the harsh judgment that it was tainted with "racism and a totalitarian spirit." The work was Arnold Rose and Caroline Rose, *America Divided* (New York, 1948), which Powell treats briefly (142–43).

21. Horace Kallen, *Cultural Pluralism and the American Idea* (Philadelphia, 1956), 98.

22. Ibid., 50, 51–52, 55.

23. Ibid., 97.

24. Ibid., 204–5.

25. Ibid., 109, 197ff. For other indications of Kallen's raising of science, democracy, and secularism (which he amalgamated together) to the level of civil religion, see his "Democracy's True Religion," *Saturday Review of Literature*, 34 (July 28,

1951), 6–7, 29–30; Kallen, "Secularism as the Common Religion of a Free Society," *Journal for the Scientific Study of Religion*, 4 (1965), 145–51; and Kallen, *Secularism Is the Will of God* (New York, 1954).

26. For fuller treatment of matters discussed in this paragraph and the two following, see Gleason, "American Identity," 47ff.; and below, chap. 6. Higham, *Send These to Me*, 218–21, provides insights to which I am much indebted.

27. Gunnar Myrdal, *An American Dilemma* (1944; New York, 1962), 1004.

28. Robin M. Williams, Jr., *The Reduction of Intergroup Tensions* (New York, 1947), 7.

29. Goodwin Watson, *Action for Unity* (New York, 1947); William E. Vickery and Stewart G. Cole, *Intercultural Education in American Schools* (New York, 1943); Nicholas V. Montalto, "The Forgotten Dream: A History of the Intercultural Education Movement, 1924–1941" (Ph.D. diss., University of Minnesota, 1978), esp. 143–44; Peter I. Rose, *The Subject Is Race* (New York, 1968), esp. 75ff.

30. In 1944 upwards of four thousand American psychologists subscribed to a "Psychologists' Manifesto" dealing with war, peace, and human nature. The third proposition states: "Through education and experience people can learn that their prejudiced ideas about the English, the Russians, the Japanese, Catholics, Jews, Negroes, are misleading or altogether false. They can learn that members of one racial, national, or cultural group are basically similar to those of other groups, and have similar problems, hopes, aspirations, and needs. Prejudice is a matter of attitudes, and attitudes are to a considerable extent a matter of training and information." Gardner Murphy, ed., *Human Nature and Enduring Peace. Third Yearbook of the Society for the Psychological Study of Social Issues* (Boston, 1945), 455–56. Cf. also Gordon W. Allport, *The Nature of Prejudice* (1954; New York, 1958), 477–80.

31. Lewis M. Killian, "Black Power and White Reactions: The Revitalization of Race-Thinking in the United States," *Annals*, 454 (March, 1981), 43.

32. It was for these reasons that Arnold and Caroline Rose rejected cultural pluralism so vehemently; see their *America Divided*, 166–74.

33. There was some effort to promote use of the term *integration* in place of *assimilation*, even in contexts other than black/white relations, the argument being that integration conveyed more clearly that the relationship involved was mutual, a "two-way street" of influence and adaptation. See W. D. Borrie, ed., *The Cultural Integration of Immigrants* (Paris, 1959), 92–94, 292. M. R. Davie's "Our Vanishing Minorities," In Francis J. Brown and Joseph Roucek, eds., *One America: The History, Contributions, and Present Problems of Our Racial and National Minorities*, rev. ed. (New York, 1946), 540–51, was more complacent about the disappearance of minorities than his title might suggest, but he favored cultural pluralism as a strategy of liberal assimilation. Myrdal, *American Dilemma*, 51–53, assumes the near complete assimilation of immigrants, and so does W. Lloyd Warner and Leo Srole, *The Social Systems of American Ethnic Groups* (New Haven, Conn., 1945), 295–96.

34. On mass society, see Daniel Bell, "Modernity and Mass Society: On the Varieties of Cultural Experience," in Arthur M. Schlesinger, Jr., and Morton White, eds., *Paths of American Thought* (Boston, 1963), 411–31, 574–77. Cf. also Marshall Sklare, "Ethnic-Religious Groups and Publicly Subsidized Pluralism," *School and Society*, 87 (May 23, 1959), 261.

35. See below, chap. 6 for fuller treatment and citation of evidence. Cf. Erik H. Erikson, *Childhood and Society*, 2d ed. (1950; New York, 1963), 282.

36. Daniel Bell, ed., *The Radical Right* (1955; Garden City, N.Y., 1964 [orig. pub. 1955 as *The New American Right*]), 75–95, 129, 216–17, 319; Edward A. Shils,

The Torment of Secrecy (Glencoe, Ill., 1956), 77ff.; David Riesman, *Individualism Reconsidered* (Garden City, N.Y., 1955), 120–21. Cf. also the ominous remarks of A. L. Kroeber on the potential totalitarian dangers implicit in "Assimilation and Uniformity," in his *Anthropology: Culture Patterns and Processes* (New York, 1963), 249–50, which is a reprint of certain chapters of the 1948 edition of Kroeber's *Anthropology*.

37. David Nicholls, *Three Varieties of Pluralism* (New York, 1974) is an excellent brief discussion that treats critically American political pluralism, distinguishing it from the British pluralist school that dates back to F. W. Maitland and J. N. Figgis, and from the "plural society" approach of a recent group of sociologists and anthropologists. Another British commentary (critical) on the American political pluralists is Bernard Crick, "The Strange Death of the American Theory of Consensus," *Political Quarterly*, 43 (1972), 46–59.

38. David Truman, *The Governmental Process* (New York, 1951) is generally regarded as the first of the pluralist works of the 1950s. Other works stressing the pluralist antidote to mass society and extremism are William Kornhauser, *The Politics of Mass Society* (Glencoe, Ill., 1959); and Shils, *Torment of Secrecy*, esp. 223–38. Seymour M. Lipset, *Political Man* (Garden City, N.Y., 1960) discusses authoritarianism, crosscutting pressures, and the "limited warfare" conception of American politics.

39. See, for example, Horace Kallen, "'E Pluribus Unum' and the Cultures of Democracy," *Journal of Educational Sociology*, 16 (February, 1943), 329–32; Kornhauser, *Politics of Mass Society*, 5; Riesman, *Individualism Reconsidered*, 106.

40. See Kallen, "Democracy's True Religion," 29–30.

41. Paul Blanshard was the best-known liberal critic of Catholicism; see his *American Freedom and Catholic Power* (Boston, 1949) and *Communism, Democracy, and Catholic Power* (Boston, 1951); and James M. O'Neill, *Catholicism and American Freedom* (New York, 1952), a Catholic reply to Blanshard.

42. See George Huntston Williams, Waldo Beach, and H. Richard Neibuhr, "Issues between Catholics and Protestants at Midcentury," *Religion in Life*, 23 (Spring 1954), 163–205; John J. Kane, *Catholic-Protestant Conflicts in America* (Chicago, 1955); and Edward A. Purcell, Jr., *The Crisis of Democratic Theory: Scientific Naturalism and the Problem of Value* (Lexington, Ky., 1973), 164ff., 179–80, 203–4, 224–25, 241.

43. Conant discussed these matters in lectures in 1952 and included a slightly reworked version in his *Education and Liberty* (Cambridge, Mass., 1953); quotations from 80–81. In his memoirs, *My Several Lives* (New York, 1970), Conant devotes chap. 34 to the episode and reproduces one of his 1952 lectures (665–70). He also notes here (470) that he did not actually use the word *divisive* himself; but he grants that his statement could be translated as "independent schools are divisive" and that "it would have seemed like a quibble" to object that he did not use it.

44. See the editorial from the *Boston Pilot* reproduced in Conant, *Education and Liberty*, 140–41.

45. John Courtney Murray, S. J., *We Hold These Truths* (New York, 1960), 147. The person quoted by Murray was Robert E. Rodes, Jr., a Catholic law professor.

46. Ibid., 15.

47. *Christian Century*, 68 (June 13, 1951), 701–03, 704–09. Will Herberg, *Protestant-Catholic-Jew: An Essay in American Religious Sociology*, rev. ed. (Garden City, N.Y., 1960 [orig. ed. 1955]), 236–37, discusses this "much-noted editorial," which is also alluded to more generally in *Catholicism in America. A Series of Articles from the Commonweal* (New York, 1954), 153–54.

48. *Christian Century*, 68 (June 13, 1951), 703. For the "plural society" writers, see Powell, "Concept of Cultural Pluralism," 230–51; and Pierre L. van den Berghe, "Pluralism," in John J. Honigmann, ed., *Handbook of Social and Cultural Anthropology* (Chicago, 1973), 961ff.

49. Robert F. Creegan, "Subsidized Pluralism," *School and Society*, 86 (January 18, 1958), 32–34; supplemented by Creegan, "Quality and Freedom through Pluralism," ibid., 87 (May 23, 1959), 248–51.

50. The presentations at the symposium were published in *School and Society*, 87 (May 23, 1949), 246–67.

51. Ibid., 260–63.

52. Ibid., 251–53, 259–60 (emphasis in original).

53. Ibid., 253–56. Creegan, "Quality and Freedom through Pluralism" also favored subsidized pluralism at the symposium.

54. Ibid., 264–67.

55. Murray, *We Hold These Truths*, x. The entire book is relevant, but see esp. 5–24, 125–39.

56. The issues discussed in this paragraph and the three that follow came to a fairly clear focus in the following exchange of articles: Daniel Callahan, "The New Pluralism: From Nostalgia to Reality," *Commonweal*, 78 (September 6, 1963), 527–31; Francis Canavan, "New Pluralism or Old Monism," *America*, 109 (November 9, 1963), 556–60; Philip Gleason, "Pluralism and the New Pluralism," *America*, 110 (March 7, 1964), 308–312.

57. Powell, "Concept of Cultural Pluralism," 180 for Herberg's articulating a new form of pluralism; ibid., 186–95 for analysis of the book.

58. Herberg, *Protestant-Catholic-Jew*, chaps. 1–4.

59. Ibid., chaps. 6–10.

60. Ibid., chaps. 5, 11.

61. Nathan Glazer and Daniel P. Moynihan, *Beyond the Melting Pot* (Cambridge, Mass., 1963), 314–15. Powell, "Concept of Cultural Pluralism," 197–203, discusses this work as bringing to full articulation the conception of racial and religious groups as the basic elements in pluralism.

62. Glazer and Moynihan, *Beyond the Melting Pot*, Preface and 290.

63. Ibid., 12–14, 313.

64. Ibid., 16, 17. The passage quoted is italicized in the book.

65. See the review by G. Paulding in the *Reporter*, 29 (October 10, 1963), 59.

66. Gordon, *Assimilation in American Life*, 130–31, 160–232. Other notable features of the book are Gordon's discussion of the interaction of class and ethnic factors, his introduction of the concept of the "ethclass," and his historical review of theories of assimilation in separate chapters entitled "Anglo-Conformity"—a term that he effectively introduced into the discussion of ethnic affairs—"The Melting Pot," and "Cultural Pluralism." The book, Gordon wrote, was ultimately concerned with problems of prejudice and discrimination, and the concluding chapter was devoted to spelling out the implications of Gordon's theoretical analysis for improving intergroup relations. Powell, "Concept of Cultural Pluralism," 204–17, is a helpful summary and commentary.

67. Gordon, *Assimilation in American Life*, chap. 3, "The Nature of Assimilation," esp. 70–71.

68. Ibid., 69, 74, 80, 82.

69. Ibid., 75–78.

70. Ibid., 80–81.

71. Ibid., 157–59; also, "To understand . . . that acculturation without massive structural intermingling at primary group levels has been the dominant motif in the American experience of creating and developing a nation out of diverse peoples is to comprehend the most essential sociological fact of that experience" (114).

72. Michael M. Passi, "Mandarins and Immigrants: The Irony of Ethnic Studies in America since Turner" (Ph.D. diss., University of Minnesota, 1971), 225–26. Cf. also John Horton, "Order and Conflict Theories of Social Problems as Competing Ideologies," *American Journal of Sociology*, 71 (1966), 701–13; and Higham, *Send These to Me*, 225–26, 228–29.

73. The best introduction to the revival of ethnicity is Mann, *The One and the Many*, chaps. 1–2. Perry L. Weed, *The White Ethnic Movement and Ethnic Politics* (New York, 1973) is narrower in focus but also quite informative. David R. Colburn and George E. Pozzetta, eds., *America and the New Ethnicity* (Port Washington, N.Y., 1979) is a useful collection of readings. My own interpretation, which agrees in general with Mann's, is developed more fully in "American Identity," 52–55.

74. See Glazer and Moynihan, *Beyond the Melting Pot*, 17–18; Nathan Glazer, *Affirmative Discrimination: Ethnic Inequality and Public Policy* (New York, 1975); Leo A. Despres, ed., *Ethnicity and Resource Competition in Plural Societies* (The Hague, 1975).

75. Colburn and Pozzetta, *America and the New Ethnicity* includes a selection on women's liberation which characterizes the United States as "the most exploitative, brutal, and complex oppressor nation in the history of western imperialism" (67).

76. The most ambitious critiques were Orlando Patterson, *Ethnic Chauvinism: The Reactionary Impulse* (New York, 1977); and Howarrd F. Stein and Robert F. Hill, *The Ethnic Imperative* (University Park, Pa., 1977).

77. See Murray Friedman, ed., *Overcoming Middle Class Rage* (Philadelphia, 1971), 15–53, 269–78. On the American Jewish Committee's depolarizing work, see also Mann, *One and Many*, 25ff. William Greenbaum, "American in Search of a New Ideal: An Essay on the Rise of Pluralism," *Harvard Educational Review*, 44 (1974), 411–40 is extremely vague and diffuse, but it seems to be a participationist version of pluralism. As the abstract of the article put it, Greenbaum "recommends support of pluralistic institutions and communities, setting policies that honor diversity as a way of maintaining unity, and, at the same time, developing a new, universal ideal."

78. *Ethnic Heritage Studies Centers*. Hearings before the General Subcommittee on Education of the Committee on Education and Labor, House of Representatives, 91st Cong., 2d session, on H.R. 14910 (Washington, D.C., 1970), 175, 44, 130, 163–65, 283–84.

79. Lillian Stanton, review of Harold Coy, *Chicano Roots Go Deep*, in *Michiana Magazine, South Bend Tribune*, December 21, 1975.

80. Hare, quoted in the *Chicago Sun-Times*, March 25, 1969. For the implications of community control, see Leonard J. Fein, "The Limits of Liberalism," *Saturday Review*, 53 (June 6, 1970), 83–85, 95–96.

81. See Joseph W. Scott, "Ethnic Nationalism and the Cultural Dialectics: A Key to the Future," in Ronald Weber, ed., *America in Change; Reflections on the 60s and 70s* (Notre Dame, Ind., 1972), 63–64.

82. Deloria, quoted in Friedman, *Middle Class Rage*, 276. See also George Feaver, "Wounded Knee and the New Tribalism," *Encounter*, 44 (February, 1975), 28–35.

83. L. Paul Metzger, "American Sociology and Black Assimilation: Conflicting Perspectives," *American Journal of Sociology*, 76 (1970–71), 629. Michael Novak, *The*

Rise of the Unmeltable Ethnics (New York, 1972) combines strident antiassimilationism with the proclamation of perduring ethnicity.

84. Passi, "Mandarins and Immigrants"; Powell, "Concept of Cultural Pluralism"; Montalto, "Forgotten Dream," pp. 53–54; Nicholas V. Montalto, "The Intercultural Education Movement, 1924–1941: The Growth of Tolerance as a Form of Intolerance," in Bernard J. Weiss, ed., *American Education and the European Immigrant: 1840–1940* (Urbana, Ill., 1982), 143 (for pluralism of deception). For the comments on the flawed pluralism of reformers of Indian education, see Ronald K. Goodenow, "The Progressive Educator and Native Americans," *History of Education Quarterly*, 20 (1980), 207–16. Goodenow acknowledges assistance from Montalto (214n.).

85. Montalto, "Forgotten Dream," xi.

86. See Killian, "Black Power and White Reactions," esp. 49–54; Pierre van den Berghe, "The Benign Quota: Panacea or Pandora's Box," *American Sociologist*, 6, no. 3 (1971), 40–43; van den Berghe, *Race and Racism; A Comparative Perspective*, 2d ed. (New York, 1978), xxviii–xxix; and Glazer, *Affirmative Discrimination*.

87. On the distinction between "primordialists" and "optionalists" (also known as "circumstantialists" or "instrumentalists"), see Peter K. Eisinger, "Ethnicity as a Strategic Option: An Emerging View," *Public Administration Review*, 38 (January–February 1978), 89–93; Pierre L. van den Berghe, *The Ethnic Phenomenon* (New York, 1981), 17–18, 256, 261.

88. Van den Berghe, *Ethnic Phenomenon*, Preface and chaps. 1–2; quotations from 18, xi.

89. Ibid., xi–xii; van den Berghe, *Race and Racism*, xviii–xxii.

90. Van den Berghe, *Race and Racism*, xx for universalist ideology; ibid., xxvii–xxix for critique of ethnic revival, which is also criticized in his *Ethnic Phenomenon*, 227–28.

91. R. Fred Wacker, "Assimilation and Cultural Pluralism in American Social Thought," *Phylon*, 40 (1979), 325–33, esp. 330–32; Wacker, "The Fate of Cultural Pluralism within American Social Thought," *Ethnic Groups*, 3 (1981), 125–38. Less directly relevant are Wacker, "An American Dilemma: The Racial Theories of Robert E. Park and Gunnar Myrdal," *Phylon*, 37 (1976), 117–25; and Wacker, "Culture, Prejudice and an American Dilemma," *Phylon*, 42 (1981), 255–61.

92. Ronald Takaki, "The Myth of Ethnicity: Scholarship of the Anti-Affirmative Action Backlash," *Journal of Ethnic Studies*, 10 (1982), 17–42 is an extreme example; van den Berghe, *Ethnic Phenomenon*, 224–28 advances a generally similar interpretation, citing Patterson, *Ethnic Chauvinism* as an authority for interpreting ethnicity as "an alibi for race and class."

93. M. G. Smith, "Ethnicity and Ethnic Groups in America: The View from Harvard," *Ethnic and Racial Studies*, 5 (1982), 1–22; quotation from 10; see 7–9 for the importance of race and "phenotype"; 11 for monumental confusion.

94. Milton Gordon, "Models of Pluralism: The New American Dilemma," *Annals*, 454 (March, 1981), 178–88. Gordon adumbrated the distinction in "Towards a General Theory of Racial and Ethnic Group Relations," in Nathan Glazer and Daniel P. Moynihan, eds., *Ethnicity: Theory and Experience* (Cambridge, Mass., 1975), 105–6. Cf. also Charles B. Keely, "Immigration and the American Future," in Lance Liebman, ed., *Ethnic Relations in America* (Englewood Cliffs, N.J., 1982), 30–33.

95. Gordon, "Models of Pluralism," 187.

96. See, for example, David A. Hollinger, "Two Cheers for the Melting Pot," *Democracy*, 2 (1982), 89–97; Stephan Thernstrom, "Ethnic Groups in American History," and Nathan Glazer "Politics in a Multiethnic Society," in Liebman, *Ethnic Relations in America*, esp. 4–5, 9–12, 18–20, 148–49.

|| 4 ||

Minorities (Almost) All

The prominent role played by the concept of the minority, or the minority group, in American social thought first called itself to my attention when I was working on "American All," and that essay (chapter 6 in this collection) devotes a couple of paragraphs to the introduction and early usage of the expression. An invitation to take part in a conference on the life and work of Louis Adamic, sponsored by the Immigration History Research Center of the University of Minnesota and held in St. Paul in May 1981, furnished the occasion for a first effort at elaboration. Since Adamic, a Slovenian immigrant and writer on ethnic affairs, came from the part of Europe that was the classic locus of the "minorities problem," it seemed appropriate to inquire how the American understanding of minorities differed from the European. The preliminary sketch of the topic presented at the Adamic conference was never published, and I was unable to do more with it for several years. Another conference, this time sponsored by the Smithsonian's Woodrow Wilson Center and National Museum of American History, brought me back to the minority concept again. The essay that follows is a slightly revised version of the paper presented at that conference in June 1989.

According to the on-line catalogue system in my university library, the Library of Congress currently employs well over three hundred subject headings under the general rubric "Minorities." This fact, daunting to the researcher, strikingly confirms the salience of the minority concept in contemporary American life. Indeed, we are so accustomed to hearing the word used in the sociological sense with which the Library of Congress headings are primarily concerned that we assume it has always been used widely in that sense. For that reason it comes as a surprise to discover that the standard historical dictionaries of American usage published around midcentury do not include a sociological definition of the word *minority*, nor does a well-known dictionary of contemporary usage that dates from the same era.[1]

Webster's Third New International Dictionary, published in 1961, marks a lexical breakthrough since it includes the following definition of *minority*: "a group differing from the predominant section of a larger group in one or more characteristics (as ethnic background, language, culture, or religion) and as a result often subjected to differential treatment and esp. discrimination."[2] This indicates that general usage had caught up with that of social scientists. But considering that academic discussions of intergroup relations had employed *minorities* in this sense for a quarter-century, one would have to say that the process of popularization had taken a long time. This fact, along with the tremendous vogue it has since enjoyed, justifies our taking a closer look at American usage of the term *minority* over time.

In the following pages, my aim is to identify the point at which the term began to be used in what we think of as its conventional sociological sense and to trace the historical evolution of its usage since that time. Obviously such an approach requires interpretation of what various users meant by the term and permits speculation as to how its usage is related to broader shifts in the climate of opinion. But despite these critical elements, my exposition is intended to be primarily *descriptive* in the sense that it aims to explain what others had in mind when they spoke of minorities, not to measure the accuracy of their usage against some ideal conceptual norm. To keep the discussion within bounds, I have concentrated rather narrowly on *minority*, forgoing systematic comparison with related terms (e.g., caste, ethnicity, pluralism), and eschewing substantive discussion of the issues of racism, prejudice, and discrimination involved in the contexts where it was applied.

In the nineteenth century, Americans spoke of a young person's being in his or her minority, meaning not being of age legally; they also used the term in its political sense, as in "minority party" or "minority report." They did not, however, use it in what we think of as its conventional sociological sense, that is, as designating a subgroup of the population. This usage seems to derive from Europe's "national minorities," concern for whose "rights" increased with the growth of nationalism after the Congress of Vienna.[3] Americans who followed European affairs may have been familiar with this application of the term, but it attracted little attention if the periodical indexes of the 1890s are a reliable guide. Not until after World War I did Americans begin to encounter *minorities* in this sense.

It was the minorities issue at Versailles, the so-called minorities treaties, and the continuing problems of European minorities in the 1920s that first alerted Americans to the sociological possibilities of the word. Jews, a classic minority in several European lands, played a leading role in urging protection for minorities at the peace conference, and American Jews were a particularly influential element in their councils.[4] Hence it is plausible to assume that Jews were more conscious of the term and idea than other Americans in the 1920s. General interest magazines, however, paid no attention to the issue until late in the decade. Nothing turns up in the *Reader's Guide to Periodical Literature* until the volume for 1925–28, and only two of the nine articles indexed there appeared before September 1927. All of them dealt with the minority situation in Europe, as did the great bulk of the twenty-seven listed for the years 1929–32; the only one explicitly focused on this country lamented the activities of organized pressure groups in politics.[5]

The sudden burst of interest in the minority issue resulted from the troubles it was causing in Europe. One writer, who said 1929 seemed "destined to be the 'year of minorities,' " reviewed complaints being taken to the League of Nations by several "disgruntled minorities" who were among "the more strident voices in Europe's cacophonic chorus of pro-test." This language, to say nothing of the same writer's sardonic allusion to "growling Ruthenians, scowling Macedonians, [and] howling Turks," suggests that Americans found the spectacle of national minority bick-ering distasteful—an attitude wholly in line with the repugnance Carlton Hayes had taught them to feel for nationalism, especially in the extreme forms it had assumed in the "war-breeding zone" of Central Europe.[6] In short, the context in which Americans first heard about minorities of the sociological sort was not such as to make the term an attractive one.

It was against this somewhat unpromising background that the term *minority* was effectively introduced into the American discussion of what was till then usually called "race relations."[7] The work that did so was Donald Young's *American Minority Peoples: A Study in Racial and Cul-tural Conflicts in the United States* (1932). Young, who became exec-utive director of the Social Science Research Council the year his book came out, proposed "to give a new perspective to academic discussions of American race relations" while also providing comprehensive coverage of the history and present status of all the groups represented among "our minority peoples."[8] The weakness of the existing literature, he thought, was that the many books written about individual groups con-veyed the impression "that Negro-white relations are one thing, while Jewish-Gentile, Oriental-white, and other race relations are vastly differ-ent from each other." Young was convinced, however, "that the problems and principles of race relations are remarkably similar, regardless of what groups are involved; and that only by an integrated study of all minority peoples in the United States can a real understanding and sociological analysis of the involved social phenomena be achieved."

Race in the biological sense, Young went on to say, was not the subject of his study. As it was employed in popular parlance, *race* encompassed cultural as well as biological features; Young would use it in that loose sense because the people whose attitudes he was studying did, but he did not consider race, as such, to be the determinative factor in intergroup relations. Addressing the problem of terminology directly, Young observed that the English language lacked a word that could be applied with perfect adequacy to "groups which are distinguished by biological features, alien national cultural traits, or a combination of both." He proposed therefore to speak of "minorities of racial or national origin," "American minorities," or "minority peoples" as synonyms for *race* as it was popularly understood.

Young's terminological innovation was positive in that it provided a way to talk about population groups without calling all of them "races," which helped shift the focus away from the biological factor in discussions of intergroup relations. Besides directing attention away from inherited racial qualities as the key element in group behavior, use of the new term implicitly drew attention to the importance of a group's position in the overall structure of society, which was also an important methodological contribution.[9] But with respect to the more strictly semantic aspect of the question, Young performed less impressively.

He realized he was introducing a neologism and felt constrained to justify it briefly. "To most of us," he wrote, "the word 'minority' has political implications in that it calls to mind a political party which is not in power. Since it is never used with that meaning in this book, no confusion should result from its present special application." But this, if I may quote myself, was surely "straining at a gnat."[10] The real likelihood of confusion arose not from usage of the word in political contexts but from its association with the "nationalities problem" in Europe. Granting that there had not been much American interest in the European minorities issue, Young's failure to refer to it, either in explaining his terminology or in the course of his six-hundred-page book, is both remarkable in itself and symptomatic of the parochial focus of much subsequent commentary on American minorities.

Judging from its relatively rapid acceptance, the new term filled a need. It was absorbed into the vocabulary of New Deal liberalism as applied to group relations, being associated with emphasis on the analytical importance of the culture concept, with acceptance of cultural pluralism as a social ideal, and with the rejection of nationalism, ethnocentrism, and prejudice as group norms or personal attitudes. This general cluster may be found in the work that constituted the first significant appearance of the term after Young's book, a special issue of *Progressive Education* (March 1935) devoted to the problems of minorities.[11] Young himself laid heavy stress on the importance of the culture concept in his *Research Memorandum on Minority Peoples in the Depression* (1937). And the appearance in the same year of Brown and Roucek's compendious *Our Racial and National Minorities*—a miniencyclopedia of American ethnic groups that was destined to be reprinted in 1946 and 1952—confirmed the place of *minorities* as a key term in socially enlightened discussion of intergroup relations.[12]

While its indigenization in the strictly American discussion was positive (i.e., associated with progressive-liberal values), a carry-over of its unappealing European associations was always possible. Young, as we have seen, ignored the whole European scene, and so, for the most part, did those whose use of the term we have noted so far.[13] At the same time, commentators on European minorities failed to relate them in any way to the "American minority peoples" Young had identified. Thus the article on "Minorities, National" in the *Encyclopaedia of the Social Sciences* dealt exclusively with the European situation, and H. A. Miller, who alerted readers of the *Annals* to "The Menace of Minorities," concentrated on central Europe, with sidelong glances at the Middle East, British imperial territories, and East Asia. And even though Brown and Roucek included an essay on European minorities, the "comparison and contrast" it promised was internal to Europe; nothing was said about American minorities, although the author did affirm that only "the method of democracy" could obviate the dangers inherent in the minority situation of central Europe.[14]

But as the likelihood of European war increased, and as interreligious tensions mounted in the United States, it became more difficult to ignore the possibility that American minorities might develop, as Europe's had, into "human dynamite."[15] Nazi exploitation of the claims of German minorities in Czechoslovakia and Poland reinforced uneasiness about American minorities, which the noisy antics of the German-American Bund and the openly pro-Fascist orientation of many Italian-American newspapers did nothing to allay.[16] After the outbreak of hostilities in 1939, suspicion of minorities fed on the specter of the fifth column, which subsequent research has shown was practically nonexistent even in Europe, but which was taken very seriously at the time. Indeed, Louis

Adamic's *Common Ground*, a journal quite sympathetic to minorities, treated seriously a 1940 book that estimated the potential fifth column in America at one million. Three years later, Louis Wirth's research memorandum on minorities in wartime still maintained that the fifth column could "no longer be regarded as a myth."[17]

The relocation of the Japanese-Americans and our national shame over that action should not mislead us into thinking that only hysterical yahoos were concerned about potential disloyalty on the part of minorities. Besides Wirth, the well-informed and liberally disposed Joseph S. Roucek expressed concern, and the anti-Fascist Max Ascoli described Mussolini's propaganda as intended to make "Italian-Americans a national minority with all the ugly implications of such a position.[18]

In these circumstances, it became important to differentiate American minorities from those of Europe—sufficiently important, indeed, that the western hemisphere states formally resolved three times between 1938 and 1942 that the concept of "national minorities" as understood in Europe had no application in the American republics. Wirth agreed that the European concept "differ[ed] widely" from that prevailing in the United States, and Gunnar Myrdal formulated the "fundamental difference" with aphoristic pithiness: "The minority peoples of the United States are fighting for status within the larger society; the minorities of Europe are mainly fighting for independence from it."[19]

Survey Graphic's "Calling America" issue (February 1939), which was devoted to "The Challenge to Democracy," illustrated how the analytical task of differentiating American from European minorities often blended with policy prescriptions designed to keep the former from coming to resemble the latter. The general subject of minorities was a leading theme of the issue, and several writers explained how American minority groups, most of which were composed of persons who had come as voluntary immigrants in search of a better life, differed from the compact and historically rooted national minorities of Europe. These commentators likewise agreed in prescribing democratic tolerance and equality as remedies for potential problems involving American minorities.[20]

The war, when it came, reinforced the "Americans All, Immigrants All" theme, thus situating the minorities issue solidly within the great ideological revival of the wartime years when the principles of democracy were hailed as the basis on which everyone should unite in the struggle against totalitarianism. *Common Ground*, a publication devoted explicitly to improving intergroup relations in the context of genuine democratic unity, repeated the lesson tirelessly: Everyone must rally to the cause of freedom and work for victory; but democracy must at the same time be made *real*, which meant eliminating prejudice and discrimination, welcoming cultural diversity, and according all minority groups the dignity that was rightfully theirs as full partners in a genuinely democratic national community.[21]

In this context, Louis Wirth elaborated the concept of the minority group which has remained classical in American usage. Wirth, like other students of Robert E. Park in his generation of Chicago-trained sociologists, was deeply interested in ethnicity and intergroup relations.[22] He had already written much on minority groups but evidently felt by the end of the war that the concept needed clarification. His essay "The Problem of Minority Groups" appeared in *The Science of Man in the World Crisis* (1945), edited by Ralph Linton. The titles of both book and essay were significant, reflecting as they did the widely shared beliefs that the social sciences had much to contribute in a world in crisis and that intergroup relations were one of the most problematic aspects of the situation, both nationally and internationally.[23]

"We may define a minority," Wirth wrote thirteen years after the term came into use in this country, "as a group of people who, because of their physical or cultural characteristics, are singled out from the others in the society in which they live for differential and unequal treatment and who therefore regard themselves as objects of collective discrimination." In addition to this compact formulation, Wirth enlarged on several other distinguishing features of minorities. Important among these are: 1) the existence of a minority implies the existence of a dominant group enjoying higher social status and greater privileges; 2) minority status entails exclusion from full participation in the life of the society; 3) minorities are treated as peoples set apart, look upon themselves in that same light, and consequently develop attitudes and behavioral forms that exaggerate their distinctiveness and isolation; and 4) the minority concept is not "statistical," which means that a minority can outnumber the dominant group but still remain a minority in terms of its subordinate relationship to the latter.[24]

Wirth also offered a typology of minorities, listing four varieties, which he called "pluralistic," "assimilationist," "secessionist," and "militant."[25] These categories were ostensibly applicable to minorities anywhere, and Wirth made several references to the European scene, among other things praising the nationalities policy of the Soviet Union (as a number of other American observers had done).[26] But his approach was decisively shaped by American expectations about minorities. Thus he suggested that pluralistic minorities, which demanded toleration for their distinctive existence, would normally evolve into assimilationist minorities, which wanted full status for their members within the host society. Only if pluralistic minorities were rejected by the host society were they likely to become secessionist minorities, demanding economic and political autonomy as well as cultural toleration. Militant minorities were clearly a morbid variety since they demanded not toleration, or even autonomy, but domination over all other groups in a society. In other words, the dynamic process Wirth built into his typology (which he said reflected "crucial successive stages in the life-cycle of minorities generally") was shaped by the American expectation of individual assimilation for minority group members, rather than by the European aspiration for collective autonomy for solidaric groups.[27] He tacitly admitted as much in lamenting that, when they dealt with the minorities question, the peacemakers at Versailles had stressed group self-determination rather than guarantees for the rights of individuals.[28]

Wirth's definition had a far more lasting influence than his typology. Its main effect was to fix firmly in the concept of the minority the element of *victimization*. In his compact definition quoted above, Wirth said only that minorities "regard[ed] themselves as objects of collective discrimination," but the essay as a whole made clear that this perception was to be accepted as accurate. After Wirth, the element of victimization was given sharper focus by other commentators, such as Arnold and Caroline Rose, who wrote, "The mere fact of being generally hated because of religious, racial, or nationality background is what defines a minority group." [29]

The Roses were extreme in speaking of hatred as the defining element. Ordinarily, minorities were said to be victims of *prejudice*. But since prejudice had by midcentury come to be viewed as the product of a diseased mind, that was perhaps not so different in its pathological connotations from the way the Roses had put it.[30] Note, however, that if being a victim of hatred and prejudice was intrinsic to minority status, it would seem almost perverse for minorities to wish to perpetuate their own existence. In that sense, these formulations—like Wirth's typology—were unconsciously predicated on the American assumption that minorities ought naturally to disappear into the larger society as a result of their members' being accepted on a fully equal basis with everyone else.

By the late 1940s, the discussion of minority groups was thus being carried on in terms that were heavily loaded, both emotionally and ideologically, and were at the same time somewhat paradoxical in their implications. Among the assumptions that seemed to underlie the discussion were the following:

1. If true Americanism were practiced, there would be no minority groups because no one would be denied equality or treated in discriminatory fashion; however,
2. minority groups existed because prejudice and hatred caused Americans to depart from their own ideals and indulge in discriminatory behavior; from which one might conclude that
3. it was unnatural for minority groups to exist, and sound social policy should aim at their elimination; yet
4. the democratic ideology required toleration of minority groups, and the widely praised ideal of cultural pluralism seemed to prescribe their nurture and preservation.

In this complex and confusing situation one thing was, nevertheless, unmistakably clear: in any contest between a minority group and the "dominant group," the moral advantage always lay with the former. Minorities, after all, were defined as victims, and their antagonists were presumed by the same definition to be guilty of harboring prejudice toward, if not hatred of, members of minority groups, and of practicing discrimination against them. This definition of the situation amounted to a tremendous form of moral and social power in the hands of minorities; eventually it made practically everyone want to be included in that category.[31]

In the quarter-century after Wirth's essay appeared, sociological usage of the term/concept burgeoned prodigiously. Although the phenomenon requires more detailed research, several generalizations may be ventured at this point.

In the first place, study of and teaching about minorities expanded tremendously at all levels of education. In elementary and secondary schools, an "intercultural education" movement pioneered in the late thirties by Rachel Davis-DuBois blossomed after the war. Even so, the American Council on Education warned in 1949 that treatment of minorities in school textbooks was grievously inadequate—a finding that was to be confirmed again and again over the next two decades.[32] At the college level, a dozen major textbooks on "minorities" or "race relations" appeared between 1948 and 1955. In roughly the same period, the overall total of published articles and books "of a professedly learned character" topped one thousand. Ten years later, Peter I. Rose learned from a national survey that no fewer than 719 institutions of higher education were offering courses in the field—many of which, he reported with surprise, followed basically the same format as that worked out by Robert Park, Louis Wirth, and Everett C. Hughes when the course was first introduced at the University of Chicago in the late 1930s.[33]

This tremendous academic expansion went on within the context of constantly intensifying public concern over improving intergroup relations in general and over *the* "race issue" in particular—that is, over the question of how to achieve equality for black people—which became the most important domestic problem facing the country by the mid fifties.[34] The factor of external public concern not only fueled the expansion of academic studies; it also confirmed the tendency to focus on prejudice and discrimination (which was also influenced by the salience of psychological perspectives in the academic world at midcentury), and it infused supposedly "scientific" work with powerful strains of moralism and ideology—points to which we have already alluded and to which we shall return.[35]

The close association of minority studies with public policy issues also reinforced the preexisting tendency of academics to concentrate their attention on the minority situation in the United States. This probably did more than anything else to make the American approach to the minority issue parochial, but the virtual disappearance of the "national minority" question in postwar Europe contributed to the same result, because that was the only place outside the United States where it had ever claimed the attention of Americans.[36] Everett C. and Helen M. Hughes took critical note of their colleagues' parochialism as early as 1952, even suggesting that it reflected an ethnocentric bias, but these minatory observations had little effect.[37] The most ambitious comparative work done by American scholars in the fifties—Charles Wagley and Marvin Harris's *Minorities in the New World*—was a summary of individual studies sponsored by the United Nations Educational, Scientific, and Cultural Organization (UNESCO). Eventually, the tacit assumption that minorities were a distinctively American phenomenon was made explicit by Edgar Z. Friedenberg, who stated in 1965 that "the minority group is a special American institution, created by the interaction between a history and an ideology which are not to be duplicated elsewhere."[38]

Several commentators voiced reservations about, or suggested modifications of, the minority concept in the postwar decade. Thus Joseph Schneider considered the term misleading except when applied to groups striving to perpetuate "cultural and spacial [sic] isolation"; both Oscar Handlin and Will Herberg thought its usage inappropriate in the American context; E. K. Francis proposed several revisions of the concept, as did William Petersen and other scholars, including Wagley and Harris.[39] These qualifications did not, however, dislodge Wirth's formulation from its position of definitional preeminence.[40] Neither did they result in the concept's being used with greater precision; on the contrary, it grew ever more capacious and diffuse.

The increasing imprecision of the minority concept resulted largely from its application to more and more elements in American society. As I indicated above, African-Americans emerged as the key minority in the postwar decade. Although several prominent students of race relations, including Gunnar Myrdal, had earlier maintained that African-Americans were more of a caste than a minority, the latter term prevailed.[41] The leading black sociologist, E. Franklin Frazier, adopted it in his influential work *The Negro in the United States* (1949); indeed, he drew explicitly on Wirth's typology in arguing that African-Americans were an "assimilationist minority."[42]

Religious groups had also been included among American minorities by Young and other early users of the term. Park spoke of Jewish communities in Europe as "classic examples of . . . racial minorities," and Nazi anti-semitism, along with the prominent role played by Jewish refugee scholars in the study of prejudice, especially the project that culminated in *The Authoritarian Personality* (1950), greatly enhanced the visibility of Jews as a minority group.[43] Catholics too were conventionally included under that rubric, but Thomas T. McAvoy, C.S.C., broadened its application considerably by treating the history of the Catholic church in the United States from the minority perspective. His usage reflected the new currency of the term, as did that of the sociologist John L. Thomas, S.J., who analyzed the American Catholic family in terms of its minority status. Another scholar, John J. Kane, suggested that Catholic sociologists themselves might be considered a minority group.[44]

The question of whether women should be thought of as a minority group was examined in 1951 from all the angles characteristic of race relations study at that time (e.g., social distance, caste vs. class, the marginal woman, etc.). It is still discussed, although the subquestions have, of course, changed.[45] By the early 1970s, the minority concept was being stretched even further, and in less conventional directions, by a growing tendency among sociologists to merge the study of "social deviance" with that of minorities. Thus anthologies began to appear dealing with "the other minorities"—homosexuals, youth, the aged, the physically handicapped, the emotionally disturbed, the poor, drug users, alcoholics, convicts and ex-convicts, and others on the margins of society.[46]

What accounts for this consistent pressure to expand the boundaries of an ostensibly undesirable social classification? Why have we experienced, as two recent writers put it, "the emergence of groups *claiming* minority status"?[47] The answer, already noted in passing, is that to be classified as a minority adds tremendously to the moral and political leverage of such a group. Because minorities are by definition victims of unequal treatment, their complaints enjoy prima facie justification and their claims for redress an automatic moral legitimacy. Some of these linkages were implicit from the earliest days of American usage, and Wirth's definition made them more explicit. But it was the civil rights/ black revolution that drove the connections home and made minority status seem insupportable because its very existence violated the principle of equality. African-Americans were the minority whose struggle for equality increasingly dominated the moral landscape and furnished the primary perspective from which minority matters were viewed from the days of Wirth and Myrdal to the era of black power and beyond. In other words, the actuality of the minority situation as it affected blacks dramatized and confirmed the theoretical linkages implicit in the definition of the minority group and in usage of the term.

But the black example would have been without effect—or at least its effect would have been greatly diminished—without the nation's historic theoretical commitment to equality as a fundamental value. Indeed, it was precisely *because* equality was so basic that the unequal status and treatment accorded African-Americans (and other minorities) could be portrayed as intolerable. Petersen drew attention to this dimension of the situation when he wrote, "The very idea of a minority suffering from discrimination implies a democratic moral judgment"; and Friedenberg's statement that the minority group was "a special American institution" is defensible only if interpreted in this sense.[48]

The commitment to making equality a meaningful reality in American society is intrinsic to the development that has given the term *minority* its present ubiquity and its unprecedented practical importance. That development is affirmative action—the policy initiated by the federal government (and widely adopted thereafter by other governmental bodies and private institutions) whereby the victims of past injustice are to be compensated by means of various positive measures, including what critics of affirmative action regard as de facto quotas in hiring, promotion, admission to educational institutions, and the conferral of other benefits. The whole matter is quite technical, immensely complicated, and highly controversial.[49] I will try to hold all three of these qualities to a minimum in the following discussion; for my purpose is not to provide a substantive analysis of all the issues but simply to indicate the impact affirmative action has had on usage of the term *minority*.

The most important shift in usage is that the term has acquired a new, quasi-legal status. That status, however, applies only to certain "designated," or "protected," minorities and not to all the groups that might hitherto have been thought of as minorities or might still be so considered in the nonlegal sense. The process by which this came about is obscure, but action taken in 1969 by the Department of Labor's Office of Federal Contract Compliance (OFCC) constitutes an important landmark.

The OFCC, created in 1965 to oversee nondiscrimination and affirmative action in all fields of activity in which the federal government purchased goods and services from private contractors, was especially concerned to increase the employment of blacks in construction work, an area where they had been largely excluded by union-controlled apprenticeship programs. The approach it finally settled on was the "Philadelphia Plan," which required contractors in that city to seek out and employ "minorities" in proportion to their availability in the local labor market. The "goals" and "timetables" called for in the Philadelphia Plan seemed to critics indistinguishable from forbidden quotas, and the ensuing controversy made its implementation doubtful until late in 1969. But even before the OFCC definitively won that battle, it issued the first version of Order No. 4, which universalized the Philadelphia Plan by extending its basic requirements to all federal contractors, not just construction contractors in a given locality. After two more years of tinkering, Revised Order No. 4 went into effect, thus applying on a much broader scale the goals, timetables, and concept of "underutilization" pioneered in the Philadelphia Plan.[50]

In all this, *minorities* figured prominently. The term was, of course, very familiar from general usage; it had also been employed, although not given great prominence, in earlier federal efforts to enforce nondiscrimination.[51] What was new about Revised Order No. 4 was the greatly enhanced visibility it gave to the term and the broader scope of its application in respect to benefits for persons belonging to certain groups. According to one count, *minority* occurred in various forms no fewer than sixty-five times in the order, but it was nowhere defined, nor was there any listing of the groups that fell within that category.[52]

Although the American people were often said to be "minorities all," the new measure did not really contemplate making everyone eligible for special attention as "members of an 'affected class' who, by virtue of past discrimination continue to suffer the present effects of that discrimination."[53] A listing of designated minorities was obviously required, and one was soon added. But the failure of the first version of Revised Order No. 4 to provide such a listing and its continuing failure to define what made a group a minority in the relevant sense suggest that the terminology was employed by federal administrators without much systematic reflection.[54] That is understandable enough, given the immense contemporary popularity of the term. But it also entailed a serious weakness because *minority's* popularity made it elastic and imprecise—despite the fact that in the then-prevailing context of racial crisis, " 'minorities' essentially meant blacks."[55]

Federal administrators had begun inquiring about the number of "Negro" and "other minority" employees on the payrolls of government contractors in the 1950s, but the first listing directly linked with what became Revised Order No. 4 occurs in a appendix to a version of the Philadelphia Plan that was issued June 27, 1969. It stated that, for purposes envisioned in the sample reporting form, "the term minority means Negro, Oriental, American [Indian], and Spanish Surnamed American."[56] But that was only the beginning in the new phase of development. The data-collecting and record-keeping requirements imposed by the bureaucratization of affirmative action throughout the whole range of activities affected by federal oversight soon led to variations in categorization. Those discrepancies in turn led to efforts to rationalize the whole system according to which the "minorities" eligible for affirmative action programs were to be identified. (Women, who were included as an affected class in Revised Order No. 4, did not figure directly in these efforts, since they were provided for on a coequal "women and minorities" basis.[57])

Two large-scale projects aimed at achieving terminological consistency were undertaken in the seventies. A group called the Federal Interagency Committee on Education (FICE) made a start in 1974–75, establishing five standard categories and definitions for purposes of minority data collection in the educational area: 1) white, not of hispanic origin (which was, of course, not a minority); 2) black, not of hispanic origin; 3) Hispanic; 4) American Indian or Alaskan native; and 5) Asian or Pacific islander. But since the educational institutions FICE dealt with had to respond to other agencies, for example, the Equal Employment Opportunity Commission (EEOC), which employed different categories, FICE proposed that governmentwide standards be developed for designating minorities. This assignment was turned over to an ad hoc "Task Force on Race/Ethnic Categories," which included representatives from FICE and other federal agencies involved in this kind of data collection, such as EEOC, the United States Commission on Civil Rights, and the Bureau of the Census. This body confirmed FICE's overall scheme of categories, but with some modification in definitions of membership. For example, persons from the Indian subcontinent were now included among Asians, which made them a new-style "minority"; and American Indians or Alaskan natives now had to "maintain cultural identification through tribal affiliation or community recognition," in addition to "having origins in any of the original peoples of North America."[58]

Mind-numbing though it may be, the foregoing sketch provides only the barest introduction to the complications that overtook the minority concept in the era of affirmative action. We cannot venture into the legal labyrinth, which includes convolutions that strike the uninitiated as truly mysterious. As an example of the latter, consider the process that transformed Justice Harlan F. Stone's passing allusion to "discrete and insular minorities," originally embedded in a footnote to a 1938 case dealing with the regulation of adulterated milk, into what some who write on affirmative action regard as the normative definition of a minority.[59]

Justice Lewis Powell's ruminations on "minorities" in the famous Bakke decision (1978) deserve quotation at length since they have been cited by other students as illustrating the difficulty of "deciding which minorities are minorities in American society." It was no longer possible, Powell wrote:

> to peg the guarantees of the Fourteenth Amendment to the struggle for equality of one racial *minority*. During the dormancy of the Equal Protection Clause, the United States had become a nation of *minorities*. Each had to struggle . . . to overcome the prejudices not of a monolithic majority, but of a "majority" composed of various *minority groups*. . . . As a nation filled with the stock of many lands, the reach of the Clause was gradually extended to all ethnic groups seeking protection from official discrimination. . . .
>
> The concepts of "majority" and "*minority*" necessarily reflect temporary arrangements and political judgments. . . . The white "majority" is itself composed of various *minority groups*, most of which can lay claim to a history of prior discrimination at the hands of the state and private individuals. Not all of these groups can receive preferential treatment and corresponding

judicial tolerance of distinctions drawn in terms of race and nationality, for then the only "majority" left would be the new *minority* of White Anglo-Saxon Protestants. There is no principled basis of deciding which groups would merit "heightened judicial solicitude," and which would not.[60]

With this kind of ambiguity acknowledged in what came to be viewed as the U.S. Supreme Court's guideline opinion on affirmative action, it is small wonder that a lower court could speak of any given minority's "drifting" into, and later out of, protected status "depending on the circumstances of the times, and the shifts in recognition of ethnic and racial equality by the majority."[61]

Beset to this degree by what even sympathetic commentators call "definitions [that] are almost absurdly vague," affirmative action has come in for much criticism.[62] With respect to minority terminology, it is almost impossible to separate semantic from substantive objections—for the very good reason that in this area labels have consequences. The following sampler suggests the range of positions from which objections have been raised to the new minority-talk.

One of the earliest critics of affirmative action to single out the term *minority* as an example of the "Orwellian" thinking of the "affirmative action shock troops" was Senator James Buckley of New York, who excoriated the whole policy as "wrong, wrong, wrong" in a 1973 Senate speech.[63] He it was who counted sixty-five occurrences of the term—but no definition—in Revised Order No. 4 and traced the first listing of designated minorities to the June 1969 Labor Department document mentioned above. Buckley also pointed out that while other official statements acknowledged that Jews and various Catholic ethnic groups had also suffered discrimination, they were excluded from protection under affirmative action. From this he inferred that the protected categories would continue to expand indefinitely, making the "absurdity of the exercise . . . self-evident."[64] His fundamental objection, however, was to the principle itself: making ethnic and racial criteria the basis for differential treatment contradicted "everything that the civil rights movement has sought to achieve."

Buckley, who had been primed for his attack by academics indignant over the affirmative action programs newly imposed on colleges and universities by the Department of Health, Education, and Welfare's Office for Civil Rights, entered into the *Congressional Record* ten articles and speeches critical of this policy. In general, these articles reflected the position that was coming to be known as neoconservative. Sidney Hook,

Paul Seabury, and Earl Raab were among the authors represented; two of the articles had appeared in *Commentary*; and another was a statement made by an officer of the Queens Jewish Community Council. The issue of quotas figured prominently in the objections of the neoconservatives, understandably so in the case of those who were Jewish.[65]

The most systematic critique mounted from this perspective was Nathan Glazer's *Affirmative Discrimination*, first published in 1975 and issued in paperback three years later. Glazer, who cited Buckley's speech and several of the articles reproduced with it in the *Congressional Record*, objected to the designation of minorities on principle and pronounced the groups then listed "a strange mix." Ten years later the semantic situation was, if possible, even worse. "The conception of 'minority,' " Glazer declared, "is so muddled that there is considerable dispute over just who we mean [in using it]." Although the law did not recognize "official minorities," public policy nevertheless defined "various categories as minorities deserving some special protection or attention." Oddly enough, the vast majority of legal immigrants entering the United States in the mid-eighties belonged to "the four somewhat official minority groups" and were therefore eligible upon entry for special assistance ostensibly justified on the basis of discrimination suffered earlier in American history.[66]

Spokesmen for European ethnic groups, who considered themselves minorities but were classed in the omnium gatherum "White, not of Hispanic origin," objected strenuously to their exclusion from benefits. They had difficulty making their voices heard, but in 1979 the United States Commission on Civil Rights sponsored a "consultation" at which their complaints were aired. Most germane here is the point made by the executive director of the Polish American Congress, who reported that he had searched vainly, both in the law and in government regulations, for "a clear definition of the word 'minority.' " Not finding one, he concluded that "the word 'minority' is used as a code word. It's used to mask different things, depending on how a person wants to use it and what groups he wants to please." A representative of Ukrainian-Americans who quoted Louis Wirth in the course of his remarks expressed the same sentiments: *minority* would have to be eliminated as "a functionally meaningless term . . . or expanded to include all groups who have been . . . [discriminated against]."[67]

Before turning to usage commentators who take the other side in the controversy over affirmative action, we should take note of two who are not directly involved in it—Henry Fairlie and Tom Wolfe. Fairlie, a British journalist who covered American public affairs for many years, included *minority* among the terms he discussed in an *Atlantic Monthly* article entitled "The Language of Politics." Citing Ortega y Gasset's *Revolt of the Masses* (1930) as his authority, he claimed that its meaning had been reversed since that book appeared, for then *minority* meant "the privileged at the top . . . [not] the underprivileged at the bottom." That was wildly off target (at least for American usage), but Fairlie came closer to a real novelty when he pointed out that to speak of people as "minorities" amounted to "identifying an individual or a group by one of his or its characteristics, which was taken to be determining."[68] Here he seemed to have in mind the practice of referring to an individual as "a minority" if he or she happens to belong to one of the designated categories. One heard this frequently by the mid-1980s, and Tom Wolfe's acute ear picked it up. In his *Bonfire of the Vanities* (1987), Peter Fallow, an English journalist, muses to his fellow Brits about the protagonist's habit of "hitting minorities, black boys, women." Then, calling his companions' attention to the grotesqueries of American usage, Fallow inquires, "Have you noticed the way the Yanks refer to women as a minority?" To which one of them predictably responds, "The poor mother tongue."[69]

Most writers favorable to affirmative action treat the term as unproblematic, but a few spokespersons for "designated minorities" (who presumably benefit from the policy) have found fault with it. Sometimes dissatisfaction is grounded in the generalized feeling that to be labeled a minority stigmatizes people and robs them of self-esteem.[70] Thus Yolanda T. DeMola roundly asserted that the time had come "to forsake a term most blacks and Hispanics consider prejorative and degrading." Although her position was not developed in detail, DeMola clearly recognized that "getting rid of minority" would entail modifications in affirmative action as a policy. She seemed willing to contemplate that possibility, noting that affirmative action is divisive in its effects and that "anti-discrimination laws already on the books" would, if strictly enforced, bring about the results it is intended to achieve. Others who dislike the term for similar reasons seem not to realize that dropping the term would require rethinking the policy.[71]

Although most blacks are strongly in favor of affirmative action, there has been some criticism of the terminology of minorities on the grounds that it erodes the uniqueness of black claims. C. Eric Lincoln puts the point in the strongest terms by calling it a "sinister policy" that lumps blacks with other "minorities."[72] Harold Cruse develops the same theme in language only slightly less harsh. Thus he speaks of "the civil rights spoils system" and deplores the fact that blacks have been "buried . . .

in civil rights anonymity" by the use of the same term to cover all groups, white and nonwhite, and by its further expansion through the minorities-and-women formula. Cruse does not call for abandonment of the term but insists that is employment not be allowed to obscure the special claims of blacks. "In America," he writes in a formulation that seems self-consciously Orwellian, "there are minorities, but then there are other minorities; some minorities are equal, but some are more or less equal than others." Blacks are emphatically not to be equated with "white ethnics," even though the latter "are in fact minorities." Women, however, are not a minority. The practical equation of their claims with those of blacks—the minority that opened the way for, and legitimized, all other minority groups claims—has, in Cruse's view, "relegat[ed] race discrimination to the back burner as a public policy issue"; ratification of the Equal Rights Amendment would "*constitutionally* submerge the *nonwhite minority group*, effectively burying it as a political and/or legal issue."[73]

This kind of sensitivity to possible conflicts of interest *among* "minorities"—which became more of a reality in the late 1980s when tensions flared between blacks and Hispanics and, to a lesser extent, between blacks and Asians[74]—may be obscurely related to some not yet firmly established shifts in terminology. Thus two specialists in intergroup relations concerned to defuse ethnic conflict in Chicago note that the designation, "African American . . . takes blacks out of black-white context and places then in an ethnic framework, opening up new possibilities for building coalitions around civil rights and other issues."[75] A development more germane to our interest has to do with the expression *people of color*. At least two proponents of the new "multiculturalism" seem to regard this expression as preferable to *minority*. The evidence is too fragmentary to permit firm conclusions, but one might speculate that *people of color* owes part of its appeal to its implicit limitation of the special status accorded "designated minorities" to those distinguished by a racially linked phenotypical feature.[76]

Among discussions by academic sociologists, the one that deals most systematically with the semantics of minority terminology is an article by Barton Meyers. As befits one who writes from a Marxist perspective, Meyers takes the history of the term into account. His historical review is incomplete, however, being confined mainly to locating the term's origins in talk of European "national minorities"; he also treats at length, and critically, the writings of Louis Wirth. For reasons not adequately explained, Meyers accords a privileged conceptual status to *national minorities* and interprets Wirth's use of *minority group* (a term he incorrectly credits Wirth with coining) as an improper universalization of an expression that was earlier embedded in "the historically concrete social situation in Europe." He also makes heavy going of Wirth's liberal individualism and suggests that the "clearly and fundamentally flawed" term *minority group* actually established itself in usage because it "erects a veiled defense of the status quo through the use of obscure language and the posing of misleading questions." Since "concrete, historical analysis" shows that power relations are what really matter, Meyers proposes that *minority group* be dropped and "that people who belong to groups which are collective targets for prejudice, discrimination, and domination be referred to as *oppressed groups*."[77]

Meyers also criticizes Wirth for saying that the sociological concept of minority is not a matter of statistics and can therefore be applied to groups that actually constitute the majority of the population in question.[78] In this he has much company, including, perhaps most influentially, Michael Banton of the University of Bristol. Banton argues that the minority concept is an essential tool in sociological analysis of intergroup relations but that its use can be made more flexible and precise by adhering to the literal sense of the term: "a category consisting of less than half the numbers of some named population." According to Banton's view, blacks in South Africa are not simply a minority, as Wirth would have it on the basis of their subordinate status; rather, they are a numerical majority which is at the same time a political minority internally subdivided into various ethnic and linguistic minorities. This way of using the concept allows us to take note of the existence of "minorities within minorities, and the varying extent to which political, religious and other boundaries coincide"—an analytical advantage with important practical consequences since "it is the divisions within groups and cross-cutting ties between groups which usually keep conflicts within bounds and often open up possibilities of their resolution."[79]

Banton's interpretation of the minority concept has attained a certain authority by being embodied in two recent reference works, a dictionary of social science and an encyclopedia of sociology.[80] That does not guarantee it will be generally adopted by academics, much less that it will displace Wirthian victimization as the crucial element in the prevailing American understanding of minorities. But his position is worth noting as another indication of dissatisfaction with the term as it is used at present.

Additional minor variations on *minorities* could be noted, but enough has been said to furnish the basis for some concluding observations.[81]

The first of these has to do with the periodization of usage and semantic development of the term, which can be summarized as follows:

1. After its effective introduction by Donald Young in 1932, *minority* (in the sociological sense) was quickly indigenized in American usage.

2. In the era of World War II, American minorities were sharply distinguished from the nationalistic and historically persistent minorities of Europe, and what might be called the liberal-individualistic understanding of the minority phenomenon was built into the classic elaboration of the concept worked out by Louis Wirth, which also fixed the notion of victimization as a key element in the definition of a minority.

3. In the postwar generation *minority* became an indispensable term in discussions of intergroup relations and general social commentary. Its application was progressively extended to more and more groups, but the central impetus to the whole development was the civil rights/black revolution, which tended to confirm the associations between minority status, victimization, and the drive to make equality a reality in American society.

4. After the dismantling of legally enforced racial segregation and the subsequent shift of attention to overcoming the effects of prior discrimination, *minority* acquired new significance as a quasi-legal category. The new meaning associated with affirmative action programs did not, however, extend to all groups previously thought of as minorities. Only those formally designated as such were minorities in the new sense. Membership in one of these designated minorities made a person eligible for officially sanctioned benefits that were not available to nonmembers of that group.

The most recent semantic shift is by far the most controversial and has occasioned considerable criticism of the term. The criticism tends, however, to be incidental to a substantive critique of affirmative action as a policy, rather than taking the form of a systematic critical analysis of the minority concept as such. Among the critiques reviewed above, only Meyers's and Banton's are of the latter sort.

That minority usage has become more controversial is explainable on both practical and theoretical grounds. Practically, the latest modulation of usage is associated with the emergence of a two-track system in which "designated minorities" are more favorably situated than what we might call "unrecognized minorities," since the former are entitled to benefits denied to the latter. But there are no clearly established, or explicitly agreed upon, criteria by which to distinguish designated minorities from the unrecognized variety. This situation, in which significant benefits are awarded on the basis of informal criteria that are subject to ad hoc modification, naturally generates controversy over what constitutes "minority" status, who ought to be included, and whose special claims are in peril of being submerged by promiscuous expansion of the category.

The absence of clear, consistent, and rationally defensible criteria for designated minority status is, in itself, a serious theoretical weakness in the two-track system. As critics such as Glazer point out, the designated minorities are "a strange mix," some included because of race, others on the basis of language or culture, and still others by reason of geographic origin. This defect may well account for the recent promotion of *people of color* as an appropriately inclusive designation for the groups eligible for compensatory benefits; however, those who favor this expression have not yet mounted a purposeful campaign to displace *minority*.

A related but more basic theoretical issue is whether group membership—defined on the basis of race, ethnicity, or anything of the sort— *should* entitle a person to benefits not available to other citizens. In other words, the new understanding of minorities raises the fundamental question of whether rights are to be understood as appertaining to *groups*, and to individuals in consequence of their belonging to those groups, or to *individuals* in their character as persons and citizens, with no regard to other forms of group membership.[82] This is not the place to embark on a theoretical analysis of that issue. What is pertinent here is that the problem is implicit in the new usage of *minority* and that this fact helps account for the controversy that has marked its development in the affirmative action era. We ought also to note, however, that insofar as the new usage implies a group rights interpretation of the minority concept, it represents a 180-degree shift away from the individualistic understanding of the concept expounded by Wirth and toward the group-centered "national minorities" version that he and other commentators of his generation explicitly rejected.

It likewise seems clear that the new usage implies an understanding of *minority* quite different from Young's, as well as from Wirth's. Young, the reader will recall, believed "that the problems and principles of race relations are remarkably similar, regardless of what groups are involved." He introduced *minority* as a generic term applicable to all sorts of groups, and it has been accounted a virtue of this word that it lessened the terminological emphasis upon race at a time when the study of intergroup relations was struggling to extricate itself from a racial paradigm shot through with invidious assumptions. Now, however, we have a two-track minority system, and there is an unmistakable tendency to identify *race* as the most important factor that qualifies a designated minority for benefits. Other ethnic groups, formerly thought of as minorities by virtue of distinctive nonracial characteristics, are assumed to have escaped the victimization suffered by racially identifiable groups and are therefore not entitled to affirmative action benefits.[83]

Given the massive fact of American slavery and its consequences for blacks, one can understand how this line of thinking established itself in their case—even, perhaps, its extension to other racially defined groups such as Asians and American Indians. But something as important as the relegitimizing of race as a criterion for differential treatment of American citizens—and differential treatment that is legally enforceable—surely requires more explicit recognition and debate than it has so far received. The degree to which this relegitimizing has actually taken place is in itself debatable, as is the question of how the new racialism resembles, or differs from, the racism of an earlier day. Whatever one may think of those questions, it seems to me indisputable that the prevailing terminology of minorities obscures rather than clarifies what is really at issue. And it would be a great pity, as well as a great irony, if a new kind of racialism were permitted to take root unnoticed while we are bemused by minority-talk.

NOTES

Source: American Quarterly, 43 (September 1991): 392–425. Reprinted by permission of the publisher.

1. See the appropriate entries in William A. Craigie and James R. Hulbert, *A Dictionary of American English on Historical Principles*, 4 vols. (Chicago, 1938–44); Mitford M. Mathews, *A Dictionary of Americanisms on Historical Principles*, 2 vols. (Chicago, 1951); and Bergen Evans and Cornelia Evans, *A Dictionary of Contemporary American Usage* (New York, 1957). The one-volume, abridged edition of H. L. Mencken, *The American Language*, edited by Raven I. McDavid, Jr. (New York, 1963), does not include an index entry for *minority*.

2. *Webster's New International Dictionary of the English Language* 2d ed., unabridged (Springfield, Mass., 1934), in both its 1934 and 1953 versions, gives only a European-type sociological definition for *minority*, namely, "the body of nationals of any state forming a small but appreciable part of the population of a neighboring state." In *Webster's Third New International Dictionary*, unabridged (Springfield, Mass., 1961), the sociological definition has two parts, the first covers minorities of the European type, as above, while the second, which I have quoted in the text, covers the American type.

3. See C. A. Macartney, *National States and National Minorities* (London, 1934), esp. 157–59, 161, for the beginnings of formal diplomatic recognition of, and protection for, nationality rights. Concerning the German word *Nationalitaet*, Hugh Seton-Watson, *The "Sick Heart" of Europe* (Seattle, 1975), 8, states that it, and its Hungarian cognate, were deliberately introduced as "a category at a lower level than a nation" to

designate "distinct cultural communities" that were known to exist but were *not* to be considered "nations."

4. Oscar I. Janowsky, *The Jews and Minority Rights (1898–1919)* (New York, 1933), 388. Supposed Jewish influence in reference to the minorities issue in Poland became an election issue in 1920 among Polish-Americans in Chicago. See Edward R. Kantowicz, *Polish-American Politics in Chicago 1888–1940* (Chicago, 1975), 117–18.

5. "Tyranny of Minorities in American Life," *Current History*, 34 (July 1931), 543–46.

6. T. R. Ybarra, "Disgruntled Minorities," *Outlook*, 151 (March 13, 1929), 408; Carlton J. H. Hayes, *Essays on Nationalism* (New York, 1926), esp. 257–60. See also Oscar I. Janowsky, *Nationalities and National Minorities (With Special Reference to East-Central Europe)* (New York, 1945), part 1 of which is captioned "The Explosive Nature of the Nationalities Problem in the War-Breeding Zone of East-Central Europe." For the best short treatment of the minorities problem under the League of Nations, see Inis L. Claude, *National Minorities: An International Problem* (Cambridge, Mass., 1955), chaps. 1–3.

7. Robert E. Park, though primarily identified with the expression *race relations*, occasionally applied the term *minority* to American groups in the 1920s, but he did so much more frequently after the appearance of Donald Young's *American Minority Peoples: A Study in Racial and Cultural Conflicts in the United States* (New York, 1932). In 1939 Park commented explicitly upon its being a term recently introduced after having "acquired its meaning in a European rather than American context." For pre-1932 usages, see Robert E. Park, *Race and Culture* (Glencoe, Ill., 1950), 165, 228 (for generic political sense); 218, 298 (for European sense); 233, 249, 368–69 (for application to American groups); for post-1932 usages, 84 (for quotation from year 1939), 99, 106, 107, 113, 115, 133, 137, 186, 194, 197, 309, 311, 312. For other examples of early usage, see Geroid Tanquary Robinson, "Racial Minorities," in Harold E. Stearns, ed., *Civilization in the United States* (New York, 1922), 351–79; Reinhold Niebuhr, *Leaves from the Notebooks of a Tamed Cynic* (1929; New York, 1957), 124.

8. The following discussion is based on Young, *American Minority Peoples*, xi–xiv. For Young's career, see his obituary, *New York Times*, April 22, 1977.

9. See Peter I. Rose, *The Subject Is Race* (New York, 1968), 69–71. The displacement in the late twenties of "race" by "culture" as an explanatory factor in intergroup relations is strikingly summed up in Stanley Coben, "The Assault on Victorianism in the Twentieth Century," *American Quarterly*, 27 (December 1975), 610–14.

10. See below, chap. 6; quotation from Young, *American Minority Peoples*, xiii–xiv.

11. *Progressive Education*, 12 (March 1935) contains articles by Alain Locke, Rachel Davis-DuBois, and twelve other less prominent contributors. More generally, see below, chap. 6; Richard Weiss, "Ethnicity and Reform: Minorities and the Ambience of the Depression Years," *Journal of American History*, 66 (December 1979), 566–85.

12. Donald Young, *Research Memorandum on Minority Peoples in the Depression* (New York, 1937), 220–21 (for culture concept), 8 (for comment on "the increasing use of the term minority peoples"); Francis J. Brown and Joseph S. Roucek, eds., *Our Racial and National Minorities* (New York, 1937). The term was also used in inter-religious work. See Newton D. Baker, Carlton J. H. Hayes, Roger W. Straus, eds. *The American Way: A Study of Human Relations among Protestants, Catholics, and Jews*

(Chicago, 1936), index heading "Minorities"; "The Cooperation of Religions" (editorial), *Commonweal*, 25 (December 11, 1936), 169–70.

13. Bruno Lasker's review of Young, *American Minority Peoples* (*Survey*, 68 [December 1932], 661) makes a passing comparison with European minorities; other fleeting mentions are found in Alain Locke, "Minorities and the Social Mind," *Progressive Education*, 12 (March 1935), 142; and Donald R. Taft, "Problems Arising from Minorities," in Brown and Roucek, *Our Racial and National Minorities*, 18–19.

14. Max H. Boehm, "Minorities, National" in Edwin R. A. Seligman and Alvin Johnson, eds., *Encyclopaedia of the Social Sciences*, 15 vols. (New York, 1930–35), 10:518–25; H. A. Miller, "The Menace of Minorities," *Annals*, 175 (September 1934), 60–64; Joseph Chmelar, "National Minorities in Central Europe, A Comparison and Contrast," in Brown and Roucek, *Our Racial and National Minorities*, 770–80. Louis Wirth, "Types of Nationalism," *American Journal of Sociology*, 41 (May 1936), 723–37 touches briefly on the difference between minorities in Europe and in America but does not discuss it at length.

15. Thus a respected Catholic spokesman, responding to the charge that his church was linked with Fascism, warned that "our democracy is breaking up into self-conscious mutually antagonistic minorities." American Catholics, he added, had the worst case of "minority-itis" in their history, one of whose symptoms was their receptivity to Father Charles E. Coughlin's anti-Semitic tirades. George N. Shuster, "A Catholic Defends His Church," *New Republic*, 97 (January 4, 1939), 246–48. See also Harry C. Wolfe, *Human Dynamite: The Story of Europe's Minorities* (New York, 1939).

16. It is revealing, for example, that the "war supplement" of a school encyclopedia included an entry "Minorities," which began by noting that Americans, familiar with a country where persons of differing ethnic stocks blended into the general population in a generation or so, had difficulty understanding why Europe should be "plagued by *minorities*, that is, by groups of people who refuse to become loyal citizens of the nations in which they live, and strive instead to join some other nation, or to set up governments of their own." The entry also included a map showing "The Many Minorities Which Trouble Europe." See *War Supplement to Compton's Pictured Encyclopedia* (Chicago, 1939), 57–58.

17. *Common Ground*, 1 (Winter 1941), 98–99. The book reviewed was George Britt, *The Fifth Column Is Here* (New York, 1940); Louis Wirth, "The Effect of War on American Minorities: A Research Memorandum" (Social Science Research Council mimeo, 1943), 9 (copy in Wirth Papers, Regenstein Library, University of Chicago). See also Wirth, "Morale and Minority Groups," *American Journal of Sociology*, 47 (November 1941), 415–33.

18. Wirth, "Effect of War on Minorities," 6, 7, speaks matter-of-factly, of the relocation of the Japanese-Americans; for the more general problem, see also his lecture, "The Present Position of Minorities in the United States," in Hu Shih et al., *Studies in Political Science and Sociology* (Philadelphia, 1941), 150–56. See Roucek, "Group Discrimination and Culture Clash," in Robert M. MacIver, ed., *Civilization and Group Relationships* (New York, 1945), 67, and the other articles by Roucek cited there; Max Ascoli, "The Italian Americans," in Robert M. MacIver, ed., *Group Relations and Group Antagonisms* (New York, 1944), 36. Louis Adamic also spoke of *minority* as a bad European word; see his *From Many Lands* (New York, 1940), 301.

19. Claude, *National Minorities*, 57; Wirth, "Effect of War on Minorities," 3; Gunnar Myrdal, *An American Dilemma*, (1944; New York, 1962), 50. See also Francis Deak, "Eastern European Nationality and Ethnic Groups," in MacIver, *Group Relations and Group Antagonisms*, 12–13.

20. Oscar I. Janowsky, "Minorities: Pawns of Power," *Survey Graphic*, 28 (February 1939), 76–80; William Allan Neilson, " 'Minorities' in Our Midst," ibid., 101–3. See also Maurice R. Davie, "Minorities, A Challenge to American Democracy," *Journal of Educational Sociology*, 12 (April 1939), esp. 454–56.

21. See below, chaps. 6–7; Deborah Ann Overmyer, " 'Common Ground' and America's Minorities, 1940–1949: A Study in the Changing Climate of Opinion" (Ph.D. diss., University of Cincinnati, 1984).

22. The best discussion is Fred Matthews, "Louis Wirth and American Ethnic Studies: The Worldview of Enlightened Assimilationism, 1925–1950," in Moses Rischin, ed., *The Jews of North America* (Detroit, Mich., 1987), 123–43; but see also Elizabeth Wirth Marvick, "Louis Wirth: A Biographical Memorandum" and the list of Wirth's publications in Louis Wirth, *On Cities and Social Life: Selected Papers*, ed. Albert J. Reiss, Jr. (Chicago, 1964), 332–50.

23. Wirth, "The Problem of Minority Groups," in Ralph Linton, ed., *The Science of Man in the World Crisis* (New York, 1945), 347–72; reprinted in Louis Wirth, *Community Life and Social Policy: Selected Papers*, ed. Elizabeth Wirth Marvick and Albert J. Reiss (Chicago, 1956), 237–60; and in Wirth, *On Cities and Social Life*, 244–69. For confidence in the social beneficence of the social sciences, see below, chap. 5.

24. Wirth, *On Cities and Social Life*, 245–47. For earlier attempts to define a minority group, see Francis J. Brown, "The Meaning of Minorities," in Brown and Roucek, *Our Racial and National Minorities*, 4–7; Stewart G. Cole, "The Meaning of the Term: *Minorities*," *Frontiers of Democracy*, 6 (April 15, 1940), 205.

25. Wirth, *On Cities and Social Life*, 253–63. Wirth had earlier worked out a somewhat similar typology of nationalism; see the 1936 article, "Types of Nationalism," as reprinted in *On Cities and Social Life*, 106–21.

26. For American admiration of Soviet nationalities policy, see James H. Powell, "The Concept of Cultural Pluralism in American Social Thought, 1915–1965" (Ph.D. diss., University of Notre Dame, 1971), 115–17.

27. Wirth's liberal individualism—reflected in this interpretation of minority group dynamics—is the central theme of Matthews, "Louis Wirth and American Ethnic Studies."

28. Wirth's lament is the more striking because, according to an authoritative study, the treaties *did* make individual rights the foundation of the whole system of minority protection and *did not* go as far in recognizing "group rights" as representatives of the national minorities wanted. See Claude, *National Minorities*, 18–20, 37.

29. Arnold Rose and Caroline Rose, *America Divided* (New York, 1948), 3. Arnold M. Rose, "Minorities," in David L. Sills, ed., *International Encyclopedia of the Social Sciences*, 18 vols. (New York, 1968–79), 10:365–70 is much more nuanced.

30. The salience of the concept of "prejudice" in scholarship on minorities is indicated in the title of the leading textbook: George Eaton Simpson and J. Milton Yinger, *Racial and Cultural Minorities: An Analysis of Prejudice and Discrimination*, 5th ed. (New York, 1985 [orig. ed. 1953]). A major review of the literature noted that "it is always considered 'bad' to be prejudiced," because prejudice involves "a failure of rationality *or* a failure of justice *or* a failure of human-heartedness in an individual's attitude toward members of another ethnic group." John Harding et al., "Prejudice and Ethnic Relations," in Gardner Lindzey and Elliott Aronson, eds. *Handbook of Social Psychology*, 2d ed. (Reading, Mass., 1968), 4–6 and passim. In another such review, Herbert Blumer observed that much race relations work in the decade after World War II "stemmed from the view that racial prejudice originates from deficient

personal organization." Blumer, "The United States of America," in issue devoted to "Research on Racial Relations," *International Social Science Bulletin*, 10 (1958), 425. See also Franz Samelson, "From 'Race Psychology' to 'Studies in Prejudice': Some Observations on the Thematic Reversal in Social Psychology," *Journal of the History of the Behavioral Sciences*, 14 (1978), 265–78, esp. 269.

31. William Petersen emphasized the moral dimension of the American definition of minorities. Distinguishing them from simple "pressure groups," he criticized the tendency for pressure groups to claim the moral advantage that belongs by right only to true minorities. But he also scored the "opportunism" of minority groups that "behave like a pressure group and at the same time demand the protection morally due a minority." See Peterson, *The Politics of Population* (Garden City, N.Y., 1964), 235–37. (An earlier version of this essay, entitled "Prejudice in American Society: A Critique of Some Recent Formulations," appeared in *Commentary*, 26 [October 1958], 342–48.)

32. Nicholas V. Montalto, "The Forgotten Dream: A History of the Intercultural Education Movement, 1924–1941" (Ph.D. diss., University of Minnesota, 1978); William E. Vickery and Stewart G. Cole, *Intercultural Education in American Schools* (New York, 1943); Committee on the Study of Teaching Materials in Intergroup Relations, *Intergroup Relations in Teaching Materials* (Washington, D.C., 1949); Lloyd Marcus, *The Treatment of Minorities in Secondary Textbooks* (New York, 1961); Michael B. Kane, *Minorities in Textbooks: A Study of Their Treatment in Social Studies Texts* (Chicago, 1973). For an example of the studies carried out by states, see Michigan Department of Education, *A Report on the Treatment of Minorities in American History Textbooks* (Lansing, Mich., 1968, mimeo.)

33. Morton B. King, Jr., "The Minority Course," *American Sociological Review*, 21 (February 1956), 80–83; Blumer, "United States," 403; Rose, *Subject Is Race*, 9, 75–76.

34. The process by which the black-white issue emerged as *the* national (rather than regional) "race problem" needs more study. As late as 1952, two Chicago sociologists prominent in the study of intergroup relations spoke of the shift of focus from immigrant assimilation to black-white relations as a recent phenomenon. See Everett C. Hughes and Helen M. Hughes, *Where Peoples Meet* (Glencoe, Ill., 1952), 31. See also David W. Southern, *Gunnar Myrdal and Black-White Relations: The Use and Abuse of An American Dilemma, 1944–1968* (Baton Rouge, La., 1987), esp. chap. 8. Vernon J. Williams, Jr., *From a Caste to a Minority: Changing Attitudes of American Sociologists toward Afro-Americans, 1896–1945* (Westport, Conn., 1989), although very informative, does not illuminate the shift mentioned above.

35. It is interesting in this connection that Louis Wirth devoted much of his energy between 1944 and 1950 to the melioristic activities of the American Council on Race Relations, a Chicago-based group of which he was the principal founder and director. For a summary of its activities, see, "The Role of the American Council on Race Relations," in *American Council on Race Relations Report*, 5 (August 1950), 1–4. A penciled notation on the copy of this report in the Wirth Papers at the University of Chicago indicates that it was written by Wirth for the issue of the *Report* which announced the termination of the council's activities. For general comment, see Harding et al., "Prejudice and Ethnic Relations," 1–6; Blumer, "United States," 405–8; and Robin M. Williams, Jr., *The Reduction of Intergroup Tensions* (New York, 1947).

36. Janowsky, *Nationalities and National Minorities*, which appeared in 1945, was the major work by an American. For later analyses of the issue as it carried over into the United Nations era, see Claude, *National Minorities*, and J. A. Laponce, *The*

Protection of Minorities (Berkeley, Calif., 1960). A recent German study attempts to integrate minority theory with a theory of imperialism. See Riita Yletyinen, *Sprachliche und kulturelle Minderheiten in den USA, Schweden und der Bundesrepublik Deutschland: Ein minderheiten- und bildungs-politischer Vergleich* (Frankfurt am Main, 1982).

37. Hughes and Hughes, *Where Peoples Meet*, esp 8ff.; see also John Higham, *Send These to Me: Jews and Other Immigrants in the Urban American* (New York, 1975), 217–18.

38. Charles Wagley and Marvin Harris, *Minorities in the New World: Six Case Studies* (New York, 1958); Edgar Z. Friedenberg, "The Image of the Adolescent Minority," reprinted in Edward Sagarin, ed., *The Other Minorities: Nonethnic Collectivities Conceputalized as Minority Groups* (Waltham, Mass., 1971), 95–107; quotation from 95. Petersen, *Politics of Population*, 237 comments acutely on the similaries and differences between American minorities and those elsewhere in the world.

39. Joseph Schneider, "On the Problem of America's Cultural Minorities," *Journal of Educational Sociology*, 20 (February 1947), 366–75; Oscar Handlin, "Group Life within the American Pattern," *Commentary*, 8 (November 1949), 413; Will Herberg, *Protestant-Catholic-Jew, An Essay in American Religious Sociology*, rev. ed. (Garden City, N.Y., 1960 [orig. ed. 1955]), 43, n. 18; E. K. Francis, "Minority Groups—A Revision of Concepts," *British Journal of Sociology*, 2 (1951), 219–29; Francis, "Variables in the Formation of So-Called 'Minority Groups,' " *American Journal of Sociology*, 60 (July 1954), 6–14; Francis, "Minority Groups in the United States of America," offprint in my possession identified as from *Integration Bulletin*, c. 1955; Petersen, *Politics of Population*, 232–37; Wagley and Harris, *Minorities in the New World*, 1–11; R. A. Schermerhorn, "Minorities: European and American," *Phylon*, 20 (1959), 178–85.

40. Thus the most recent (1985) edition of the leading textbook not only quotes Wirth's definition, but it also makes use of his typology; see Simpson and Yinger, *Racial and Cultural Minorities*, 9, 13–14.

41. For the caste versus minority debate, see Williams, *From Caste to Minority*, 160ff.; for Mydral's reservations on the term *minority* as applied to Negroes, see *American Dilemma*, 50ff., 667.

42. E. Franklin Frazier, *The Negro in the United States*, rev. ed. (New York, 1957), 680; see Williams, *From Caste to Minority*, 172–73.

43. Park, *Race and Culture*, 84; T. W. Adorno et al., *The Authoritarian Personality* (New York, 1950), esp. v–vii, on the background of the study; Martin Jay, *The Dialectical Imagination: A History of the Frankfurt School and the Institute of Social Research, 1923–1950* (Boston, 1973), 217–18 and chap. 7. Marcus, *Minorities in Secondary School Textbooks*, and Kane, *Minorities in Textbooks*, which were sponsored by the Anti Defamation League of B'nai B'rith, also gave prominence to Jews as a minority group.

44. Thomas T. McAvoy, "The Formation of the Catholic Minority in the United States, 1820–1860," *Review of Politics*, 10 (January 1948), 13–34; John L. Thomas, *The American Catholic Family* (Englewood Cliffs, N.J., 1956), esp. chap. 1; and John J. Kane, "Are Catholic Sociologists a Minority Group?" *American Catholic Sociological Review*, 14 (March 1953), 2–12.

45. Helen Mayer Hacker, "Women as a Minority Group," *Social Forces*, 30 (October 1951), 60–69; William H. Chafe, *Women and Equality: Changing Patterns in American Culture* (New York, 1977), 4–6, 174–76; Anthony Gary Dworkin and Rosalind J. Dworkin, *Minority Report: An Introduction of Racial, Ethnic, and Gender Relations*, 2d ed. (New York, 1982), 15.

46. Sagarin, *Other Minorities*, chap. 1; Robert W. Winslow, ed., *The Emergence of Deviant Minorities* (New Brunswick, N.J., 1972).

47. Dworkin and Dworkin, *Minority Report*, 15 (emphasis added).

48. Petersen, *Politics of Population*, 235; Friedenberg, "Image of the Adolescent Minority."

49. The literature on affirmative action is mainly legal and/or polemical. For a detailed historical account of its emergence, see Hugh Davis Graham, *The Civil Rights Era: Origin and Development of National Policy, 1960–1972* (New York, 1990). Lawrence H. Fuchs, *The American Kaleidoscope: Race, Ethnicity, and the Civic Culture* (Middletown, Conn., 1990), chaps. 21–23 provides a comprehensive recent assessment; William R. Beer, "Sociology and the Effects of Affirmative Action: A Case of Neglect," *American Sociologist*, 19 (Fall 1988), 218–31 complains it has been little studied by sociologists; Meyer Weinberg, *Racism in the United States: A Comprehensive Classified Bibliography* (Westport, Conn., 1990), 1–10 lists some 130 titles dealing with affirmative action.

50. Graham, *Civil Rights Era*, chaps. 11 and 13 and pp. 412–13. See also Benjamin B. Ringer, *"We The People" and Others: Duality and America's Treatment of Its Racial Minorities* (New York, 1983), 366–77. For the text of Revised Order No. 4, see 36 *Federal Register* 17444, 31 August 1971; and 36 *Federal Register* 23152, 4 December 1971.

51. For this background, see Harold Orlans, "The Politics of Minority Statistics," *Society*, 26 (May-June 1989), 24–25; Ringer, *We the People*, 351–66.

52. Senator James Buckley (R., New York) is the source of the count; see *Congressional Record*, 93d Cong., 1st sess., vol. 119, pt. 13, p. 16431. The text of Revised Order No. 4 given in 36 *Federal Register* 23152, 4 December 1971 includes no listing of minority groups, but a later version (43 *Federal Register* 49249, 20 October 1978) lists the affected groups as: "Blacks, Spanish-surnamed Americans, American Indians, and Orientals." This version, which was still in effect through the 1980s, differs from the supposedly uniform listing (discussed below) that was worked out in the 1970s.

53. Quoted by Ringer, *We the People*, 378. See Gerald Leinwand, *Minorities All* (New York, 1971).

54. Herbert Hammerman, the first chief of the EEOC's "reports unit," has recently stated that the listing of minorities used by EEOC (and later adopted in the Philadelphia Plan) was inherited from earlier agencies' forms and "was the product of sheer historical accident." Hammerman, " 'Affirmative Action Stalemate': A Second Perspective," *Public Interest*, 93 (Fall 1988), 131. Cf. Graham, *Civil Rights Era*, 328.

55. Graham, *Civil Rights Era*, 329, 286–87.

56. Quoted in Buckley speech, *Congressional Record*, 16431. Cf. Graham, *Civil Rights Era*, 328. For inquiries in the 1950s, see Orlans, "Minority Statistics."

57. Graham, *Civil Rights Era*, 412–13, stresses the importance of Revised Order No. 4 for the women's movement.

58. John Lescott-Leszczynski, *The History of U.S. Ethnic Policy and Its Impact on European Ethnics* (Boulder, Colo., 1984), 49–51. On the definition of racial categories as they affected higher education, and on FICE's activities, see also Alexander W. Astin, *Minorities in Higher Education* (San Francisco, 1982), 214–16. For a convenient collection of relevant federal laws and regulatory guidelines, see Floyd D. Weatherspoon, *Equal Employment Opportunity and Affirmative Action: A Sourcebook* (New York, 1985), 295–401.

59. The case is United States v. Carolene Products Co., 304 U.S. 144, 152 n. 4 (1938); for acceptance as normative, see Leslie W. Dunbar, "Government for All the People," in Dunbar, ed., *Minority Report: What Has Happened to Blacks, Hispanics,*

American Indians, and Other Minorities in the Eighties (New York, 1984), 192; for discussion see Graham, *Civil Rights Era*, 369 and the literature cited there.

60. Quoted from Board of Regents of the University of California v. Bakke, 438 U.S. 265 (1978), in Bette Novit-Evans and Ashton Wesley Welch, "Racial and Ethnic Definition as Reflections of Public Policy," *Journal of American Studies*, 17 (1983), 434 (emphasis added).

61. See Arthur Larson and Lex K. Larson, *Employment Discrimination: Race, Religion, and National Origin* (New York, 1988), vol. 3, section 94.21(b), pp. 20/26–20/27, citing Ortega v. Merita Insurance Co., 433 F. Supp. 135 (N.D. Ill. 1977).

62. Quotation from Evans and Welch, "Racial and Ethnic Definition," 435.

63. *Congressional Record*, pp. 16429–32. For a reference to Orwellian "newspeak" from the opposite side of the ideological fence, see Herman Schwartz, "Affirmative Action," in Dunbar, *Minority Report*, 63.

64. Although this has not happened to the extent Buckley feared, some expansion has taken place, Arch Stokes, *Equal Opportunity Handbook for Hotels, Restaurants, and Institutions* (Boston, 1979), 4–5, lists more than two dozen groups (from "affectional preference" to "weight") which may be able to claim special protection with respect to employment; and Andrew Hacker, "Affirmative Action: The New Look," *New York Review of Books*, October 12, 1989, 63 reports that the University of California-Berkeley has added Filipinos and the disabled to the groups eligible for preferential admission and that City University of New York has taken similar action with respect to Italian-Americans. For an unsuccessful effort to have Hasidic Jews included among groups eligible for minority "set-aside" programs, see Fuchs, *American Kaleidoscope*, 454.

65. *Congressional Record*, 16432–57. For a more recent critique of the same sort, see Harvey C. Mansfield, Jr., "Affirmative Action versus the Constitution," in W. Lawson Taite, ed., *A Melting Pot or a Nation of Minorities* (Austin, Tex., 1986), 91–110.

66. Nathan Glazer, *Affirmative Discrimination: Ethnic Inequality and Public Policy* (New York, 1975), esp. 73–76; Glazer, ed., *Clamor at the Gates: The New American Immigration* (San Francisco, 1985), 226, 236. For more recent statements, see Glazer, "The Future of Affirmative Action," in Phyllis A. Katz and Dalmas J. Taylor, eds., *Eliminating Racism: Profiles in Controversy* (New York, 1988), 329–39; and Glazer, "The Affirmative Action Stalemate," *Public Interest*, 90 (Winter 1988), 99–114. The fullest response to Glazer is Ringer, *We the People*, 408–23; for more general defenses of affirmative action, with some attention to critics, see Schwartz, "Affirmative Action," 58–74; and Ira Glasser, "Affirmative Action and the Legacy of Racial Injustice," in Katz and Taylor, *Eliminating Racism*, 341–57.

67. *Civil Rights Issues of Euro-Ethnic Americans in the United States: Opportunities and Challenges*. A Consultation Sponsored by the United States Commission on Civil Rights, Chicago, Illinois, 3 December 1979 (Washington, D.C., n.d.), 381, 550. The same sentiment was expressed in Stan Chlebek's letter to the editor, captioned "Don't Say Minority," *Chicago Tribune*, February 22, 1989.

68. Henry Fairlie, "The Language of Politics," *Atlantic Monthly*, 235 (January 1975), 28–29. Fairlie insists that the sense he indicates was "the normal way in which the word was used" when Ortega's book was published. Although his example has been sanctified by inclusion in J. A. Simpson and E. S. C. Weiner, eds., *The Oxford English Dictionary*, 2d ed. (Oxford, 1989), his contention as to usage is clearly wrong for the United States, whatever may be the case in Great Britain.

69. Tom Wolfe, *Bonfire of the Vanities* (New York, 1987), 499; see also 254. Some

language watchers object to this usage and its acceptance by recent standard dictionaries; see James J. Kilpatrick, "Cases before Court of Peeves Include Redundancies and Use of 'Minority,' " *South Bend Tribune*, September 30, 1990.

70. The psychological impact of minority group status on members of minority groups has been a prominent theme in the literature of intergroup relations. See, for example, Gordon W. Allport, *The Nature of Prejudice*, 25th anniversary ed. (Reading, Mass., 1979), chap. 9, "Traits Due to Victimization." Norman Mailer's formulation, quoted in a leading college history textbook, is highly idiosyncratic: "What characterizes the sensations of being a member of a minority group is that one's emotions are forever locked in the chains of ambivalence—the expression of an emotion forever releasing its opposite—the ego in perpetual transition from the tower to the dungeon and back again. By this definition nearly everyone in America is a member of a minority group, alienated from the self by a double sense of identity and so at the mercy of a self which demands action and more action to define the most rudimentary borders of identity." See John M. Blum, et al., *The National Experience, Part 2. A History of the United States since 1865*, 5th ed. (New York, 1981), 896.

71. Yolanda T. DeMola, "Let's Get Rid of 'Minority,' " *America*, 157 (October 31, 1987), 284–85; Edward K. Braxton, "Loaded Terms: What's in a Name?" *Commonweal*, 116 (June 2, 1989), 328–29. See also William Simpson's letter to the editor, captioned "History Suppressed," in *Chicago Sun-Times*, April 19, 1984.

72. C. Eric Lincoln, *Race, Religion, and Continuing American Dilemma* (New York, 1984), 211–21.

73. Harold Cruse, *Plural but Equal: A Critical Study of Blacks and Minorities and America's Plural Society* (New York, 1987), 52–69, 360, 362–70, 378, 380–91; quotations from 364, 362, 53, 365, 381.

74. Linda Chavez, "Rainbow Collision," *New Republic*, 203 (November 19, 1990), 14–16. A proponent of multiculturalism (whose overall ideological stance is far to the left of Chavez's) recently expressed concern about the kind of "inter-minority strife that puts serious constraints on a cooperative multiculturalism." See George Yudice, "Latino Identity and the Reconceptualization of 'America' as a Multicultural Society," paper given at the convention of the American Studies Association, New Orleans, November, 1990.

75. Marcia E. Lazar and David G. Roth, "Managing Chicago's Ethnic Conflict," *Chicago Tribune*, May 22, 1989.

76. The editors of a widely used multicultural anthology speak for a small but influential group when they state that "ethnic, minority populations . . . [are] usually defined as 'people of color.' " See Rick Simonson and Scott Walker, eds., *The Graywolf Annual Five: Multi-Cultural Literacy* (St. Paul, Minn., 1988), xi. An educationist prominent in the effort to establish ethnic studies as part of the elementary and secondary curriculum notes that "educators and social scientists are increasingly referring to groups such as African Americans, Hispanics, and Asian Americans as *people of color* rather than as ethnic minorities." This, he explains, is due "in part" to the fact that in California "students of color constitute majorities" in many classrooms; but beyond that, "educators and social scientists are becoming more aware that many terms and concepts used in the past do not accurately and sensitively describe ethnic realities today." See James A. Banks, *Teaching Strategies for Ethnic Studies*, 5th ed. (Boston, 1990), 15.

77. Barton Meyers, "Minority Groups: An Ideological Formulation," *Social Problems*, 32 (October 1984), 1–15. The word *group* was so commonly used in discussions of immigration and race relations that its extension to "minorities" was quite natural.

For use of *minority group* in 1937, see Brown, "The Meaning of Minorities," 5. In 1939, Robert E. Park commented explicitly on the increasing use of the expression *minority group*. Park, *Race and Culture*, 84.

78. Meyers, "Minority Group," 6. Here Meyers cites several other authorities who criticize Wirth on this point, but not Banton, whose position is discussed below.

79. Michael Banton, *Racial and Ethnic Competition* (Cambridge, 1983), 130–31. For more extended discussion of Wirth's formulation, see Banton, *The Idea of Race* (London, 1977), 146ff.

80. G. Duncan Mitchell, ed., *A New Dictionary of the Social Sciences* (New York, 1979), 127; Michael Mann, ed., *The International Encyclopedia of Sociology* (New York, 1984), 243. Banton wrote the entry on "minority" in these two works. See also Pierre L. van den Berghe's critique of the term "Minorities," in E. Ellis Cashmore, *Dictionary of Race and Ethnic Relations* (London, 1984), 167–68. Richard F. Morrisoe, *Minority Groups* in the *Encyclopedia of Sociology* (Guilford, Conn., 1974), 187–88, treats substantive issues of economics, education, etc., as they affect "racial and ethnic minorities" but offers no definition of the term beyond alluding to the "current flux in meaning."

81. Yudice, "Latino Identity" speaks of " 'minoritarian' movements"; Friedenberg, "Image of the Adolescent Minority" distinguishes between "hot-blooded minorities" (blacks and Latins), and "long-suffering minorities" (Jews and women). The idea that the sociological concept of minority should be understood in the not-of-legal-age sense was toyed with by R. L. Bruckberger, O.P., a French priest-observer of American society, and by Isidro Lucas of the University of Chicago. The former was admonishing his American coreligionists to become more "mature"; the latter meant to indicate that *minority* carried the implication of abridged rights "as if the [minority] person were a chronic minor." See R. L. Bruckberger, "The American Catholics as a Minority," in Thomas T. McAvoy, ed., *Roman Catholicism and the American Way of Life* (Notre Dame, Ind., 1960), 40–48; and Isidro Lucas, "Bilingualism and Higher Education: An Overview," *Ethnicity*, 8 (1981), 306.

82. For a group rights interpretation that squints toward a Calhounesque "concurrent majority," see Nicholas Appleton, *Cultural Pluralism in Education: Theoretical Foundations* (New York, 1983), 229–30 and the literature cited there.

83. This line of thinking is avowed or clearly implied in Ringer, *We the People*; Cruse, *Plural but Equal*; Lincoln, *Continuing American Dilemma*; Dunbar *Minority Report*, 192n.; and in many other recent writings, for example, M. G. Smith, critique of the *Harvard Encyclopedia of American Ethnic Groups*, in *Ethnic and Racial Studies*, 5 (1982), 1–22. See also above, chap. 3.

|| 5 ||

Identifying Identity: A Semantic History

As I noted in the Introduction, this essay is a direct offshoot of my contribution to the *Harvard Encyclopedia of American Ethnic Groups*. Convinced that a reference work covering the experience of over one hundred different immigrant peoples should also provide an entry on the host society to whose culture these groups had to adjust, the editors called for a discussion of "American identity." Their insistence that such an entry must focus on the national "identity" was a product of the intellectual vogue enjoyed by the term, the development of which is traced here. But I did not yet know that when approached to write the article. All I knew was that it had to be about "American identity," and that a survey of national characteristics such as optimism, individualism, and the like, was not what the editors had in mind. Given the elusive, not to say mystifying, quality of the term *identity*, my first task was obviously to decide in my own mind just what the subject of the essay actually was. Hence my first draft began with a sketchy history of the term that clarified it enough to allow me to proceed with the substantive discussion. Having served its deck-clearing function, and not being necessary to the substantive discussion as such, the prefatory semantic history was cut from the published version of an already lengthy entry, "American Identity and Americanization."[a]

The essay that follows here is an expanded version of the discarded preamble to the encyclopedia entry. Its elaboration owes much to the encouragement of Lewis Perry, who was editor of the *Journal of American History*, where it was first published, and to the anonymous readers who critiqued it at that time.

Today we could hardly do without the word *identity* in talking about immigration and ethnicity. Those who write on these matters use it casually; they assume the reader will know what they mean. And readers seem to feel that they do—at least there has been no clamor for clarification of the term. But if pinned down, most of us would find it difficult to explain just what we do mean by *identity*. Its very obviousness seems to defy elucidation: identity is what a thing is! How is one supposed to go beyond that in explaining it? But adding a modifier complicates matters, for how are we to understand identity in such expressions as *ethnic identity*, *Jewish identity*, or *American identity*?

This is a question to which the existing writings on ethnicity do not provide a satisfactory answer. There are helpful discussions, to be sure, but none seems altogether adequate, at least not from the historian's viewpoint. The historically minded inquirer who gains familiarity with the literature, however, soon makes an arresting discovery—*identity* is a new term, as well as being an elusive and ubiquitous one. It came into use as a popular social science term only in the 1950s. The contrast between its handling in two standard reference works dramatizes its novelty. The *International Encyclopedia of the Social Sciences*, published in 1968, carries a substantial article on "Identity, Psychosocial," and another on "Identification, Political." The original *Encyclopaedia of the Social Sciences*, published in the early 1930s, carries no entry at all for *identity*, and the entry headed "Identification" deals with fingerprinting and other techniques of criminal investigation.[1]

So striking a shift demands investigation. In the following pages I will attempt to show that the semantic history of the word *identity* casts useful light on its ambiguities of meaning and also upon certain aspects of recent American thought. The investigation proceeds in three phases. Part one, which traces the emergence and diffusion of the term, is brief and descriptive. In the second section of the essay, I have singled out the work of Erik H. Erikson and of certain sociologists as the principal sources of interest in identity and have analyzed some of the complications that arise from the differing interpretations of the concept that they advance. The final section is more interpretive in the historical sense, since it focuses on those aspects of recent American cultural history that seem to me most relevant in explaining why the term *identity* caught on so quickly.

Identity comes from the Latin root *idem*, "the same," and has been used in English since the sixteenth century. It has a technical meaning in algebra and logic and has been associated with the perennial mind-body problem in philosophy since the time of John Locke. The meaning of *identity* in this philosophical context is close to its meaning in ordinary usage, which is given as follows by the *Oxford English Dictionary* (*OED*): "the sameness of a person or thing at all times or in all circumstances; the condition or fact that a person or thing is itself and not something else; individuality, personality. *Personal identity* (In *Psychology*), the condition or fact of remaining the same person throughout the various phases of existence; continuity of the personality."[2]

The *OED*'s first two usage citations illustrating psychological "personal identity" are from Locke's *Essay concerning Human Understanding* (1690) and David Hume's *Treatise on Human Nature* (1739). This tends to corroborate Robert Langbaum's assertion that identity did not take on psychological connotations until the empiricist philosophers called into question what he calls "the unity of the self." The unity of the self was not a problem so long as the traditional Christian conception of the soul held sway, but it became a problem when Locke declared that a man's "Identity . . . consists in nothing but a participation of the same continued Life, by constantly fleeting Particles of Matter, in succession vitally united to the same organized Body." Langbaum argues that Locke and Hume "use the word *identity* to cast doubt on the unity of the self," and he has written a book to show how writers from William Wordsworth to D. H. Lawrence reacted to this challenge to the integrity of "the self."[3]

This tradition of usage is obviously very important; it invested identity with great intellectual significance and moral seriousness. But it was a restricted, quasi-technical tradition. Most of the time people who used the word *identity* in reference to personality or individuality did so in a looser, more informal manner. The *OED* gives two examples of this vernacular usage, as we might call it: "He doubted his own identity, and whether he was himself or another man" (from Washington Irving's *Sketch Book*, 1820); and "Tom . . . had such a curious feeling of having lost his identity, that he wanted to reassure himself by the sight of his little belongings" (from E. Garrett's *At Any Cost*, 1885).[4]

Identity was sometimes casually employed in this vernacular manner by writers discussing immigration, but it did not represent an important analytical concept. Oscar Handlin's classic book *The Uprooted* (1951) is perhaps the last major work in the field of which that could be said. Handlin used *identity* or *identify* a half-dozen or so times, but it was not a key term, and the contexts suggest that he was employing it in an unself-conscious manner as part of the ordinary vocabulary of common discourse. A particularly telling example is the passage in which he contrasts the immigrant's loneliness and isolation in the New World to his secure niche in the ancestral village: "In the Old Country, this house in this village, these fields by these trees, had had a character and identity of their own. They testified to the peasant's *I*, had fixed his place in the visible universe." Here the word refers not directly to the peasant's psyche but to the distinctive physical surroundings of his once familiar world. The connection with psychological identity is very clear—indeed, the passage reminds us of Tom and his little belongings—but Handlin does not use the term in the way that contemporary usage had led us to expect. On the contrary, in looking back at the book one is struck at its virtually complete absence. The book's themes are expressed, and its tone established, not by *identity* but by words such as *uprootedness*, *alienation*, and *loneliness*.[5]

With Will Herberg's *Protestant-Catholic-Jew* (1955) we have turned a corner. Not only do the words recur again and again, but identity and identification are, in a sense, what the book is all about. They are central to the interpretation of the problem Herberg set out to explore, namely, the place of organized religion in American life in the 1950s. Religion, he said, had become the most satisfactory vehicle for locating oneself in society and thereby answering the "aching question" of identity, Who am I? Ethnic identity figured prominently in the discussion because Herberg argued that the ethnic identities of an immigrant-derived population had transformed themselves into religious identification with organized Protestantism, Catholicism, or Judaism through the workings of Hansen's law ("What the son wants to forget the grandson wants to remember") and the triple melting pot. In short, Herberg interpreted the whole situation in terms of what was already being called "the search for identity."[6]

C. Vann Woodward's essay "The Search for Southern Identity," published in 1958, used the term without enclosing it in quotation marks or explicitly defining it, but it carried the new weight of meaning that *identity* was acquiring in the mid 1950s. W. L. Morton's *Canadian Identity*, published a few years later, likewise regarded the word as entirely unproblematic.[7] A rash of other publications used *identity* in title or subtitle in the late 1950s, and in 1960 the editors of an anthology entitled *Identity and Anxiety* drew attention to a marked shift from concern over conformity to concern with identity.[8] Three years later the editor of another volume of readings could introduce the opening section, headed "Identity," with the remark: "It is common knowledge that identity becomes a problem for the individual in a rapidly changing dynamic and technological society such as we have in America." The collection included a selection by Kenneth Keniston in which he listed *identity* among "the most appealing moral terms of our time."[9]

Robert Penn Warren highlighted the importance identity had assumed by the mid 1960s in his *Who Speaks for the Negro?* (1965): "I seize the word *identity*. It is a key word. You hear it over and over again.

On this word will focus, around this word will coagulate, a dozen issues, shifting, shading into each other. Alienated from the world to which he is born and from the country of which he is a citizen, yet surrounded by the successful values of that new world, and country, how can the Negro define himself?"[10] Negroes were far from being alone in having identity problems. American Catholics fairly luxuriated in them. Martin Marty remembers being told by some Catholic collegians who were enthusiastically applauding a priest who had just renounced his priesthood: "You'll never understand what an identity crisis the Catholic Church gave each one of us." Others managed to preserve a better humor in their travail—at Harvard University notices were posted facetiously announcing that Catholic students were holding an "Identity Crisis" at a specified time and place.[11]

By the early 1970s Robert Coles could lament that the terms *identity* and *identity crisis* had become "the purest of clichés." A 1972 book, *The Identity Society*, which stated among other things that Vietnam was the first war fought by an "identity society," offered corroborative evidence for that judgment. *Identity* had reached the level of generality and diffuseness that A. O. Lovejoy complained of many years earlier with respect to the word *romantic*: it had "come to mean so ·many things that, by itself, it means nothing. It has ceased to perform the function of a verbal sign."[12] There is little point in asking what *identity* "really means" when matters have reached this pass. The more pertinent questions are, What can we find out about the specific channels through which the word passed into such widespread use? and, What elements in the intellectual background of its emergence help explain its extraordinary popularity? To the first of these questions we now turn.

Erikson was the key figure in putting the word into circulation. He coined the expression *identity crisis* and did more than anyone else to popularize *identity*. In his usage *identity* means something quite definite, but terribly elusive. In fact, the subtlety of Eriksonian identity helps account for the vagueness that soon enveloped the term, for his ideas are of the sort that cannot bear being popularized without at the same time being blunted and muddied.

Erikson admits that identity, as he conceives it, is hard to grasp because it concerns "a process 'located' *in the core of the individual* and yet also *in the core of his communal culture*, a process which establishes, in fact, the identity of those two identities."[13] What he seems to mean by this Delphic deliverance is that identity involves an interaction between the interior development of the individual personality, understood in terms derived from the Freudian id-ego-superego model, and the growth of a sense of selfhood that arises from participating in society, internalizing its cultural norms, acquiring different statuses, and playing different roles. As the individual passes through the eight stages of the life cycle distinguished by Erikson, the ego undergoes certain experiences and confronts various tasks, distinctive to each stage. These experiences and tasks are related to biological maturation, but they are also intrinsically linked through social interaction to the milieu in which one finds oneself; the features of that milieu are in turn conditioned by the historical situation of the culture that shapes the social world in which the individual and his or her fellows exist. An identity crisis is a climactic turning point in this process; it is the normal occurrence of adolescence, but it can also be precipitated by unusual difficulties further along in the life cycle.

This conception of identity developed from Erikson's clinical experience as a psychoanalyst working chiefly with children, and from reflection upon his own life experience as a European refugee intellectual who traveled widely in the United States and was acquainted with some of the leading social scientists of his generation. The rise of Adolf Hitler and World War II contributed to his interest in the interaction between large-scale historical movements and the development of individual personality, and it was against the background of World War II that Erikson first began to use the term *identity*.

Knowledge of his work was at first confined to professionals in psychology and related fields, but by the late 1950s his reputation began to reach a larger public. The appearance in 1963 of a second edition of *Childhood and Society* (originally published in 1950) was a major event. As other books followed in quick succession over the next few years, Erikson and his ideas became something of a cultural phenomenon. His study of Mahatma Gandhi won both a Pulitzer Prize and a National Book Award. These honors, plus a biography by Coles in 1970, provided the occasion for extensive treatment of Erikson in mass circulation magazines. His being selected in 1973 to deliver the prestigious Jefferson Lectures in the Humanities testified to Erikson's high standing among intellectual opinion leaders.[14]

Erikson's influence was crucial, but his writings were not the only source from which the terminology of identity passed into general circulation. On the contrary, Erikson was concerned as early as 1958 to distinguish his version of identity from other usages; the following year he insisted that identity formation, as he understood it, began where the notion of "identification" left off. By the late 1960s the terminological situation had gotten completely out of hand, and Erikson tried once more to set the record straight. Identity was not the same as role playing, he wrote; it was not just self-conception or self-image, and it was not simply an answer to the faddish question, Who am I?[15]

The mentions of identification and role playing provide useful clues to follow up in searching for other sources of interest in identity. The term *identification* was introduced by Sigmund Freud to designate the process by which the infant assimilates to itself external persons or objects. It became a key element in psychoanalytical explanations of socialization in children; through the 1940s its use was confined almost exclusively to psychologists.[16] Gordon W. Allport was still using "identification" primarily in connection with childhood development in his influential *Nature of Prejudice* (1954), but his discussion is significant because it implied a more general applicability for the concept and linked it with ethnicity. Conceding that the term was loosely defined, Allport said that it conveyed "the sense of emotional merging of oneself with others." Then he illustrated its operation:

> One of the areas where identification may most easily take place is that of social values and attitudes. . . . Sometimes a child who confronts a social issue for the first time will ask his parents what attitude he should hold. Thus he may say, "Daddy, what are we? Are we Jews or gentiles; Protestants or Catholics; Republicans or Democrats?" When told what "we" are, the child is fully satisfied. From then on, he will accept his membership and the ready-made attitudes that go with it.[17]

Identification understood in this sense is very closely related to role theory and reference group theory. That is, identification is involved in the process by which persons come to realize what groups are significant for them, what attitudes concerning them they should form, and what kind of behavior is appropriate. Both role theory and reference group theory were new; they were also gaining rapidly in acceptance among sociologists and social psychologists. As they did so, the theoretical relevance of identification—and the inseparably linked notion of identity—was brought home to other social scientists besides the psychologists who had first used these terms.[18]

Ralph Linton's *Study of Man* (1936) introduced role theory, showed how the concept of social role was intimately linked with that of social status, and made it possible for these two concepts to be "systematically incorporated into a developing theory of social structure."[19] Role theory quickly became a major conceptual perspective for sociology, but as Nelson N. Foote pointed out in 1951, it lacked "a satisfactory account of motivation." To explain why people were willing to be cast in certain roles, accepting the statuses that accompanied those roles, Foote proposed identification as the basis for a theory of motivation in social interaction.[20]

Explicitly distinguishing his use of the term from Freud's, Foote defined *identification* as "appropriation of and commitment to a particular identity or series of identities" on the part of an individual. Identification "proceeds by *naming*," he added, for to appropriate and be committed to an identity meant that one accepted the name (that is, assignment to a certain category) given by others on the basis of family lineage, religion, work activity, and other attributes. Appropriation of these identities by an individual transformed social ascriptions into elements of an evolving sense of selfhood and was experienced as a process of self-discovery and self-actualization. But identities of this sort were not imposed by society in an absolute way, and as one grew older and was exposed to a greater variety of social situations, one could combine and modify identities by conscious choice more effectively than was possible for a child or young person.[21]

Foote's article firmly linked identification with role theory; in doing so it laid great stress on a kind of "identity" that was different from Erikson's and closer to what I have called the vernacular meaning of the word. Foote did not mention reference group theory, perhaps because it was so new when he wrote. It was, however, quite compatible with his analysis since it dealt with the way in which a person's attitudes, values, and sense of identity were shaped by alignment with, or rejection of, "reference groups" that had significance for the individual, either positively or negatively. The expression *reference group* was coined only in 1942, and for the first few years its use was confined to social psychologists. In 1950 Robert Merton and Alice S. Kitt (later Alice S. Rossi) brought the concept to the attention of the larger sociological community in a path-breaking essay. Seven years later this discussion, revised and enlarged, was given much greater visibility in the second edition of Merton's very influential *Social Theory and Social Structure*, which devoted no fewer than 161 pages to reference groups. Being primarily interested in systematic structural analysis, Merton did not lay much emphasis on identity or identification. He did, however, point out the relevance of reference group theory to these matters, and by so greatly augmenting the prestige of a sociological approach to which they were intimately related, he contributed importantly to popularizing the terminology of identity.[22]

Identity eventually gained an even more prominent place in the vocabulary of the sociological school known as symbolic interactionists. Emerging as a self-conscious group around 1940, the symbolic inter-actionists were especially interested in the way social interaction, me-diated through shared symbolic systems, shaped the self-consciousness of the individual. They did not at first use the word *identity* in analyzing this sort of interaction because the founding fathers of the approach, Charles Horton Cooley and George Herbert Mead, had spoken instead of "the self," and that continued to be the preferred term through the 1960s. By that time, however, *identity* had also become a "stock technical term" for symbolic interactionists.[23] Erving Goffman and Peter L. Berger played important roles in popularizing this sociological understanding of identity since their works reached a more general audience than that constituted solely by academic specialists. Goffman shifted from the ter-minology of "the self" to that of "identity" in his 1963 work, *Stigma*. In the same year, Berger's popular *Invitation to Sociology* featured identity quite prominently in its treatment of role theory and reference group theory, dramaturgical sociology, and the phenomenological approach.[24]

By the mid 1960s, the word *identity* was used so widely and so loosely that to determine its provenance in every context would be im-possible. But enough has been said to show that sociological traditions of usage in role theory, reference group theory, and symbolic interac-tionism constituted important feeder streams supplementing the prin-cipal source of popularization, Eriksonian psychology. Besides helping to popularize the term, sociological usage also contributed to its uncer-tainty of meaning because the kind of identity that sociologists had in mind was not the same as that contemplated by Erikson.

The two approaches differ most significantly on whether identity is to be understood as something internal that persists through change or as something ascribed from without that changes according to circum-stance. For Erikson, the elements of interiority and continuity are indis-pensable. Working within the Freudian tradition, he affirms that identity is somehow "located" in the deep psychic structure of the individual. Identity is shaped and modified by interaction between the individual and the surrounding social milieu, but, change and crisis notwithstand-ing, it is at bottom an "accrued confidence" in the "inner sameness and continuity" of one's own being.[25]

The sociologists, on the other hand, tend to view identity as an artifact of interaction between the individual and society—it is essentially a matter of being designated by a certain name, accepting that desig-nation, internalizing the role requirements accompanying it, and behav-ing according to those prescriptions. Foote is explicit here, and Berger asserts not only that identities are "socially bestowed" but that they "must also be socially sustained, and fairly steadily so." He adds pointedly that this sociological view of personality challenges the assumption of continuity in the self. "Looked at sociologically, the self is no longer a solid, given entity. . . . It is rather a process, continuously created and re-created in each social situation that one enters, held together by the slender thread of memory."[26] Another sociologist, acknowledging Goffman's influence, goes even further by equating identity with social relationship. "We have treated social relationship and identity as merely different terms for referring to the same phenomena: the establishment of mutually recognized, expected sequences of behavior in a transaction. Identity refers to the individual's sequence of acts; relationship refers to the ensemble of acts made up by the sequences of all the parties involved."[27]

Obviously we are back at the problem of "the unity of the self," the emergence of which Langbaum associates with the writings of Locke and Hume. Indeed, it is striking how closely the formulation just quoted parallels Locke's contention that "Identity . . . consists in nothing but a participation of the same continued Life, by constantly fleeting Particles of Matter." The reappearance in new form of what we might call the philosophical problem of the soul is of considerable interest in itself, but it is also related to an issue more immediately relevant to students of ethnicity, namely, whether ethnic identity is something primordially given or optionally cultivated.

The distinction between these two interpretations emerged only recently; it has not, to my knowledge, been systematically explored.[28] Briefly, the difference between the two approaches is that primordialists regard ethnicity as a given, a basic element in one's personal identity that is simply there and cannot be changed, while optionalists hold that ethnicity is not an indelible stamp impressed on the psyche but a dimension of individual and group existence that can be consciously emphasized or deemphasized as the situation requires. This disagreement obviously involves a fundamental issue concerning ethnic identity, and it just as obviously parallels the difference between the Eriksonian and the sociological understanding of identity itself.

The parallel rests on the centrality of the question of continuity or permanence to both sets of contrasting interpretations. In the case of identity, Erikson insists that an inner continuity of personality perdures through all the changes the individual undergoes in passing through the stages of the life cycle, while the interactionists envision a flickering succession of identities adopted and shed according to the requirements of different social situations. In respect to ethnicity, the primordialists plump for permanence, whereas the optionalists believe that ethnicity can, within certain limits, be assumed or put aside by conscious choice.

The analogy between these two sets of interpretations is striking. But since it has never been pointed out before, much less studied in detail, its implications are not wholly clear. One might ask, for example, whether a person who accepts the Eriksonian version of personal identity is thereby committed to a primordialist position on ethnic identity. The two positions are beautifully congruent, but I would not be prepared to argue that the one logically entails the other. On the other hand, consistency would surely require an interactionist on personal identity to adopt the optionalist view of ethnicity. The key point for the present discussion, however, is that the analogy brings out clearly the basic equivocation embedded in discussions of identity (including ethnic identity) as a result of the fact that different users assign different meanings to the term. For Eriksonians/primordialists, identity is deep, internal, and permanent; for interactionists/optionalists, identity is shallow, external, and evanescent. It is bad enough that, in many contexts of usage, one cannot tell which of these very different interpretations is intended. Much worse is the likelihood that many who speak of identity are completely oblivious of the equivocation and hence do not themselves know which of the interpretations they intend.

Confusion arising from this source and from other perplexities of terminology bedevils discussion at every level from popular journalism to scholarly analysis.[29] Hearings recently held by the United States Commission on Civil Rights on "Civil Rights Issues of Euro-Ethnic Americans" furnish an instructive example from the broad area of debate over social policy. The "consultation," as it was officially designated, took place in 1979 and provided a sounding board for white ethnic spokespersons unhappy about programs of the affirmative action type. Several of the witnesses likewise expressed misgivings about the label *Euro-ethnic*, which led Geno Baroni to observe: "We argue about terminology—even the name of this meaning. . . . We don't have the language to describe ourselves, and America has no national sense of identity."[30] Irving M. Levine, like Baroni a pioneer of the new ethnicity, was equally troubled about Americans' inability to understand the nature of identity. The situation was not helped by the careless way terms relating to race and ethnicity are used, even by judges, and Levine suggested that it was time for the United States Commission on Civil Rights "to clear up some of the definitions."[31]

Especially interesting were the remarks of Francis X. Femminella. Noting that other witnesses had "talked about ethnic identity," Femminella delivered a brief disquisition on "ethnic *ego* identity . . . a very special kind of a concept." His purpose was not merely to clarify the ambiguities left by other testimony but also to refute the claim that ethnic groups could not perpetuate themselves without some degree of self-segregation. Invoking Erikson's authority, he argued that a person internalizes the social heritage of his or her group at so deep a level that it is "damn close" to being "genetically inheritable." For that reason, ethnic communities need not seal themselves off from others; rather, "if that heritage is there, then the ethnic communities will go on irrespective of whether they have a locale."[32]

These observations illustrate the affinity between Eriksonian identity and primordialist ethnicity. The linkage has important implications from the viewpoint of advocacy, for the intimate association thus established between personal identity and ethnic heritage makes plausible the argument that ethnic cultures require some sort of official recognition if the self-esteem of individuals is not to suffer damage. The respect for the dignity of the individual demanded by the democratic ideology is thereby extended to cover ethnic cultures that sustain the sense of personal self-worth.[33] Femminella did not develop this aspect of the matter, but his remarks suggest another strategic use of this perspective in controversy. For the Eriksonian theoretical framework, "where," as Femminella put it, "you can get something going," made it possible for him to avoid the taint of racialism while asserting that ethnicity would perdure indefinitely without any need for potentially divisive group self-segregation.

But of course every position has the defect of its virtues. The defect here is that so strong a primordialist argument inevitably suggests the conclusion that, if ethnicity is bound to persist anyhow, there is no great need for new social policies designed to foster or protect it. The optionalist view is much better adapted for arguing in favor of new social policies because it stresses the role of situational factors in shaping ethnic identity. Since the participants in the Euro-ethnic consultation were overwhelmingly in favor of changes in policy, it is not surprising that they also made use of the optionalist argument. Paul J. Asciolla was most explicit: he said that "the concept of ethnicity as a factor in American culture" would "diminish or indeed vanish" if it were not "kept alive consciously."[34]

No one pointed out the contradiction between Femminella's position and that of Asciolla. Very likely it was not even noticed; we are so accustomed to hearing ethnic identity talked about in both ways that the contradictory implications pass us by. From the viewpoint of advocacy, it would not have been very adroit to call attention to the equivocation of terminology anyhow, for it is clearly advantageous to be able in certain contexts to argue that ethnic identity is fixed and in others to affirm that it is malleable. But much as the controversialist may like having terms that mean whatever the rhetorical situation requires, equivocation of this sort is fatal to efforts to achieve a clear theoretical grasp of the issues. It is likewise a grievous handicap to the forging of sound social policy through rational debate. On that account, bringing such equivocation out into the open is of more than purely academic interest.

Having sketched the popularization of the term and having investigated its provenance and some of its complexities, we turn now to the matter of causes, seeking to answer the question, Why did *identity* so quickly become an indispensable term in American social commentary? A full answer would take more space than is available here, but some comments are required to round out the semantic history of identity. We will first consider the mystique of the social sciences and the vogue of national character studies, which are best thought of as mediating conditions that contributed to the popularization of the term. Then we will look briefly at more substantive causes for concern with identity.

The mystique of the social sciences is relevant to the popularization of identity because the new usage derived from the technical vocabulary of psychology and sociology; for that reason, it shared in the aura of cognitive authority surrounding the social sciences at midcentury. Although they had emerged as autonomous disciplines around 1900, the social sciences came into their own only after World War I. They developed a strong corporate sense in the 1920s and created a major support institution in the Social Science Research Council (SSRC), which quickly attracted large-scale funding from philanthropic foundations. By the end of the decade, the social scientific disciplines had matured sufficiently to make possible the publication of a monumental collaborative work, the *Encyclopaedia of the Social Sciences*, which appeared between 1930 and 1935. The New Deal opened new opportunities for public service for economists and other social scientists. Then came World War II. That really brought the social scientists out of their ivory towers and set them to work for their country, as Stuart Chase observed in an admiring survey of the wartime accomplishments and postwar prospects of the social sciences.[35]

Chase's book *The Proper Study of Mankind* (1948) illustrates the way the war enhanced the prestige of the social sciences. It was undertaken at the suggestion of officials of the SSRC and Carnegie Corporation, who "followed the project step by step" and provided financial support.

The roll call of scholars who encouraged Chase and provided information on the "mine of fresh material accumulated during the war" constituted a veritable who's who of the social sciences. The book itself explained the scientific method and reviewed its achievements—many of which were war related—in such fields as human relations, public opinion polling, and learning theory. Reviewers hailed the book as a valuable reconnaissance that indicated directions for future research, and it sold well enough to justify a revised edition in 1956. By that time the intellectual authority of the social sciences seemed to Chase so well established that he said "an intelligent layman" would hesitate to form a judgment on "complicated questions about crime or sex or the federal budget without some background in social science—perhaps a course or two in college, or in the extension field."[36]

As supporting evidence for this dictum Chase might have cited the role played by social scientific evidence in the fight for racial desegregation. He might likewise have pointed to the vast readership enjoyed by David Riesman's *Lonely Crowd* (1950) and the almost equal success of William H. Whyte, Jr.'s *Organization Man* (1956). With the publication in 1959 of Vance Packard's *Status Seekers*, "pop sociology" had come of age as a literary genre with mass appeal.[37]

These developments testify to the belief, widely held by lay people as well as by academic intellectuals, that the social sciences could unlock the secrets of the human condition.[38] This belief goes a long way toward explaining why *identity* caught on so quickly in the 1950s. Although the word had been used in the vernacular sense for a long time, the kind of identity talked about by psychologists and sociologists seemed to refer to something deeper, more mysterious, and more important. It was a matter of universal concern, since everyone had an identity, but to fathom its involvement in harrowing "searches" and agonizing "crises" one had to call on the special expertise of the social scientist. The association of the term *identity* with the social sciences thus added to its intellectual cachet, making it part of the conceptual equipment of the approach that offered the best hope of solving the problems besetting American society.

Among the many problems facing American society in the years after World War II, understanding the national character would probably not strike us today as one meriting high priority. Yet self-understanding is always important, and in that era the study of national character was regarded as one of the most exciting frontier areas of the social sciences.[39] The vogue of national character studies is particularly relevant for us because Erikson had close connections with the group of social scientists who pioneered a new approach to the subject, and it was against the background of national character studies that he began to put the term *identity* into circulation.

The belief that different human groups are marked by distinctive characteristics is at least as old as Herodotus, but it had fallen into disrepute in the 1930s as a result of its association with racialism. The new era of scientifically respectable study of national character was inaugurated in World War II by a group of scholars who were called upon by agencies of the United States government to apply their skills to such questions as how civilian morale could best be maintained or what kind of propaganda could be most effectively employed against the enemy. Margaret Mead was the best-known scholar involved, and she led the way in applying to these questions the methods worked out in the 1930s by the culture-and-personality school of anthropologists. She was one of the founders of this school, which combined psychological assumptions and ethnographic observation in the effort to discover how group norms and attitudes were stamped on the personalities of individuals belonging to different cultures. From this mode of investigation to the study of national character was only a short step, and Margaret Mead later stated explicitly that what were called culture-and-personality studies in the 1930s "would today [1961] be called . . . 'national character' [studies]."[40] The degree of scientific prestige attained by this approach is best illustrated in the postwar Tensions Project, an ambitious collaborative investigation initiated by UNESCO and supported by the SSRC, which relied heavily on the national character perspective in its effort to find ways of reducing "tensions affecting international understanding." And in 1954 the historian of nationalism Louis L. Snyder spoke respectfully of the developing "science of national character."[41]

There were national character studies of other peoples—Ruth Benedict's book on the Japanese, *The Chrysanthemum and the Sword* (1946), being especially notable—but studies of the American character were the most popular. Margaret Mead's *And Keep Your Powder Dry* (1942) opened the era in which studies of the American character became a leading growth sector of the knowledge industry and almost the reason for being of the new discipline (or disciplinary holding company) of American studies.[42] The key point for us is that American character studies dealt directly with the relationship of the individual and society and explored the problem of whether, to what extent, or how the individual's personality, character, or "identity" was shaped by the culture in which he or she was a participant.

A direct connection can be shown between this general development and the introduction of the term *identity*, since Erikson was closely associated with the social scientists engaged in wartime national character studies. He prepared memoranda for the Committee for National Morale on the stresses of life on submarines, on interrogating German prisoners of war, and on the feasibility of making psychological observations in internment camps. His major contribution was an inquiry into Hitler's success in winning the loyalty of German youth by embodying in himself the anxieties and fantasies of a generation that experienced national humiliation, cultural crisis, and economic collapse. Margaret Mead cited this study in *And Keep Your Powder Dry*, and Coles has stressed its importance when discussing the impact of the war on Erikson's thinking about identity.[43]

Erikson knew and admired Margaret Mead's work on the American character, and he first worked out his ideas on the interaction between "ego identity" and "group identity" in the context of the wartime investigation of national character.[44] The 1946 article "Ego Development and Historical Change" was published in a specialized psychoanalytical journal and was clinically oriented, but it also showed marked affinities with national character studies since Erikson was concerned with the way in which the individual's social heritage (group identity) affected the development of personality (ego identity). It was essential, he wrote, "to correlate a patient's childhood history with the history of his family's sedentary residence in prototypical areas (East), in 'backward' areas (South), or in 'forward' areas (Western and Northern frontier), as these areas were gradually incorporated into the American version of the Anglo-Saxon cultural identity." In emphasizing polarities in the American group identity, Erikson was taking over an insight first elaborated by one of his wartime co-workers, Gregory Bateson, in a paper "Morale and National Character." As heir to a history of extreme contrast and abrupt changes, said Erikson, the "functioning American . . . bases his final ego-identity on some tentative combination of dynamic polarities such as migratory and sedentary, individualistic and standardized, competitive and cooperative, pious and free-thinking, etc." Touching on the challenges of the war experience, Erikson spoke of the "subliminal panic" that accompanied "the large scale testing of the American identity" in the war. "Historical change," he declared, "has reached a coercive universality and a global acceleration which is experienced as a threat to the emerging American identity."[45]

Erikson reworked much of this material for the chapter of *Childhood and Society* (1950) entitled "Reflections on the American Identity." This chapter marks a milestone in the semantic history of *identity* because it was the first major publication in which the expression *American identity* was used as the equivalent of *American character*. Reverting again to the subject of polarities, Erikson began by observing that virtually all characteristically American traits have opposites that are likewise characteristically American. "This, one suspects," he continued in the second sentence of the chapter, " is true of all 'national characters' or (as I would prefer to call them) national identities."[46] Although distinctive in being based primarily on Erikson's clinical experience as a psychoanalytical therapist, the chapter was clearly in the tradition of commentaries on the American character. Thus Erikson made reference to Vernon Louis Parrington's work, alluded to the legacies of Puritanism and the frontier, and touched on many other familiar themes of national character commentary.[47]

That *identity* could be used alternatively for *character* in an era when national character studies were extremely popular doubtless helped to smooth the way for its rapid acceptance. But that is surely not a sufficient explanation for the enormous success of the term. *Identity*, after all, gained much greater currency than *character* ever had, and its popularity continued long after the vogue of national character studies was forgotten. Its having been launched in the favorable climate created by the interest in national character studies and its prestige as a term taken from the technical vocabulary of social science must therefore be understood as factors that mediated its popularization rather than being regarded as decisive causes.

What, then, *was* the decisive cause? The most important consideration, I would say, was that the word *identity* was ideally adapted to talking about the relationship of the individual to society as that perennial problem presented itself to Americans at midcentury. More specifically, *identity* promised to elucidate a new kind of conceptual linkage between the two elements of the problem, since it was used in reference to, and dealt with the relationship of, the individual personality and the ensemble of social and cultural features that gave different groups their distinctive character.

The relationship of the individual to society has always been problematic for Americans because of the surpassing importance in the national ideology of the values of freedom, equality, and the autonomy of the individual. Alexis de Tocqueville analyzed in classical fashion how democratic principles and equalitarian social conditions gave rise to an "individualism" (a word he effectively introduced into the lauguage) that tended to shrivel a man's consciousness of solidarity with his fellows, throwing him forever back upon himself alone and threatening to "shut [him] up in the solitude of his own heart."[48] He did not, of course, use

the term *identity* in this connection, but it is impossible for today's reader
not to think of "identity problems" on encountering Tocqueville's un-
cannily modern diagnosis of the psychological strains created by uncertainties of status and his description of the strange restlessness that made
Americans "serious and almost sad even in their pleasures."[49] It is also
easy to understand why there was in the 1950s an admiration for Tocqueville that approached veneration, for "the isolation of the individual
and the atomization of society" that he described in Jacksonian times
anticipated the discovery of mass society that loomed so large in the
landscape of American social commentary at midcentury.[50]

The post–World War II critique of mass society drew on a variety of
sources, but what gave it compelling urgency and made it a matter of
general concern was undoubtedly the frightening rise of totalitarianism
followed by the catastrophe of world war. Refugee intellectuals, who had
special reason to abhor totalitarianism, were important contributors to
the critique of mass culture, and one influential group—the so-called
Frankfurt School, whose "dialectical method" fused Marxist and Freudian perspectives—saw in American society tendencies that could well
eventuate in totalitarianism and that were already producing "authoritarian personalities" susceptible to fascism.[51] The relation of the individual to society was the crucial issue for critics of mass society, who discussed it in terms of "alienation," "anxiety," "anomie," "ethnocentrism,"
"status consciousness," "conformity," and "the need for belonging." Riesman introduced "other-directedness," and the title of his book—*The
Lonely Crowd*—epitomized the central problem: personal isolation in a
mass society. Handlin's book *The Uprooted*, published a year after Riesman's volume, explored a different dimension of American social experience, but it also put into circulation a term—*uprootedness*—that added
a new strain of poignance to the interpretation of the relation of the
individual to American society.

In these circumstances the questions, Who am I? and, Where do I
belong became inevitable. Identity was, in a sense, what the discussion
was all about. As Erikson noted in 1950, "we begin to conceptualize
matters of identity at the very time in history when they become a problem." The study of identity, he believed, was "as strategic in our time as
the study of sexuality was in Freud's time."[52] Understood as a concept
of the social sciences, "identity" thus gained its original currency because
of its aptness for discussing one of the issues that dominated the American intellectual horizon of the 1950s, "the survival of the person in mass
society."[53] In those days the characteristic problem centered on "the
search for identity," which was thought to arise primarily from the in-

dividual's feeling of being rootless and isolated in a swarming, anonymous throng. In the next decade the cultural climate changed drastically, and the mass society problem receded far into the background. But the word *identity* did not decline with the fading interest in the problems that first called for employment of the concept; on the contrary, it gained even greater popularity. The problem of the relation of the individual to society assumed new forms in the turmoil of the 1960s, but identity was more relevant than ever—only now it was of "identity crises" that one heard on every hand.

Few who lived through that troubled time would deny that the expression *identity crisis* spoke with greater immediacy to the American condition than the formula *search for identity*. For the nation did go through a profound crisis—social, political, and cultural—between the assassination of John F. Kennedy and the resignation of Richard Nixon. The ingredients of the crisis—racial violence, campus disruptions, antiwar protests, cultural upheaval, and the abuse of official power and betrayal of public trust—need no elaboration. The point is that the national crisis translated itself to the ordinary citizen as a challenge to all individuals to decide where they stood with respect to the traditional values, beliefs, and institutions that were being called into question, and with respect to the contrasting interpretations being offered of American society, American policies, and the American future. In other words, the national crisis brought about a reexamination on a massive scale of the relationship between the individual and society. That was the relationship with which identity dealt, and in innumerable cases the reexamination was sufficiently intense to make the expression *identity crisis* seem very apt.

Within the context of cultural crisis, the revival of ethnicity deserves special attention as perhaps the most important legacy of the 1960s so far as usage of *identity* is concerned. There is in the nature of the case a close connection between the notion of identity and the awareness of belonging to a distinctive group set apart from others in American society by race, religion, national background, or some other cultural marker. As a matter of fact, Erikson alluded to the acculturation of immigrants immediately after drawing attention in 1950 to the timeliness of identity as an analytical concern. Looking back twenty years later, he underscored his own experience as an immigrant in tracing the developing his thinking about identity: "It would seem almost self-evident now how the concepts of 'identity' and 'identity crisis' emerged from my personal, clinical, and anthropological observations in the thirties and forties. I do not remember when I started to use these terms; they seemed naturally grounded in the experience of emigration, immigration, and American-ization."[54]

That is certainly plausible. But the connection between Erikson's personal experience and his sensitivity to identity problems doubtless seemed clearer by 1970 because of the growth of interest in ethnicity in the intervening years and because of the new respectability gained by ethnic consciousness. In the late 1940s, assimilation was thought to have eroded immigrant cultures almost entirely, and the lingering vestiges of group consciousness seemed not only archaic but also potentially dys-functional as sources of ethnocentrism, antiintellectualism, and isola-tionist sentiment.[55] Even Herberg, who first stressed the linkage between ethnicity and the search for identity, believed ethnic identities were being replaced by religious identities. The black revolution of the 1960s and the subsequent emergence of the new ethnicity changed all that. These movements affirmed the durability of ethnic consciousness, gave it le-gitimacy and dignity, and forged an even more intimate bond between the concepts of ethnicity and identity. And these developments not only took place against the background of the national identity crisis; they were also dialectically related to it—that is, ethnic or minority identities became more appealing options because of the discrediting of traditional Americanism brought about by the racial crisis and the Vietnam War.[56] As Nathan Glazer pointed out in 1975, a situation had by then developed in "the ecology of identities" in which, for the first time in American history, it seemed more attractive to many individuals to affirm an ethnic identity than to affirm that one was simply an American.[57] The evidence cited earlier from the consultation on Euro-ethnics indicates that ethnic identity is still perceived to be closely related to group concerns and social policy, which supports the contention that the ethnic revival has had the most enduring effect on usage of the term *identity*.

Thus far the semantic history of *identity*. What can we conclude from it? Three reflections of special relevance for historians suggest themselves. The first is simply a plea for wider application of the historical approach as a method for clarifying ambiguous concepts. Not many American historians have undertaken investigations of this sort, although there are a few outstanding examples.[58] Without claiming to have cleared up all the problems associated with identity, I would argue that the present study has brought to light much that was not known about it before and that could never have been discovered by purely systematic conceptual analysis.

Second, I would suggest that historians interested in problems involving identity acquaint themselves with the sociological writings about the subject in addition to resorting to the works of Erikson. There are, as we have seen, important differences between the two interpretations. Erikson's is by far the better known; for certain purposes, however, the sociological perspective may offer a more useful conceptual framework for analyzing socio-historical influences on identity than Erikson's primarily psychological approach.[59] In any case, familiarity with both brings into sharper focus the distinctive assumptions of each and thereby assists historians in reaching their own conclusions as to how the concept of identity should be handled.

The final point to be emphasized is the obvious one that historians need to be very careful in talking about identity and highly critical in assessing the way others talk about it. The term can legitimately be employed in a number of ways. It may, for example, mean no more than that a person or group is known by a certain name, but it may also be used in reference to the distinguishing characteristics marking whatever is known by that name or to the ensemble of cultural features that collectively constitutes the larger reality with which a person or group is identified through a certain name.[60] Erikson seems at times to encompass all of these senses in his notion of identity, but his characteristic emphasis is on a crucial psychic ingredient, something within the personality of the individual that makes it possible "to experience one's self as something that has continuity and sameness, and to act accordingly."[61] Adding to the already great likelihood of confusion arising from this array of possible meanings is the ambiguity stemming from the fact that the sociologists most apt to talk about identity understand it in a quite different way.

For these reasons, responsible use of the term demands a lively sensitivity to the intrinsic complexities of the subject matter with which it deals and careful attention to the need for precision and consistency in its application. But of course its enormous popularization has had just the opposite effect: as *identity* became more and more of a cliché, its meaning grew progressively more diffuse, thereby encouraging increasingly loose and irresponsible usage. The depressing result is that a good deal of what passes for discussion of identity is little more than portentous incoherence, and the historian need not be intimidated into regarding it as more than that.[62] What is called for, rather, is confidence in the traditional critical skills of the historical craft. By applying them with care, historians can make a contribution to better understanding of a significant problem in contemporary American culture.

NOTES

Source: Journal of American History, 69 (March 1983), 910–31. Reprinted by permission of the publisher.

a. See Stephan Thernstrom, Ann Orlov, and Oscar Handlin, eds., *Harvard Encyclopedia of American Ethnic Groups* (Cambridge, Mass., 1980), 31–58. The words "and Americanization" were added by the editors after the essay was completed. For a sketch of the approach it follows, see the opening paragraphs of chap. 6, "Americans All."

1. David L. Sills, ed., *International Encyclopedia of the Social Sciences,* 18 vols. (New York, 1968–79), 7:57–65; Edwin R. A. Seligman and Alvin Johnson, eds., *Encyclopaedia of the Social Sciences,* 15 vols. (New York, 1930–35), 7:573-74. A discussion that is opaque to the reader not well versed in the tradition of continental philosophical psychology is David J. de Levita, *The Concept of Identity* (New York, 1965). More useful is Arnold Dashefsky, ed., *Ethnic Identity in Society* (Chicago, 1976), esp. 5–9. Examples of recent discussions by social scientists are Frank A. Salomone and Charles H. Swanson, "Identity and Ethnicity: Ethnic Groups and Interactions in a Multi-Ethnic Society," *Ethnic Groups,* 2 (May 1979), 167–83; and Kwen Fee Lian, "Identity in Minority Group Relations," *Ethnic and Racial Studies,* 5 (January 1982), 42–52.

2. The definition quoted in the text is the second given for *identity.* The first, not germane here, is: "The quality or condition of being the same in substance, composition, nature, properties, or in particular qualities under consideration; absolute or essential sameness; oneness." OED, s.v. *identity.*

3. Ibid.; Robert Langbaum, *The Mysteries of Identity: A Theme in Modern Literature* (New York, 1977), 25.

4. OED, s.v. *identity.*

5. Oscar Handlin, *The Uprooted* (Boston, 1951), 105, 185, 188, 194, 239, 280, 304. *Identity* is not used as a technical term in William Carlson Smith's synthesis of the sociological literature on immigrant assimilation. Smith, *Americans in the Making: The Natural History of the Assimilation of Immigrants* (New York, 1939).

6. Will Herberg, *Protestant-Catholic-Jew: An Essay in American Religious Sociology* (Garden City, N.Y., 1955), 24–31, 40–44.

7. C. Vann Woodward, "The Search for Southern Identity," *Virginia Quarterly Review,* 34 (Summer 1958), 321–38; W. L. Morton, *The Canadian Identity* (Madison, Wis., 1961).

8. Allen Wheelis, *Quest for Identity* (New York, 1958); Helen Merrell Lynd, *On Shame and the Search for Identity* (New York, 1958); Erik H. Erikson, *Identity and the Life Cycle: Selected Papers* (New York, 1959); Anselm Strauss, *Mirrors and Masks: The Search for Identity* (Glencoe, Ill., 1959); Maurice R. Stein, Arthur J. Vidich, and David Manning White, eds., *Identity and Anxiety: Survival of the Person in Mass Society* (Glencoe, Ill., 1960), 25.

9. Hendrik M. Ruitenbeek, ed., *Varieties of Modern Social Theory* (New York, 1963), 3, 100. Elsewhere Ruitenbeek asks, "Who, thirty years ago, would have thought that the problem of identity would become one of the most crucial issues for the searching individual in our society?" Ibid., xii–xiii. See also Roger L. Shinn, ed., *The Search for Identity: Essays on the American Character* (New York, 1964).

10. Robert Penn Warren, *Who Speaks for the Negro?* (New York, 1965), 17.

11. Martin E. Marty, *By Way of Response* (Nashville, 1981), 19. The Harvard University episode is reported in Erik H. Erikson, *Identity: Youth and Crisis* (New York, 1968), 15–16.

12. Robert Coles, review of Erik H. Erikson, *Dimensions of a New Identity*, in *New Republic*, June 8, 1974, 23; William Glasser, *The Identity Society* (New York, 1972), 43; Arthur O. Lovejoy, *Essays in the History of Ideas* (Baltimore, Md., 1948), 232.

13. Erikson, *Identity: Youth and Crisis*, 22. For the best introduction to Erik H. Erikson's writings, see ibid.; Erikson, *Identity and the Life Cycle*; Erikson, *Childhood and Society* (New York, 1950).

14. An informative biography that provides extensive commentary on Erikson's writings is Robert Coles, *Erik H. Erikson: The Growth of His Work* (Boston, 1970). See also Erik H. Erikson, "Autobiographic Notes on the Identity Crisis," *Daedalus*, 99 (Fall 1970), 730–59; H. Stuart Hughes, *The Sea Change: The Migration of Social Thought, 1930–1965* (New York, 1975), 217–32. For journalistic coverage, see David Elkind, "Erik Erikson's Eight Stages of Man," *New York Times Magazine*, April 5, 1970, 25–27, 84, 87, 89, 90, 92, 110, 112, 114, 117, 119; Robert Coles, "Profiles: The Measure of Man—I," *New Yorker*, November 7, 1970, 51–131; Coles, "Profiles: The Measure of Man—II," ibid., November 14, 1970, 59–138; Webster Schott, "Explorer of Identity," *Life*, November 27, 1970, 24; review of Robert Coles, *Erik H. Erikson*, *Time*, November 30, 1970, 51–52; "Erik Erikson: The Quest for Identity," *Newsweek*, December 21, 1970, 84–89. The Jefferson Lectures were published as Erik H. Erikson, *Dimensions of a New Identity: The 1973 Jefferson Lectures in the Humanities* (New York, 1974).

15. Erik H. Erikson, "Identity and Uprootedness in Our Time," in Ruitenbeek, *Varieties of Modern Social Theory*, 59–60; Erikson, *Identity and the Life Cycle*, 112–13; Erikson, *Identity: Youth and Crisis*, 23, 314.

16. Jack Rothman, *Minority Group Identification and Intergroup Relations: An Examination of Kurt Lewin's Theory of Jewish Group Identity* (New York, 1965), 14–19; Gordon W. Allport, "The Historical Background of Modern Social Psychology," in Gardner Lindzey, ed., *Handbook of Social Psychology*, 2 vols. (Cambridge, Mass., 1954), 1:24.

17. Gordon W. Allport, *The Nature of Prejudice* (Reading, Mass., 1954), 293–94.

18. In 1950 a sociologist associated with the Menninger Clinic began an article by asking: "What concern can sociology have, one might ask, with such a strictly psychological phenomenon as identification?" Louisa P. Holt, "Identification: A Crucial Concept for Sociology," *Bulletin of the Menninger Clinic*, 14 (September 1950), 164–73.

19. Ralph Linton's paternity of role theory as a systematic conceptual perspective is categorically asserted by Robert Merton, *Social Theory and Social Structure* (Glencoe, Ill., 1957), 368n. See also Ralph Linton, *The Study of Man: An Introduction* (New York, 1936), 113–31.

20. Nelson N. Foote, "Identification as the Basis for a Theory of Motivation," *American Sociological Review*, 16 (February 1951), 14–21.

21. Ibid., 17–19. See also Everett C. Hughes and Helen M. Hughes, *Where Peoples Meet: Racial and Ethnic Frontiers* (Glencoe, Ill., 1952), 102.

22. Robert K. Merton and Alice S. Kitt, "Contributions to the Theory of Reference Group Behavior," in Robert K. Merton and Paul F. Lazarsfeld, eds., *Continuities in Social Research: Studies in the Scope and Method of "The American Soldier"* (Glencoe, Ill., 1950), 40–105; Merton, *Social Theory and Social Structure*, 225–386. For allusions to identification and the introduction of the term *reference group*, see ibid., 269, 275–76, 277.

23. Andrew J. Weigert, "Identity: Its Emergence within Sociological Psychology,"

typescript, 1982 (in possession of Andrew J. Weigert). For general treatments, see Bernard N. Meltzer, John W. Petras, and Larry T. Reynolds, *Symbolic Interactionism: Genesis, Varieties, and Criticism* (London, 1975); Paul Elliott Rock, *The Making of Symbolic Interactionism* (Totowa, N.J., 1979).

24. Erving Goffman, *The Presentation of the Self in Everyday Life* (Garden City, N.Y., 1959); Goffman, *Stigma: Notes on the Management of Spoiled Identity* (Englewood Cliffs, N.J., 1963); Peter L. Berger, *Invitation to Sociology: A Humanistic Approach* (Garden City, N.Y., 1963). The importance of Anselm Strauss's *Mirrors and Masks* in putting the word *identity* into the working vocabulary of symbolic interactionists is stressed by Weigert, "Identity," 10–11.

25. For discussion of the evolution of Erikson's concept of identity, see Coles, *Erikson*, 165–79, 265.

26. Foote, "Identification," 14–21; Berger, *Invitation to Sociology*, 100–106.

27. Thomas J. Scheff, "On the Concepts of Identity and Social Relationship," in Tamotsu Shibutani, ed., *Human Nature and Collective Behavior: Papers in Honor of Herbert Blumer* (Englewood Cliffs, N.J., 1970), 205. See also the discussion of Erving Goffman's term *identity kit*, which refers to "the assortment of role identities that each individual carries with him," in William M. Newman, "Multiple Realities: The Effects of Social Pluralism on Identity," in Dashefsky, *Ethnic Identity in Society*, 40.

28. The distinction was, I believe, first broached by Nathan Glazer and Daniel P. Moynihan in commenting on the contributions to a volume of essays that they edited. See Glazer and Moynihan, eds., *Ethnicity: Theory and Experience* (Cambridge, Mass., 1975), 19–20. They called the two approaches "primordialist" and "circumstantialist," but the term *optionalist* was substituted for *circumstantialist* in Peter K. Eisinger, "Ethnicity as a Strategic Option: An Emerging View," *Public Administration Review*, 38 (January–February 1978), 89–93. See also Pierre L. van den Berghe, *The Ethnic Phenomenon* (New York, 1981), 17–18, 256, 261.

29. Calling for "deobfuscation" of identity, Carlos H. Arce says that the scholarly literature on Chicano identity "demonstrates the confused commingling of disparate phenomena and the failure to develop consistent conceptual definitions." He also speaks of the "conceptual morass" of earlier work on Mexican-American communities. Carlos H. Arce, "A Reconsideration of Chicano Culture and Identity," *Daedalus*, 110 (Spring, 1981), 182–83.

30. *Civil Rights Issues of Euro-Ethnic Americans in the United States: Opportunities and Challenges*. A Consultation Sponsored by the United States Commission on Civil Rights, Chicago, Illinois, 3 December 1979 (Washington, D.C., n.d.), 590. For other observations about the term *Euro-ethnic*, see ibid., 76, 584.

31. Ibid., 12, 8.

32. Ibid., 284.

33. As John W. Briggs has noted, it is "the central tenet of the 'new ethnicity' movement that group identity and roots are vitally important to personal identity, character, and psychological well-being." See Briggs, review of Patrick J. Gallo, *Old Bread, New Wine, American Historical Review*, 87 (April 1982), 544. This theme recurs frequently in the 1970 hearings on the bill to establish ethnic heritage studies centers. See *Ethnic Heritage Studies Centers*. Hearings before the General Subcommittee on Education of the Committee on Education and Labor, House of Representatives, on H.R. 14910, 91st Cong., 2d sess. (Washington, D.C., 1970), 1, 22, 23–24, 129, 135, 175–76, 255, 256, 263, 267.

34. *Civil Rights Issues of Euro-Ethnic Americans*, 284, 569.

35. Stuart Chase, *The Proper Study of Mankind*, rev. ed. (New York, 1956), x.

Another observer stated at the time: "During World War II the social scientist took his place, with dignity, alongside the medical and physical scientist. To the contributions of the physicist, the chemist, and the technologist were added the contributions of the anthropologist, economist, political scientist, psychologist, psychiatrist, and sociologist. . . . This phenomenal acceleration in the development and productivity of the social sciences, though occurring under the compulsion of war, may yet prove at least one great boon to mankind." Charles E. Hendry, Foreword, in Goodwin Watson, *Action for Unity* (New York, 1947), x. For a more recent survey of the subject, see Gene M. Lyons, *The Uneasy Partnership: Social Science and the Federal Government in the Twentieth Century* (New York, 1969), 80–123.

36. For the role of the SSRC and Carnegie Corporation, and for the listing of social science informants, see Stuart Chase, *The Proper Study of Mankind* (New York, 1948), xv–xx; quotation from Chase, *Proper Study* (1956), 307.

37. David Reisman, *The Lonely Crowd: A Study of the Changing American Character* (New Haven, Conn., 1950); William H. Whyte, Jr., *The Organization Man* (New York, 1956); Vance Packard, *The Status Seekers: An Explanation of Class Behavior in America and the Hidden Barriers That Affect You, Your Community, Your Future* (New York, 1959). For the role of social scientific evidence in the struggle for desegregation, see Kenneth B. Clark, "The Social Scientist as an Expert Witness in Civil Rights Litigation," *Social Problems*, 1 (June 1953), 5–10; Brown v. Board of Education of Topeka, 347 U.S. 483; Richard Kluger, *Simple Justice: The History of Brown v. Board of Education and Black America's Struggle for Equality* (New York, 1976), 315–45, 556–57.

38. Still another indication of this belief was the 1950 decision of the Ford Foundation "to throw its great financial resources behind the effort 'to advance human welfare' through the application of scientific methods and techniques to the study of human behavior." Heniz Eulau called this "a milestone in the development of modern social science" and "an act of faith . . . that social science is ready to contribute to the solution of the manifold problems which vex mankind." Heinz Eulau, "Social Science at the Crossroads," *Antioch Review*, 11 (March 1951), 117–28.

39. Cf. Alex Inkeles and Daniel J. Levinson, "National Character: The Study of Modal Personality and Sociocultural Systems," in Lindzey, *Handbook of Social Psychology*, 2:977–1020; Milton Singer, "A Survey of Culture and Personality Theory and Research," in Bert Kaplan, ed., *Studying Personality Cross-Culturally* (Evanston, Ill., 1961), 43–57.

40. Margaret Mead, "National Character and the Science of Anthropology," in Seymour Martin Lipset and Leo Lowenthal, eds., *Culture and Social Character* (New York, 1961), 17.

41. Louis L. Snyder, *The Meaning of Nationalism* (New Brunswick, N.J., 1954), 162–87. On the Tensions Project, see Otto Klineberg, *Tensions Affecting International Understanding: A Survey of Research* (New York, 1950); and Morroe Berger, " 'Understanding National Character'—and War," *Commentary*, 11 (April 1951), 375–86.

42. Ruth Benedict, *The Chrysanthemum and the Sword: Patterns of Japanese Culture* (Boston, 1946); Margaret Mead, *And Keep Your Powder Dry: An Anthropologist Looks at America* (New York, 1942). For a useful guide to the immense literature on American character, see Michael McGiffert, "Selected Writings on American National Character," *American Quarterly*, 15 (Summer 1963), 271–88. Other illuminating discussions are Thomas L. Hartshorne, *The Distorted Image: Changing Conceptions of the American Character since Turner* (Cleveland, 1968); E. Adamson Hoebel, "Anthropological Perspectives on National Character," *Annals*, 370 (March 1967), 1–7;

David E. Stannard, "American Historians and the Idea of National Character," *American Quarterly*, 23 (May 1971), 202–20.

43. Mead, *And Keep Your Powder Dry*, 274; Coles, *Erikson*, 84–100, 421.

44. Erik Homburger Erikson, "Childhood and Tradition in Two American Indian Tribes," *Psychoanalytic Study of the Child*, 1 (1945), 348n. In 1950 Erikson stated, "It would be impossible for me to itemize my over-all indebtedness to Margaret Mead." Erikson, *Childhood and Society*, 13.

45. Erik Homburger Erikson, "Ego Development and Historical Change," *Psychoanalytic Study of the Child*, 2 (1946), 373–74, 378, 388. Gregory Bateson, "Morale and National Character," in Goodwin Watson, ed., *Civilian Morale: Second Yearbook of the Society for the Psychological Study of Social Issues* (Boston, 1942), 71–91. There is a strong likelihood that Erikson was acquainted with Gregory Bateson's polarities approach, since the latter was at the time married to Mead and his general assistance is acknowledged in Erikson, *Childhood and Society*, 14.

46. Erikson, *Childhood and Society*, 244.

47. Erikson did not change this chapter in the 1963 edition of the book, but he added a rather murky endnote. Erikson, *Childhood and Society*, 2d ed. (New York, 1963), 324–25.

48. Alexis de Tocqueville, *Democracy in America*, ed. Jacob Peter Mayer (Garden City, N.Y., 1969), 506–8.

49. Ibid., 536. Two recent critics of "the prevalent American piety toward the self" who cite Alexis de Tocqueville's discussion are Philip Rieff, *The Triumph of the Therapeutic: Uses of Faith after Freud* (New York, 1966), 62, 69–70; and Christopher Lasch, *The Culture of Narcissism: American Life in an Age of Diminishing Expectations* (New York, 1978), 9.

50. The quotation is from Yehoshua Arieli, *Individualism and Nationalism in American Ideology* (Cambridge, Mass., 1964), 196. For interest in Tocqueville in the 1950s, see John Higham, Leonard Krieger, and Felix Gilbert, *History: The Development of Historical Studies in the United States* (Englewood Cliffs, N.J., 1965), 221–22. For an introduction to the discussion of mass society, see Daniel Bell, "Modernity and Mass Society: On the Varieties of Cultural Experience," in Arthur M. Schlesinger, Jr., and Morton White, eds., *Paths of American Thought* (Boston, 1963), 411–31, 574–77.

51. Martin Jay, *The Dialectical Imagination: A History of the Frankfurt School and the Institute of Social Research, 1923–1950* (Boston, 1973), 212–52. See also Hughes, *Sea Change*, 134–88.

52. Erikson, *Childhood and Society*, 242.

53. This was the subtitle of Stein, Vidich, and White, eds., *Identity and Anxiety*. See also Winston White, *Beyond Conformity* (Glencoe, Ill., 1961), 50–52.

54. Erikson, *Childhood and Society*, 242; Erikson, *Life History and the Historical Moment* (New York, 1975), 43. The wording here varies slightly from Erikson's first published autobiographic reflections, in Erikson, "Autobiographic Notes on the Identity Crisis," 747–48. Interestingly, Erikson did not say in the 1970 version that the connection between immigration and his interest in identity problems "seem[ed] almost self-evident."

55. See chap. 6.

56. This interpretation is developed more fully in Philip Gleason, "American Identity and Americanization," in Stephan Thernstrom, Ann Orlov, and Oscar Handlin, eds., *Harvard Encyclopedia of American Ethnic Groups* (Cambridge, Mass., 1980), 52–55. See also Arthur Mann, *The One and the Many: Reflections on the American Identity* (Chicago, 1979), 1–45.

57. Nathan Glazer, *Affirmative Discrimination: Ethnic Inequality and Public Policy* (New York, 1975), 177–78.

58. Arthur E. Bestor, Jr., "The Evolution of the Socialist Vocabulary," *Journal of the History of Ideas*, 9 (June 1948), 259–302; Donald Fleming, "Attitude: The History of a Concept," *Perspectives in American History*, 1 (1967), 287–365; John Higham, "Ethnic Pluralism in Modern American Thought," in Higham, *Send These to Me: Jews and Other Immigrants in Urban America* (New York, 1975), 196–230; Job L. Dittberner, *The End of Ideology and American Social Thought: 1930–1960* (Ann Arbor, Mich., 1979), 1–101, on the introduction and early diffusion of the concept of ideology among American intellectuals.

59. For an impressive example, see Peter Berger, "Modern Identity: Crisis and Continuity," in Wilton S. Dillon, ed., *The Cultural Drama: Modern Identities and Social Ferment* (Washington, D.C., 1974), 158–81.

60. Thus in some contexts *American identity* has the same meaning as *American character*, while in others it is equivalent to *American nationality*. C. Vann Woodward uses *identity* to designate a distinctive regional heritage in his "Search for Southern Identity," 321–38; and *identity* is synonymous with *nationality* in Morton, *Canadian Identity*.

61. Erikson, *Childhood and Society*, 38.

62. See, for example, Vine Deloria, Jr., "Identity and Culture," *Daedalus*, 110 (Spring 1981), 13–27.

Part Two

World War II and American Identity

|| 6 ||

Americans All

This essay follows a methodological approach somewhat different from that employed in the previous chapters. Although close attention is paid to semantic complexities, the primary focus here is on a major historical experience—participation in World War II—which profoundly shaped the way Americans thought of themselves as a people, both at the time and for a long generation thereafter.[a] That the war had this effect on our collective sense of national identity was the most important intellectual discovery I made in working up the entry for the *Harvard Encyclopedia of American Ethnic Groups*. "Americans All" was the first article to appear as an offshoot of that project, and its relation to the overall interpretation advanced there is sketched in the introductory section of the essay.

A shorter version of "Americans All" was presented at the 1980 meeting of the European Association for American Studies, held in Amsterdam, and appeared among the papers published from that convention in the volume entitled *The American Identity: Fusion and Fragmentation*.[b] The expanded version that follows here was published in the *Review of Politics* for October 1981. Although several of the issues it deals with are also treated in other essays included in this volume, I have not attempted to eliminate duplication of coverage. "Americans All" has its own integrity as a first effort to sketch the broad outlines of the war's impact on our national self-understanding, and I let it stand in the form it had in that first attempt.

Although it is four decades since the United States entered World War II, some aspects of the nation's wartime experience are still virtually unstudied. Military and diplomatic historians have labored productively for many years, but historians interested in American social and intellectual developments are just beginning to turn their attention to the wartime era. Recent general studies by Richard Polenberg and John M. Blum are especially welcome since, by drawing greater attention to the period, they should stimulate further research.[1] There is much left to be done because the war affected practically every dimension of American life. The present essay deals with one of its less obvious effects—the way in which it shaped the thinking of a whole generation on the subject of American identity.

The expression *American identity* had not yet come into use in World War II. In those days people spoke instead of American nationality or American character. All of these terms are elusive and, in many cases, simply vague. We need not enter into all the semantic complications, but a few preliminary comments are required for the discussion that follows.[2] In the first place, we should note that the underlying question in many contexts where these terms appear is, What does it mean to be an American? Although a straightforward and seemingly simple question, it raises issues of the deepest sort about the values we hold as a people, the goals we should pursue, the loyalties we may legitimately cherish, and the norms of conduct we ought to follow. These issues are not only controversial in that Americans will disagree about the appropriate answers; they are also inherently difficult in that they are subtle, complex, and resistant to perspicuous formulation. In view of these facts it is not surprising that discussions of American identity have historically been marked by a good deal of conceptual unclarity and impassioned misunderstanding.

From the earliest days of our national existence, elements of ideology and ethnicity have figured prominently in these discussions. *Ideology* here refers to the foundational values of freedom, equality, and commitment to self-government under law which served as the justification for the colonies' separation from the mother country, and on which the Founding Fathers erected the constitutional fabric. The ideological element in American identity, in other words, comprises the universalistic political and social principles for which the Republic stands, and through adherence to which individuals identify themselves with the nation. *Ethnicity*, on the other hand, refers to the more particularistic dimensions of group consciousness that have marked the American people, or portions of them, causing them to think of themselves, and to be thought of by others, as belonging to a distinctive community, set apart from others by race, religion, language, national derivation, or some combination of these and other cultural features.

A historical review of the evolution of American thinking on identity shows that ideological and ethnic elements have interacted in complex ways and that their relative salience has varied from one epoch to another. For the revolutionary and immediate postrevolutionary generations, ideological themes predominated strongly. In the years 1830–60, however, religion—specifically the Roman Catholicism of so many immigrants—became the focal point in controversies over what it meant to be an American. In fact, the word *Americanization* was first used to refer to immigrant assimilation in the Know-Nothing debates of the 1850s. Ethnic elements attained their greatest salience in the era that spanned the years from 1890 to the mid 1920s. Religious feeling still ran high, and by then Jews were numerous enough to play a prominent role, especially since they produced writers who helped establish the terms of discourse with respect to national identity. Israel Zangwill, who put the symbol of the melting pot in circulation, and Horace Kallen, who propounded the theory of cultural pluralism, were both Jews. In this era racialism was triumphant, both as scientific doctrine and as popular sentiment. Combining with the chauvinism brought on by the war, and with postwar cultural panic, racialist nativism brought about a reversal of America's century-old tradition of almost completely unrestricted immigration.

In the half-century that has passed since the climax of nativism in the 1920s, there was first an ebbing and then (after the mid 1960s) a resurgence of the ethnic dimension in thinking on national identity. When ethnicity was most recessive (from about 1940 to the early 1960s) the ideological aspect of American identity was given greater emphasis than it had received since the days of the Founding Fathers. In the following pages we will explore some of the factors related to the decline of attention to the ethnic dimension after the mid 1920s and·then examine the role played by World War II in accentuating the ideological conception of American identity.

Nineteen twenty-four is the place to begin, because the passage that year of the national origins quota law ended a century of massive overseas immigration, satisfied the demands of the restrictionists, and permitted Americans hitherto alarmed about the immigrant peril to relax. As a result, the 1924 law inaugurated an era in which ethnic concerns faded from consciousness as important public issues. It is true that religious and ethnocultural feelings played a prominent role in the Al Smith campaign of 1928, but that contest proved a kind of epilogue to the era when passions of this sort loomed large in public controversy.[3]

The Great Depression was most decisive in pushing ethnocultural considerations into the background, but a reassessment of the concept of race contributed to this result by undercutting traditional ideas about group life. These shifting views on the nature of group life and intergroup relations become rather complicated, and they demand careful analysis.

The traditional view, which dominated in the late nineteenth century and reached its climax in the first two decades of the twentieth, held that inborn racial qualities determined the kind of culture a people could create. Since cultures could be ranked on a scale from lower to higher, and since race and nationality blurred together, the old racial theory jibed nicely with restrictionists' claims that the new immigrants from eastern and southern Europe were overwhelming and degrading American culture. Indeed, it gave shape through the national origins device to the kind of restriction enacted in the 1924 law. The national origins principle was not abandoned in law till the mid sixties, but the racial theory it embodied had been discredited long before. World War II confirmed the shift at the level of popular thinking, but the crucial change in educated opinion came in the fifteen years before the war.

Social scientists were the first to repudiate the older racialism. Among them, the anthropologists—Franz Boas first of all—claim pride of place, not merely because they led the way in the critique of racialism, but also because the anthropological concept of culture replaced race as the key to understanding human groups. Boas had struggled for many years against the view that cultural phenomena were racially linked, but his interpretation did not attain the status of anthropological orthodoxy until the 1920s. Thereafter a sharp disjunction was posited between race as the realm of the biologically determined and culture as the domain of learned behavior, human creativity, and spiritual freedom.[4]

The incompatibility of this view with the older racialism was obvious, and by 1930 social scientists had nearly all discarded the latter, even though it required some of them to repudiate their previously published opinions.[5] Not so obvious at first were the far-reaching implications of the culture concept as an analytical and interpretive principle. Boas enlarged on some of these matters in a 1928 volume entitled *Anthropology and Modern Life*, of which a reviewer said that it annihilated "the bases of almost all the prejudices and passions on which modern society rests."[6] But two of Boas's students were even more effective in bringing the anthropological perspective to the attention of the general reading public.

The first was Margaret Mead. Her *Coming of Age in Samoa* informed a wide readership in 1928 that adolescence was not the psychologically stressful experience in Samoa that it was in Western society because of culturally conditioned differences in family structure, attitudes toward sex, and so on. The youthful anthropologist—only twenty-three when she went to Samoa—underscored the implications of her study for Americans. Besides the general point that personality was shaped by cultural norms and institutions, she stressed the relativity of such norms and institutions, the need for tolerance and open-mindedness in evaluating human conduct, and the desirability of educating American youngsters in such a way as to enable them to choose without feelings of guilt among the many competing value systems and styles of life offered by the heterogeneous society in which they dwelt.[7]

Ruth Benedict was also a student of Franz Boas, and her book *Patterns of Culture* (1934) reaffirmed the message of cultural relativism and the need for tolerance. Yet this work, probably the most widely read anthropological study ever written, was even more important in popularizing the view that a culture was not simply a collection of discrete institutions and traits but an integrated complex, more or less tightly organized around some animating vision, central motif, or generalized attitude toward reality. So understood, a culture had to be viewed holistically, for none of its specific features could be adequately grasped without reference to the pattern of which they formed a part. A culture was something like an art style—it represented the collective response of a people to what Benedict called the "great arc" of human possibilities. This did not mean that all cultures were equally appealing; but appreciating the diversity of cultures helped to liberate one from the imperatives of one's own culture and provided a perspective from which to assay its dominant traits.[8]

By the eve of World War II, the culture concept was fast becoming "the foundation stone of the social sciences."[9] Even historians—a group notoriously laggard in matters methodological—saw the light by 1939, when the program chairman for their annual convention decided that "the time was ripe for a discussion of the cultural approach and for an attempt to try it out in different fields." The first group of topics treated in the published version of the sessions dealt with immigration history under the rubric "Cultural Groups." Not all the contributors drew the same inferences from the culture concept, however; one distinguished scholar even suggested that nativism might be a very positive thing from the cultural perspective, since by retarding the assimilation of immigrants it helped preserve cultural diversity.[10]

Differences in interpretation were natural enough because the anthropological concept was rather spongy in itself, and because it overlay older, more informal, senses of the word *culture*. In addition, sociologists had also done much work on human groups, and, as the two disciplines mutually influenced and borrowed from each other, their terminologies "half-blended in a grand confusion."[11] Since these obscurities of terminology shrouded real conceptual ambiguities, we must look more closely at what the sociologists were doing and at some of the more problematic terms that were used in the discussion of ethnic affairs.

What Franz Boas and Columbia University were to anthropology, Robert E. Park and the University of Chicago were to sociology. One authority dates the beginnings of scientific sociology in the United States from the publication of *The Polish Peasant in Europe and America*, by Park's colleague and friend, W. I. Thomas, and his Polish associate, Florian Znaniecki.[12] Personal difficulties led to Thomas's departure from Chicago about the time the book was published in 1918, but Park carried on the tradition and made racial and ethnic relations a leading specialization as sociology came of age. And although the lay person often has trouble distinguishing between the work of a sociologist and an anthropologist, there was a significant difference between the Parkian approach and that of the anthropologists.

Because of their fascination with culture, anthropologists were predisposed toward an internalist approach to the study of human groups— they focused primarily on the group considered in itself, its norms, institutions, and the patterns that gave it coherence. They spoke of acculturation and cultural change, to be sure, but these matters were logically secondary, since one had to understand a culture before one could analyze its modifications. There was thus an implicit tendency toward what we might call analytical isolationism—considering each group as an isolated unit—and the characteristic work of anthropologists was carried out in remote corners of the earth, among primitive groups whose cultures could be grasped in the round.[13]

Park's intellectual disposition was very difficult.[14] He had been a newspaperman before turning to academic life, and the metropolis was his natural milieu. For him the primary fact about group life in the modern world was not that each group had its own distinctive culture but that all groups were being thrown into contact with each other, were reacting to each other, and were mutually influencing each other in all sorts of ways. Getting an intelligible grip on this melee was one of the chief tasks of social science, and to do that, one obviously needed a perspective that highlighted the processes of interaction *between* groups rather than the peculiarities of each group considered in itself.

Park's formulation of the interaction process became famous as the "race relations cycle." It envisioned a four-stage sequence, of which the first was competition. Here the groups involved might not even be aware of their relationship to each other, since competition was mostly a matter of economic interdependence mediated through the marketplace, the division of labor, and so on. The stage of conflict ensued when groups became aware of their interconnection and strove to get the better of each other by divers means, the most extreme of which was war. Accommodation, the third stage, represented "the unstable equilibrium achieved by conflicting parties who became weary of the struggle . . . and agreed . . . to limit their claims and coexist with potential rivals." In the final stage, assimilation, the groups in question forged more intimate links by what Park called "a process of interpenetration and fusion in which persons and groups acquire the memories and sentiments and attitudes of other persons and groups, and, by sharing their experience and history, are incorporated with them in a common cultural life."[15]

Although he spoke of "a common cultural life," Park did not visualize it as requiring a high degree of cultural integration. Rather, he believed a modern society could function effectively if its constituent elements all conformed to a minimum of general norms that enabled them to get along together and cooperate in carrying out essential collective tasks.[16] He departed here from the view implicit in much anthropological work that there was something intrinsicially unhealthy about a society whose cultural features were not all of a piece. This difference is quite important because it suggests that the Parkian version of "assimilation" could accommodate a greater amount of internal diversity than could the anthropological concept of culture, despite the fact that culture rather than assimilation was usually associated with the idea of tolerance for diversity. The difference noted above is also significant because it reflected a really crucial divergence between the Parkian and the anthropological approaches—that is, Park's interaction model of group relations was a dynamic one in which conflict and change were built in, whereas the view popularized by Ruth Benedict squinted toward stasis and made contact with outsiders a problematic business.[17]

This perhaps puts too fine a point on the contrast, but it was nevertheless real. And it was important, for it involved different criteria for evaluating the health of a society. Conflict, for Park, was not necessarily a morbid symptom; nor were differences in interests, goals, and values among the constituent groups making up the society. In Benedict's perspective, however, these would be morbid symptoms, for her interpretation of culture assumed internal coherence and harmony as fundamental requirements for social health. This underlying contrast was not brought clearly into the open and analyzed in the 1930s, with the result that submerged ambiguities persisted in the discussion of acculturation, assimilation, tolerance for diversity, and other matters related to ethnicity. The conceptual situation was made even more complex by semantic uncertainties associated with other terms that figured prominently in the discussion. We will look at three of these terms—*minority*, *ethnocentrism*, and *prejudice*.

The term *minority*, or *minority group*, entered the discussion in 1932 when Donald Young gave the title *American Minority Peoples* to a general study of group relations in the United States. He introduced the term because there was no other word that embraced strictly racial groups, those set off by "alien national cultural traits," and those (such as Asians) in which biological and cultural features combined. Young wanted an inclusive term, for he regarded the problems and principles of group relations as being "remarkably similar," no matter what groups were involved. In other words, he agreed with Park that interaction between groups was more significant than their inborn qualities. His minority concept caught on quickly and weakened the older racialism, not merely by providing an alternative term for racial groups, but by redirecting attention toward the *placement* of groups in the social order as a whole.[18]

Young knew he was introducing a neologism of sorts, and he justified it briefly in his Preface. "To most of us," he wrote, "the word 'minority' has political connotations in that it calls to mind a political party which is not in power." Since he avoided this usage in his book, he did not think his "special application" would cause confusion.[19] But this was straining at a gnat! The real potential for confusion, and the explosive political connotations, derived from the use of the same word for years in connection with the "minorities problem" of Central Europe. This Young simply overlooked. But as his terminology entered into general circulation, the question naturally arose whether American minorities were like those of Europe and, if so, whether they might not be dangerous, since the latter were associated with extreme nationalism and the threat of Balkanization. Nazi exploitation of minority resentments, and the fifth column menace, magnified the peril in the later thirties. Hence, though discussion of American minorities usually stressed the need for tolerance and mutual understanding, there was also an undercurrent of uneasiness and latent hostility.[20]

In contrast to minority, "ethnocentrism" was a concept that aroused quite unambiguous feelings. It was a bad thing, and everyone was against it. But, if not ambiguous, this was at least puzzling, since ethnocentrism was the by-product—or was it the cause?—of the tight cultural cohesion that anthropologists seemed to regard as healthy in primitive groups. Indeed, the term had been introduced in William Graham Sumner's ethnological classic, *Folkways* (1906), among a cluster of coinages (including the perennial favorites, *in-group* and *out-group*) all of which referred to the phenomenon of intense group solidarity.[21] Why, then, had the concept become so repugnant by the 1930s? The article on ethnocentrism in the *Encyclopaedia of the Social Sciences* (1931) throws some light on the question.

The author, George P. Murdock, a leading anthropologist, quoted Sumner's definition of ethnocentrism as "that view of things in which our own group is the center of everything, and all others are scaled and rated with reference to it." This implied not simply approval for one's fellows, but fear, suspicion, and hostility toward outsiders and their ways. Ethnocentrism, Murdock declared, was a manifestation of the herd instinct; essentially irrational and primitive, it resembled the "group egotism" Wolfgang Koehler had observed among apes. Conceding that it had survival value, Murdock stressed its negative effects in causing friction between groups, and he linked it to such contemporary phenomena as chauvinistic nationalism, race prejudice, and lynchings. Such fruits proved how undesirable ethnocentrism was, and Murdock noted hopefully that education might diminish its force and promote "toleration, catholicity and cosmopolitanism" in its place. He concluded with just a touch of disciplinary smugness—not to call it professional ethnocentrism—by claiming that the social sciences were particularly well suited to promote intergroup understanding because they specialized in explaining cultural diversities.[22]

Well, perhaps. But these social scientists failed to address a question that seems obvious to us. To wit: If ethnocentrism is so destructive, does that not discredit ethnicity itself as a legitimate principle of group cohesion? Admittedly, it's a lot easier for us to ask the question today, since we have the term *ethnicity* and they didn't. But those who commented on these matters in the thirties were certainly acquainted with what we now call ethnicity. That was what they usually had in mind in talking about cultural groups, and the notion of cultural pluralism was based on the assumption that ethnic diversity was a good thing and should be preserved. But, to repeat, how could such diversity be a good thing if the ethnocentrism that was central to preserving ethnic distinctiveness was such a bad thing? Since the question was never put in those stark terms, it was, of course, never answered.[23] But neither was it ever made clear— and perhaps it was not even recognized—that the remedies recommended for ethnocentrism (i.e., tolerance and cosmopolitanism) would inevitably work against the preservation of ethnocultural diversity because they were bound to weaken the internal solidarity of groups and blur the boundaries between them.[24] Indeed, these remedies were actually prescriptions for assimilation, scandalous as this assertion might seem to our latter-day prophets of pluralism and ethnicity.

Robert Park would not have been scandalized by such an assertion.[25] Recall that the assimilation he described envisioned groups, formerly in conflict, getting along by mutual give-and-take. Assimilation presumed enough agreement on basic matters to permit a peaceable common life, but beyond that people were free to do as they pleased. The situation was best exemplified in the great cities, where all sorts of groups pursued their special interests or followed their distinctive ways. The urbane cosmopolitan might savor this spectacle of diversity. The ordinary citizen was more apt to ignore it, either from pure indifference or from a careless attitude of live and let live. Both reactions were acceptable forms of tolerance in the Parkian system.

While Park thus prized tolerance, he was not unduly scandalized by *prejudice*. This statement strikes the modern ear as scandalous in itself, because prejudice has come to be viewed as a pathological attitude, the mark of a diseased mind. But this psychological view of prejudice was hardly adumbrated before 1939, and it established itself firmly only in the next decade, the appearance in 1950 of *The Authoritarian Personality* being the decisive landmark. In the twenties and thirties, the concept of prejudice was very much in flux. Or, more accurately, it was gradually *becoming* a technical concept besides being an everyday term of ordinary discourse. It had not yet emerged as a generalized something-in-itself that could act as an independent variable. Thus one finds no entry under "Prejudice" in the *Encyclopaedia of the Social Sciences*, and the heading "Race Prejudice" yields only: "See Race Conflict."[26]

Which brings us back to Park and why it is possible to say, without slandering his memory, that he was not unduly scandalized by prejudice. Competition and conflict were built into his theory of intergroup relations. Feelings of antagonism between groups naturally accompanied these phases of the race relations cycle. Prejudice considered as a form of hostility, or a predisposition toward it, was quite intelligible within this theoretical framework. In 1924, Park suggested that prejudice might be understood as a disposition to maintain the "social distance" between groups and that it was most apt to be called into play when change threatened to disturb the relative statuses of groups. Four years later, he distinguished between racial prejudice and racial antipathy—the former being a conservative, but quite rational, resistance to status-threatening change; the latter referring to the quasi-instinctive repugnance aroused by perceived differences between races, especially those connected with the sense of smell.[27]

The distinction never caught on.[28] It is true that some commentators of the thirties stressed the role of prejudice in maintaining exploitive economic relationships, which was roughly in line with Park's view that prejudice was more a rational than an irrational phenomenon.[29] But the general drift of thinking was in the opposite direction. One reason for this was the belief that prejudice sprang from ethnocentrism and was therefore grounded in the same primitive herd instinct.[30] Ultimately more important was that prejudice was increasingly claimed as a subject appropriate for psychological, rather than sociological, analysis.

Park's concept of social distance played a role here. After being put into operation by Emory S. Bogardus, who devised a way to measure it on a friendliness-hostility scale, it became an important element in the early development of attitudinal surveys.[31] Among the social psychologists, prejudice was associated from the first with "stereotyping,"[32] and other less than fully rational operations, and, because of the survey techniques employed, the focus of interest shifted from relations between groups to the attitudinal makeup of individuals. Psychoanalytical perspectives came into prominence after 1940, especially as a result of the work of the refugee scholars linked to the strongly Freudian Frankfurt School, whose outlook shaped the research that went into *The Authoritarian Personality* and many other studies of prejudice in the postwar decade.[33] As a result of these developments, prejudice and discrimination came to be accounted for in terms of intolerant personality structure rather than conflicting group interests.

Besides establishing the psychoanalytical perspective, the refugee scholars reoriented the study of prejudice by giving much greater prominence to anti-Semitism. This was obviously the result of Hitlerism and the war. Perhaps the reader has wondered if we would ever get to the war. We are almost there; but first let me sum up the situation on the eve of its outbreak, adding a few descriptive generalizations about matters that cannot be discussed in detail.

The first generalization is that, despite all the conceptual ambiguities, there was growing evidence of sympathetic interest in minority groups and their place in American life.[34] The prevailing assumption in the late thirties was that national minorities were being assimilated rapidly but that the racial split was a more stubborn matter and might even have the permanence of a caste division.[35] Most observers regarded assimilation benignly, but many were also troubled by the decline of diversity. Almost no one contemplated the indefinite perpetuation of immigrant cultures without change, but forced Americanization programs were uniformly deprecated.[36] There was also a quickening of interest in second-generation immigrants, whose marginal status between two cultures was believed to entail much psychic distress. The popular Slovenian-born writer Louis Adamic spoke of a "psychological civil war" being waged in the souls of new Americans, and he campaigned for equality of emphasis on "Ellis Island and Plymouth Rock."[37]

Accompanying the sympathetic concern for minorities and cultural diversity was severe disapproval of nationalism, ethnocentrism, and prejudice.[38] The grotesque but frightening rise of Nazi racism not only reinforced this disapproval but made the whole matter more urgent because organized anti-Semitism was growing by leaps and bounds in the United States.[39] At the same time, the noisy antics of the German-American Bund and the pro-Fascist orientation of much of the Italian-American press raised questions about the commitment to American principles of some minority group members.[40] Worries of this sort led to systematic efforts to promote intergroup understanding and national unity on the basis of tolerance and mutual respect. In 1937 the Progressive Education Association set up the Commission on Intercultural Education; the next year the association made "Education for Democracy" the special theme of its work, a campaign that continued into the 1940s.[41]

Motives such as these prompted the U.S. Office of Education to sponsor a series of twenty-four radio broadcasts in 1938–39 dealing with ethnic groups and their contributions to American life. Entitled "Americans All . . . Immigrants All," the series was made available on records for use by schools and civic groups. It was a prototype of much that was to come in its insistence on the themes of tolerance and diversity in the name of "the preservation of the ideals, aims, and spirit for which our democracy stands."[42]

A few months after "Americans All" was aired, war erupted in Europe. It exerted a profound influence on the matters we have been discussing and on the general question of how ethnicity and ideology figured in the national identity. The first notable effect of the war was that, by making the need for national unity more compelling, it intensified the efforts that were already under way to cut down prejudice, improve intergroup relations, and promote greater tolerance of diversity.[43] With the very large exception of the removal of the Japanese-Americans from the West Coast, the government's record was good in this area. Despite uneasiness on the "minorities" issue, German-Americans and Italian-Americans did not become the objects of popular suspicion or official repression.[44] Internal tensions resulting from wartime population shifts, increasing Negro militance, and other social changes did cause serious concern, however, especially after outbursts of racial violence in Los Angeles and Detroit in 1943. Gunnar Myrdal's monumental *American Dilemma*, which came out the following year, underscored the need for action, and by the end of the war no fewer than 123 national organizations were active on the race relations front.[45]

The second and most crucial result of the war was that it stimulated a great ideological reawakening.[46] It was in the context of this revival that activities in the sphere of intergroup relations took place. Myrdal's volume is revealing here, for his principal theme was the contradiction between American racial practice and "the American Creed"—the system of values which Myrdal believed Americans were genuinely committed to. He predicted that the war would hasten the resolution of the dilemma posed by this contradiction because the ideological nature of the conflict made it increasingly glaring and intolerable.[47] He was quite right. But over and above the racial problem, what stands out in retrospect is that the monstrous contrast of Nazism galvanized Americans to a new appreciation of their own ideological values. By 1940, even the detached skeptic Carl Becker was sufficiently aroused to vindicate "Some Generalities That Still Glitter"; and he acknowledged in doing so that Hitlerism was what threw the merits of democracy into bold relief. At about the same time, Max Lerner emphasized the importance of knowing "what we believe in, what America stands for," and the need for "a new tough-mindedness in the service of a set of fervent convictions." The respected newsman Raymond Gram Swing chaired a Council for Democracy organized in the fall of 1940 the purpose of which was "to crystallize and instill in the minds of Americans the meaning, value, and workability of democracy as a dynamic, vital creed—just as Nazism, Fascism, and Communism are to their adherents." Symbolically, Bill of Rights day, marking the 150th anniversary of the ratification of the first ten amendments, fell on the first Sunday after Pearl Harbor and was commemorated by a radio drama written by Norman Corwin and entitled "We Hold These Truths."[48]

The ideological revival had a powerful, but somewhat paradoxical, effect on thinking about intergroup relations, ethnocultural affairs, and national identity. The substance of its message, and its practical effect, was strongly assimilationist in tendency. That is, what was actually being urged—indeed, required—was ideological consensus as the basis for harmonious intergroup relations. Yet the message was couched in the language of pluralism and diversity and gave rise to the confused impression that some sort of particularism either already was or should become the basis of the American identity. We must look into this more closely before turning to a third notable effect of the war, the stimulus it gave to explicit studies of the American character.

The statement of purposes adopted by the Common Council for American Unity illustrates several of these points. This group—the reorganized version of a society long interested in ethnic affairs—stated its first aim in these words: "To help create among the American people the unity and mutual understanding resulting from a common citizenship, a common belief in democracy and the ideals of liberty, the placing of the common good before the interests of any group, and the acceptance, in fact as well as in law, of all citizens, whatever their national or racial origins, as equal partners in American society."[49] The statement went on to call for appreciation of the contributions of each group, for tolerance of diversity, for the creation of an American culture "truly representative" of all the people, for an end to prejudice, and for assistance to immigrants who encountered difficulties in adjusting to American life.

Here ethnicity and pluralism of a sort are prominently featured, but it is clearly ideology—a shared commitment to certain universalistic values—that makes Americans what they are. Acceptance of all groups on an equal basis and tolerance for diversity are not in themselves constitutive of Americanism; rather, they derive as corollaries from "a common belief in democracy and the ideals of liberty." The role of the war in sensitizing the Common Council for American Unity to these matters was made explicit in the first issue of its journal, *Common Ground*, which began publication in the fall of 1940: "Never has it been more important that we become intelligently aware of the ground Americans of various strains have in common . . . that we reawaken the old American Dream, which in its powerful emphasis on the fundamental worth and dignity of every human being, can be a bond of unity no totalitarian attack can break."[50]

But because the "American Dream" was vague, or at least multivalent, and because totalitarianism meant forced uniformity—the barbarous *Gleichschaltung* of the Nazis—it was an easy transition to the view that diversity as such was the essence of the American system. The transition was made almost inevitable by the popularization of the term *cultural pluralism*. Horace Kallen coined this term in 1924, contrasting the ideal for which it stood to assimilation or Americanization.[51] In his original formulation, cultural pluralism prescribed the indefinite perpetuation of immigrant cultures and envisioned the United States as a federation of ethnic nationalities rather than being a country with a nationality of its own. While extreme and unrealistic, this was at least fairly clear. Kallen's concept attracted almost no attention for a number of years. By the time the expression came into general usage in World War II, the original meaning had faded from memory, and the notion of cultural pluralism became hopelessly amorphous.[52] In most cases, it signified merely that the speaker believed diversity was a good thing and always to be prized—unless, of course, it was "divisive," for divisiveness was somehow bad, even though pluralism was good. Yet the term also carried with it some of the portentous freight that the culture concept had accumulated in the thirties, and it seemed to be terribly important since it was often equated with democracy. Kallen himself claimed in 1943 that cultural pluralism defined "both the material and spiritual intent of the four freedoms."[53]

But the real mystification created by this kind of usage was that it effectively concealed the fact that so-called cultural pluralism was predicated upon, and made possible by, a high degree of consensus.[54] Ostensibly it repudiated assimilation; in fact, it embodied assimilation because it assumed that everyone agreed about basic matters that were actually distinctive to the United States, at least in their centrality to the life of the nation, rather than being universally held by the common consent of mankind. Illustrative of such matters are: acceptance of a democratic system of government; respect for the principle of equality before the law; recognition of the dignity of the individual and the rights of minorities; willingness to uphold free speech, freedom of religion, etcetera, and to abide by constitutional guidelines, as interpreted by the courts, in the settlement of disputes. Kallen came close to recognizing the importance of agreement on fundamentals when he wrote in 1956 that cultural pluralism was "grounded on and consummated in the American Idea."[55] But by then the mischief was done. The popularization of the term in the preceding decade created a situation in which we have been unable ever since to talk about ethnicity and national identity without dealing in terminology that confuses the analytical task rather than clarifying it.

The third aspect of wartime influence on thinking about American identity—the boom in national character studies—stands in definite opposition to the pluralism-and-diversity motif just discussed. It is the aspect of wartime influence most explicitly related to our subject because the expression *American identity* came to be used synonymously with *American character*. In contrast to the emphasis on diversity, however, national character studies stressed the presence of common traits—not to say uniformity—among Americans. Even so, we find that immigration the development of American character studies even more interesting is that our friends the cultural anthropologists pioneered in making the kind of scientific investigations that were said to redeem the study of national character from crude racialism and to elevate it above the level of more belletristic speculation.

This all came about, as Margaret Mead later explained, when she and other social scientists such as Ruth Benedict and Erik Erikson were called upon by agencies of the government to apply their skills to such questions as how civilian morale might be maintained, or what kind of propaganda was most likely to influence the enemy.[56] To answer these questions, the social scientists turned to the techniques of the culture-and-personality school of anthropologists, who combined psychological assumptions and ethnographic observation in trying to identify the "basic personality structure" impressed on individuals by the norms of the group to which they belonged. "By the end of the war," Mead wrote, "the term 'national character' was being applied to studies that used anthropological methods from the field of culture and personality, psychiatric models from psychoanalysis, statistical analysis of attitude tests, and experimental models of small-group process."[57]

Mead's *Coming of Age in Samoa* had been one of the earliest culture-and-personality studies; in the 1942 volume *And Keep Your Powder Dry*, she contributed the first of the new national character studies. Despite her claims to the contrary, there was little that was scientific about the book, a loose and rambling affair written in a style of impressionistic omniscience and intended as a contribution to the war effort. Yet the assertion that an American character really did exist carried much weight coming from an anthropologist intimately acquainted with half a dozen exotic cultures. Aside from her emphasis on parent-child relationships, there was nothing terribly novel about the Americans she described— moralistic, ambivalent about aggressiveness, oriented toward the future, and inclined to interpret success or failure as an index of personal merit. A certain ideological interest attaches to her statement that postwar planning would have to eliminate those "social behaviors which automatically preclude the building of a democratic world" and her (unsuccessful) effort to show that such a commitment did not violate the principle that cultural differences were all to be tolerated.[58] But what is more pertinent here is that Mead singled out an aspect of immigrant assimilation as having paradigmatic significance for understanding the American character.

References to immigration recur frequently throughout the book, and its most striking interpretive metaphor is developed in chapter 3,

"We Are All Third Generation." Mead's point was not so much that many Americans actually were the grandchildren of immigrants but that nearly all had the kind of "character structure" that resulted from growing up in a family of second-generation parents and third-generation children. She described the outlook produced by this familial setting in these words:

> Father is to be outdistanced and outmoded, but not because he is a strong representative of another culture . . . [and] not because he is a weak and ineffectual attempt to imitate a new culture; he did very well in his way, but he is out of date. He, like us, was moving forwards, moving away from something symbolized by his own ancestors, moving towards something symbolized by other people's ancestors. . . . [We need not rebel against Father. We merely need to pass him.] And to pass him it is only necessary to keep on going and to see that one buys a new model every year. Only if one slackens, loses one's interest in the race towards success, does one slip back.[59]

Mead's colleague in national character work, Geoffrey Gorer, pushed the analysis back a generation further. His book *The American People* (1948), begins with a chapter entitled "Europe and the Rejected Father," depicting the problem of the first-generation immigrant who must abandon much of his past in order to become an American. The immigrant, alas, cannot transform himself completely; the Old World still clings to him, and he becomes an object of scorn to his American-born offspring, who reject their father as role model and authority figure. "It is this break of continuity between the immigrants of the first generation and their children of the second generation which is . . . of major importance in the development of the modern American character," Gorer announced. He then proceeded to elaborate this insight along Freudian lines in explaining Americans' lack of respect for authority, the marginal family role of fathers as compared to mothers, and so on.[60]

For Mead and Gorer, then, the "ethnic"—that is, the immigrant or person of immigrant derivation—is a prototypically American figure, *not* because of any distinctiveness of cultural heritage but for exactly the opposite reason, namely, because he or she exhibits in extreme degree the "character structure" produced by the *American* experience of change, mobility, and loss of contact with the past. This interpretation differed drastically from what the celebration of diversity and cultural pluralism might lead one to anticipate about the American character, but it accorded nicely with the interpretation offered by Oscar Handlin in

The Uprooted, a work that shaped an entire generation's understanding of the immigrant experience. Published in 1951 when interest in the American character was near its zenith, the book began with the assertion that "the immigrants *were* American history," and the central metaphor of uprootedness was easily transferable to Americans generally. After all, Handlin explained, the "experience of displacement" was the crucial thing; having undergone it, the immigrants "were on the way toward being Americans almost before they stepped off the boat."[61]

Handlin did not fail to note that migration meant liberation and that uprootedness called forth new creative energies, but the tone of the book was elegiac: it was the immigrant's alienation that impressed itself upon the reader. Within a few years, people would be talking about this sort of thing in terms of identity problems and identity crises. Indeed, these terms have become so indispensable that it is almost a shock to note their absence from Handlin's conceptual armamentarium. But *identity* in this sense derives primarily from the work of Erik Erikson, and he was just beginning to put the term in circulation. His book *Childhood and Society*, published only a year before *The Uprooted*, marks its real introduction. It is also a landmark in American character studies since the chapter entitled "Reflections on the American Identity" was the first major publication to equate American character and American identity.[62]

Erikson did not give immigration the same prominence as did Mead or Gorer, but he mentioned it, and what he says is interesting: "We begin to conceptualize matters of identity at the very time in history when they become a problem. For we do so in a country which attempts to make a super-identity out of all the identities imported by its constituent immigrants." In an autobiographical account published twenty years later, Erikson, an immigrant himself, quoted this passage and added that the terms *identity* and *identity crises* seemed to grow out of "the experience of emigration, immigration, and Americanization." Identity problems, he said, "were in the mental baggage of generations of new Americans, who left their motherlands and fatherlands behind to merge their ancestral identities in the common one of the self-made man."[63]

All this put the ethnics right in the middle of things as far as understanding the American character was concerned. It also suggested, however, that they might be particularly prone to the characteristic defects of Americans. Uprooted as they were, alienated, unsure of their identities, were the ethnics also more anxious about status than other Americans? Were they more obsessively conformist? More rigid in their thinking? More intolerant? More ethnocentric?

This was potentially a matter for grave concern, since these qualities of mind and disposition marked "the authoritarian personality." And here we return momentarily to the study of prejudice. Recall that it was beginning to turn toward psychology in the later 1930s and soon became strongly psychoanalytical under the influence of refugee scholars from Europe. But with the key group—the Frankfurt School—psychology was closely interwoven with the critique of modern society, since their so-called dialectical method represented a fusion of Marxist and Freudian elements. This was the orientation within which the study of anti-Semitism was undertaken that resulted in the publication in 1950 of *The Authoritarian Personality*. Given this background, it is understandable that prejudice is implicitly interpreted there not simply as a psychological disorder but as a highly ideological kind of disorder produced by the stresses of an advanced capitalist society. Frustrated by the contradictions of bourgeois civilization, and seeking to "escape from freedom," typical prejudiced individuals were naturally disposed to authoritarianism—in short, they were potential Fascists and the degree of their susceptibility could be measured on the famous F-scale.[64]

No sooner had this diagnosis been offered than the eruption of McCarthyism seemed to confirm it. Here was a political movement exhibiting semihysterical rigidities in thinking and a total incapacity to tolerate ambiguities. It was clearly Fascist in tendency, according to the best qualified observers, and demanded explanation in terms of social psychology. Analysis of this kind was soon forthcoming, and was authoritatively summed up in the volume edited by Daniel Bell under the title *The New American Right* (1955). And who do we find singled out here as the population group most susceptible to the status anxieties and resentments mobilized by McCarthy? Ethnics, of course. The point was made by several of the contributors, most notably by Richard Hofstadter, whose concept of "pseudoconservatism" was taken straight from *The Authoritarian Personality*, and who likewise referred to Margaret Mead's "we-are-all-third-generation" view of the American character.[65]

A decade later, Hofstadter qualified much of his analysis, noting that some of his remarks about immigrant authoritarianism were "gratuitously speculative," and regretting in general his "excessive emphasis" on "the clinical side of the problem."[66] By that time interest in the American character had fallen off sharply, while ethnicity and the American ideology stood on the verge of the seismic transvaluation that would occur in the midst of the Vietnam War, whose effects on thinking about American identity were just the opposite of those of World War II. In the cultural crisis brought on by Vietnam, the racial upheaval, the counterculture, women's liberation, and Watergate, the ideological dimension of the American identity was severely discredited and ethnicity assumed greater positive salience than it had ever had before. But that is another story. What is now in order is a reflective look back at the epoch we have just sketched.

To summarize, then, the argument advanced in this essay is that World War II shaped the self-understanding of Americans, not only with respect to the nation's role in world affairs but also in regard to what we now call the American identity. Following upon a period in which ethnic factors had receded from prominence in discussions of national identity, the war gave unprecedented salience to the ideological dimension. For a whole generation, the question, What does it mean to be an American? was answered primarily by reference to "the values America stands for": democracy, freedom, equality, respect for individual dignity, and so on. Since these values were abstract and universal, American identity could not be linked exclusively with any single ethnic derivation. Persons of any race, color, religion, or national background could be, or become, Americans. Hence, "Americans all . . . Immigrants all!" Historically, however, particularistic ethnic loyalties ("racial," religious, nationality, etc.) had been obscurely, but intimately, interwoven with the commitment to universalistic political and social principles as ingredients in the citizen's sense of Americanness—and this was true of those comprising "old American stock" just as much as it was for the more recently arrived Americans. The war-related emphasis on ideology should therefore be understood as the accentuation of one element—albeit a crucially important one—in a preexisting mix of beliefs, attachments, and loyalties.

Prewar developments, both social and intellectual, reshaped the context within which wartime thinking on national identity took place. Our understanding of these complex shifts is dim, however, because they have been so little studied by historians. The key developments, in my view, were: the discrediting of racialism, both intellectually and morally; the growth of the social sciences and the increasing attention given to group life and group relations by anthropologists and sociologists; the emergence of the culture concept as the most influential analytical perspective employed in the human sciences; the sketching out by Robert Park of a contrasting conflict theory of assimilation; the growing recognition that the problems of minorities, and intergroup relations generally, constituted serious social issues; and the closely related beliefs that ethnocentrism and prejudice exacerbated these problems, while the promotion of tolerance for diversity would mitigate them.

Given the relative newness of social scientific study of human relations and the elusive nature of the phenomena being studied, it is not
surprising that the terms of discourse were sometimes vague and that
latent tensions existed among the concepts employed. Special difficulties
surrounded the culture concept and the relation in which it was thought
to stand with respect to other important concepts. Thus, though the
words were often used interchangeably, *acculturation* and *assimilation*
derived from different disciplinary approaches and reflected different
kinds of assumptions. When Everett and Helen Hughes spoke of the
terminologies of anthropology and sociology having "half-blended in a
grand confusion," *acculturation* and *assimilation* figured foremost
among the examples they gave.[67]

Besides the uncertainty as to whether these two widely employed
terms meant the same thing—or, if not, wherein they differed—there
was also a problem built into the relationships that were thought to exist
between the concepts of culture, tolerance for diversity, and ethnocentrism. In most discussions, tolerance for diversity was positively linked
with the culture concept, while ethnocentrism was looked upon as the
exact opposite of the cultural understanding preached by the exponents
of the Boas-Mead-Benedict viewpoint. These relationships, however, are
not logically entailed in the concepts themselves. As Robert Redfield
wrote in criticism of the doctrine of cultural relativity: "It cannot be
proved, from the proposition that [cultural] values are relative, that we
ought to respect all systems of values. We might just as well hate them
all."[68] And, in fact, tolerance for diversity comes close to being flatly
inconsistent with the culture concept as such if we understand it as
referring to a self-contained, cohesive ensemble of values and norms that
operates holistically in guiding people's lives. Shocking as it may seem,
it is ethnocentrism rather than tolerance that is implicit in the culture
concept considered in itself. Robert Park was therefore correct in observing that "when we speak of culture . . . we think of a small, familiar,
ethnocentric group."[69]

If the conventional wisdom on these matters was so illogical, the
question naturally arises as to how it ever got established. A general and
a more particular explanation can be suggested. The general explanation
is that the proponents of the culture concept were themselves sophisticated cosmopolitans; their personal values and outlook transcended the
relatively narrow boundaries of any single culture. This enabled them to
appreciate the good things to be found in the ways of life of the peoples
they studied as anthropologists and disposed them to urge their fellow
citizens still locked within the ethnocentric confines of their own tra-

ditional culture to be more broad-minded and tolerant. Considered in this light, it is not dealing in paradox to say that tolerance of diversity is a function of assimilation, since it comes easiest to those who have detached themselves somewhat from a specific familial, local, or ethnic tradition and have learned to get along with others whose background differs from their own.

But something besides cosmopolitanism was involved. A more particular motive impelling the Boasian anthropologists to leap from the empirical observation that cultural diversity existed to the ethical imperative that it should be tolerated, or even prized, derived from the fact that they were alienated from, and critical of, their own culture, which they regarded as notably repressive and intolerant. Mead, Benedict, and other leading disciples of Boas formed their views in the 1920s and were inevitably affected by the prevailing disaffection from American civilization felt by the intellectuals of the day. Edward Sapir openly avowed his preference for the "genuine" culture of American Indians over the "spurious" civilization of modern America; Margaret Mead contrasted the emotionally crippling effects of the Puritanical American family to the freer and healthier sexual codes and child-rearing patterns of the South Pacific; and the implications of Ruth Benedict's admiring report on the calm and noncompetitive communalism of Zuñi culture were equally clear.[70] In affirming that cultural diversity should teach Americans tolerance, these writers were really saying that other cultures were preferable in some respects and that modifications of American culture in those directions were desirable.

Ethnocentrism very likely came to be thought of as opposed to the cultural approach because chauvinistic nationalism was one of the features of American life in the 1920s that intellectuals found most repugnant. The relativistic tolerance of diversity preached by the anthropologists was clearly opposed to nativist prejudice, or to ethnocentrism understood in that sense, with the result that the built-in relationship between ethnocentrism and the close cultural cohesion prized by Benedict was lost to view.

The concept of assimilation was also affected by the intellectuals' reaction against chauvinism, but the situation in this case was much more complicated. Understood as the belief that many different elements would voluntarily fuse into one American people, assimilation was an ideal as old and honorable as the national motto, E pluribus unum. The term acquired negative connotations of intolerance in the twenties, however, through association with fanatical drives for hundred-percent Americanization. Besides these usages, sociologists employed it as a neutral scientific term: in Park and Burgess's famous *Introduction to the Science of Sociology*, assimilation designated the final stage in a natural process of social interaction discoverable anywhere in the world, not just in the United States. And Park later sketched out—but did not develop systematically—a version of assimilation that left much room for diversity within the framework of agreement on fundamentals. As a practical reality, assimilation made a "great leap forward" after the immigration restriction law of 1924 drastically cut back the influx of immigrants.[71] The advance of assimilation was regarded benignly, on the whole, since it reduced the likelihood of intergroup friction and enabled minority group members to participate more fully in American life. But there were also regretful murmurs about the decline of diversity entailed by assimilation. All of these crosscurrents (in addition to its uncertain relation to acculturation) made *assimilation* a somewhat problematic term by the eve of World War II.

Discussions of ethnicity, intergroup relations, and national identity were thus complex and burdened with submerged confusions when the war came along. It clarified some matters (by making democratic values the touchstone of American identity), but made others more baffling than ever (by formulating the demand for unity in terms of pluralism). The treatment in the second part of this article, despite being exploratory and incomplete, raises more issues than can be systematically analyzed here. I will therefore close, not with a conclusion, but with some retrospective observations.

First, it should be noted that the practical effect of wartime experience was assimilative in the sense that it enhanced national unity and a common sense of national belongingness. Commenting in 1952 on the war as an integrating force in American life, Robin Williams pointed out that its impact "galvanized into concerted action a wide range of previously discordant segments of the society." He added that service in the armed forces, no matter how unpleasant at the time, constituted for millions of young men and women a common experience "which in the end left a new residue of shared values and traditions." And two more recent investigators have stressed the effects of the war in broadening the horizons and hastening the assimilation of second- and third-generation immigrants in the Pittsburgh area.[72]

More directly relevant to our interest, of course, was the great ideological reawakening of the wartime years which simultaneously: 1) promoted national unity on the basis of value consensus; 2) exalted toleration and respect for cultural differences as the means of attaining intergroup harmony; and 3) stimulated curiosity about the way in which the American social and cultural environment shaped persons of all derivations toward a common national type.

One aspect of the ideological revival not mentioned earlier which deserves notice is the remarkable contrast it affords to the situation in the 1920s with respect to the attitudes held by intellectuals concerning American culture. In the twenties intellectuals were alienated. Americanization had assumed forms hateful to liberals such as Horace Kallen; anthropologists such as Sapir, Mead, and Benedict were repelled by the shallowness and discontinuity of American civilization. In World War II, however, intellectuals (including Kallen, Mead, and Benedict) rallied to the nation. Simple patriotism in a time of danger was no doubt a factor; but in the battle against Nazism, America stood for universalistic values dear to the intellectual community. As Carl Becker explained, the rational and humane values that democracy affirmed were "older and more universal than democracy" itself, to say nothing of their being older than the American nation.[73] Yet the United States based itself on these values, and in the war it was their foremost champion. Since intellectuals are the ones who articulate a people's understanding of itself, their identification with the national cause goes far toward accounting for the generally positive and strongly ideological interpretation of national identity that established itself during the wartime era.

But the very generality and abstractness of American values meant that they were subject to divergent interpretations that gave rise to divisive conflicts over whose was the correct understanding of true Americanism. An ironic instance was reported in a 1944 symposium entitled "Approaches to National Unity." The symposium was the fifth sponsored by a group called the Conference on Science, Philosophy, and Religion in Their Relation to the Democratic Way of Life, which had been formed in 1940; after its second meeting, "certain philosophical humanists, positivists, and naturalists" withdrew because they were offended by the religious pronouncements of various participants in the original group. Hence there was by 1943 a rival Conference on the Scientific Spirit and the Democratic Faith, whose members regarded as dangerously undemocratic the views of some of their erstwhile collaborators in the search for unity.[74]

Of the same sort, but more serious and long-lasting, were the issues of loyalty and un-Americanism that reached a climax in the McCarthy era. The nature of the Cold War contest with Communism, both on the world scene and as a potential source of internal subversion, heightened the ideological dimension, but the wartime stress on commitment to American values made it inevitable that fissures in national unity would open up along ideological rather than ethnic fault lines. Hence the national loyalty of Catholics was not called into question, despite the sharp controversies that broke out in the late forties between Catholics and Protestants, Jews, and secular liberals. On the contrary, it was because national identity was defined in ideological rather than ethnic terms that "to be an Irish Catholic became *prima facie* evidence of loyalty. Harvard men were to be checked; Fordham men would do the checking."[75]

There were thus very definite limits to the toleration of diversity in the ideological sphere. In the broader area of intergroup relations, however, tolerance was the touchstone, and to the degree that it was formulated in terms of cultural pluralism it became almost impossible to determine what the limits of tolerance were, if there were any, or, in many cases, even to determine what was being talked about. In battling against totalitarian enemies, it was understandable, as John Higham has written, that Americans should exalt the principle of diversity. But he goes on to say, "The astonishing fact about the emphatic endorsement of cultural pluralism in the postwar years was not its occurrence but rather a general unwillingness or inability to assess critically its relation to the apparently contrary imperative of national integration." As diversity was hailed, even while divisiveness was deplored, the "traditions of pluralism and assimilation blurred into a rosy haze."[76]

To make matters worse, a group of political scientists who analyzed American society in terms of interest groups and crosscutting pressures became known as "pluralists."[77] The relationship of this perspective to that of cultural pluralism was never clarified and possibly not even adverted to at the time. But the growing tendency to speak of pluralism without the modifier *cultural* made the term even more generalized and abstract, as did usages such as *pluralistic*, and *pluralistically*. Also, cultural pluralism itself can be appealed to by persons who have significantly different goals in mind. What might be called a cosmopolitan version of cultural pluralism appeals to persons relatively detached from any specific ethnic tradition as a general vision of a society made up of diverse groups, all interacting harmoniously without losing their distinctiveness. But cultural pluralism can equally well stand for a highly particularistic vision when appealed to by persons who care little about the overall design of American society but are passionately determined to preserve their (often quite "ethnocentric") group traditions.[78]

In short, cultural pluralism in all its ambiguities and complexities is the crucial legacy of World War II with respect to American identity. The frequency with which it is invoked today testifies to its continuing relevance to our present efforts to define what it means to be an American.

A great deal more study is needed to clarify the circumstances of its popularization in the wartime era and the vicissitudes of its conceptual evolution since then.

NOTES

Source: Review of Politics, 43 (April 1981), 483–518. Reprinted by permission of the publisher.

a. A more recent article on one aspect of this topic is Richard W. Steele, "The War on Intolerance: The Reformulation of American Nationalism, 1939–1941," *Journal of American Ethnic History*, 9 (Fall 1989), 9–35.

b. Rob Kroes, ed., *The American Identity: Fusion and Fragmentation* (Amsterdam, 1980).

1. John M. Blum, *V Was for Victory: Politics and American Culture during World War II* (New York, 1976); Richard Polenberg, *War and Society: The United States, 1941–1945* (Philadelphia, 1972); Polenberg, *One Nation Divisible: Class, Race, and Ethnicity in the United States since 1938* (New York, 1980), esp. chaps. 1–3. (My citations are to the Penguin paperback edition of this work, which comprises vol. 7 of the Pelican History of the United States [Harmondsworth, 1980]). Cf. also Jim F. Heath, "Domestic America during World War II: Research Opportunities for Historians," *Journal of American History*, 58 (1971), 384–414.

2. The following paragraphs are based on my article, "American Identity and Americanization," in Stephan Thernstrom, Ann Orlov, and Oscar Handlin, eds. *Harvard Encyclopedia of American Ethnic Groups* (Cambridge, Mass., 1980), 31–58. The present essay is an expansion of matters discussed in that article, esp. 47–50, and makes use of some of the same evidence and formulations found there.

3. John Higham, *Strangers in the Land: Patterns of American Nativism, 1860–1925* (New Brunswick, N.J., 1955), chap. 11, describes both the passage of the national origins law and the rapid ebbing of nativist sentiment thereafter. Allan J. Lichtman, *Prejudice and the Old Politics: The Presidential Election of 1928* (Chapel Hill, N.C., 1979), the most recent analysis of the 1928 election, stresses the religious issue above all other ethnocultural factors.

4. It is worth nothing that in Melville J. Herskovits's brief sketch of Boas's work the principal substantive chapters are headed: "Man, the Biological Organism,"; "Man, the Culture-Building Animal"; and "Man, the Creator." Cf. Herskovits, *Franz Boas* (New York, 1953). The best discussion of Boas's career and influence is George W. Stocking, Jr., *Race, Culture, and Evolution: Essays in the History of Anthropology* (New York, 1968), esp. chaps. 7–11.

5. The social scientists' abandonment of racism in the 1920s is strikingly summed up in Stanley Coben, "The Assault on Victorianism in the Twentieth Century," *American Quarterly*, 27 (December 1975), 610–14. Cf. also Thomas F. Gossett, *Race: The History of an Idea in America* (Dallas, Tex., 1963), 416–30.

6. Freda Kirchwey, review of Franz Boas, *Anthropology and Modern Life*, in *Nation*, 127 (December 19, 1928), 689.

7. Margaret Mead, *Coming of Age in Samoa* (New York, 1928). The work is subtitled *A Psychological Study of Primitive Youth for Western Civilisation*. In the Preface to a reprint of the book (New York, 1973), Mead writes: "When this book was written, the very idea of culture was new to the literate world. The idea that our every

thought and movement was a product not of race, not of instinct, but derived from the society within which an individual was reared, was new and unfamiliar." Stocking observes, incidentally, that "it was not Boas but his students who were largely responsible for the elaboration and development of the anthropological concept [of culture]. Stocking, *Race, Culture, and Evolution*, 231.

8. Ruth Benedict, *Patterns of Culture* "Sentry Edition" (Boston, 1959 [orig. ed. 1934]). In a preface, Margaret Mead comments on its influence in popularizing the anthropological notion of culture. See chaps. 2 and 3 for cultural diversity and cultural integration; chaps. 7 and 8 for applications to contemporary America and the need for tolerance.

9. Stuart Chase, *The Proper Study of Mankind* (New York, 1948), 50, 59–86, 275–76, 289–90; quotation from 59. The essays collected in Louis Schneider and Charles Bonjean, eds., *The Idea of Culture in the Social Sciences* (Cambridge, 1973) are extremely informative. For examples of emphasis on the culture concept in the 1930s, see Otto Klineberg, *Race Differences* (New York, 1935), pt. 3, "The Cultural Approach"; Donald Young, *Research Memorandum on Minority Peoples in the Depression* (New York, 1937), 220–21.

10. Caroline F. Ware, ed., *The Cultural Approach to History* (New York, 1940); quotation from 15; 81 for R. A. Billington's comment about the "unpleasant conclusion" concerning nativism. Cf. also the difference between Carlton C. Qualey's view of "The Transitional Character of Nationality Group Culture," 82–84, and the "Summary of the Discussion," by Caroline Ware and others, 86–89.

11. Everett C. Hughes and Helen M. Hughes, *Where Peoples Meet* (Glencoe, Ill., 1952), 30–31. For the overlapping of the anthropological and the older humanist senses of the word *culture*, see Stocking, *Race, Culture, and Evolution*, 69–90, 195–233.

12. John Madge, *The Origins of Scientific Sociology* (New York, 1962), chap. 3.

13. Melville J. Herskovits, *Acculturation* (New York, 1938), esp. 22–23, 49–50, 51. Walter Goldschmidt recently began an article by stating, "The natural habitat of the cultural anthropologist is the world of native, preliterate, tribal, and peasant communities." Further on he adds that the two distinctive marks of the anthropological approach, cultural relativism (meaning the need to understand each culture in its own terms) and holism, both had "their source in that vanishing environment of ethnographic fieldwork." Goldschmidt, "Should the Cultural Anthropologist Be Placed on the Endangered Species List?" in Harry R. Garvin, ed., *New Dimensions in the Humanities and Social Sciences* (Lewisburg, Pa., 1977), 15, 19.

14. The best treatment of Park is Fred H. Matthews, *Quest for an American Sociology: Robert E. Park and the Chicago School* (Montreal, 1977). See also the discussion of Park in Leon Bramson, *The Political Context of Sociology* (Princeton, N.J., 1961); and Robert E. L. Faris, *Chicago Sociology 1920–1932* (Chicago, 1967). Robert E. Park, *Race and Culture* (Glencoe, Ill., 1950), collects twenty-nine of Park's papers, published from the teens to the 1940s. It also contains a very brief autobiographical note.

15. This follows Matthews, *Quest for an American Sociology*, 160–62, who refers to Park's model as "the interaction cycle, or cycle of group interaction." Park used a slightly different set of labels ("contacts, competition, accommodation and eventual assimilation") in a 1926 paper, "Our Racial Frontier on the Pacific," in which he spoke explicitly of "The Race Relations Cycle." See Park, *Race and Culture*, 149–51. The sequence of competition, conflict, accommodation, and assimilation as presented in Matthews is taken from chaps. 8–11, which have those titles, of Robert E. Park and Ernest W. Burgess, *Introduction to the Science of Sociology*, 2d ed. (Chicago, 1924).

For later critiques of the race relations cycle, see Stanford M. Lyman, "The Race Relations Cycle of Robert E. Park," *Pacific Sociological Review,* 11 (Spring 1968), 16–22; L. Paul Metzger, "American Sociology and Black Assimilation: Conflicting Perspective," *American Journal of Sociology,* 76 (1970–71), 627–47; and Ernest A. T. Barth and Donald L. Noel, "Conceptual Frameworks for the Analysis of Race Relations: An Evaluation," *Social Forces,* 50 (March 1972), 333–48, as reprinted in Thomas F. Pettigrew, ed., *The Sociology of Race Relations; Reflection and Reform* (New York, 1980), 418–22.

16. Matthews, *Quest for an American Sociology,* 167–69. See also Park's article, "Assimilation, Social" in Edwin R. A. Seligman and Alvin Johnson, eds., *Encyclopaedia of the Social Sciences* 15 vols. (New York, 1930–35), 2:281–83, which is not included in the essays collected in *Race and Culture,* but which Matthews calls "Park's most concentrated theoretical discussion of assimilation."

17. In an important essay contrasting "genuine" and "spurious" versions of culture, Edward Sapir in 1924 wrote that a genuine culture was "inherently harmonious, balanced, self-satisfactory," and "not a spiritual hybrid of contradictory patches." Such a culture could not tolerate the thousand "spiritual maladjustments" to be found in the spurious modern American culture. Sapir preferred the "well-rounded life of the average participant in the civilization of a typical American Indian tribe," before that culture was destroyed by contact with white civilization. Sapir, "Culture, Genuine and Spurious," *American Journal of Sociology,* 29 (1924), 410, 416. Coben, "Assault on Victorianism," 607–8, discusses this article.

18. Donald Young, *American Minority Peoples: A Study in Racial and Cultural Conflicts in the United States* (New York, 1932), xii–xiii. The classical formulation of the concept of the minority group is Louis Wirth, "The Problem of Minority Groups," in Ralph Linton, ed., *The Science of Man in the World Crisis* (New York, 1945), 347–72. Cf. also Peter I. Rose, *The Subject Is Race* (New York, 1968), 69–71; E. B. Reuter, "Racial Theory," *American Journal of Sociology,* 50 (May 1943), 452–61; E. F. Frazier, "Sociological Theory and Race Relations," *American Sociological Review,* 12 (June 1947), 265–71.

19. Young, *American Minority Peoples,* xiii–xiv.

20. Max H. Boehm, "Minorities, National," in Seligman and Johnson, *Encyclopaedia of the Social Sciences,* 10:518–25 deals with the European kind of minorities and does not mention American minorities. Cf. also Donald R. Taft, "Problems Arising from Minorities," in Francis J. Brown and Joseph S. Roucek, eds., *Our Racial and National Minorities* (New York, 1937), 18–32; Roucek, "Minorities—a Basis of the Refugee Problem," *Annals,* 203 (May 1939), 1–17; Roucek, editorial, *Journal of Educational Sociology,* 12 (April 1939), 449–50; Stewart G. Cole, "Europe's Conflict of Cultures," in Robert M. MacIver, ed., *Group Relations and Group Antagonisms* (New York, 1944), 121–56; Oscar I. Janowsky, "Ethnic and Cultural Minorities" in ibid., 157–70; George Britt, *The Fifth Column Is Here* (New York, 1940); Polenberg, *One Nation Divisible,* 42–45. Gunnar Myrdal, *An American Dilemma* (1944; New York, 1962), 50, notes the difference between minorities in the United States and Europe: "The minority peoples of the United States are fighting for status within the larger society; the minorities of Europe are mainly fighting for independence from it."

21. William Graham Sumner, *Folkways* (Boston, 1906), 12ff.

22. Seligman and Johnson, *Encyclopaedia of the Social Sciences,* 5:612–13. For Murdock's relation to Sumner, and some differences between his approach to anthropology and that of the Boasian school, see George P. Murdock, ed., *Studies in the Science of Society* (New Haven, Conn., 1937), xiii–xv.

23. The issue was just below the surface in some discussions. In explaining the need to go beyond tolerance to sharing values, Rachel Davis-DuBois warns, "we must not allow people to be so proud of their own culture that they can see no good in that of others. This disease the sociologists call ethnocentrism. We can avoid this by putting emphasis on . . . sharing our values so that new values will emerge which will have in them the best of those which have gone into the merging. . . . The term 'cultural democracy' will describe this process—a thinking, feeling and acting together, on a basis of equality." R. Davis-Dubois, "Sharing Cultural Values," *Journal of Educational Sociology*, 12 (April 1939), 482–86. Along the same lines, "we misconceive group prejudice when we think of it as primarily a prejudice *against* some one or more particular groups: as anti-Semitism, anti-Catholicism, anti-Anything-in-particular. It is instead at bottom a prejudice *in favor* of 'My Own Group' as against *all* others, 'pro-us' prejudice eternal, live, and waiting, ready to be focussed and intensified against *Any* Other Group." Karl N. Llewellyn, "Group Prejudice and Social Education," in R. M. MacIver, ed., *Civilization and Group Relationships* (New York, 1945), 13 (italics in original).

24. This point was implicit in Billington's observation that nativists did more to make immigrants preserve their cultural heritage than disciples of the immigrant-gifts approach did. Cf. Ware, *Cultural Approach*, 81.

25. The following discussion owes much to Matthews, *Quest for an American Sociology*, 167–74.

26. I have found no historical study of the development of the concept of prejudice. John Higham's "Anti-Semitism and American Culture," in his *Send These to Me: Jews and Other Immigrants in Urban America* (New York, 1975), 174–95, contains relevant material. Higham states that in the nineteenth century " 'Prejudice' was defined as a prepossession *for or against* anything, formed without due examination of the facts. No one supposed that it might be reified . . . [or] that it referred distinctively to negative judgments of minorities and therefore connoted a certain kind of exclusionist mentality" (176). Gordon W. Allport still used *prejudice* in this loose and generalized way in an article written in 1935 for a handbook of social psychology. The article dealt with "Attitudes," and, in the section headed "Prejudgment and Prejudice," Allport wrote that a preexisting attitude so strong that it "seriously distorts perception and judgment . . . [is called] a *stereotype*, a *prejudice*, or sometimes, more loosely, . . . a *logic-tight compartment*." Allport illustrated the workings of prejudice by reference to experiments in which respondents were asked to rate the literary quality of selected passages, all of which were in fact written by the same author, although they were labeled as being the work of different authors. Prejudice was revealed by the consistency with which respondents rated passages supposedly written by authors they admired more highly than other passages alleged to be works of lesser-known writers. Other experimental results cited by Allport dealt with preferential ranking of racial and national groups, but it is clear that Allport did not regard *prejudice* as referring primarily to negative judgments of minorities or as connoting what Higham calls an "exclusionist mentality." Cf. Gordon W. Allport, "Attitudes," in Carl A. Murchison, ed., *Handbook of Social Psychology* (1935; New York, 1967), 814–16. Myrdal, *American Dilemma*, 52n., 1141, expresses his dissatisfaction with the conceptual fuzziness of the term *prejudice*. Eugene L. Horowitz's study " 'Race' Attitudes," undertaken as a part of the Myrdal study and published in Otto Klineberg, ed., *Characteristics of the American Negro* (New York, 1944), 138–247, provides evidence of a marked shift in the understanding of prejudice around 1940. The term hardly appears at all in the body of Horowitz's study, which is a descriptive summary of numerous investigations

of racial attitudes in children and other population groups. When he turns to "Suggested Hypotheses for Future Research," however, prejudice suddenly becomes the major conceptual category, although no effort whatever is made to relate the heavily psychological hypotheses concerning the origins of prejudice to the evidence adduced in the previously reviewed studies of racial attitudes. Horowitz's study also reveals, incidentally, the degree of uncertainty still prevailing around 1940 as to the content of the concept of attitude. On this general problem, see Donald Fleming, "Attitude: The History of a Concept," *Perspectives in American History*, 1 (1967), 287–365.

27. Cf. Park, "The Concept of Social Distance" (1924), 256–60, and "The Bases of Race Prejudice" (1928), 230–43, both in his *Race and Culture*.

28. Emory S. Bogardus followed the distinction slavishly in his *Immigration and Race Attitudes* (Boston, 1928), 30ff., a book dedicated to Robert Park. Eight years later, however, Donald R. Taft conflated racial antipathies with race prejudice, specifically including "Olfactory, Tactual, Gustatory, and Visual Experiences" among the "Types of Experiences Leading to Race Prejudice." See Taft, *Human Migration* (New York, 1936), 332.

29. Cf. Richard Weiss, "Ethnicity and Reform: Minorities and the Ambience of the Depression Years," *Journal of American History*, 66 (December, 1979), 574–75.

30. Everett R. Clinchy, "Prejudice and Minority Groups," in Brown and Roucek, *Our Racial and National Minorities*, 538–39.

31. Fleming, "Attitude," 342ff.; John Harding et al., "Prejudice and Ethnic Relations," in Gardner Lindzey, ed., *Handbook of Social Psychology*, 2 vols. (Cambridge, Mass., 1954), 2:1021.

32. The concept of the stereotype was introduced in Walter Lippman, *Public Opinion* (New York, 1922).

33. Fleming, "Attitude," 351ff.; Harding et al., "Prejudice," 1021; Martin Jay, *The Dialectical Imagination. A History of the Frankfurt School and the Institute of Social Research, 1923–1950* (Boston, 1973), chap. 7. Horowitz's "Suggested Hypotheses" (see above, n. 26) is also relevant in this context. Arnold M. Rose, "The Causes of Prejudice," in Francis E. Merrill et al., *Social Problems* (New York, 1950), 402–25 is an excellent review of the literature on the eve of the publication of *The Authoritarian Personality*.

34. Weiss, "Ethnicity and Reform" provides evidence of sympathetic interest in minorities in the late 1930s. It is also interesting that immigration historiography reached a new level of sophistication and visibility with the publication of a cluster of outstanding works between 1938 and 1941: Ray Allen Billington, *The Protestant Crusade, 1800–1860. A Study of the Origins of American Nativism* (New York, 1938); Carl Wittke. *We Who Built America. The Saga of the Immigrant* (New York, 1939); Marcus L. Hansen. *The Atlantic Migration 1607–1860* (Cambridge, Mass., 1940); Hansen, *The Immigrant in American History* (Cambridge, Mass., 1940); Theodore Blegen, *The Norwegian Immigration to America: The American Transition* (Northfield, Minn., 1940); Oscar Handlin, *Boston's Immigrants; A Study in Acculturation* (Cambridge, Mass., 1941).

35. The prevailing view on assimilation was well presented in William C. Smith's excellent synthesis of the existing sociological and historical literature, *Americans in the Making: The Natural History of the Assimilation of Immigrants* (New York, 1939). The assumption of rapid and nearly complete assimilation of immigrants is also reflected in Ruth Benedict's curious essay, "Race Problems in America," *Annals*, 216 (July 1941), 73–78. Myrdal, *American Dilemma*, 51–53 comments on the difference in expectation about the assimilation of Negroes as contrasted to persons of immigrant

stock. John Dollard's *Caste and Class in a Southern Town* (New York, 1937) gave new prominence to the concept of caste in racial matters; see also Allison Davis et al., *Deep South: A Social Anthropological Study of Caste and Class* (Chicago, 1941).

36. A particularly authoritative statement of concern over the decline of diversity may be found in: National Resources Commission, *Problems of a Changing Population* (Washington, D.C., 1938), 249–51, which reflects a strong Deweyan influence. For the other points see, for example, Francis J. Brown, "Minority Groups and Their Communities," in Brown and Roucek, *Our Racial and National Minorities*, 570–72; and more generally, James H. Powell, "The Concept of Cultural Pluralism in American Social Thought, 1915–1965" (Ph. D. diss., University of Notre Dame, 1971), 79ff., esp. 106–12.

37. Nicholas V. Montalto, "The Forgotten Dream: A History of the Intercultural Education Movement, 1924–1941" (Ph. D. diss., University of Minnesota, 1978), chap. 2 is a useful review of the concern over the second-generation problem which discusses Adamic, 67–73. Adamic is also discussed in Daniel E. Weinberg, "The Foreign Language Information Service and the Foreign Born, 1918–1939: A Case Study of Cultural Assimilation Viewed as a Problem in Social Technology" (Ph. D. diss., University of Minnesota, 1973), 158–62, 172–73, 177. Cf. also Weiss, "Ethnicity and Reform," 579–82; Rudolph Vecoli, "Louis Adamic and the Contemporary Search for Roots," *Ethnic Studies*, 2 (1978), 29–35. Adamic's concerns in the late 1930s are best approached through his books *My America, 1928–1938* (New York, 1938), esp. 185–259, and *From Many Lands* (New York, 1940), esp. 291–301.

38. In 1926, Carlton J. H. Hayes, the principal authority on nationalism, concluded that it was "the indivisible source of grave abuses and evils," such as a spirit of exclusiveness and narrowness, a tendency toward social uniformity, a tendency to increase the docility of the masses, an unhealthy concentration on war, jingoism, imperialism, and intolerance. Hayes predicted that nationalism, if not mitigated, would be "an unqualified curse to future generations." Cf. Hayes, *Essays on Nationalism* (New York, 1926), 257–60.

39. Donald S. Strong reported in 1941 that of 119 anti-Semitic organizations in the United States at that time, all but five had been formed since 1933. Cited in Rose, "Causes of Prejudice," 416. Myrdal, *American Dilemma*, 53, 1186n. notes the growth of anti-Semitism in the late thirties. As a newcomer to the United States in 1938, Myrdal felt that anti-Semitism "probably was somewhat stronger than in Germany before the Nazi regime." The belief that anti-Semitism was growing was disputed on the basis of public opinion surveys by Otto Klineberg, "Race Prejudice and the War," *Annals*, 223 (September 1942), 191–93. Cf. also Higham, *Send These to Me*, 184–93; Polenberg, *One Nation Divisible*, 40–42.

40. For the Bund, see Frederick Luebke, "The Germans," in John Higham, ed., *Ethnic Leadership in America* (Baltimore, Md., 1978), 83–85; Sander Diamond, *The Nazi Movement in the United States, 1924–1941* (Ithaca, N.Y., 1974). For the Italians, see John P. Diggins, *Mussolini and Fascism: The View from America* (Princeton, N.J., 1972), 340–52. Diggins states that "until the summer of 1940 there was no question that Italian-Americans in general were solidly behind Mussolini" (349).

41. Patricia A. Graham, *Progressive Education: From Arcady to Academe* (New York, 1967), 81–84, 93, 105–8. Cf. also Montalto, "Forgotten Dream."

42. Montalto, "Forgotten Dream," chap. 6 provides interesting details on the Americans All" project. J. Morris Jones, *Americans All . . . Immigrants All. A Handbook for Listeners* (Washington, D.C., Federal Radio Education Committee, n.d.), and Jones, *Americans All . . . Immigrants All. A Manual* (Washington, D.C. Federal Radio Edu-

cation Committee, n.d.) provide commentary and suggestions for using the recordings. For somewhat similar hortatory collections, see *The Atlantic Presents We Americans* (Boston, 1939); Alain Locke and Bernhard J. Stern, eds., *When Peoples Meet: A Study of Race and Culture Contacts*, rev. ed. (New York, 1945 [orig. 1942]); ed. Arnold Herrick and Herbert Askwith, eds., *This Way to Unity: For the Promotion of Good Will and Teamwork among Racial, Religious, and National Groups* (New York, 1945).

43. From the viewpoint of intellectual content, the most substantive effort was a series of lectures sponsored at Columbia University by the Institute for Religious Studies beginning in 1942 and continuing for several years thereafter. The Columbia sociologist Robert M. MacIver was the leading figure in the series and the editor of volumes that it produced: *Group Relations and Group Antagonisms* (New York, 1944); *Civilization and Group Relationships* (New York, 1945); *Unity and Difference in American Life* (New York, 1947); and *Discrimination and National Welfare* (New York, 1949). MacIver's book *The More Perfect Union: A Program for the Control of Inter-Group Discrimination in the United States* (New York, 1948) grew out of his concern with intergroup relations. Cf. also Higham, *Send These to Me*, 218ff.

44. Cf. Everett V. Stonequist, "The Restricted Citizen," *Annals*, 223 (September 1942), 149–56. This volume of the *Annals* is devoted to "Minority Peoples in a Nation at War." See also Polenberg, *One Nation Divisible*, 59–60, 78–85.

45. Joseph S. Roucek, "Group Discrimination and Culture Clash," in MacIver, *Civilization and Group Relationships*, 39–69 is an informed discussion of wartime tensions and their implications; Robin M. Williams, Jr., *The Reduction of Intergroup Tensions* (New York, 1947), 7 gives the figure of 123 national organizations. For more general accounts see Neil A. Wynn, "The Impact of the Second World War on the American Negro," *Journal of Contemporary History*, 6 (May 1971), 42–54; Harvard Sitkoff, "Racial Militancy and Interracial Violence in the Second World War," *Journal of American History*, 58 (December 1971), 661–81; Polenberg, *One Nation Divisible*, 69–78.

46. *Common Ground*, 1 (Spring 1941), 133 lists the following books as timely treatments of "America's current 'urgency' and her future": George S. Counts, *The Prospects of American Democracy* (New York, 1938); Max Lerner, *It Is Later Than You Think: The Need for a Militant Democracy* (New York, 1938); Edward L. Bernays, *Speak Up for Democracy* (New York, 1940); John Chamberlain, *The American Stakes* (Philadelphia, 1940).

47. Myrdal, *American Dilemma*, esp. chap. 45, "America Again at the Crossroads." Robert E. Park discussed the influence of the war and the ideological issue on race relations in his essay "Race Ideologies," in William F. Ogburn, ed., *American Society in Wartime* (Chicago, 1943), 165–83; reprinted in Park, *Race and Culture*, 301–15. Writing to a former student after the Detroit race riot of 1943, Park said he was less concerned with stopping race riots than with stopping the fact that Negroes always lost them. Then he added, "I am in favor of winning the present war and this [racial conflict] seems to be merely one aspect of the war—war on the home front" (quoted in Matthews, *Quest for an American Sociology*, 189).

48. Carl Becker, "Some Generalities That Still Glitter," *Yale Review*, 29 (June 1940), 649–67; Max Lerner, quoted in Louis Adamic, "This Crisis Is an Opportunity," *Common Ground*, 1 (Autumn 1940), 73; Swing's Council for Democracy statement quoted in ibid., 1 (Winter 1941), 79; for Bill of Rights Day, see *New York Times Magazine*, December 14, 1941; and Polenberg, *One Nation Divisible*, 53. Alain Locke pointed out in 1941 that "democracy has encountered a fighting antithesis, and has awakened from considerable lethargy and decadence to a sharpened realization of its

own basic values." Locke, "Pluralism and Intellectual Democracy," in Conference on Science, Philosophy and Religion in Their Relation to the Democratic Way of Life, Second Symposium, *Science, Philosophy and Religion* (New York, 1942), 206. His point is repeated almost verbatim in Locke and Stern, *When Peoples Meet*, 735.

49. The statement of purposes was carried on the inside cover of the magazine published by the council, *Common Ground*. Weinberg, "Foreign Language Information Service" traces the history of the Common Council's predecessor group from 1918 to 1939; see 172–77 for the reorganization that brought the Common Council into existence.

50. *Common Ground*, 1 (Fall 1940), 103. The sociologist James G. Leyburn likewise stressed the role of the war in bringing home a realization of the ideological nature of American identity. Discussing ethnicity and Americanization, he stated: "What really stirs our hearts and minds is our set of ideals and values. Often we do not realize explicitly what these are until they are threatened. But in the present crisis we know with our inmost being how dear to us are our American ideals of democracy, decency, and individual freedom, our belief in free speech and in free elections and in the right to worship as we choose, our family mores, our religious faith, our respect for certain symbols which convey these ideals to our attention (the American flag, for example)." Leyburn, "The Problem of Ethnic and National Impact from a Sociological Point of View," in David F. Bowers, ed., *Foreign Influences in American Life* (Princeton, N.J., 1944), 60.

51. On Kallen and cultural pluralism, see Powell, "The Concept of Cultural Pluralism," chap. 1; Higham, *Send These to Me*, chap. 10; Milton M. Gordon, *Assimilation in American Life* (New York, 1964), chap. 6; and Gleason, "American Identity and Americanization," 43–46.

52. Higham, *Send These to Me*, 220–21; Powell, "Concept of Cultural Pluralism," chap. 4; Weiss, "Ethnicity and Reform," 578–82.

53. Kallen, " 'E Pluribus Unum' and the Cultures of Democracy," *Journal of Educational Sociology*, 16 (February 1943), 329–32.

54. Higham brings this out in his brilliant essay on pluralism in *Send These to Me*, 197–98, 211–13, 230.

55. Kallen, *Cultural Pluralism and the American Idea* (Philadelphia, 1956), 97. Cf. Gleason, "American Identity and Americanization," 50.

56. The literature on national character is very large, but two essays by Margaret Mead are especially useful in pinning down the connection with wartime needs. See Mead, "The Study of National Character," in Daniel Lerner and Harold D. Lasswell, eds., *The Policy Sciences* (Stanford, Calif., 1951), 79–85; Mead, "National Character and the Science of Anthropology," in Seymour M. Lipset and Leo Lowenthal, eds., *Culture and Social Character* (New York, 1961), 15–26. Thomas L. Hartshorne, *The Distorted Image: Changing Conceptions of the American Character since Turner* (Cleveland, Ohio, 1968), chaps. 6–7 sets the new approach to national character studies in context. Revaluations of the late 1960s, when the concept had lost most of its attractiveness, may be found in E. Adamson Hoebel, "Anthropological Perspectives on National Character," *Annals*, 370 (March 1967), 1–7; Daniel Bell, "National Character Revisited: A Proposal for Renegotiating the Concept," in Edward Norbeck et al., eds., *The Study of Personality* (New York, 1968), 103–20; David E. Stannard, "American Historians and the Idea of National Character," *American Quarterly*, 23 (May 1971), 202–20.

57. Mead, "National Character and the Science of Anthropology," 18. Cf. also Margaret Mead and Rhoda Metraux, eds., *The Study of Culture at a Distance* (Chicago,

1953); and Morroe Berger, " 'Understanding National Character'—and War," *Commentary*, 11 (April 1951), 375–86.

58. Margaret Mead, *And Keep Your Powder Dry: An Anthropologist Looks at America* (New York, 1942), 239ff., comprises Mead's unsuccessful effort to reconcile cultural relativism with a commitment to the imperatives of democratic ideology. She resorted to the analogy of disease, arguing that postwar reconstruction should treat institutions that breed Fascism as "dangerous viruses," while the individuals infected by these institutions should be regarded as "carriers of fatal social diseases" (245). Quotation in text from 255.

59. Ibid., 52–53.

60. Geoffrey Gorer, *The American People: A Study in National Character* (New York, 1948), 26.

61. Oscar Handlin, *The Uprooted* (Boston, 1951), 3, 305.

62. Erik H. Erikson, *Childhood and Society* (New York, 1950), 244–83. Erikson used *American identity* in the sense of "American character" in "Ego Development and Historical Change," *Psychoanalytic Study of the Child*, 2 (1946), 359–96, but that technical journal had a very limited readership. Robert Coles, *Erik H. Erikson* (Boston, 1970), is an informative biography that provides extensive commentary on Erikson's writings.

63. Erikson, *Childhood and Society*, 242; Erikson, " 'Identity Crisis' in Autobiographic Perspective," in his *Life History and the Historical Moment* (New York, 1975), 43. Cf. also Erikson, "Identity and Uprootedness in Our Time," in his *Insight and Responsibility* (New York, 1964), 83–107.

64. Cf. Jay, *Dialectical Imagination*, 217–218 and chap. 7 passim, esp. 226–34. Max Horkheimer and Samuel H. Flowerman, "Foreword to Studies in Prejudice," in T. W. Adorno et al., *The Authoritarian Personality* (New York, 1950), v–vii provides some background information on the anti-Semitism project. Theodor W. Adorno, "Scientific Experiences of a European Scholar in America," *Perspectives in American History*, 2 (1968), 355–65 is a commentary by the principal investigator. Fleming, "Attitude," 352–57 discusses *The Authoritarian Personality* within the context of attitudinal surveys. Referring to the "Aesopian" terminology developed by the Frankfurt group while in America at a time when "Marx and Marxism could not be mentioned," Henry Pachter notes that "they used Hegel or 'German idealism' as code words. They said alienation when they meant capitalism, reason when they meant revolution, and *Eros* when they meant proletariat. . . . When the success story of the word *alienation* in America is written the contribution of the Institute people will receive its due acknowledgment." Pachter, "On Being an Exile," in Robert Boyers, ed., *The Legacy of the German Refugee Intellectuals* (New York, 1972), 36.

65. Richard Hofstadter, "The Pseudo-Conservative Revolt," in Daniel Bell, ed., *The Radical Right* (Garden City, N.Y., 1964), 75–95. (*The Radical Right* is an expanded and updated version of *The New American Right*, originally published in 1955.) For references to ethnics by other contributors, see *Radical Right*, 129, 216–17, 319. At about the same time, Samuel Lubell offered an ethnic explanation for isolationism. See Lubell, *The Future of American Politics* (New York, 1952), 132.

66. Hofstadter's second and third thoughts are found in Bell, *Radical Right*, 97–103; and Hofstadter, *The Paranoid Style in American Politics* (New York, 1965), 56n., 66–92.

67. Hughes and Hughes, *Where Peoples Meet*, 30–31.

68. Robert Redfield, *The Primitive World and Its Transformations* (Ithaca, N.Y., 1953), 147.

69. Park, *Race and Culture*, 18.

70. Coben, "Assault on Victorianism," 605–8; F. H. Matthews, "The Revolt against Americanism: Cultural Pluralism and Cultural Relativism as an Ideology of Liberation," *Canadian Review of American Studies*, 1 (Spring 1970), 4–31, esp. 16ff., Sapir, "Culture, Genuine and Spurious"; Mead, *Coming of Age in Samoa*; Benedict, *Patterns of Culture*.

71. Higham, *Send These to Me*, 211–12 speaks of the "great leap forward" in assimilation.

72. Robin M. Williams, Jr., *American Society; A Sociological Interpretation* (New York, 1952), 527; Howard F. Stein and Robert F. Hill, *The Ethnic Imperative* (University Park, Pa., 1977), 35–36, 82ff.; Polenberg, *One Nation Divisible*, 46–54, 57.

73. Becker, "Some Generalities," 666–67.

74. See Ordway Tead, "Survey and Critique of the Conference on Science, Philosophy, and Religion," in Lyman Bryson, Louis Finkelstein, and Robert M. MacIver, eds., *Approaches to National Unity: Fifth Symposium* (New York, 1945), 783–92. Cf. the proceedings of the first conference held by the secessionist group, entitled *The Scientific Spirit and the Democratic Faith* (New York, 1944).

75. Nathan Glazer and Daniel P. Moynihan, *Beyond the Melting Pot* (Cambridge, Mass., 1963), 271.

76. Higham, *Send These to Me*, 220–21.

77. Ibid., 225–27.

78. The distinction between these two versions of pluralism has never been developed systematically, but see ibid., 197–99, 228–29; and David A. Hollinger, "Ethnic Diversity, Cosmopolitanism and the Emergence of the American Liberal Intelligentsia," *American Quarterly*, 27 (1975), 133–51, esp. 142.

|| 7 ||

The Study of American Culture

Given the range of intellectual and cultural effects described in the previous essay, one would naturally expect to find that World War II had some influence on the academic study of American culture, and especially on the newly emerging discipline of American studies, which took the national culture as its special province. What is surprising in this connection is not the existence of such influence but that no one called attention to it until the war had been over for almost forty years.

It is true, of course, that very little systematic study has been devoted to the evolution of American studies, so we are pretty much in the dark about all aspects of its history. But this is a discipline whose founders lived through the war as adults. These people and their first-generation students dominated the field at least into the 1970s. And yet the published record establishes quite clearly that World War II simply does not figure in the collective memory of Americanists as a formative moment in the development of their discipline. (I am speaking of the United States; as is pointed out in the essay, the development of American studies abroad was quite clearly a by-product of the war).

The reason for this puzzling omission, I suspect, is that the cultural tasks reinforced by the war—tasks such as articulating the nation's values, reappropriating its spiritual heritage, and understanding the strengths and weaknesses of the American character—seemed so intrinsic to the new discipline, so entwined in its basic fabric, that it never occurred to academic Americanists that an "external" factor such as the war could have had anything to do with their interest in these matters. That is, of course, speculative. But the evidence presented in this essay shows that the war set off a massive ideological reawakening that was closely related to key themes in American studies; in addition, wartime developments in national character studies fed directly into one of the leading preoccupations of postwar Americanists, understanding the American character or (as Erik Erikson called it) American identity.

Although my own aquaintance with American studies as a field goes back to the mid fifties, a quarter-century passed before I awoke to the possibility that World War II had influenced its development. The connection first struck me when I was working on the essay for the *Harvard Encyclopedia of American Ethnic Groups*, but it is not developed there; the article reprinted here was written for the 1984 bibliographical issue of the *American Quarterly*, which dealt with war and American culture.

Despite the fact that World War II immediately preceded the great burgeoning of academic programs in American studies, our conventional understanding of the rise of the movement ignores the war and, by doing so, denies it any role in the development of American studies. Very little research has been devoted to the subject, but what might be called the "folk history" of American studies runs like this: The movement had its beginnings in the 1920s with scattered efforts among professors of literature and history to develop an integrated approach to the study of the national culture; it took on more formal shape in the 1930s with establishment of the first degree programs in American civilization at Harvard, Yale, and Pennsylvania; and it expanded rapidly in the next decade by a natural process of growth, the launching of *American Quarterly* (1949) and the founding of the American Studies Association (1951) being the culminating marks of its maturation. My purpose here is not to dispute the chronology of this "folk history" but to call attention to, and in a small way to compensate for, its failure to accord any positive importance to World War II as a factor in the development of American studies.[1]

Considering the vast scale and significance of World War II as an episode in the national experience, there is a prima facie case for assuming that it had some impact on academic efforts to understand and interpret American life and culture. In what follows, I will specify the case in three areas: 1) the growth of American studies abroad; 2) the wartime revival of the democratic ideology and its relation to the "cultural" understanding of American identity; and 3) the impetus given by the war to national character studies, which interacted with the ideological revival to stimulate great interest in the problem of defining the American character. In developing the second and third points I make no claim that the war alone was responsible for subsequent developments in American studies. All I hope to establish is that it was an important factor in the evolution of American studies as an academic movement and that its influence warrants further study.

With respect to the expansion of American studies abroad, the connection with the war is patent. The United States emerged from the conflict in 1945 as one of two global superpowers and the bastion of the free world. Sigmund Skard underlines the significance of this fact in tracing the development of American studies in Europe. Besides the political, economic, and military factors that made America much more important to Europeans than it had been before, Skard adds that they felt the need for a deeper understanding of "the common cultural foundations of the West, including the United States." Robert E. Spiller, one of the founders of the movement, also calls attention to the impact of the war on the growth of American studies in Europe.[2]

Concerning the second point, my contention is that World War II powerfully reinforced existing tendencies toward cultural nationalism, gave great prominence to the ideological dimension of American identity (that is, to the ideas and values for which the nation stands), and forged a link between the democratic ideology and the idea of culture that became central to the American studies approach.

Evidence of growing self-consciousness about the distinctiveness of American culture was discernible in the twenties and gained ground rapidly in the next decade. By 1930 students of American literature were, according to Spiller, "virtually committed to the gigantic task of restudying the American past from the point of view of a literary history which was nationalistic without being chauvinistic and which attempted to discover the relationship between the literature actually produced in America and its immediate sources in cultural evolution."[3] In the same period, Frederick Jackson Turner's distinctively American frontier thesis, Vernon L. Parrington's Jeffersonianism, and Charles A. Beard's democratic progressivism were in the asendancy among historians, while the History of American Life series, which began to appear in 1927 under the general editorship of Arthur M. Schlesinger, Sr., and Dixon Ryan Fox, betokened a new determination to include the whole of the national culture in the historian's purview. Indeed, the desire to capture and record the day-to-day experiences of the American people was widely shared by artists, scholars, and literate Americans, as Alfred Kazin noted long ago in his book, *On Native Grounds* (1942). In the concluding chapter, "America! America!" Kazin interpreted the contemporary interest in regionalism, the collection of folklore, and the preparation of film documentaries as manifestations of a cultural nationalism that was not "blind and parochial," but an "experience in national self-discovery."[4] Warren Susman has called attention to Kazin's judgment and develops many of the same points in a highly suggestive essay, "The Thirties." He emphasizes the importance assumed by the anthropological concept of culture in those years, points out that its acceptance coincided with the popularization of expressions such as *American way of life* and *American dream*, and argues that the literary nationalism of the decade reflected a "complex effort to seek and to define America as a culture and to create the patterns of a way of life worth understanding."[5]

These tendencies were buttressed and given a sharp ideological focus by the mounting threat of Nazi power. Kazin hinted at this development by linking the evidence of cultural nationalism with the international crisis. The emergence of the United States as "the repository of Western culture in the world overrun by Fascism," he declared, lent urgency to the effort "to recover America *as an idea*." In fact, by 1939 a mighty democratic revival was under way which continued into the wartime years and shaped the outlook of a whole generation. A few recent scholarly works have touched on one aspect or another of the democratic revival of World War II, but it has yet to be surveyed in its entirety.[6]

Observers at the time were aware that a requickening of the democratic spirit was taking place. "The American people are talking democracy over again," was the way Benson Y. Landis put it in introducing a lengthy reading list on the subject of democracy that was published by the American Library Association in January 1940. This particular listing included some 290 titles, many of which were annotated, arranged under twenty-nine headings. It was not the only such guide to "books for democracy" to be published in the wartime era. Yet listings of this sort could not keep pace with the flood of new publications.[7] The *Book Review Digest*'s cumulative index for the years 1937–1941 lists 132 titles under the heading "Democracy," and the entries in the *Reader's Guide* likewise testify to a rising wave of magazine articles on democracy that crested just about the time that the United States entered the war.[8]

Anthologies on democracy, such as Irwin Edman and Herbert W. Schneider's *Fountainheads of Freedom* (1941), and Norman Cousins's *A Treasury of Democracy* (1942), were also published in these years.[9] Another collection, Bernard Smith's *Democratic Spirit* (1941), brought together American writings, mostly selections from classic authors such as Jefferson, Emerson, and Whitman. In his introduction, however, Smith emphasized the relevance of democratic principles in the contemporary crisis, and he included a selection from Lewis Mumford's *Faith for Living* (1940), a militantly anti-fascist work controversial because of the author's stringent critique of prevailing intellectual trends that had sapped America's spiritual fiber.[10] Democracy was, of course, a recurrent theme in *American Issues* (1941), the famous anthology edited by Willard Thorp, Merle Curti, and Carlos Baker. The final selection in the volume devoted to "The Social Record," a speech by the progressive educator, George S.

Counts, spoke directly to the contemporary crisis. This address, which was given only a few weeks after the collapse of France, reveals vividly how the stunning onslaught of Nazi panzers convinced many American observers that civilization itself was imperiled and galvanized them to a passionate affirmation of democratic principles.[11]

The same reaction prompted the formation of ad hoc groups dedicated to defining, defending, and promoting democracy. Among the earliest and most important with respect to intellectual substance was the Conference on Science, Philosophy, and Religion in Their Relation to the Democratic Way of Life. Its organizers began their work in the fall of 1939, enrolled seventy-nine leading scholars as founding members in June, 1940, and held their first symposium three months later. These gatherings, the printed proceedings of which often ran to well over five hundred pages, were held annually through the war years and for over a decade thereafter.[12] A breakaway group, dissatisfied with the strongly religious orientation of the original conference, organized itself as a rival Conference on the Scientific Spirit and Democratic Faith and began meeting in 1943.[13] In the meantime, two other groups had appeared on the scene. The Council for Democracy, headed by the respected news commentator, Raymond Gram Swing, mobilized some eighty well-known scholars and writers to instill in the American people the conviction that democracy was "a real, dynamic burning creed worth fighting for."[14] A few months after the Council for Democracy was formed, another group calling itself the Committee of Fifteen published a manifesto entitled *The City of Man: A Declaration on World Democracy* (1941), which exhorted Americans—in language that would have been dismissed as bombastic under other circumstances—to meet their responsibilities to civilization.[15]

Besides these newly formed groups, the educational establishment threw itself into the campaign to promote democracy. The Progressive Education Association had already taken up the cause of "Education for Democracy," and in the critical summer months of 1940 special statements on that theme were issued by the American Council on Education, the Educational Policies Commission of the National Education Association, and the faculty of Teachers College, Columbia University.[16] At the same time, the Foreign Language Information Service, an organization long active in the field of ethnic affairs, transformed itself into the Common Council for American Unity and began to publish *Common Ground* in an effort to reinforce national unity by rallying America's diverse and often hostile ethnic groups around the universal principles of democracy.[17]

People occasionally wearied of hearing about democracy—in 1941 Justice William O. Douglas reported hearing an audience cheer the boast of a speaker that he had not used the word in his talk[18]—but on the whole the people responded positively to the message of democratic patriotism. One indication was the enthusiasm that greeted the *Ballad for Americans*, a rousing cantata by John Latouche and Earl Robinson. This musical review of the national heritage included generous mention of minority group representatives and "wave[d] the flag for tolerance," as *Newsweek* put it. Paul Robeson introduced *Ballad for Americans* in a November 1939 radio broadcast and in doing so set off a frenzy of applause in the studio audience that lasted twenty minutes after the broadcast went off the air. MGM snapped it up for a movie; high school choruses performed it across the country; and Horace Kallen was still recommending it warmly to teachers of English in 1946.[19]

The democratic revival was fully in line with national policy as enunciated by President Franklin D. Roosevelt, who spoke of making the United States "the arsenal of democracy," proclaimed the "four freedoms" in his annual message to Congress in January 1941, and devoted his third inaugural address to a meditative reflection on the democratic faith that was challenged by the international threat as it had earlier been challenged on the domestic front by the depression.[20] The first lady, Eleanor Roosevelt, elaborated her own views in a book called *The Moral Basis of Democracy* (1940).[21]

An alphabetically arranged sampling will give some indication of the range and stature of the authors who wrote on democracy and the world crisis during this period: Herbert Agar, *A Time for Greatness* (1942); Jacques Barzun, *Of Human Freedom* (1939); Carl Becker, *Modern Democracy* (1940), and *New Liberties for Old* (1940); Edward L. Bernays, *Speak Up for Democracy* (1940); James B. Conant, *Our Fighting Faith* (1942); George S. Counts, *The Prospects of American Democracy* (1938); Carl J. Friedrich, *The New Belief in the Common Man* (1942); Sidney Hook, *Reason, Social Myths and Democracy* (1940); William T. Hutchinson, ed., *Democracy and National Unity* (1942); Max Lerner, *It's Later Than You Think: The Need for a Militant Democracy* (1938); Robert M. MacIver, *Leviathan and the People* (1939); Archibald MacLeish, *The Irresponsibles* (1940), *A Time to Speak* (1940), and *The American Cause* (1941); Thomas Mann, *The Coming Victory of Democracy* (1938); Charles E. Merriam, *The New Democracy and the New Despotism* (1939), *What Is Democracy?* (1941), and *On the Agenda of Democracy* (1941); Lewis Mumford, *Men Must Act* (1939), and *Faith for Living* (1940); Jerome Nathanson, *Forerunners of Freedom* (1941); Wilfrid Parsons,

Which Way, Democracy? (1939); Ralph Barton Perry, *Shall Not Perish From the Earth* (1940), and *On All Fronts* (1942); T. V. Smith, *The Democratic Tradition in America* (1941), and *Discipline for Democracy* (1942); Ordway Tead, *New Adventures in Democracy* (1939); M. L. Wilson, *Democracy Has Roots* (1939); and Carl Wittke, ed., *Democracy Is Different* (1941).

Besides these topical treatments, a number of works that formed the basic reading for American studies were published at this time and may be related to the democratic revival. Ralph H. Gabriel's *Course of American Democratic Thought* (1940), for example, appeared in the midst of the revival and contributed to it. Democracy was a recurrent theme in Merle Curti's *Growth of American Thought* (1943), the first edition of which concluded with the question that cut through all others—would democracy survive the challenge of totalitarianism and war? A second edition of Carl Becker's already classic *Declaration of Independence* (1922) was issued in 1942 with prefatory remarks by the author on its pertinence to the times. Perry Miller's *New England Mind: The Seventeenth Century* (1939) added new depth to the understanding of American origins; and Ralph Barton Perry's *Puritanism and Democracy* (1944) highlighted the connection between the Puritan heritage and the national ideology. Other important historical works reaffirmed American principles at least by implication: Charles A. and Mary R. Beard, *The American Spirit* (1942); Arthur Ekirch, *The Idea of Progress in America, 1815–1860* (1944); Alice Felt Tyler, *Freedom's Ferment* (1944); and Arthur M. Schlesinger, Jr., *The Age of Jackson* (1945).

In literature, the landmark study *American Renaissance* by F. O. Matthiessen appeared in 1941. It provided "the sort of assurance that we need" in a time of crisis, Spiller observed in a review, because it showed that the nation had developed, and its literature had expressed, "a native myth of the democratic man, capable of all the range of experience of the traditional heroic man." Matthiessen was pleased that Spiller "singled out the democratic strain," for he thought other reviewers had underestimated this aspect of the book.[22] Very likely the same sensitivity to the timeliness of the democratic myth was felt by many of the contributors to the *Literary History of the United States* (1948), the production of which was planned by Spiller and his collaborators in the wartime years.[23] The ideological note was strongly sounded by at least one of the contributors to the first volume produced by Princeton's Program in American Civilization, *Foreign Influences in American Life* (1944),[24] and the ethos of a democratic society was explored in Dixon

Wector's *Hero in America* (1941) and Constance Rourke's *Roots of American Culture* (1942).

Somewhat removed from the history-and-literature mainstream of American studies during its formative years were two books that demand attention nevertheless. Reinhold Niebuhr's *Children of Light and the Children of Darkness: A Vindication of Democracy and a Critique of Its Traditional Defense* (1944) was perhaps the most profound and original work produced in the democratic revival. It illustrated the relevance of traditional religious ideas to the crisis of the times, and its reception testified to the degree to which secular thinkers were impressed.[25] Gunnar Myrdal's *American Dilemma: The Negro Problem and Modern Democracy* (1944) deserves notice because it stressed the ideological issue so heavily. The "American Creed," Myrdal stated at the outset, was what held the country together. The dilemma to which his title referred arose precisely because Americans were failing to live up to its prescriptions in the area of race. Yet the "American Creed," though distinctively American, was at the same time universal, for it was simply an expression of "the common democratic creed" that was derived from "humane ideals as they have matured in our common Western civilization over a number of centuries."[26]

Myrdal's remarks touch on some of the central themes of the democratic revival. Listing them will perhaps help to specify the contention that World War II influenced the development of American studies.

1. We note first that the monstrous contrast of Nazism (and to a lesser extent, totalitarianism in general) was the primary cause of the democratic revival. Carl Becker acknowledged this fact in reaffirming "Some Generalities That Still Glitter," and Alain Locke said, "Democracy has encountered a fighting antithesis, and has awakened from its considerable lethargy and decadence to a sharpened realization of its own basic values."[27] The "interventionists" in the great debate over American foreign policy were prominent early exponents of the revival and to some extent made *democracy* a party term; the "isolationists," however, were equally devoted to democracy—they simply disagreed about how to preserve it.[28] The important point is that even intellectuals critical of American social, economic, and cultural weaknesses were aroused by the brutality and terrifying power of the Nazi regime to a warmer appreciation of democratic principles and institutions.

2. Indeed, the threat posed by Nazism to all civilized values led many American observers to identify democracy and its defense with the preservation of Western civilization as such. Mumford's 1939 tocsin, *Men*

Must Act, made the logical sequence quite clear: the fourth chapter was entitled "The Barbarian Alternative"; the fifth, "Democracy Equals Civilization"; and the sixth, "The Challenge of the American Heritage."[29] Others more detached from the polemics of the neutrality debate also perceived the same associations, as the previously quoted comments of Kazin and Myrdal suggest. Yet controversy arose because different observers stressed contrasting elements in the heritage of Western civilization and offered divergent prescriptions for overcoming the crisis. Especially severe was the split between the "relativists," who linked democracy with scientific naturalism and the experimental approach, and the "absolutists," who insisted that the survival of democracy hinged on a return to religion and perennial truths in philosophy and social thought.[30]

3. Despite the controversy, virtually everyone agreed that the United States stood for certain ideas and values, whether they were called "democracy," "the American Creed," "the American Dream," or simply "promises." Ideology, in other words, was the essential element in the national identity. As James Truslow Adams explained, it was ideas that made us a nation.[31] Eleanor Roosevelt agreed and went on to draw an important moral:

> We know that this country is bound together by an idea. The
> citizens of this country belong to many races and many creeds.
> They have come here and built a great Nation around the idea
> of democracy and freedom. . . . [The present crisis challenges
> us] to preserve what this country was founded to be, a land
> where people should have the right to life, liberty, and the pur-
> suit of happiness, regardless of race or creed or color. We have
> not achieved it. We are very far from it in many ways, but we
> know that that is what we must achieve.[32]

4. As this quotation makes clear, the ideas that America stood for were *normative*—they were meant to guide conduct. Talk—or belief—without action was not enough. Democracy was thus more than a political system or an institutional arrangement: it was a way of life. This formula was incorporated into the title of the Conference on Science, Philosophy, and Religion in Their Relation to the Democratic Way of Life, which had strong support from religious traditionalists, but it was also a favorite theme of progressive thinkers like Boyd H. Bode and Sidney Hook.[33] The most influential spokesman for the progressive version of democracy as a way of life was undoubtedly John Dewey, for whom, as J. H. Randall,

Jr., noted, "the democratic life, pursued in conscious unity of interaction with one's fellows," took on religious quality.[34]

5. But a normative way of life was a *culture*, as anthropologists explained the concept that was rapidly becoming "the foundation stone of the social sciences."[35] Appropriately enough, it was John Dewey who nailed down the connection in his *Freedom and Culture* (1939). Alluding to the work of the anthropologists, he declared that the idea of culture put the problem of the individual and society on a new footing. Now the task was to discover the kind of culture that promoted democratic living. In Dewey's thinking, democracy was indissolubly bound to the experimental method and had to be struggled for on "as many fronts as culture has aspects: political, economic, international, educational, scientific and artistic, religious."[36] Although the most eminent, Dewey was not the only American thinker who espoused a cultural interpretation of democracy. So many others took the same view that eventually America, understood as a functioning democratic culture, itself became normative—that is, America as a practical instance of democracy came to be equated with the abstract ideal of democracy.

Edward A. Purcell's *Crisis of Democratic Theory: Scientific Naturalism and the Problem of Value* (1973) provides a brilliant analysis of the complex intellectual matrix within which this development occurred.[37] For our purposes, however, the main point is one with which Purcell is not concerned, namely, that the cultural interpretation of democracy brought the ideological revival into close interaction with American studies because understanding the national culture holistically is the task Americanists have always set for themselves. Besides being the implicit (and sometimes explicit) premise of the American studies approach,[38] the idea of culture is also closely related to the wartime boom in national character studies; hence it carries us over to the final topic to be outlined here, the connection between the war and the vogue of American character studies.

Interest in the American character naturally accompanied the democratic revival. The concept of national character had fallen into disrepute in the 1930s because of its association with racial stereotypes, and James Truslow Adams still used quotation marks in November 1940 when he discussed the American "national character" in the context of "the ideas that make us a nation." Three years later he devoted a full-length book to *The American: The Making of a New Man* (1943).[39] More influential, however, was Arthur M. Schlesinger, Sr.'s handling of Crèvecoeur's question, "What then is the American, this new man?" in his December 1942 presidential address before the American Historical Association. This rich and provocative analysis of the American character was published a month later in the *American Historical Review*, and it reappeared as the opening essay in Schlesinger's *Paths to the Present* (1949). Yet influential as they were, Schlesinger's treatment and Denis Brogan's well-known *American Character* (1944) were relatively old-fashioned analyses by scholars trained in the humanities.[40] What was new in World War II was the claim of social scientists to be pioneering a new approach that redeemed the concept of national character from the taint of racialism and elevated it above the plane of mere belletristic speculation. By the end of the war, people spoke respectfully of the "science of national character," and for the next ten years it was looked upon as an exciting and important area of study in the social and behavioral sciences.[41]

The war played a crucial role in these developments. When the United States became involved in the conflict, anthropologists and other social scientists were called upon by agencies of the government to apply their skills to such questions as how civilian morale could be maintained, what kind of propaganda could be most effectively employed against the enemy, and how American troops should conduct themselves in foreign lands to minimize friction with the indigenous populations. To answer these questions, scholars such as Margaret Mead and Ruth Benedict applied the perspective of the culture-and-personality school of anthropology, which combined psychological assumptions and ethnographic observation of child-rearing patterns in an effort to determine how the "basic personality structure" characteristic of different cultures was stamped upon the psyches of individuals growing up in those cultures.[42] From here it was only a short step to the study of national character, which the war had made "a matter of grave practical importance," as Ruth Benedict later wrote. Direct observation of enemy populations was impossible in wartime, but techniques were developed for assessing cultures "at a distance" by means of interviews with native informants, analysis of literature, films, and so on. In response to wartime needs, social scientists plunged into this sort of national character analysis with what Margaret Mead later described as a "kind of fervor."[43]

Unlike Ruth Benedict, who worked for two years for the Office of War Information, Margaret Mead did not sign on full time with a defense agency. She was, however, actively involved in war-related work as a member of the Committee for National Morale, as executive secretary of the National Research Council's Committee on Food Habits, and as an informal emissary sent to Great Britain to help improve relations between the British people and the American troops who were crowding into that country. Mead was also the best-known social scientific proponent of national character studies. Her book *And Keep Your Powder Dry: An Anthropologist Looks at America* (1942), marked the opening of a new epoch in American character studies.[44]

Written in a few weeks, the book was intended as a contribution to the war effort. "Freedom's battles must be fought by freedom's own children," Mead declared, and to do so most effectively they had to know the strengths and weaknesses of their collective personality. Her analysis of the American "character structure" was strictly scientific, she insisted.[45] Yet that claim could be justified only on the supposition that, since she thought of herself as a social scientist, she regarded all of her judgments as the products of scientific reasoning. Actually, the book was fully as impressionistic as any humanist's discussion of American character, though it was, of course, distinctively shaped by Mead's anthropological perspective and her unusually extensive field experience.

It was also deeply influenced by the democratic revival, which was near its climax when the book appeared. Though not uncritical of American ways, Mead was a decided partisan of democracy, which she understood in the cultural sense—that is, as the name for "a type of behavior and an attitude of mind which runs through our whole culture."[46] More than that, Mead argued that since culture determines character, and since culture itself is learned behavior, a more democratic world order could be brought into being by the application of social engineering techniques. Indeed, she implied that the American drive for success, and the need Americans felt to be morally right in the purposes they pursued, demanded nothing less as the ultimate goal of the war effort than the creation of a new democratic world. There were problems to be sure—such as reconciling democracy with social engineering and finding a way to combine tolerance for diversity with the imperatives of world order—but Mead thought they could be overcome.[47] Thus her book, the last chapter of which was entitled "Building the World New," embodied a nationalistic internationalism that some would consider characteristically American and that anticipated the hubris that postwar social scientists were to display about their ability to reduce "tensions affecting international understanding" through techniques such as the analysis of national characters.[48]

Mead's discussion of the American character as such was plausible, but unsurprising; many time-honored themes (individualism, success orientation, the melting pot, the legacies of Puritanism and the frontier) were treated explicitly or lurked just below the surface.[49] The most original part of the book was her emphasis on the fixing of cultural characteristics by childhood socialization and her discussion of patterns of family interaction as a formative influence on the American personality structure. Thus while it was important that a leading anthropologist so roundly affirmed the existence of national character as a scientifically reputable reality, it was perhaps even more important that Mead's highly informal treatment of the subject overlapped at so many points with traditional approaches and thereby tacitly conveyed the impression that anyone could become a scientific commentator by spicing the standard literary and historical materials with a few concepts taken from social psychology.

Mead's *And Keep Your Powder Dry* and Benedict's book on the Japanese, *The Chrysanthemum and the Sword* (1946), were the first major social scientific studies of national character, although there were several shorter essays and many allusions to the subject during the wartime years.[50] In the postwar period the floodgates opened. Among the most significant works by social scientists were Geoffrey Gorer's *American People* (1948), a prepublication summary of which appeared in *Life* magazine; Erik H. Erikson's "Reflections on the American Identity," which was chapter eight of *Childhood and Society* (1950); David Riesman's fabulously popular *Lonely Crowd: A Study of the Changing American Character* (1950); and David Potter's *People of Plenty: Economic Abundance and the American Character* (1954), a provocative attempt by a historian to appropriate the methodological insights of the culture-and-personality school.[51]

There is no room to document the assertion that the effort to understand the American character was central to American studies in the decade after World War II. Yet as anyone familiar with the movement in those days could testify, that was almost its definition. Despite the pretensions to clinical rigor on the part of social scientists, national character was an inescapably diffuse notion referring broadly to the body of ideals, values, and cultural traits held in common by the members of a given national culture. Hence, as Max Lerner pointed out at the time, the American character was spoken of interchangeably with the American mind, the American spirit, the American tradition, the American creed, the American civilization (the phrase Lerner himself preferred), or the American way of life.[52] Yet these were precisely the topics in which the increasingly self-conscious devotees of American studies were interested. Whether they approached their task by elucidating American symbols and myths, by employing traditional literary or historical methods of narrative and textual analysis, or by drawing on the social sciences, they could all legitimately think of themselves as seeking to illuminate the mysteries of the American character. What I have tried to show here is that World War II exerted a profound though hitherto unrecognized influence on their work by giving new visibility and respectability to national character studies and, even more decisively, by causing American scholars to appreciate more deeply the positive values embodied in the nation's social, political, and cultural traditions.

NOTES

Source: American Quarterly, 36 (1984), 343–58. Reprinted by permission of the publisher.

1. For an example of the "folk history" of American Studies, see the retrospective review by one of the founders of the movement, Robert E. Spiller, "American Studies, Past, Present, and Future," in Joseph J. Kwiat and Mary C. Turpie, eds., *Studies in American Culture: Dominant Ideas and Images* (Minneapolis, Minn., 1960), 207–20. Concerning the war, Tremaine McDowell's pioneering book, *American Studies* (Minneapolis, Minn., 1948), 24 says only, "The actualities of World War II made many professors and many students dissatisfied with the more restricted varieties of academic specialism, and eager to grapple with knowledge in more inclusive terms." Two other early commentators on the movement were sensitive to the danger of excessive nationalism but did not associate that peril with the war. See Richard H. Shryock, "The Nature and Implications of Programs in American Civilization," *American Heritage,* 3 (April 1949), 36–37; Arthur E. Bestor, Jr., "The Study of American Civilization: Jingoism or Scholarship?" *William and Mary Quarterly,* 9 (1952), 3–9. More recently, Leo Marx alluded to the "overheated nationalism that accompanied World War II and its Cold War aftermath," but he did not develop the point in connection with the growth of American Studies. See Marx, "Thoughts on the Origin and Character of the American Studies Movement," *American Quarterly,* 31 (1979), 399–400. Recent, and quite helpful, general studies that fail to take the war into account are: Gene Wise, " 'Paradigm Dramas' in American Studies: A Cultural and Institutional History of the Movement," ibid., 293–337; Guenter H. Lenz, "American Studies—Beyond the Crisis? Recent Redefinitions and the Meaning of Theory, History, and Practical Criticism," in Jack Salzman, ed., *Prospects: An Annual Journal of American Cultural Studies,* 7 (New York, 1982), 53–113. It is also revealing that David Marcell's comprehensive bibliography, *American Studies: A Guide to Information Services* (Detroit, 1982) provides no index heading for World War II.

2. Sigmund Skard, *American Studies in Europe: Their History and Present Organization,* 2 vols. (Philadelphia, 1958), 1:38–42, 71ff., 169ff., 292ff.; Robert E. Spiller, "The Fulbright Program in American Studies Abroad: Retrospect and Prospect," in Robert H. Walker, ed., *American Studies Abroad* (Westport, Conn., 1975), 4–5. See also Max Beloff. "The Projection of America Abroad," *American Quarterly,* 1 (Summer, 1949), 23–29.

3. Robert E. Spiller, "Those Early Days: American Literature and the Modern Language Association," in Spiller, *Late Harvest: Essays and Addresses in American Literature and Culture* (Westport, Conn., 1981), 210.

4. John Higham, Leonard Krieger, and Felix Gilbert, *History: The Development of Historical Studies in the United States* (Englewood Cliffs, N.J., 1965), 171–97; Alfred Kazin, *On Native Grounds* (New York, 1942), 488.

5. Warren I. Susman, "The Thirties," in Stanley Coben and Lorman Ratner, eds.,

The Development of an American Culture, 2d ed. (New York, 1983), 220ff., quotation from 227.

6. Kazin, *On Native Grounds,* 488–89; Richard H. Pells, *Radical Visions and American Dreams: Culture and Social Thought in the Depression Years* (New York, 1973), 359–64 is critical of the revival; Geoffrey Perrett, *Days of Sadness, Years of Triumph* (New York, 1973), 123–26 is patronizing; James J. Martin, *American Liberalism and World Politics, 1931–1941,* 2 vols. (New York, 1964), 2:930–74, 1139–88 provides much information on related matters such as the attitudes of intellectuals toward totalitarianism and war.

7. Benson Y. Landis, comp., "Democracy: A Reading List," *ALA Bulletin,* 34, no. 1, pt. 2 (January 1940), 53–68; Bernard Smith, "Books for Democracy," *Publishers' Weekly,* 140 (September 20, 1941), 1077–79; "Reading List for Democracy," *Saturday Review of Literature,* 25 (February 21, 1942), 12, 18–20.

8. The volume of the *Reader's Guide* covering mid 1935 to mid 1937 lists 92 articles under the heading "Democracy." The next four volumes yield the following tallies: for 1937–39, 194 entries; for 1939–41, 245 entries; for 1941–43, 175 entries; for 1943–45, 88 entries.

9. Irwin Edman and Herbert W. Schneider, eds., *Fountainheads of Freedom* (New York, 1941); Norman Cousins, ed., *A Treasury of Democracy* (New York, 1942).

10. Bernard Smith, ed., *The Democratic Spirit: A Collection of American Writing from the Earliest Times to the Present Day* (New York, 1941), xxv–xxxiii, 887–92. For a brief discussion of the controversy surrounding Mumford's book, see William L. O'Neill, *A Better World: The Great Schism: Stalinism and the American Intellectuals* (New York, 1982), 32–35.

11. Willard Thorp, Merle Curti, and Carlos Baker, eds., *The Social Record,* vol. 1 of *American Issues* (Philadelphia, 1941), 1017–22.

12. Van Wyck Brooks describes the formation of this organization in "Conference on Science, Philosophy and Religion in Their Relation to the Democratic Way of Life," in *Science, Philosophy, and Religion: A Symposium* (New York, 1941), 1–10. Among the scholars represented in this volume are: Moses Hadas, Robert M. MacIver, Pitirim A. Sorokin, Mortimer J. Adler, Jacques Maritain, Albert Einstein, and Harold D. Lasswell. For a complete listing of the published proceedings of the conference, see Conference on Science, Philosophy, and Religion in Their Relation to the Democratic Way of Life, *The Ethic of Power: The Interplay of Religion, Philosophy and Politics,* ed. Harold D. Lasswell and Harlan Cleveland (New York, 1962), 465–66.

13. Among the members of the breakaway group were Brand Blandshard, John Dewey, Horace Kallen, Eduard C. Lindeman, Jerome Nathanson, and Herbert W. Schneider. Three collections of papers were published by this group: *The Scientific Spirit and Democratic Faith* (New York, 1944); *The Authoritarian Attempt to Capture Education* (New York, 1945); and Jerome Nathan, ed., *Science for Democracy* (New York, 1946). Ordway Tead discusses the split in his "Survey and Critique of the Conference on Science, Philosophy, and Religion," in Lyman Bryson, Louis Finkelstein, and Robert M. MacIver, eds., *Approaches to National Unity: Fifth Symposium* (New York, 1945), 783–92.

14. *New York Times,* 10 October 1940.

15. Committee of Fifteen, *The City of Man: A Declaration on World Democracy* (New York, 1941). Among the names on the title page of this booklet were: G. A. Borgese, Van Wyck Brooks, Dorothy Canfield Fisher, Alvin Johnson, Hans Kohn, Thomas Mann, Lewis Mumford, Reinhold Niebuhr, and Gaetano Salvemini.

16. Patricia A. Graham, *Progressive Education: From Arcady to Academe* (New York, 1967), 81–84, 105–08; I. L. Kandel, *The End of an Era: Educational Yearbook*

of the International Institute of Teachers College, Columbia University, 1941 (New York, 1941), 100–19.

17. See chap. 6.

18. Douglas, who told this story in a speech given before the Commonwealth Club of San Francisco, treated democracy very reverently. It was no "mere shibboleth" but "a word to fill the heart with pride." See William O. Douglas, "The Function of Democracy," in *Representative American Speeches 1940–1941*, which is vol. 15, no. 1, of the Reference Shelf (New York, 1941), 225.

19. *Newsweek*, 15 (March 25, 1940), 40; Horace M. Kallen, "Of the American Spirit," *English Journal*, 35 (1946), 293–94. I remember taking part in a performance of "Ballad for Americans" in my own high school during the war years.

20. *Public Papers and Addresses of Franklin D. Roosevelt, 1940: War—and Aid to Democracies* (New York, 1941), 643, 672; *Public Papers and Addresses of Franklin D. Roosevelt, 1941: The Call to Battle Stations* (New York, 1950), 3–7.

21. In the interest of saving space, no additional publication information will be given for this title, or others adduced as evidence of interest in the topic of democracy, unless a page citation is needed. Full bibliographical information is easily accessible through standard reference works such as *The National Union Catalog: Pre-1956 Imprints*.

22. Spiller's review and Matthiessen's letter responding to it are reprinted in Robert E. Spiller, *Milestones in American Literary History* (Westport, Conn., 1977), 55–57, 53.

23. See Spiller, "History of a History: The Story Behind *Literary History of the United States*," in Spiller, *Milestones*, 111–28.

24. "What really stirs our hearts and minds is our set of ideals and values. Often we do not realize explicitly what these are until they are threatened. But in the present crisis we know with our inmost being how dear to us are our American ideals of democracy, decency, and individual freedom, our belief in free speech and in free elections and in the right to worship as we choose, our family mores, our religious faith, our respect for certain symbols which convey these ideals to our attention (the American flag, for example)." James G. Leyburn, "The Problem of Ethnic and National Impact from a Sociological Point of View," in David F. Bowers, ed., *Foreign Influences in American Life* (Princeton, N.J., 1944), 60.

25. For discussion, see Edward A. Purcell, Jr., *The Crisis of Democratic Theory: Scientific Naturalism and the Problem of Value* (Lexington, Ky., 1973), 243–47.

26. Gunnar Myrdal, *An American Dilemma*, 2 vols. (New York, 1944), 1:3, 25.

27. Carl Becker, "Some Generalities That Still Glitter," *Yale Review*, 29 (June 1940), 649–67; Alain Locke, "Pluralism and Intellectual Democracy," in *Science, Philosophy, and Religion: Second Symposium* (New York, 1942), 206. See also Purcell, *Crisis of Democratic Theory*, chap. 7; Robert Allen Skotheim, *Totalitarianism and American Social Thought* (New York, 1971), chap. 3.

28. For an example of the interventionist position on democracy, see William Allen White, ed., *Defense for America* (New York, 1940), 107–14; for the isolationist position, Anne Morrow Lindbergh, *The Wave of the Future* (New York, 1940), 24–25, 36–41. For a survey of the secondary literature, see Justus D. Doenecke, "Beyond Polemics: An Historiographical Re-Appraisal of American Entry in World War II," *History Teacher*, 12 (1979), 217–51.

29. Lewis Mumford, *Men Must Act* (New York, 1939). In a later chapter on revitalizing democracy at home, Mumford acknowledged "that it is only by comparison with totalitarian countries that democracy may be said to flourish in America" (144).

30. Purcell, *Crisis of Democratic Theory*, chaps. 8–12; Tead, "Survey and Critique."

31. James Truslow Adams, "The Ideas That Make Us a Nation," *New York Times Magazine*, November 24, 1940, 3, 24.

32. Quoted in U.S. Office of Education, *Helping the Foreign-Born Achieve Citizenship*, pamphlet no. 21 in Education and National Defense Series (Washington, D.C., 1942), 1.

33. Boyd H. Bode, *Democracy as a Way of Life* (New York, 1943); chap. 13, "The Democratic Way of Life," comprises the whole of the section headed "Credo" in Sidney Hook, *Reason, Social Myths, and Democracy* (New York, 1940). The *Journal of Legal and Political Sociology*, which began publication in October 1942, devoted its first issue to "Democracy and Social Structure," with contributions by Robert M. MacIver, Karl N. Llewellyn, Georges Gurvitch (founder of the *Journal*), David Riesman, Talcott Parsons, Robert Merton, and Kingsley Davis. For an illuminating discussion of Merton's essay "A Note on Science and Democracy," see David A. Hollinger, "The Defense of Democracy and Robert K. Merton's Formulation of the Scientific Ethos," in *Knowledge and Society: Studies in the Sociology of Culture Past and Present*, vol. 4, *Current Perspectives on the History of the Social Sciences*, ed. Robert A. Jones and Henrika Kuklick (Greenwich, Conn., 1983), 1–15.

34. J. H. Randall, Jr., "The Religion of Shared Experience," in *The Philosopher of the Common Man: Essays in Honor of John Dewey to Celebrate His Eightieth Birthday* (1940; New York, 1968), 110–11, 122. See also, in the same collection, John Dewey, "Creative Democracy—The Task Before Us," 220–28. For a general study, see Jerome Nathanson, *John Dewey: The Reconstruction of the Democratic Life* (New York, 1951), esp. chap. 4, "Democracy as a Way of Life."

35. Stuart Chase, *The Proper Study of Mankind* (New York, 1948), 59. See also Susman, "Thirties," 220ff.; Louis Schneider and Charles Bonjean, eds., *The Idea of Culture in the Social Sciences* (Cambridge, 1973).

36. John Dewey, *Freedom and Culture* (New York, 1939), 27, 13, 173.

37. See Purcell, *Crisis of Democratic Theory*, esp. 211–17, and chaps. 13–14.

38. For explicit prescription of the anthropological concept of culture, see Richard E. Sykes, "American Studies and the Concept of Culture: A Theory and Method," *American Quarterly*, 15 (1963), 253–70; Jay Mechling, Robert Meredith, and David Wilson, "American Culture Studies: The Discipline and the Curriculum," ibid., 25 (October 1973), 363–89. For tensions caused by the social science approach in one institution, see Murray G. Murphey, "American Civilization at Pennsylvania," ibid., 22 (1970), 495–97.

39. Adams, "Ideas That Make Us a Nation," 3; Adams, *The American: The Making of a New Man* (New York, 1943). For the discrediting of national character by racial associations, see David Potter, *People of Plenty: Economic Abundance and the American Character* (Chicago, 1954), 26, 31, 32, 38, 57. In this connection, it is interesting that a comprehensive survey of "alleged American characteristics, ideals, and principles," which was published in 1941, did not once make use of the expression *national character* and the closest it came to *American character* was in a reference to "the amazing diversity of American life and character." See Lee Coleman, "What Is American? A Study of Alleged American Traits," *Social Forces*, 19 (1941), 492–99. The major historical analysis of American character studies is Thomas L. Hartshorne, *The Distorted Image: Changing Conceptions of the American Character since Turner* (Cleveland, Ohio, 1968); and among the most recent additions to this immense literature are Rupert Wilkerson, "American Character Revisited," *Journal of American*

Studies, 17 (1983), 165–87; and Alex Inkeles, "The American Character," *Center Magazine*, 16 (November–December 1983), 25–39. See also Michael McGiffert, "Selected Writings on American National Character," *American Quarterly*, 15 (1963), 271–88; Thomas L. Hartshorne, "Recent Interpretations of the American Character," in Jefferson B. Kellog and Robert H. Walker, eds., *Sources for American Studies* (Westport, Conn., 1983), 307–14.

40. Arthur M. Schlesinger, Sr., "What Then Is the American, This New Man," *American Historical Review*, 48 (1943), 225–44; reprinted in Schlesinger, *Paths to the Present* (New York, 1949), 1–22. D. W. Brogan, *The American Character* (New York, 1944).

41. Otto Klineberg, "A Science of National Character," *Journal of Social Psychology*, 19 (February 1944), 147–62; Louis L. Snyder, *The Meaning of Nationalism* (New Brunswick, N.J., 1954), 162–87; Alex Inkeles and Daniel J. Levinson, "National Character: The Study of Modal Personality and Sociocultural Systems," in Gardner Lindzey, ed., *Handbook of Social Psychology*, 2 vols. (Cambridge, Mass., 1954), 2:977–1020; Milton Singer, "A Survey of Culture and Personality Theory and Research," in Bert Kaplan, ed., *Studying Personality Cross-Culturally* (Evanston, Ill., 1961), 43–57.

42. Margaret Mead, "The Study of National Character," in Daniel Lerner and Harold D. Lasswell, eds., *The Policy Sciences* (Stanford, Calif., 1951), 79–85; Mead, "National Character and the Science of Anthropology," in Seymour M. Lipset and Leo Lowenthal, eds., *Culture and Social Character* (New York, 1961), 15–26.

43. Ruth Benedict, "The Study of Cultural Patterns in European Nations," *Transactions of the New York Academy of Science*, 2d ser., 8 (1946), 274; Margaret Mead and Rhoda Metraux, eds., *The Study of Culture at a Distance* (Chicago, 1953); Sol Tax et al., eds., *An Appraisal of Anthropology Today* (Chicago, 1953), 136.

44. For Benedict, see Judith Schachter Modell, *Ruth Benedict: Patterns of a Life* (Pittsburgh, 1983), 266ff. For Mead's wartime activities, see William L. Partridge and Elizabeth M. Eddy, "The Development of Applied Anthropology in America," in Eddy and Partridge, eds., *Applied Anthropology in America* (New York, 1978), 28–29; Mead, "The Application of Anthropological Techniques to Cross-National Communication," *Transactions of the New York Academy of Sciences*, 2d ser., 9 (February 1947), 133–52. John Higham notes that "the revival of serious discussion of national character by scholars" seems to date from Mead's book and Arthur Schlesinger's article "What Then Is the American, This New Man?" Higham, Krieger, and Gilbert, *History*, 221, n. 18.

45. Margaret Mead, *And Keep Your Powder Dry: An Anthropologist Looks at America* (New York, 1942), 24–26, 10–11, 213.

46. Ibid., 20.

47. Ibid., chaps. 10–13. See also Mead, "The Comparative Study of Culture and the Purposive Cultivation of Democratic Values," in *Science, Philosophy, and Religion: Second Symposium*, 56–69; Mead, "The Comparative Study of Cultures and the Purposive Cultivation of Democratic Values, 1941–1949," in Lyman Bryson, Louis Finkelstein, Robert M. MacIver, eds., *Perspectives on a Troubled Decade: Science, Philosophy and Religion, 1939–1949* (New York, 1950), 87–108.

48. See Otto Klineberg, *Tensions Affecting International Understanding; A Survey of Research* (New York, 1950); Robert C. Angell, "UNESCO and Social Science Research," *American Sociological Review*, 15 (1950), 282–86; Robert Endleman, "The New Anthropology and Its Ambitions: The Science of Man in Messianic Dress," *Commentary*, 8 (September 1949), 284–91; and Morroe Berger, " 'Understanding National Character'—and War," ibid., 11 (April 1951), 375–86.

49. Mead listed the features of the American character as follows: 1) is geared to success and movement; 2) is ambivalent about aggressiveness; 3) measure success quantitatively in comparison with contemporaries; 4) interprets success and failure as indications of moral worth; 5) is uninterested in the past; 6) is oriented toward the future; and 7) is ambivalent toward other cultures. *And Keep Your Powder Dry*, 193–94.

50. On Benedict's book, see Modell, *Ruth Benedict*, 279ff. For wartime essays: Gregory Bateson, "Morale and National Character," in Goodwin Watson, ed., *Civilian Morale: Second Yearbook of the Society for the Psychological Study of Social Issues* (Boston, 1942), 71–91; Erik H. Erikson, "Hitler's Imagery and German Youth," *Psychiatry*, 5 (1942), 475–92; Kurt Lewin, "Cultural Reconstruction," *Journal of Abnormal and Social Psychology*, 38 (March 1943), 166–73. Lewin's essay resembles Mead's book in its concern with inculcating democratic cultural values.

51. Geoffrey Gorer, *The American People: A Study in National Character* (New York, 1948); Gorer, "The American People," Life, 23 (August 18, 1947), 94–98, 100, 103–4, 106, 109–10, 112; Erik H. Erikson, *Childhood and Society* (New York, 1950); David Riesman, *The Lonely Crowd: A Study of the Changing American Character* (New Haven, Conn., 1950); Potter, *People of Plenty*, chap. 2 provides an excellent historical discussion of the development of the culture-and-personality approach.

52. Max Lerner, "The Idea of American Civilization," *Journal of Social Issues*, 7 (1951), 30–39. The definition of national character as embracing ideals, values, and cultural traits is also taken from this essay, which was revised as chap. 2 of Lerner's *America as a Civilization* (New York, 1957). Margaret Mead discussed national character as an area of common interest to historians and anthropologists in one of the early volumes of *American Quarterly*. See Mead, "Anthropologist and Historian: Their Common Problems," *American Quarterly*, 3 (1951), 8–9.

|| 8 ||

Pluralism, Democracy, and Catholicism: Religious Tensions

One aspect of wartime experience that has been largely forgotten, both in the popular mind and by historians, is the effect the war had on religion and religious groups in American society. Yet the crisis of war restored religious ideas to intellectual respectability, enhanced the prestige of "neo-orthodox" thinkers such as Reinhold Niebuhr, and stimulated such rapid growth in church membership that people spoke in the postwar years of a popular "revival of religion." A different dimension of religious change saw Protestant cultural hegemony challenged by the breakthrough of Catholics and Jews to new levels of public visibility and influence. So noticeable was the combined effect of these changes that social scientists began to treat religion as a marker of group boundaries almost as important as race.

While the essays in part 3 touch on several aspects of the postwar religious scene, they do not pretend to offer a comprehensive survey of the topic. This chapter explores religious tensions in the postwar years, specifically the controversies that broke out between Catholics on the one hand and Protestants and secular liberals on the other. It could just as well have been included under the heading "Religion and American Diversity," but I have placed it in part 2 because of the central role played in the controversies by the war-related ideological themes of authoritarianism, democracy, and pluralism.

My attention was first drawn to the "Catholic question" as a complication of pluralism when I was working on the essay published here as chapter 3, and the reader will see that Horace M. Kallen, the father of cultural pluralism, figures prominently in this chapter too. It was first presented at the 1985 meeting of the Southern Historical Association in Houston, Texas and published a year and a·half later in the *Review of Politics*.

After World War II bitter controversy broke out in the United States between Catholics, on the one hand, and Protestants and liberals on the other. Although important issues were involved, these controversies have attracted almost no scholarly attention. Donald Crosby's book on Catholics and McCarthyism is the only full-scale monograph dealing with any aspect of the controversies of which I am aware.[1] My intention here is to draw attention to two additional aspects of the controversy which touch on matters that are still of interest and in need of much more study by historians. These are: 1) ambiguities in the concept of pluralism; and 2) a tendency that emerged in the critique of Catholic authoritarianism to treat democracy as a civil religion. But before taking up these issues we must look briefly at the development of "the Catholic issue" between the Al Smith campaign of 1928 and the end of World War II.

The 1928 election was, of course, the high point of anti-Catholic sentiment in the twentieth century.[2] The extreme to which no-popery was carried aroused considerable sympathy for Catholics, however, and the next few years were marked by improved interreligious feeling. The Depression, which crowded cultural issues off center stage, was basic to this development, but as an important element in the Democratic coalition, Catholics also benefited from Franklin D. Roosevelt's election. As president, Roosevelt appointed more Catholics to office than anyone ever had before. Catholics may also have benefited in a more diffuse way from the concern for improved intergroup relations that emerged in the context of New Deal liberalism.[3]

After 1935 this mellowing was sharply offset by a series of developments that poisoned relations with liberals and Protestants. Concentrating first on the liberals (though recognizing that many Protestants were included in this group), we note that Father Charles E. Coughlin's shift to an anti–New Deal position in 1935–36 alerted liberals to the Fascistic tendencies of his activities.[4] Thereafter his growing extremism on the menace of Communism, his open anti-Semitism after 1938, and the sometimes violent behavior of his Christian Front followers contributed to the linkage between Catholicism and Fascism which many American liberals took for granted by the end of the decade. In New York City, where much liberal opinion was formed, Catholic anti-Semitism (and Christian Front hooliganism) reflected not just the influence of Coughlin but also Irish Catholic frustration over losses sustained in the 1930s to the growing political, economic, and cultural power of the city's Jewish community.[5]

Most decisive in reawakening hostility to the Catholic church, however, was the Spanish Civil War.[6] Public opinion favored the Loyalists by a wide margin, and to liberals the war was a clear-cut contest between

Fascism and democracy in which the Catholic church had shown its true colors by rallying to the Fascists. American Catholic opinion was almost as strongly pro-Franco; according to Catholic commentators, the real issue was Communism, which they believed dominated the Republican side and which they held primarily responsible for the Loyalists' campaign of persecution against the church in Spain. The ideological conflict could hardly have been more direct. What was even more alarming to the liberals, however, was that the Catholic church seemed to be dictating American foreign policy by mobilizing the political influence of Catholic voters.

The episode that solidified this impression was Catholic opposition to lifting the embargo on arms sales to the Spanish Republicans. Although scholars are divided on whether Catholic influence was in fact decisive in keeping the embargo in force, liberals were convinced that it was, and it made them furious.[7] To Harold Ickes, caving in to Catholic pressure was "the mangiest, scabbiest cat" that could possibly be let out of the bag, and he freely predicted that it would generate an anti-Catholic backlash.[8] Even the semireclusive literary scholar Van Wyck Brooks was deeply upset by the specter of "Political Catholicism." He had lost sleep over it, he confided to Lewis Mumford. "For the Catholic Church is growing so bold in this country. It defeats every measure for decent living." Yet how could one combat it without arousing the furies of ignorant no-popery?[9]

The liberal case against the Catholic church was summed up in 1939 in George Seldes's *Catholic Crisis*, a book that one reviewer thought (incorrectly) might "become the *novissimum testamentum* of the rapidly growing American anti-Catholic reaction."[10] To Seldes the Catholic church was clearly in league with Fascism. Support for Franco was the centerpiece, but Vatican softness toward Germany and Italy, and opposition to liberalism and Communism, buttressed his case. The domestic scene Seldes covered with a farrago of evidence ranging from Father Coughlin and anti-Semitism to Catholic ties with corrupt politicians (especially Boss Hague) and objectionable pressure group tactics brought to bear on Congress, state legislatures, the press, the film industry, and private groups or individuals who espoused causes of which Catholics disapproved, such as birth control.[11]

Seldes's indictment was comprehensive in its way, but it failed to bring out the point that the clash between Catholics and liberals was at bottom one of radically divergent worldviews. For Catholics, the great evil of the day was secularism—the exclusion of God from human life, personal and social—and against that evil they launched a vigorous cam-

paign in the 1930s and 1940s.[12] Essential to the campaign was a philosophical critique of the intellectual position underlying secularism; in
carrying out that critique, Catholics became involved in harsh polemics
with the thinkers they called "naturalists," the most prominent of whom
was John Dewey. As pacesetters for American liberalism, thinkers such
as Dewey already had ample reason for annoyance at Catholics; the
assault on their ideas and the degree to which religious ideas seemed to
be regaining intellectual respectability aroused them to something like
outrage.

The deepest source of bitterness was that Catholics and naturalists
each accused the other of holding principles that furnished the intellectual foundation for totalitarianism.[13] Underlying the mutual recrimina-
tion was a disagreement about how values are grounded. Catholics and
other "absolutists," as they came to be known, held that there is an
inherent structure of value in reality; that man can discern its basic
pattern, and that he is obligated to take it as his guide in the social and
political realm as well as in personal and family life. The naturalists, or
"relativists," on the other hand, denied that reality exhibited any such
inherent structure of value; they affirmed instead that man evolves his
own values from social experience and imposes them on reality.

The relativist position dominated American intellectual life in the
1930s, but those who held it were profoundly discomfited by the charge
that their own principles left them no grounds on which to object to
Hitler because all he was doing was imposing on reality a set of values
different from their own, but which they had no warrant for saying was
evil. Moreover, the charge continued, by denying that values rested on
anything more than human volition, the relativists had actually paved
the intellectual way for Hitlerism. Unable to refute the charge as formulated, the relativists simply dismissed it and brought a *tu quoque*
countercharge against the absolutists. According to their etiology, totalitarianism in politics derived from authoritarianism in thought; that in
turn was inseparable from the conviction that one could attain the truth
about things in their very essence; hence Catholics and other absolutists
were the real intellectual progenitors of totalitarianism.

This interpretation complemented the widely accepted linkage between Catholicism and Fascism, and it was the majority view of American
intellectuals. But the Catholic-absolutist critique had put secular intellectuals on the defensive for a time, and it would have required supernatural patience (to which, of course, they made no pretension) for them
not to have felt anger as well as chagrin. By the time the war ended,

they were thoroughly aroused on the subject of Catholic authoritarianism and prepared to respond vigorously to any further provocation.[14]

Protestants too had had as much as they could take of Catholic "aggressiveness." Many of them were alienated in the late 1930s for reasons already mentioned. Yet the campaign for interreligious brotherhood being promoted by the National Conference of Christians and Jews provided a countercurrent of good will. In these circumstances, President Roosevelt's 1939 appointment of Myron C. Taylor as his "personal representative" to the Vatican constituted a significant turning point in the overall climate of Protestant feeling. Because it raised the church-state issue in highly visible form, and even more because it seemed to symbolize a new status for Catholics in the national community, the Taylor appointment aroused strong Protestant opposition from groups relatively untouched by the anti-Catholic feeling generated by issues such as the Spanish Civil War.[15]

The church-state issue was sharpened in 1940 by the appearance of a book restating the traditional teaching on the desirability of Catholicism's being the established religion of the state. Separation of church and state and religious freedom were, according to this teaching, merely expedients tolerable in situations where the Catholic faith could not, for practical reasons, be established as the religion of the state. This formulation was all the more shocking because its author was John A. Ryan, the outstanding American Catholic liberal of his generation. Naturally, no non-Catholic reader was satisfied with Ryan's bland reassurance that the possibility of establishing the Catholic religion in the United States was so remote that no sensible person need feel any concern about it. Indeed, the Ryan book seemed to give the lie to the protestations by American Catholic leaders that they were sincerely committed to the American principle of religious freedom and church-state separation.[16]

The growing strength and assertiveness of American Catholics took on a more disquieting cast in the light of this revelation of what Protestants regarded as the ultimate intentions harbored by the Catholic church. Something else that heightened their anxieties was the conviction that the hierarchy was pursuing a carefully thought out plan to "take over" America and subvert the democratic ideals and values that were rooted in its Protestant heritage. The degree to which this conviction had established itself by the end of the war in the minds of the leaders of mainstream Protestantism—not just the radical fringe of traditional Catholic baiters—is made clear by an eight-part series by Harold E. Fey entitled "Can Catholicism Win America," which appeared in the

Christian Century between 29 November 1944 and 17 January 1945.[17]

Fey was an editor of the magazine; he was clearly not a bigot in the old-fashioned sense, and he conceded that any religious group had a right to try to build up its following. "But," he added, "when the extension of a religious faith becomes an avowed means of gaining political and social power looking toward clerical domination of American culture, objections are in order." The Catholic hierarchy, in Fey's view, was making a calculated grab for power that was "conceived in totalitarian terms."[18] Other Protestant writers also warned against "emergent clericalism" and pointed to abuses it had produced in other lands—"the crucifixion of liberty, political fascism, social decadence, revolutionary violence, and anti-clerical revolt."[19] The lesson for Protestants who cared about their religion and the national culture that had sprung from it was obvious: they had to arouse themselves to the danger and develop a militance of their own in behalf of the "culture of liberty."[20]

The stage was thus set for a major eruption over "the Catholic issue" when the war ended. There was nothing like the groundswell of popular no-popery that existed in the 1920s, but both Protestant and secular liberal elites felt that Catholic presumptuousness had gone too far.[21] Catholics, for their part, had so completely internalized the conviction they were underdogs in American society that they seemed unaware others regarded them as aggressors.[22] Indeed, their very heedlessness, springing from what was called "insulation from the main stream of American life and thought," was urged as a complaint against them.[23]

But Catholics might have responded that it was time for "the mainstream" to be redefined. Had they not proved their devotion to American ideals by wartime service and sacrifice? Had not the war itself discredited liberal optimism and vindicated Catholic teaching on the reality of sin and man's need for divine assistance? Was not their longstanding opposition to Communism in the process of being vindicated by postwar disillusionment and the emerging Cold War? Of course Catholics were conscious of differing from others on many issues, but they considered their position correct and thought they were equally entitled with others to try to influence the direction of national policy. From the Catholic viewpoint, this was a matter not of being presumptuous or aggressive but of asserting the legitimate claims of a large group of Americans who were no longer willing to be told by others how they should behave.

The clash was not long in coming.[24] Traditional sore points such as U.S.-Vatican relations, restrictions placed on Protestant missionaries in Latin America, and Roman ties with conservative regimes in Europe continued as significant irritants. But the quarrel over public aid for parochial schools soon emerged as the paramount issue, especially when it became interwoven with postwar attempts to provide federal aid to education, and when the U.S. Supreme Court decision in the Everson case (1947) sanctioned the use of public funds to bus parochial school children, while at the same time setting forth a very stringent definition of the "wall of separation" between church and state. The decision galvanized into action the newly formed organization Protestants and Other Americans United for the Separation of Church and State, which pursued a militantly anti-Catholic line. Later decisions of the court in the McCollum (1948) and Zorach (1952) cases steered a somewhat zigzag course with respect to religion and education and kept the school question in the forefront of controversy.[25]

Although secular liberals operated from different premises, they agreed with Protestants on the school question. Paul Blanshard's *American Freedom and Catholic Power* (1949) set forth the liberal case against Catholicism in comprehensive terms. The school issue was very prominent, but Blanshard also scored Catholic censorship, the crude use of political clout to impose a repressive morality on others, support for reactionary political regimes, disregard for civil liberties, and, most basically, the church's adherence to a hierarchical principle of organization that made it intrinsically un-American. When portions of the book appeared as a series of articles in the *Nation*, they set off a bitter quarrel in New York; the appearance of the book itself called forth an angry flood of Catholic responses. Blanshard elaborated his charge in 1951 with a second book drawing out the parallels between Catholicism and Communism as two opposed totalitarian systems.[26]

Catholics' *anti*-Communism, already a matter of great concern to liberals, took on an even more sinister cast in 1950 when it became intertangled with McCarthyism.[27] The junior senator from Wisconsin was, of course, a Catholic, and he had much Catholic support. But Catholicism itself was not the central issue in McCarthyism, and Catholics were divided in their reactions to McCarthy. Although suspicions lingered after McCarthy's downfall, "the Catholic issue" had receded from prominence by that time. The appearance in 1955 of Will Herberg's *Protestant-Catholic-Jew*, which presented a sympathetic picture of Catholicism as one of the "three great faiths of democracy," can be taken as an indication that the period of controversy was over.[28]

With this rough sketch of the background, and without attempting to treat the subject comprehensively, we turn now to the ambiguities of pluralism. Although Horace M. Kallen introduced the key term *cultural pluralism* in the twenties, it did not catch on until the end of the next decade and came into general use only in the wartime years and after. By that time it meant something quite different from what Kallen originally had in mind. Written in reaction to the hundred-percent Americanism of World War I, his original version of cultural pluralism was radically antiassimilationist. It envisaged American nationality not as a distinctive something-in-itself but as a collocation of autonomous ethnic nationalities, each of which had its own spiritual enclave, all somehow coexisting harmoniously within the political entity called the United States. When the term was taken up by the students of intergroup relations in the late thirties, however, cultural pluralism had lost its hard edge and become an enlightened form of Americanization theory. Although it laid verbal stress on diversity, its proponents acknowledged that it was "essentially a technique of social adjustment which will make possible the preservation of the best of all cultures" as contributors to the generic American culture. It was, in other words, a relaxed version of the classic melting pot ideal, which was precisely what Kallen meant to discredit and overthrow.[29]

The assimilationist version of cultural pluralism came into wider usage in the war years because it was ideally suited to the rhetorical requirements of the situation—that is, it allowed the insistence on wartime unity to be couched in the language of tolerance and respect for diversity. We were, after all, fighting a brutal totalitarian regime based on an abhorrent doctrine of racial supremacy. What united us in this desperate struggle was our common commitment to a set of ideals, the ideals of democracy—indeed, of Western civilization—among which respect for the dignity of the individual, whatever his background, loomed very large. Sharing this common ground, our differences were unimportant. Of course, we had to live up to our ideals; hence the message of tolerance for diversity, respect for cultural pluralism, took on a certain urgency. But at bottom it assumed we were more alike than different because we were "Americans All." As Louis Adamic put the matter in 1940: by respecting diversity, "we will produce unity—automatically—and make it dynamic, bring[ing] out the basic sameness of people."[30]

As this term that seemed to say one thing and mean another became ever more bland and innocuous, students of government complicated matters even more by applying the word *pluralism* to America's multigroup political system. Although it came out of a different intellectual tradition, this usage blended with *pluralism* as it was understood by commentators on intergroup relations, making the term more diffuse and generalized than ever.[31]

Catholics were conventionally included among the minorities to be cherished in our pluralistic society, and reducing religious prejudice was a time-honored goal of those committed to better intergroup relations. Catholics found the idea of pluralism congenial and were using the term freely by around 1950. By that date social scientists were also calling attention to the tendency for ethnic distinctiveness to fade into a broader social differentiation based on religion. This interpretation, fully elaborated in Herberg's triple-melting-pot thesis of 1955, suggested that cultural pluralism was resolving itself into religious pluralism, or at least that religion and race were the most basic elements in American pluralism.[32]

That, of course, was how Catholics saw the matter. Being defined as a religious minority, they regarded respect for religious differences as the foundation stone of American pluralism, which they interpreted to mean that a religious minority was warranted in pursuing its own way of life so long as it did not thereby infringe on the rights of others. Hence they were shocked when Protestants and liberals denounced as "divisive" activities that Catholics believed were wholly legitimate expressions of American pluralism.

Although occasionally referred to in the twenties and thirties, divisiveness emerged as a leading issue only in the postwar era of religious controversy when it was closely associated with the school question.[33] Not only were Catholic efforts to get public funds for their schools denounced as divisive; so also was the very existence of parochial schools, even if maintained by Catholics themselves on a fully voluntary basis. Nor could the charge always be dismissed as the work of Catholic-baiters such as Paul Blanshard. It was also made by the prestigious president of Harvard University, James B. Conant. While disclaiming any thought of weakening America's prized diversity, he nevertheless characterized parochial schools as a threat to national unity. Indeed, Conant sounded like an old-fashioned advocate of the melting pot in praising the role played by the public school in assimilating immigrants.[34]

Divisiveness was not, however, confined to the schools. Protestant observers had long warned that the hierarchy was mobilizing the Catholic faithful into religiously segregated associations as part of their campaign to take over American society. The tremendous array of institutions and societies Catholics had built up, along with the heavy stress laid on what was called "Catholic Action," lent plausibility to such fears.[35] By 1951 the danger seemed so pressing that the *Christian Century* was moved to the extreme of repudiating pluralism itself. An editorial entitled "Pluralism—National Menace" made the warning explicit, linking it with an exposé of Catholic mobilization in the city of Buffalo which was described in an accompanying article. In the face of this kind of pluralism, the editors felt no embarrassment in calling universal public education "the *sine qua non* of a homogeneous society," and in urging "straightforward, uncompromising resistance to any efforts by any group to subvert the traditional American way of life."[36]

Rejection of pluralism itself was highly anomalous, and quite unnecessary in view of the availability of *divisiveness* as a pejorative term. That is no doubt the reason the *Christian Century*'s repudiation of pluralism had no impact on general usage. But it does call attention to the puzzling relationship of pluralism and divisiveness. Why was the former overwhelmingly acclaimed while the latter was universally deplored? Was it possible to be pluralized without being somehow divided? What made one kind of diversity good and another kind bad? For enlightenment of this perplexity we turn to Horace Kallen, the inventor of "cultural pluralism.

Kallen's *Cultural Pluralism and the American Idea* (1956) was his first major treatment of the subject in thirty years, and his ideas had changed dramatically. Pluralism was no longer primarily associated with ethnic cultures and their preservation; the vision of a federation of nationalities had vanished. Rather, cultural pluralism had been extended to include the most "diverse utterance of diversities—regional, local, religious, ethnic, esthetic, industrial, sporting, and political." But Kallen was not prepared to embrace *every* kind of pluralism: absolutist or isolationist pluralism, a pluralism of noninteracting social monads, he rejected with something like indignation.[37]

Kallen's style is diffuse, and it is difficult at times to make out exactly what he is saying, but his criteria of acceptability seemed to derive from what he referred to as "the philosophy of Cultural Pluralism."[38] This philosophy envisioned reality as a perpetual flux; an unending cosmic coming and going; nothing absolute or fixed. Since this was the nature of reality in itself, pluralism—understood as recognition of this state of affairs and a willingness to accommodate to it through openness and flexibility—was obviously the appropriate social policy. A correct understanding of cultural pluralism, in other words, implied acceptance of a specific metaphysical position, although Kallen would probably have objected to calling it that, since it was, from his viewpoint, simply the way things are.

Correctly understood, pluralism was synonymous with Americanism. That was the point of Kallen's title—*Cultural Pluralism and the
American Idea*—and of the long passages given over a Whitmanesque
roll call of the prophets, symbols, doctrines, and documents that comprised "the Bible of America."[39] As this language suggests, Kallen tended
to erect Americanism into a civil religion; indeed, he conceded the point
in responding to a Roman Catholic critic who objected to his treating
Americanism as "an ultimate ideology . . . a surrogate religion." Of course
the "American Idea" was not a surrogate religion. "It is," Kallen declared,
"that apprehension of human nature and human relations, which every
sort and condition of Protestant, Catholic, Judaist, Moslem, Buddhist, and
every other communion must agree upon, be converted to and convinced
of, if they mean to live freely and peacefully together as equals, none
penalizing the other for his otherness and all insuring each the equal
protection of the law. And this," he concluded roundly, "is how the
American Idea is, literally, religion."[40]

Given this confession of faith, one begins to see why Catholics and
secular liberals were at loggerheads on pluralism and divisiveness. Kallen, who spoke with authority in this area, affirmed that pluralism and
Americanism were the same thing and that it (or they) required everyone
to accept the same substantive "apprehension of human nature and
human relations." Catholics believed almost precisely the opposite. Far
from requiring this kind of agreement, American pluralism, in their view,
designated a system that allowed people to live together in civic peace
*despite their disagreements on basic beliefs about human nature and
human relations.*[41]

The terminology in which discussions of pluralism were carried on
made it almost impossible to discern this fundamental difference of view.
The differences emerge more clearly in another article of Kallen's entitled
"Democracy's True Religion," discussion of which brings us to the second
major issue I want to touch on—the tendency to treat democracy as a
civil religion which emerged in the critique of Catholic authoritarianism.[42]

The role played by World War II in stimulating the development of
democracy as a civil religion can hardly be overestimated. The need to
mobilize the nation's spiritual resources in the desperate struggle against
totalitarianism naturally brought about a terrific emphasis on democracy
as the symbol of the values for which we fought. As a result, wartime
nationalism assumed a highly ideological form, expressing itself in fervent reaffirmations of traditional democratic ideals, the four freedoms,
and what Gunnar Myrdal called in 1944 "the American creed." Mention

of Myrdal in this context calls to mind another aspect of the situation, already alluded to in passing, namely the point that emphasis on the universalistic values of democracy as the basis of wartime unity was what made possible the seemingly paradoxical celebration of pluralism. It was, to repeat, only because the nation was united on the ideology of democracy that it was committed to tolerating diversity—and could afford to do so.[43]

All this was, in my opinion, not only understandable in the circumstances but also necessary and proper. I do not, in other words, regard what has just been said as an unmasking of something cynical or manipulative.[44] On the contrary, I cannot conceive of anything more appropriate for emphasis at the time than the traditions of democracy. But of course there were drawbacks as well. Like all developments, the emphasis on democracy was subject to its own distinctive excesses, labored under built-in difficulties, and carried negative potentialities.

The most obvious negative potentiality was realized in the semihysteria over subversion that developed in the Cold War years. Although deplorable, this kind of fixation on the danger of "un-American" tendencies was but the obverse side of wartime insistence on the democratic ideology as the touchstone of national unity.

The built-in difficulty that democracy is a highly abstract concept that means different things to different people tended to aggravate the impassioned confusion of the postwar years. Misunderstanding springing from this source led easily to suspicion of bad faith, for it is difficult not to question the honesty of an antagonist who claims to be devoted to a principle cherished by all, but who interprets it as justifying policies one believes to be perverse. While it was inherent in the situation, this difficulty was perhaps made worse by the tendency of secular liberals to think of democracy in "cultural" terms, that is, as a mode of behavior or "way of life," rather than as a set of institutional arrangements or the principles that those institutions were intended to embody.[45]

The cultural definition of democracy appealed to the liberals because it enabled them to get around the claim of the absolutists that the good society had to be based on common assent to universally binding general principles. But it inevitably implied a behavioral test of true democracy. After all, if democracy is a way of life, only those who live that way are really democrats. To the extent that they accepted a cultural definition of democracy, liberals were thus inadvertently erecting behavioral conformity into the test of authentic Americanism.

The built-in difficulties and negative potentialities already mentioned were reinforced by what I consider the distinctive excess of the wartime emphasis on democracy—namely, the tendency to invest democracy with the aura of the sacred, to exalt it to the level of a civil religion. Given democracy's close association with the deepest values of Western civilization, this kind of tendency was natural enough at a time when those values were threatened with annihilation. More often than not, it was merely an implicit tendency—illustrated, for example, in the crisis-induced association of American values and the "Judeo-Christian tradition"—but it was occasionally formulated in more explicit terms.[46] The article by Kallen referred to above is one of these explicit formulations, and it also illustrates how liberals sometimes insisted on conformity to their understanding of "the democratic way of life" as the test of true Americanism.

Kallen's article, which was popular in approach, appeared in the *Saturday Review of Literature* in July 1951.[47] Defining religion in Deweyesque terms as that which a person invests with ultimate importance and "bets his life on," Kallen proceeded immediately to the assertion that science and democracy were a religion in this sense. They were one religion because science was democracy in the realm of ideas, while democracy was "the method of science" applied to human relations. This religion was also called "secularism," a designation that Kallen accepted despite the hackles it raised in some quarters.[48]

The distinctive feature of this religion, according to Kallen, was that its "what" was a "how," by which he meant that its content was a process or method rather than a body of teachings. That method he described as "a free mobility, wherein majorities may become minorities without any loss of rights and minorities [may become] majorities without any accrual of privilege; where every majority guarantees all minorities equal liberty and equal justice and protects them from the dangers of coercion and injustice at its own hands." Attuned as it was to the cosmic flux of reality, this religion assured an "open society in which the entire miscellany of mankind may enter freely and move and have their beings in safety, all equally free to unite themselves with their fellows or to abandon one union and join another as their consciences direct, their needs prompt, and their understandings guide."[49]

This religion—which was Kallen's midcentury version of pluralism seen from a different angle—might appear terribly vague, but it was not without practical implications. For true believers like Kallen, "the democratic faith" was "the religion *of* and *for* religions"—in other words, it was superior to all other religions and had the responsibility of seeing to it that they obeyed *its* principles. No "assumption of infallibility" on the part of a subordinate faith could be tolerated, for example, nor could any other practice "repugnant to the religious life" as that was defined by the religion of science and democracy. And since "free mobility" was the crucial "what/how" of the democratic faith, it was unacceptable for any subordinate religion to impede the free coming and going of its followers by attempting to keep them apart from other religionists.[50]

From what has already been said, one might infer that the Roman Catholic church would have trouble adjusting itself to the regime of science-democracy-secularism as the religion of religions. Another area of incompatibility emerged from Kallen's discussion of ministry. Since it did not accept any "invidious distinction between the 'religious' and the other vocations of man," the democratic faith affirmed "the priesthood of all believers" and thereby consummated the liberation of the human conscience begun by the Protestant Reformation. Directly opposed to this democratic understanding of religious ministry was "clericalism," by which Kallen understood the pretension of a sacerdotal caste to special powers that were used to justify special privileges.[51]

By this point in the article it was clear that Catholicism was incompatible with the religion of science and democracy. Kallen did not shrink from the duty this laid upon him of pointing out that fact, and of exploring its implications. Indeed, he devoted at least one-fifth of his space to the peril to democracy posed by "the Roman Catholic hierarchy," which had become so "notably aggressive" in resisting the salutary processes of secularization that all non-Catholics were justifiably alarmed. He covered familiar ground in saying that the church had "declared war" on church-state separation, denounced the U.S. Supreme Court, and demanded an ambassador to the Vatican. He was more original, however, in relating these offenses to a perverted interpretation of the American principle of freedom of religion.[52]

According to the "sacerdotal argument" advanced by the Roman hierarchy, Kallen explained, freedom of religion was identified with "the liberty of a priestly craft [sic], calling themselves 'the teaching church,' to impose its authority willy-nilly." But that was, of course, wrong; freedom of religion was *not* intended to allow churches to conduct themselves in keeping with their own law, "such as the canon law." What freedom of religion really involved, Kallen declared as the exegete of the democratic faith, was "recognition by the state . . . of the liberty of the personal conscience . . . of the individual's right of private judgment which secures him from the aggressions and coercions of sacerdotal authority." In other words, it was the job of the state to make sure all the subordinate religions conducted themselves "democratically" in their dealings with their own communicants. And if they didn't, the state would presumably require them to do so.[53]

As an illustration of this extraordinary interpretation of freedom of religion and separation of church and state, Kallen pointed to the area of education. Consider the case, he said, of "an American parent believing in the Roman Catholic religion." Such persons had as much right as anyone else to send their children to the public school; but according to the law of the Catholic church, they could do so only under pain of sin. This amounted, in Kallen's view, to "suppression of the parent's right by clerical coercion," and it constituted "a violation of the Constitution."[54] He failed to specify what should be done, but since it was unconstitutional and wrong, judicial and/or legislative relief would seem to be called for—court orders or laws spelling out what the Catholic church could and could not do in maintaining its own internal discipline. Theoretically, the church might be required to do away with the hierarchy as such, since that authoritarian structure was clearly the root of the offense against the religion of science, democracy, and secularism.

Even without drawing that inference, Kallen's article confirmed precisely the point Catholics were always urging against their secular-liberal critics—namely, that the secular-liberal position amounted to a religion in itself and one that claimed the privileged status of being normative for American society. Kallen's affirmation of his own sectarian version of democracy as a civil religion was not a momentary aberration; he repeated it in 1954 and 1965.[55] Nor was he the only one to make such an affirmation in that era. J. Paul Williams, a professor of religion at Mount Holyoke, did the same, laying particular emphasis on the role of the public school in inculcating "the democratic ideal *as religion* [sic]." Williams spoke of the public school as "a veritable temple for the indoctrination of democracy" and prescribed as "*worship*" school exercises aimed at revitalizing democratic idealism. Will Herberg asserted in 1952 that "influential Jewish religious leaders" had been advocating essentially the same thing "for years."[56]

This kind of talk was an embarrassment to public school spokespersons who endorsed strict separationism and insisted that secular education was in no way identifiable with religious or "metaphysical" instruction.[57] In 1954, however, the prominent historian of American religion Sidney E. Mead chided the public for ignoring Williams's argument. Mead, who was to emerge in the 1960s as a leading apologist for American civil religion, all but explicitly endorsed Williams's dictum that "governmental agencies must teach the democratic ideal *as reli-*

gion." This, he frankly admitted, "is essentially an appeal for a State Church in the United States, and . . . [the] arguments for it largely parallel those traditionally used to defend Establishments."[58]

What Mead failed to explain was how such an establishment could get around the First Amendment, which proscribed establishments of religion without making an exception for the religion of democracy. Writers sympathetic to American civil religion do not address this problem very straightforwardly—at least not in the terms presented here. Perhaps the reason is that, for a writer such as Kallen, the word *democracy* stood for the ultimate principles underlying human life, and the idea that the Constitution could really proscribe its being "established" as the common faith of Americans was simply incoherent. But this, of course, is merely to assume that the religion of democracy cannot be proscribed because it is *true*, while it is entirely proper for false religions to be proscribed— especially (Kallen at least would add) religions as antipathetic to "democracy" as Roman Catholicism was.

It was because of this tendency to absolutize democracy, to elevate it to religious status, that Catholics, who were themselves abused as authoritarians, responded in like terms, calling their secularist critics "totalitarians" who insisted that everyone else think and act as they did.[59] While often shrill in defending themselves, Catholics were on solid ground in rejecting Kallen's "democratic faith" as the normative formulation of Americanism. At the same time, reasonable Catholics were deeply concerned to mitigate the controversies and to correct the genuine abuses their critics pointed out. Most of all, Catholics were embarrassed by commitment to an outmoded ideal of church-state union. Hence it is no accident that a revitalized American Catholic liberalism was forged in the era of controversy, the most significant achievement of which was John Courtney Murray's working out of a persuasive Catholic rationale for religious freedom and separation of church and state.[60]

But that is another story. The point of this one is that analysis of the controversies of the forties helps us to identify basic conceptual ambiguities that have persisted in more recent discussions of pluralism and democracy, religion and secular humanism.

NOTES

Source: Review of Politics, 49 (Spring 1987), 208–30. Reprinted by permission of the publisher.

1. Donald F. Crosby, *God, Church, and Flag: Senator Joseph R. McCarthy and the Catholic Church, 1950–1957* (Chapel Hill, N.C., 1978).

2. Lerond Curry, *Protestant-Catholic Relations in America: World War I through Vatican II* (Lexington, Ky., 1972), 12ff.

3. George Q. Flynn, *American Catholics and the Roosevelt Presidency, 1932–1936* (Lexington, Ky., 1976), esp. 50ff. For general coverage of the Catholic history of this period, see James Hennesey, *American Catholics: A History of the Roman Catholic Community in the United States* (New York, 1981), chaps. 18–20; Jay P. Dolan, *The American Catholic Experience: A History from Colonial Times to the Present* (Garden City, N.Y., 1985), chaps. 13–14. For concern about intergroup relations in the 1930s, see Richard Weiss, "Ethnicity and Reform: Minorities and the Ambience of the Depression Years," *Journal of American History*, 66 (December 1979), 566–85.

4. Charles J. Tull, *Father Coughlin and the New Deal* (Syracuse, N.Y., 1965), 78, 80, 82–88. See also Alan Brinkley, *Voices of Protest: Huey Long, Father Coughlin, and the Great Depression* (New York, 1982), 269–83.

5. Tull, *Father Coughlin*, chap. 6; Sheldon Marcus, *Father Coughlin: The Tumultuous Life of the Priest of the Little Flower* (Boston, 1973); David J. O'Brien, *The Renewal of American Catholicism* (New York, 1972), 118–28; Ronald H. Bayor, *Neighbors in Conflict: The Irish, Germans, Jews, and Italians of New York City, 1929–1941* (Baltimore, Md., 1978), chap. 5; George N. Shuster, "The Conflict among Catholics," *American Scholar*, 10 (January 1941), 5–16, esp. 10–11. For a Catholic response to the charge of pro-Fascism, see Theodore Maynard, "Catholics and the Nazis," *American Mercury*, 53 (October 1941), 391–400.

6. J. David Valaik, "American Catholics and the Spanish Civil War, 1931–1939" (Ph.D. diss., University of Rochester, 1964); Allen Guttmann, *The Wound in the Heart: America and the Spanish Civil War* (New York, 1962); Fredrick B. Pike, "The Background to the Civil War in Spain and the U.S. Response to the War," in Mark Falcoff and Fredrick B. Pike, eds., *The Spanish Civil War, 1936–39: American Hemispheric Perspectives* (Lincoln, Neb., 1982), 20–37.

7. J. David Valaik, "Catholics, Neutrality, and the Spanish Embargo, 1937–1939," *Journal of American History*, 54 (June 1967), 73–85, and Leo V. Kanawada, *Franklin D. Roosevelt's Diplomacy and American Catholics, Italians, and Jews* (Ann Arbor, Mich., 1982), chap. 3 tend to credit Catholic pressure with preventing the lifting of the embargo; more skeptical about the role of Catholic pressure are George Q. Flynn, *Roosevelt and Romanism: Catholics and American Diplomacy, 1937–1945* (Westport, Conn., 1976), 43–53; and Robert Morton Darrow, "Catholic Political Power: A Study of the Activities of the American Catholic Church on Behalf of Franco during the Spanish Civil War, 1936–1939" (Ph.D. diss., Columbia University, 1953), 141–50, 211.

8. Harold L. Ickes, *The Secret Diary of Harold L. Ickes* (New York, 1953–54), 2:390. The most explicit statement of Ickes's "pet theory" about anti-Catholic backlash was made to the Reverend Maurice Sheehy of the Catholic University of America in 1940; see ibid., 3:383. See also ibid., 1:687, 2:86; and Kanawada, *Roosevelt's Diplomacy*, 67, 71.

9. Van Wyck Brooks to Lewis Mumford, 12 April 1938, in Robert E. Spiller, ed., *The Van Wyck Brooks-Lewis Mumford Letters: The Record of a Literary Friendship, 1921–1963* (New York, 1970), 154.

10. George Seldes, *The Catholic Crisis* (New York, 1939). This book was reissued with a new preface and an additional chapter in 1945. The reviewer quoted in the text is Conrad H. Moehlman, *Christian Century*, 57 (January 3, 1940), 17.

11. An instance of offensive Catholic pressure used to prevent Margaret Sanger from speaking in a Congregational church in Holyoke, Mass. was later made the focal

point of an intensive study of interreligious tensions; see Kenneth W. Underwood, *Protestant and Catholic: Religious and Social Interaction in an Industrial Community* (Boston, 1957).

12. I know of no secondary account of this campaign, but see Geoffrey O'Connell, *Naturalism in American Education* (New York, 1938); National Catholic Alumni Federation, *Man and Modern Secularism: Essays on the Conflict of the Two Cultures* (New York, 1940); *Secularism: Statement Issued November 14, 1947, by the Bishops of the United States and Signed in Their Names by the Members of the Administrative Board, N.C.W.C.* (Washington, D.C., 1947). See also Hugh J. Nolan, ed., *Pastoral Letters of the American Hierarchy, 1792–1970* (Washington, D.C., 1971), 368–70, 403–408.

13. This discussion is based on Edward A. Purcell, Jr., *The Crisis of Democratic Theory: Scientific Naturalism and the Problem of Value* (Lexington, Ky., 1973); for reference to Catholic criticism of the naturalistic position, see 164ff., 179–80, 203–4, 224–25, 241. See also Donald H. Meyer, "Secular Transcendence: The American Religious Humanists," *American Quarterly*, 34 (Winter 1982), 524–42.

14. For liberal irritation with Catholics, see *The Scientific Spirit and Democratic Faith* (New York, 1944); *The Authoritarian Attempt to Capture Education* (New York, 1945); and "The New Failure of Nerve," *Partisan Review*, 10 (January–February 1943), esp. 11, 17–20, 28, 29, 50, 51, 53.

15. Curry, *Protestant-Catholic Relations*, 36ff.; Flynn, *Roosevelt and Romantism*, 20, 21, 72, 98–136; John S. Conway, "Myron C. Taylor's Mission to the Vatican 1940–1950," *Church History*, 44 (March 1975), 85–99; Gerald P. Fogarty, "Vatican-American Relations: 1940–1984," paper delivered at the Charles and Margaret Hall Cushwa Center for the Study of American Catholicism, University of Notre Dame, Fall 1984. See also Fogarty, *The Vatican and the American Hierarchy from 1870 to 1965* (1982; Wilmington, Del., 1985), 259–66, 269–71.

16. John A. Ryan and Francis J. Boland, *Catholic Principles of Politics* (New York, 1940), chaps. 22–23, esp. pp. 316–21. This was a revision of a book published originally in 1922 and entitled *The State and The Church*, which had been a focal point of controversy in the Al Smith campaign. See Francis L. Broderick, *Right Reverend New Dealer: John A. Ryan* (New York, 1963), 118–20, 170–79, 247–48.

17. After running in the magazine, the series was widely circulated as a pamphlet. A Congregational minister in Madison, Wisconsin, recommended it to his flock in the following terms: "Here is a carefully wrought study of the strategy by which Rome, weakened in Europe, hopes to make America a Catholic province, capturing Middletown, controlling the press, winning the Negro, courting the workers, invading rural America, and centralizing its power in Washington." Quoted in advertisement for the Fey pamphlet in *Christian Century*, 62 (February 28, 1945), 287.

18. Fey, "Catholicism Fights Communism," *Christian Century*, 62 (January 3, 1945), 13; Fey, "The Center of Catholic Power," ibid., 62 (January 17, 1945), 75.

19. J. A. M. (John A. MacKay), "Emergent Clericalism," *Christianity and Crisis*, 5 (February 19, 1945), 1–2. MacKay, later described by his fellow Presbyterian John Foster Dulles as "violently anti-Catholic" (Crosby, *God, Church, and Flag*, 136), issued the following warning in 1943: "No small part of the contemporary crisis is the imperiousness of the Roman Catholic hierarchy. The evidence of studied disregard for the sensibilities of non-Roman Christians in the United States is so great that, if a very serious situation is to be avoided, it will be necessary for the leaders of Roman Catholicism in this country to moderate their attitudes and alter their procedures. It is well that they should know that Protestant sentiment, more thoroughly united today

on important issues than it has been for generations, will not tolerate indefinitely the arrogance of the new Catholic policy." MacKay, "Hierarchs, Missionaries, and Latin America," *Christianity and Crisis*, 3 (May 3, 1943), 2.

20. In a discussion of the "Protestant Reorientation" that led eventually to the formation of the National Council of Churches, the *Christian Century*, 60 (October 27, 1943), 1222, cited the growing power of the Catholic church as requiring a Protestant response and added, "Only by imagining American culture as predominantly informed by one or the other of these faiths will the significance of their differences appear. Protestantism cannot be true to itself and be indifferent to the character which American civilization would take on in the event that Catholicism became the preponderant spiritual force in the nation's life." In a paper entitled "Protestantism and Democracy," originally presented in 1945, the well-known historian of American religion William Warren Sweet asserted that the basic freedoms enjoyed by Americans "are to a large degree Protestant accomplishments. And if they are to be retained, they must be preserved by a united and intelligent Protestantism." Sweet, *American Culture and Religion* (Dallas, Tex., 1951), 39. See also Charles Clayton Morrison, *Can Protestantism Win America?* (New York, 1948), esp. chaps. 1, 6 (this book, expanded from a series of articles in the *Christian Century*, was inspired by Fey's series in the same journal); James Hastings Nichols, *Democracy and the Churches* (Philadelphia, 1951), esp. 243–79; and Ronald James Boggs, "Culture of Liberty: History of Americans United for Separation of Church and State, 1947–1973" (Ph.D. diss., Ohio State University, 1978), esp. 1:63–68, which outlines the "culture of liberty" ideology as it was drawn up in 1947 by Charles Clayton Morrison.

21. For evidence from public opinion polls, see Hazel Gaudet Erskine, "The Polls: Religious Prejudice, Part I," *Public Opinion Quarterly*, 29 (Fall 1965), 486–96.

22. The Catholic tendency to interpret all criticism from non-Catholics as bigotry is reflected in the way the Jesuit weekly, *America*, reacted to Fey's series: it dismissed the articles in a brief note that characterized them as giving the "green light to Ku Kluxism." *America*, 72 (February 17, 1945), 382. The same article quoted *Time*, January 26, 1945 on how Protestants were launching "a slam-bang crusade against the Roman Catholic Church."

23. The degree to which this view was widely shared among intellectuals is suggested by the fact that Lynn T. White, Jr., considered it relevant to a wartime discussion of the future of the humanities. See White, "Conflicting Forces in the United States," in *The Humanities Look Ahead: Report of the First Annual Conference Held by the Stanford School of Humanities* (Stanford, Calif., 1943), 38.

24. For general treatments see Curry, *Protestant-Catholic Relations*, chap. 2; Boggs, "Culture of Liberty," chap. 1; John J. Kane, *Catholic-Protestant Conflicts in America* (Chicago, 1955); Anson Phelps Stokes and Leo Pfeffer, *Church and State in the United States*, rev. ed. (New York, 1964), 278–79, 436–40; Lawrence H. Fuchs, *John F. Kennedy and American Catholicism* (New York, 1967), chap. 4, esp. pp. 130–42; W. Russell Bowie, "Protestant Concern over Catholicism," *American Mercury*, 69 (September 1949), 261–73; John Courtney Murray, "The Catholic Position—A Reply," ibid., 274–83; George N. Shuster, "The Catholic Controversy," *Harper's Magazine*, 199 (November 1949), 25–32; D. W. Brogan, "The Catholic Church in America," ibid., 200 (May 1950), 40–50; George Huntston Williams, Waldo Beach, and H. Richard Niebuhr, "Issues between Catholics and Protestants at Mid-century," *Religion in Life*, 23 (Spring 1954), 163–205.

25. Diane Ravitch, *Troubled Crusade: American Education, 1945–1980* (New York, 1983), 29–41; Boggs, "Culture of Liberty," chaps. 2–5; Thomas G. Sanders,

Protestant Concepts of Church and State: Historical Backgrounds and Approaches for the Future (New York, 1964), 161–65, 257ff.; Walter W. Benjamin, "Separation of Church and State: Myth and Reality," *Journal of Church and State*, 11 (Winter 1969), 93–109, esp. 97–99.

26. Paul Blanshard, *American Freedom and Catholic Power* (Boston, 1949); Blanshard, *Communism, Democracy, and Catholic Power* (Boston, 1951). The most comprehensive Catholic reply to Blanshard was James M. O'Neill, *Catholics in Controversy* (New York, 1954). Of particular interest in view of his revisionist work in the area of Catholic church-state theory is John Courtney Murray's critique, "Paul Blanshard and the New Nativism," *Month*, 191 (1951), 214–25.

27. Crosby, *God, Church, and Flag*, esp. chap. 6.

28. Will Herberg *Protestant-Catholic-Jew: An Essay in American Religious Sociology*, rev. ed. (Garden City, N.Y., 1960), esp. chap. 10.

29. For a fuller development of these points, see Philip Gleason, "American Identity and Americanization," in Stephan Thernstrom, Ann Orlov, and Oscar Handlin, eds., *Harvard Encyclopedia of American Ethnic Groups* (Cambridge, Mass., 1980), 43–46; chap. 3, above; John Higham, "Ethnic Pluralism in Modern American Thought," in his *Send These to Me: Jews and Other Immigrants in Urban America* (Baltimore, Md., 1975), 196–230.

30. See chaps. 3, 6, above. Quotation from Louis Adamic, "This Crisis Is an Opportunity," *Common Ground*, 1 (Autumn 1940), 66; see also Adamic, *From Many Lands* (New York, 1940), 298–99. Note also the following statement, the context of which links it closely to Kallen and cultural pluralism: "We perceive that the very diversity which is the creative principle in American life is made possible by a unifying faith in the dignity and value of the individual, a unifying aspiration toward equality of opportunity and freedom for all." Foreword to issue devoted to "Intercultural Education," *English Journal*, 35 (June 1946), 286.

31. See chap. 3.

32. For examples of Catholic usage of the term, see Bryan M. O'Reilly, "Catholic America Comes of Age," *Catholic World*, 166 (January 1948), 347; Charles Donahue, "Freedom and Education: The Pluralist Background," *Thought*, 27 (Winter 1952), 542–60. The modulation of ethnic into religious identity is implied in Ruby Jo Reeves Kennedy, "Single or Triple Melting Pot?" *American Journal of Sociology*, 49 (January 1944), 331–39; is explicitly identified as a trend in Alfred McClung Lee, "Sociological Insights into American Culture and Personality," *Journal of Social Issues*, 7, no. 4 (1951), 10–14; and is made the basis of Herberg's interpretation of the religious situation of the 1950s in *Protestant-Catholic-Jew*, esp. chaps. 2–3.

33. Donahue begins his article by saying, " 'Divisive' has come to be a favorite word among those who believe that all American education ... should be tax-supported, secular, and entirely under public control." Donahue, "Freedom and Education," 542. Efforts to arouse "divisive passions" were deprecated in 1920 in what has been called "the first united expression of opposition to religious and racial prejudice in the history of the United States." See James E. Pitt, *Adventures in Brotherhood* (New York, 1955), 12–13. See also J. Paul Williams, *The New Education and Religion* (New York, 1945), 13; T. T. Brumbaugh, "How Religion Divides Us," *Christian Century*, 62 (January 31, 1945), 138–39.

34. James B. Conant, *Education and Liberty* (Cambridge, Mass., 1953), 80–81. See Conant, *My Several Lives* (New York, 1970), chap. 34 and app. 3.

35. This theme runs through the Fey series cited earlier. See also James T. Farrell, "The Pope Needs America," *Nation*, 143 (October 17, 24, 1936), 440–41, 476–77;

D. A. Saunders, "Liberals and Catholic Action," *Christian Century*, 54 (October 20, 1937), 1293–95; Seldes, *Catholic Crisis*, 53–54; Blanshard, *American Freedom*, 29–31.

36. "Pluralism—National Menace," *Christian Century*, 68 (June 13, 1951), 701–11. Herberg, *Protestant-Catholic-Jew*, 236–38, 241, discusses this "much-noted editorial" at some length. It is also referred to, specifically in the context of "the semantic confusion current in the term 'cultural pluralism,' " by Joseph Cunneen, "Catholics and Education," in *Catholicism in America: A Series of Articles from "The Commonweal"* (New York, 1954), 153–54. For another reference to the confusing way in which "cultural pluralism" was talked about by religions leaders, see John R. Seeley et al., *Crestwood Heights* (New York, 1956), 379.

37. Horace M. Kallen, *Cultural Pluralism and the American Idea* (Philadelphia, 1956), 98, 50, 55.

38. Ibid., esp. 51–52.

39. Ibid., 86ff.

40. Ibid., 206–7.

41. The paradigmatic formulation of the Catholic understanding is that of John Courtney Murray, S. J.: "The American Proposition makes a particular claim upon the reflective attention of the Catholic insofar as it contains a doctrine and a project in the matter of the 'pluralist society,' as we seem to have agreed to call it. The term might have many meanings. By pluralism here I mean the coexistence within one political community of groups who hold divergent and incompatible views with regard to religious questions—those ultimate questions that concern the nature and destiny of man within a universe that stands under the reign of God. Pluralism therefore implies disagreement and dissension within the community. But it also implies a community within which there must be agreement and consensus. There is no small political problem here. If society is to be at all a rational process, some set of principles must motivate the general participation of all religious groups, despite their dissensions, in the oneness of the community. On the other hand, these common principles must not hinder the maintenance by each group of its own different identity." Murray, *We Hold These Truths* (New York, 1960), x, 15–24.

42. Horace M. Kallen, "Democracy's True Religion," *Saturday Review of Literature*, 34 (July 28, 1951), 6–7, 29–30.

43. See above, chaps. 3 and 7. For Myrdal and the "American Creed," see his *American Dilemma* (New York, 1944), 1:3, 25.

44. In this I differ from the editors of *American Quarterly*, 36 (1984), 341, who said of my contribution that its implications might be "devastating" for students of American culture.

45. Purcell, *Crisis of Democratic Theory*, 211–17 and chaps. 13–14. For an interesting one-page example of making democracy a "folkway or mode of behavior," see C. J. Friedrich, "Comment: Democracy and Dissent," *Review of Politics*, 2 (July 1940), 379.

46. See Mark Silk, "Notes on the Judeo-Christian Tradition in America," *American Quarterly*, 36 (Spring 1984), 65–85, esp. 66–69. F. Ernest Johnson commented on the spiritualization of democracy in "Democracy and Discipline," *Christianity and Crisis*, 3 (December 13, 1943), 1–2. Herbert Agar et al., *The City of Man: A Declaration of World Democracy* (New York, 1941) is explicit in proposing a "universal religion of Democracy"; see esp. 80–85. For a Catholic critique, see Wilfrid Parsons, "Even to Contempt of God," *Commonweal*, 33 (January 24, 1941), 352–54. Lewis Mumford, who was a signer of the "City of Man" statement, quoted an English correspondent

on how democracy seemed, in the crisis of war, to be evolving toward a new kind of religion. See Lewis Mumford to Van Wyck Brooks, September 14, 1940, in Spiller, *Brooks-Mumford Letters*, 192–93.

47. Kallen, "Democracy's True Religion."

48. Ibid., 6–7, 29.

49. Ibid., 7.

50. Ibid., 7, 29.

51. Ibid., 29–30.

52. Ibid.

53. Ibid., 30.

54. Ibid.

55. Kallen, *Secularism Is the Will of God* (New York, 1954); Kallen, "Secularism as the Common Religion of a Free Society," *Journal for the Scientific Study of Religion*, 4 (1965), 145–51.

56. J. Paul Williams, *What Americans Believe and How They Worship* (New York, 1952), 371; Williams, "The Schoolmen and Religion," *School and Society*, 70 (August 13, 1949), 97–100. Williams's 1952 book had later editions in 1962 and 1969. For earlier statements by Williams along the same line, see his "Religious Education, Ignored but Basic to National Well-Being," *School and Society*, 57 (May 22, 1943), 598–600; and his *New Education and Religion*. For Herberg's assertion, see his "Sectarian Conflict over Church and State," *Commentary*, 14 (November 1952), 459.

57. See V. T. Thayer, *Public Education and Its Critics* (New York, 1954), 65–69, 142–44, 159–60.

58. Sidney E. Mead, "Thomas Jefferson's 'Fair Experiment'—Religious Freedom," *Religion in Life*, 23 (Autumn 1954), 566–79; as reprinted in Mead, *The Lively Experiment: The Shaping of a Christianity in America* (New York, 1963), 55–71, esp. 68–71. Lawrence H. Fuchs seems to take a similar position concerning the desirability of American civil religion; see his *John F. Kennedy* at the pages cited under the index heading "Americanism, culture-religion of."

59. In 1953 a prominent liberal-Catholic journalist, William P. Clancy, drew an explicit parallel between Catholic authoritarianism and doctrinaire secularism and described them both as "the fruit of that totalitarian spirit which hating diversity, demands that all existence be made over to conform to its own vision." See Clancy, "Catholicism in America," in *Catholicism in America. A Series of Articles from the Commonweal* (New York, 1954), 11–12.

60. For an early appreciation by a Protestant observer of the importance of Murray's work, see George H. Williams's contribution to Williams, Beach, and Niebuhr, "Issues between Catholics and Protestants," esp. 176–86.

Part Three

Religion and
American Diversity

|| 9 ||

Hansen, Herberg, and American Religion

The expression *Hansen's law* enjoys nothing like the popularity of terms such as *melting pot*, *pluralism*, or more recently, *diversity*, but it is quite familiar to students of immigration and ethnicity. It commemorates Marcus Lee Hansen, a great pioneering figure in the study of immigration to the United States, who encapsulated what he called "the principle of third generation interest" in these memorable words: "What the son wishes to forget the grandson wishes to remember." This striking formulation has been known as Hansen's law since Will Herberg called it that in his influential study of the postwar revival of religion, *Protestant-Catholic-Jew* (1955).

Hansen's law was first enunciated in a lecture given before the Augustana Historical Society in 1937, and the fiftieth anniversary of that event was marked by a scholarly conference on Hansen's work held at Augustana College in Rock Island, Illinois. My being invited to participate in that gathering provided the stimulus to look more closely into the way Hansen's ideas have been employed by students of American ethnic and religious history. The results, which first appeared in *American Immigrants and Their Generations* (1990), edited by Peter Kivisto and Dag Blanck, both surprised me and confirmed what I suspected.

I was surprised to discover, for example, that Hansen did not really discuss or offer evidence for the principle of third-generation interest—he simply assumed it as a given and used it as a springboard to get into the main body of his lecture. I was even more surprised to discover that the published version of the lecture attracted no notice whatsoever between 1938, when it first appeared, and 1952, when it was reprinted as a "classic essay." On the other hand, my suspicion that students of American religion were primarily responsible for giving visibility to Hansen's law was confirmed. Even there, however, it was a surprise to learn that the recovery and early popularization of Hansen's ideas were exclusively the work of Jewish scholars. This finding furnishes the occasion for some speculations toward the end of the essay on the relationship

between Jewish religion and Jewish ethnicity and on the role of World
War II in highlighting the former as opposed to the latter. All in all, the
project confirmed my belief that tracing the usage of terms and concepts
is a rewarding approach to the history of intergroup relations, ethnicity,
and religion.

Now universally regarded by scholars in the field as a classic, Hansen's
celebrated essay, "The Problem of the Third Generation Immigrant,"
attracted no notice whatsoever until fourteen years after its original publication. It was brought to the attention of *Commentary*'s readers in
November 1952 as being especially pertinent to the contemporary situation of American Jews. Three years later, Will Herberg popularized
"Hansen's law"—a term he introduced—by arguing in his widely read
Protestant-Catholic-Jew that the statement "what the son wishes to forget the grandson wishes to remember" was one of the main conceptual
keys to understanding the postwar "revival of religion." Thus the applicability of Hansen's third-generation thesis to religious phenomena was
what put his 1938 essay into general circulation. It was, indeed, in precisely this context that the essay first came to be regarded as a classic,
despite the oblivion into which it had fallen after its original publication.
These facts seem to me sufficiently intriguing to justify a closer look at
the relationship between Hansen's essay and religion. My aim is simply
to open the subject; if my observations seem at times speculative, I would
claim as warrant the venturesome example Hansen set in his original
discussion.

The original lecture being the obvious place to begin, we note first
that it was delivered under the auspices of a church-related organization—the Augustana Historical Society—to an audience whose historical
identity was inseparable from the religion around which their life as a
social collectivity was structured. Hansen was quite conscious of the
aegis under which he spoke. Indeed, he felt some concern that the
religious context might lead his audience to put an unduly narrow construction on the message he wanted to get across. This uneasiness played
no small part in shaping his treatment of "the problem of the third
generation immigrant," as a brief review of his lecture will show.[1]

Those whose expectations were formed by Herberg and other recent
commentators may feel surprise, if not bewilderment, on looking into the
original lecture; the "problem," as Hansen himself explains it, is not
what they have been led to expect. The problem is not to determine

whether such a thing as "the principle of third generation interest" actually exists, or to account for its origins, or to establish how extensively
its influence is felt. All these matters are, for Hansen, quite unproblematic. He simply *asserts* the principle as one of "the laws of history . . .
applicable in all fields of historical study" and asserts further that it
derives from an "almost universal phenomenon" of human psychology
("what the son wishes to forget the grandson wishes to remember").
Although he calls the third-generation principle a "theory," he makes no
effort to verify it in a rigorous way. Rather, he "illustrates" its operation
by more or less offhand references to the contemporary interest in the
history of the South—not disdaining to instance the case of *Gone With
the Wind*, "written by a granddaughter of the Confederacy"—and to the
emergence of immigrant historical societies.[2] Only after having dealt with
what posterity regards as the heart of the matter in a series of generalizations so impressionistic that they might be said to fall into the "arm-
chair" category does Hansen get around to the "problem."

What then *was* the problem? Simply this: How was the third generation's interest in its group heritage—assumed as a given—to be "organized and directed" in such a way as to produce the most fruitful
historiographical results? Because the Augustana Historical Society was
one of the organizations exemplifying third-generation historical interest,
the "problem" had immediate application to Hansen's audience.[3] And it
was in suggesting how they ought to deal with it that he betrayed the
uneasiness alluded to above.

Two general principles, according to Hansen, ought to guide the
third generation's historical work: it should avoid "self-laudation" and
hew to "broad impartial lines," and it should aim to "make a permanent
contribution to the meaning of American history at large." To elucidate
the former, Hansen admonished his audience on five points that related
directly to the religious matrix from which the Augustana Historical
Society sprang. They must look beyond the church in telling the story
of their past; they should study first the context in which the church
was planted and grew; they ought to give particular attention to groups
"that broke with the faith of the old country"; they were not to overlook
the political influence of the Augustana Synod; finally, they must also
pay attention to groups that were the church's "competitors in the matter
of interest, affection and usefulness."[4]

Hansen's remarks on the second general principle, although of considerable intrinsic interest, do not bear directly on the religious dimension. His guidelines on avoiding group "self-laudation" reveal very clearly,
however, that he was sensitive to the religious aspect of the immigrant's

historical heritage and group consciousness. They indicate with equal
clarity that he regarded it as something that could easily distort a group's
historical self-understanding. It would be rash to conclude, on this evidence alone, that Hansen had little historical interest in matters religious.
What the lecture does establish beyond peradventure is that he did not
find in the third-generation principle the special significance for religious
development that later commentators emphasized.

Although it is proverbially difficult to prove a negative, a strong case
can be made to show that "The Problem of the Third Generation Immigrant" was unknown to the intellectual world in general until 1952.
First, the form in which it was published—as a pamphlet by a local
historical society—gave it far less visibility than it would have had as a
journal article. Hansen quite possibly never saw it in print himself, for
he died in May of the year it was published [1938]. Thus he never had
a chance to call it to the attention of colleagues or to develop more
systematically the principle of third-generation interest. He did refer to
the principle in speaking to an audience of social workers a few weeks
after the Augustana lecture, but that talk attracted little attention at the
time and was not made known to scholars until 1979.[5] It seems reasonable to conclude that Arthur M. Schlesinger, Sr., did not know about the
Augustana lecture, for he did not include it, or make any reference to it,
in the volume of Hansen's essays that he edited as *The Immigrant in
American History*. Neither did C. Frederick Hansen say anything about
"The Problem of the Third Generation Immigrant" in a biographical
memoir of his brother, entitled "Marcus Lee Hansen—Historian of Immigration," which was published in 1942.[6]

It is true that Margaret Mead's *And Keep Your Powder Dry* (1942),
a widely read analysis of the American character, makes interpretive use
of a third-generation concept. But despite the fact that the two are sometimes mentioned together, there is no reason to believe that Mead was
acquainted with Hansen's essay. She does not refer to Hansen—or any
other historian, for that matter—in text or notes; where he perceived a
third-generation interest in ethnic roots, Mead stresses the third generation's being completely cut off from their immigrant heritage and
wishing to identify not with their grandfathers but with the "founding
fathers."[7] In contrast to the second-generation problem, which was a
sociological commonplace, not much had yet been written about the
situation of the third generation when *Keep Your Powder Dry* appeared.
But Mead's interpretation was consistent with the prevailing assumption
that the third generation was the most "fully assimilated," and we can

safely assume that Hansen had nothing to do with forming her ideas on the subject.[8]

It would be tedious to list all the relevant works of the period that do not mention Hansen's third-generation essay. But because something more ought to be said to establish the presumption that it was unknown, let us look at two particularly revealing cases. The first of these works in which we could surely expect to find a reference to the Augustana lecture, if it were known, is the compendium of articles on immigration and ethnicity edited by Brown and Roucek. The first edition, *Our Racial and National Minorities*, appeared in 1937, the year before Hansen's lecture was published; hence its nonappearance there signifies nothing. There were, however, two later editions of the book, in 1946 and 1952, both of which had the main title *One America*. Each of the later editions included a contribution by Samuel Koenig on "Second- and Third-Generation Americans." Although he cited a wide range of literature—more than fifty footnotes in a fifteen-page article—Koenig made no reference to Hansen's essay in either 1946 or 1952. Nor was that essay included in the lengthy bibliographies that accompanied each edition, although an obscure Hansen monograph of 1931 turned up in all three (among the readings listed for Portuguese Americans), and the latter two also included *The Atlantic Migration* and *The Immigrant in American History*.[9]

The second particularly revealing bit of negative evidence involves the writings of Edward N. Saveth. We know that he was much impressed by "The Problem of the Third Generation Immigrant" because he included it in his book of readings, *Understanding the American Past*.[10] That volume, however, appeared two years after Hansen's essay was republished in *Commentary*. Although Saveth cited the 1938 Augustana Historical Society publication as his source, it seems clear that his attention was called to the essay by seeing it in *Commentary*. We might draw that inference simply because he was at the time an employee of the American Jewish Committee and could therefore be expected to be familiar with the contents of the magazine it published. There is, however, more conclusive evidence, namely, Saveth's failure to allude to the third-generation essay in his earlier discussions of Hansen as an immigration historian. Although he praised Hansen's work in a 1946 *Commentary* article and in his standard monograph, *American Historians and European Immigrants, 1875–1925*, in neither case did he give evidence of acquaintance with the essay he later reprinted.[11]

If we can take it as at least provisionally established that Hansen's essay was unknown to the world at large until 1952, what were the circumstances of its immediate acceptance then as a classic? Nathan Glazer, a young scholar already deeply interested in ethnicity, came across Hansen's essay among the materials he was researching at the New York Public Library. Much struck by it, Glazer, an associate editor of *Commentary*, called the essay to the attention of his colleagues, who agreed that it would be of interest to readers of the magazine. It appeared in the November 1952 issue with a slightly altered title ("The Third Generation in America"), and with the subtitle or caption: "A Classic Essay in Immigrant History." Oscar Handlin, a frequent contributor whose recently published book *The Uprooted* made him the preeminent academic authority on immigration, added an introductory note.[12]

Although his remarks dealt mainly with Hansen's career, what Handlin had to say about the essay itself is of particular interest. After noting Hansen's message about how an immigrant group should write its own history, Handlin called attention to "the applicability to Jewish immigrants of Hansen's striking theses." Among these he mentioned the latter's "views on the second and third generation," but the point he stressed "above all perhaps" was Hansen's "prediction as to the limited survival span in America . . . of the effective *distinctive* life of the group itself." Jewish readers, Handlin thought, would be surprised to discover the parallels between their own group experience and that of others, seemingly unlike them. They might also reflect, he concluded somberly, on the distinctiveness of Jewish group life and on "whether, to what degree, and how American Jews . . . can hope to escape the complete amalgamation which Hansen seems to predict."[13] From the viewpoint of group survival, this was a distinctly pessimistic reading that stands in sharp contrast to the emphasis Will Herberg was soon to lay on the law of third-generation return.

After its republication, Saveth and Glazer were the first to take note of Hansen's essay. Saveth, as we saw, reprinted it in 1954, but his introductory comments were brief and noncommittal. Although he observed that it dealt with "the relationship of groupings in the American population to ancestral cultures," he did not draw attention to the principle of third-generation interest or speculate on its implications.[14] Glazer, who rediscovered Hansen, was also the first to stress this aspect of the essay. His treatment, unlike Saveth's, was strongly theoretical. In "Ethnic Groups in America: From National Culture to Ideology" (1954), he hailed Hansen for perceiving that the third generation tends, in some sense, "to return to the first," and he linked that perception to his own bold interpretation of the overall pattern of American ethnic development as moving from identification with relatively concrete cultural attributes (e.g., language) to a more abstract "ideological" phase. An earlier version of Glazer's discussion included a paragraph arguing that religion functioned for some immigrant groups as a transmuted form of spiritual commitment to the old country.[15] In thus including religion among the aspects of Old World culture transformed in the New World and "returned to" by third-generation immigrants, Glazer anticipated certain aspects of the interpretation Will Herberg was soon to advance in *Protestant-Catholic-Jew*.

Herberg's book was published in the fall of 1955, but *Commentary* readers had been given a preview of two chapters in the August and September issues.[16] The book attracted much attention because of the brilliant way it explained how a "revival of religion" could be taking place in a society that seemed simultaneously to be growing more and more secularized. The explanation, Herberg suggested, was to be found in the social psychology of an immigrant-derived people. The Augustana lecture provided one of the principal keys to understanding the situation, for it was in accordance with Hansen's law that members of the third generation were "returning" to the churches and synagogues as a means of reestablishing contact with their ancestral heritages. The religious dimension of an ethnic heritage was, in Herberg's view, best suited for third-generaion "remembering" for several reasons. In the first place, it had persisted more successfully than language and customs, which had been eroded by assimilation. At the same time, immigrant religious traditions had been sufficiently Americanized to suit the mentality of the third generation. Moreover, religion helped the members of the third generation to locate themselves in the "lonely crowd" by providing an answer to the "aching question" of social identity, Who am I? Finally, religion was much prized in American society, whereas foreign "nationality" was regarded as narrow, ethnocentric, even divisive.

Herberg thus portrayed the religious revival as deriving in large part from religion's function as a kind of residuary legatee of ethnic feeling. But why was religion itself so widely regarded as a good thing? Why did public figures such as President Eisenhower insist so strongly that religion was indispensable to national well-being? The reason, Herberg said in an answer that anticipated the civil religion discussion of the late 1960s and early 1970s, was that the American ideology was a profoundly spiritual construct embodying such values as freedom and individual dignity, as well as more mundane elements associated with material prosperity. As such, it had always been closely linked to religion. In the early days, the linkage was to Protestantism exclusively; with the coming of the immigrants and the adjustment of their religious traditions to the new environment, Catholicism and Judaism took their places alongside Protestantism as "the three great faiths of democracy." Hence, Protestantism, Catholicism, and Judaism were socially praiseworthy because they constituted three equally acceptable ways for the individual to manifest his or her commitment to the "spiritual values" underlying the "American Way of Life"—which was, in Herberg's view, the real religion of Americans.

Hansen's law and the process of spiritual amalgamation just described presumably accounted for the modulation of ethnic identity into religious identity which Herberg dealt with under the rubric of "the triple melting pot." Although this expression seemed to imply greater diversity (three melting pots instead of one), the phenomenon to which it referred was the gradual assimilation of a large number of different nationality groups into three major religious denominations: Protestantism, Catholicism, and Judaism. The evidence for the sociological reality of the triple melting pot was thin—Herberg relied principally on an early 1940s study of intermarriage trends in New Haven—but a number of other observers agreed that, as immigrant "nationalities" faded away, the "residual group differences . . . [were] racial and religious."[17]

In fact, the assumption that Protestants, Catholics, Jews, and Negroes (not yet called Blacks) constituted the principal social groupings in the American population is still to be found in Glazer and Moynihan's *Beyond the Melting Pot* (1963) and in Milton M. Gordon's *Assimilation in American Life* (1964).[18] Although largely forgotten in the racial turmoil and reassertion of ethnicity that ensued shortly after the publication of these works, the belief was widely held in the 1950s that religion was becoming a more important sociological category for understanding contemporary American society. Herberg's book, which was the most influential single work in establishing this view, thus simultaneously popularized Hansen's law and linked it firmly to an interpretation of the relationship of ethnicity, religion, and American culture very broadly considered.

Although Herberg treated Hansen's law as applicable to the American religious scene generally, he was, of course, best acquainted with the Jewish situation, and the evidence clearly indicates that Jews were particularly sensitive to the role of generational transition in the contemporary revival of Judaism as a religion. The very prominence of Jewish scholars in the recovery and elaboration of Hansen's essay constitutes one bit of evidence because it testifies to a special alertness to the issue on their part. The essay was reprinted in a Jewish publication, and every one of the commentators mentioned so far—Handlin, Saveth, Glazer, and Herberg—was also Jewish.

The appearance of Herberg's book brought Hansen to the attention of a wider audience. But even then, Jewish writers seemed more preoccupied by the Hansen thesis than Protestant or Catholic commentators. Thus Glazer featured it in his review of Herberg, and in an independent analysis of "The Jewish Revival in America." While reviewing Herberg favorably, Marshall Sklare cautioned against making too much of Hansen and the triple melting pot idea; and in developing the generational component of his analysis of "symbolic Jewishness" (which anticipated "symbolic ethnicity" by twenty years), Herbert Gans explained how his interpretation differed from "the well-known thesis of Marcus Hansen." C. B. Sherman maintained, a few years later, that Jews were the only group whose experience "suppl[ied] proof of Hansen's thesis."[19]

Protestant and Catholic reviewers of course took note of the generational angle, but they tended to lay greater stress on the more distinctively religious aspects of Herberg's discussion. The *Christian Century*, for example, featured the work of David Riesman and Will Herberg in an editorial entitled "The Lonely Crowd at Prayer." Although it summarized the generational interpretation (without mentioning Hansen), its main purpose was to criticize the "pallid . . . religion" that threatened to "let us all disappear into the gray-flannel uniformity of the conforming culture."[20] Herberg's earlier work had attracted favorable attention from Catholics, and they greeted *Protestant-Catholic-Jew* with enthusiasm. Immediately upon its publication, the influential Jesuit weekly, *America*, devoted a feature article to the book. Here Gustave Weigel, S. J., who was the leading American Catholic theologian involved in ecumenical activities, pronounced the sociological interpretation (including Hansen's law) "fascinating and enlightening." But he added immediately, "Dr. Herberg draws something profound, however, from the facts he reports and organizes." That more profound point had to do with Herberg's assertion that religion was considered "a good thing" because it buttressed the "American Way of Life."[21]

Weigel's reaction was typical in the sense that Catholics tended to value Herberg's work primarily for the critique it offered of the nature of American religiosity. They were impressed, to be sure, by the sociological analysis—including what one reviewer called "the interesting law of the assimilation of immigrants"[22]—but no Catholic observer seriously suggested that anything like a "third generation return" played a significant role in making American Catholicism what it was in the 1950s. Although Catholic faith and piety were flourishing, there was no "revival" in the sense of a recovery from an earlier slump. On the contrary, the Catholic community had been growing vigorously over the past generation in numbers, institutional strength, and spiritual vitality. The Catholic dimension of the post–World War II "revival of religion" was, in other words, a straight-line continuation and intensification of developments that had been evident for a long time. Catholics of Italian background were thought to be becoming more regular in their churchgoing, but that, too, was a straight-line progression rather than a reversion to an earlier pattern.

Catholic reformers of the 1950s did, to be sure, talk a great deal about the immigrant heritage of the American church. But the talk was overwhelmingly negative in its assessment of that heritage insofar as it still made itself felt in the mid twentieth century. What else but their memories of nativist hostility made Catholics so suspicious and standoffish? Why were they burdened with a siege mentality? Whence came their antiintellectualism? Why had they exerted so slight an influence on the cultural life of the nation? It was clearly time, according to Catholic reformers, for the church in America to come out of its "immigrant ghetto" and plunge into "the mainstream of American life." The hope, in other words, was not that the grandchildren of the immigrants would return to the ancestral religion, which they had never left in massive numbers; it was, rather, that they would more effectively leave behind them the psychological and cultural encumbrances that were their inheritance from immigrant days.[23]

If the Hansen thesis didn't really apply to the religious situation of American Catholics, it seemed even less appropriate as a general explanation of the religious upswing among Protestants. Their situation was illuminated by other features of Herberg's analysis—for example, the melding of religion and Americanism—but the "new immigrants" included too few Protestants for the Hansen effect to be regarded as a major factor in their situation in the 1950s. Hansen himself, as we have seen, gave no indication of thinking that the third generation would be more fervent churchgoers. What his discussion revealed was an anxiety that the continuing religious attachments of his audience might unduly restrict their study of the immigrant past. And it seems unlikely that any considerable number of later Protestant observers were persuaded that a third-generation return had much to do with the postwar revival of religion so far as it affected their own denominations.

The situation among Jews was strikingly different. Although the most widely heralded, Will Herberg was only one among a cluster of Jewish observers to point out that the generational issue was crucial to an understanding of the religious situation of American Jews and to make the further point that the heightened participation of the third generation in religious activities was to be understood in functional terms—that is, as a means of giving young Jews a sense of who they were and thereby maintaining group identity and boundaries. In addition to earlier works cited by Herberg as consistent with his interpretation (for instance, Sklare's *Conservative Judaism*), two studies (by Glazer and Gans) arriving at very similar conclusions were published so soon after he wrote that we can safely assume the authors were thinking along the same lines before they read Herberg. A few years later, Erich Rosenthal gave the impression he was merely summing up what knowledgeable observers already knew when he wrote, "It appears, then, that the basic function of Jewish education is to implant Jewish self-consciousness rather than Judaism, to 'inoculate' the next generation with that minimum of religious practice and belief that is considered necessary to keep alive a level of Jewish self-consciousness that will hold the line against assimilation."[24]

The preceding establishes that Hansen's thesis really applied much more to Jews than to Protestants or Catholics; but Herberg's exaggeration in this matter by no means vitiates his whole interpretation; nor does it dim the brilliance of his contribution to our understanding of the religious situation at midcentury. If our concern were primarily with Herberg's analysis, we should have to look further into how his exaggeration affected the overall argument of his book. But because our interest here is in Hansen's thesis as it relates to religious developments, the more pertinent line of inquiry is *why* the law of third-generation interest fits the case of Jews more closely than that of Protestants or Catholics. Because of the nature of the inquiry, the discussion that follows has a more speculative quality than that preceding it.

First, Jews might be expected to find almost any third-generation thesis particularly relevant to their situation because the American Jewish population was entering a third-generation phase in the 1950s. More than four out of five American Jews derived from the great East European migration that entered the United States in the last quarter of the nineteenth century and the first fifteen years of the twentieth.[25] This was a much higher proportion than "new immigrant" stock comprised among Catholics, to say nothing of Protestants. This meant that the fortunes of the Jewish group as a whole were linked to what happened to the grandchildren of the immigrants in a way that was not true for either of the other two major religious bodies. Little had been written about the third generation by midcentury; hence it is understandable that Hansen's essay—easily the boldest and most original discussion of the subject in existence—seemed particularly apt to Jews when it was rediscovered by a Jewish researcher, republished in a Jewish magazine, and elaborated upon by other Jewish commentators.

But there was more to it than where Jews as a group stood in terms of generational stages. Hansen's discussion of immigrant psychology involved religion more directly in the case of Jews because religion and ethnicity stood in a different relationship for them than for Catholics or Protestants. This is not the place for an elaborate discussion of the nature of Judaism or of the relation of Judaism as a religion to Jewishness as a nationality or a species of ethnicity.[26] It is, nevertheless, clear that Judaism is an "ethnic religion" in a way quite different from the manner in which Catholicism was an ethnic religion for Irish, or Polish, or Italian immigrants (to confine the discussion to Catholic groups whose religion is considered to be closely related to their ethnicity, and whose situation I know better than that of American Protestants).

From the viewpoint of Judaism as a religion, God's covenant with Abraham made his descendants a chosen race, a royal priesthood, a people set apart. God took them for His own in a special way: setting forth the law they were to follow, chastising their lapses, guiding them through the desert, overcoming their foes, and bringing them at length to the land He had promised would be theirs. In this sense, Judaism is a highly particularistic religion—one that involves a quite definite historical people, in real and identifiable times and places, under the care of a God who, although He is the creator and ruler of all, revealed Himself only to them, and promised to be with them until the end of days. Judaism, on this account, is not a missionary religion; it is something that belongs uniquely to Jews and can hardly, without changing its nature, be spread abroad to others who do not share the original inheritance. Jewishness and Judaism are thus interlinked theoretically as well as practically in a way that, for example, Irishness and Catholicism could never be, for however close the historic connection between religion and nationality, the theoretical distinction between being Catholic and being Irish—or Polish, or Italian, or whatever—could always be clearly drawn.

The intimate linkage between religion and group identity meant that when Jewish immigrants, and their children of the second generation, fell away from adherence to and the practice of Judaism as a religion—which they did in massive numbers—it left a kind of vacuum at the center of their group identity. As with all immigrants, the problematic nature of group identity was very much heightened when Jews reached the third-generation stage because, unlike their parents and grandparents, these young people did not have living memories of the beliefs and customs that had been abandoned. Moreover, upward mobility had dispersed the packed ghettos, resulting in more frequent contacts with gentiles and magnifying the danger of assimilation for a generation of Jewish youngsters who had difficulty explaining to themselves why they were different from anyone else. In these circumstances, second generation parents, who were conscious of being Jews even though they might not be believers, turned to the practice of Judaism as a religion and insisted on a modicum of Jewish religious education for their children in order, as Rosenthal put it, to "inoculate" the next generation against assimilation. The religious dimension, historically at the core of being Jewish, was thus optionally cultivated, not from strictly religious motives but as a means of giving concrete content to a group identity that could not be so easily specified in any other way.[27]

Herberg took note of the uniqueness of the Jewish situation with respect to Hansen's law, but he interpreted it differently from the interpretation offered here. In the case of Italian or Polish immigrants, he said, there was nothing left for the third generation to "remember" but the religion, so that Hansen's law resulted in "the disappearance of the 'Italianness' or the 'Polishness' of the group, or rather its dissolution into the religious community." Catholicism for these third generations, thus replaced ethnicity. In the case of the Jews, however, third-generation remembering of religion resulted in a reinforcement of ethnicity because, among the Jews alone, the "religious community bore the same name as the old ethnic group and was virtually coterminous with it."[28]

It is, perhaps, a fine point, but this seems to me almost to suggest that the difference arose from a peculiarity of labeling—"Jewishness" signifying both religion and ethnicity—rather being rooted in a more intimate substantive linkage between Judaism and Jewishness than existed between Catholicity and Italianness or Polishness. In addition, Herberg speaks as though Hansen's law operated in conventional fashion with these Catholic groups but in an anomalous way with Jews. I would maintain, rather, that Herberg offered no real evidence for its operation in any way among Catholic immigrants and that the Jews were actually the paradigmatic case of its operation, which led him to assume its application to other groups as well. The more basic difference this implies might be summarized as follows: Herberg seems to take for granted that the religion of Catholic immigrant nationalities was abandoned in the second generation and returned to by the third, in accordance with Hansen's law. I would argue, however, that the religion of these ethnic groups did not have to be "returned to" because it had persisted through all three generations—although not, to be sure, without differences in understanding and practice in which generational shifts were involved as well as other factors.

Herberg was certainly correct, however, in suggesting that American circumstances encouraged the tendency to stress the religious aspect of Jewishness at midcentury. Freedom of religion is one of the cornerstones of the American system, and the courts have often defended minority religious positions even when they affect public policy areas such as education and conscientious objection to military service; moreover, the need to cultivate feelings of tolerance, brotherhood, and interfaith understanding was preached with increasing insistence in the era of World War II. American Jews strongly supported the interfaith work of the National Conference of Christians and Jews; indeed, Nicholas Montalto has shown that this organization, formed in 1926, received most of its funding from Jewish sources during the first fifteen years of its existence.[29]

Montalto links this support to the policy pursued by the American Jewish Committee (AJC) of stressing the religious rather than the ethnic dimension of Jewishness. Writing as a convinced proponent of the new ethnicity, Montalto laments what we might call the AJC's "religious strategy" and even implies that it, rather than Hansen's law, accounted for the existence of Herberg's triple melting pot.[30] The latter point strikes me as overdrawn, but Montalto has undoubtedly called attention to matters Herberg overlooked that are highly relevant to the emergence of Judaism as one of the "three great faiths of democracy." Montalto's discussion, however, is not without significant omissions of its own.

According to Montalto, the AJC adopted the religious strategy primarily because its leadership was dominated by third- and fourth-generation German Jews, strongly assimilationist in orientation, who shared the prevailing American antipathy for "organizations smacking of ethnic separatism." On this account, he argues, they promoted a "sectarian view of Judaism" that was misguided in the long run because it involved Judaism's "denying part of itself—the ethnic part."[31] Although one can understand how an ethnic enthusiast of the 1970s might reach such a conclusion, it leaves out far too much of the background of the 1930s to be a satisfactory explanation for the heavy stress placed on the religious character of Jewishness. More specifically, it fails to give anything like adequate weight to the influence of Nazi anti-Semitism and to the overall effect of the wartime crisis in enhancing the intellectual respectability and public importance of religion. Matters, incidentally, which Herberg likewise failed to underline.

Nazi anti-Semitism must surely be regarded as the greatest single force affecting American Jewish life in the 1930s. It not only stimulated anti-Semitism in this country, but it also shaped the thinking and re-actions of Jews and other persons concerned about intergroup relations.[32] And what was the nature of Nazi anti-Semitism? It was racial—Jewish blood, even in the smallest proportion, made anyone in whom it coursed an abomination, a defiler of the Aryan purity of the Germanic *Volk*. But Nazi anti-Semitism was not only the paradigmatic exemplar of racism; it was part and parcel of an insanely elaborated form of nationalistic ethnocentrism, the dangers of which had been a staple of liberal com-mentary since the 1920s.

In view of the frightening growth of racial anti-Semitism, it was virtually unthinkable that American Jews would want to insist on the ethnic quality of their group cohesiveness and identity. To do so would seem to confirm what the Nazis were saying—the Jews were unassi-milable, an ineradicably alien racial element wherever they dwelt. For Jews even more than others, Nazism utterly discredited racism and, in doing so, also discredited related forms of collective consciousness, in-cluding what came to be called ethnicity in the 1960s. We must remem-ber that the term and concept *ethnicity* had not yet been introduced in the 1930s. People spoke much more inclusively in those days of "racial groups" and "race feeling," or of immigrant "nationalities." The kind of group consciousness later benignly characterized as "ethnic" was then associated with "ethnocentrism" and was regarded as an unalloyed social evil.[33] In these circumstances, "ethnicity" as a way of defining Jewish group identity was simply not an option. Jews could perhaps have insisted on calling themselves a nationality rather than a religion, but that would have created problems of its own. To stress the religious quality of Judaism was a far more appealing policy because it entailed none of the "loyalty" problems implicit in the terminology of nationality, and at the same time it made the struggle against anti-Semitism part of America's historic commitment to religious toleration.

Besides discrediting all forms of descent-based group feeling, Na-zism was part of broader phenomena—totalitarianism and world war— that lent new intellectual respectability to traditional religious beliefs about the reality of evil, suffering, and the demonic potentialities inherent in projects to remake the world. Although dismissed by secular Jews such as Sidney Hook as a "new failure of nerve," the intellectual revival of religion was a reality sufficiently consequential to require from liberals a vigorous counterattack on the "authoritarianism" of the "absolutists."[34] Louis Finkelstein, provost of the Jewish Theological Seminary of America, was the leading promoter of its most important institutional expression, the Conference on Science, Philosophy and Religion in Their Relation to the Democratic Way of Life. This body, organized shortly after the outbreak of war in 1939, sponsored annual symposia for two decades; its religious orientation was so pronounced at first that a group of prominent secular thinkers, including John Dewey, seceded in protest.[35]

We might plausibly assume that this kind of intellectual revitalization would make the "religious strategy" all the more appealing to American Jews. Another factor that enters the picture in this connection is the introduction of the term *Judeo-Christian tradition*, which was popularized in the wartime crisis by those who wished to emphasize that the values threatened by totalitarianism were deeply rooted in the spiritual traditions of the West.[36] Although later commentators tend to treat the term ironically, consideration of the wartime circumstances suggests a more generous interpretation of the outlook and thinking of those who put it into circulation. In any case, popularization of the expression clearly reinforced the tendency to emphasize the religious dimension of Jewishness.

These war-related factors, along with the reasons mentioned by Montalto and Herberg, operated to bring out and to underline the religious element in Jewishness—which surely helped to make the Jewish "return" to religion seem the natural, almost inevitable, way of reaffirming and maintaining the identity and coherence of the group. In the postwar era, observers such as Oscar Handlin began to insist that Jews were better understood as an ethnic group than as a religious body. But Handlin also made the same point as Glazer, Gans, and Herberg: Jewish ethnicity was increasingly coming to expression in the form of more active participation in Judaism as a religion.[37] It was this complex relationship between religion and ethnicity among American Jews as the group entered its third-generation stage that made the rediscovery of Hansen's essay so opportune. The intensity with which Jewish students of ethnicity developed his ideas testifies to the fecundity of Hansen's insight and makes the rediscovery of the Augustana lecture an important landmark in the historiography of American religion.

NOTES

Source: Peter Kivisto and Dag Blanck, eds., *American Immigrants and Their Generations: Studies and Commentaries on the Hansen Thesis after Fifty Years* (Urbana: University of Illinois Press, 1990), 85–103. Reprinted by permission of the publisher.

1. Marcus Lee Hansen, "The Problem of the Third Generation Immigrant," republication of the 1937 address with introductions by Peter Kivisto and Oscar Handlin (Rock Island, Ill., 1987). For a recent discussion see Werner Sollors, *Beyond Ethnicity: Consent and Descent in American Culture* (New York, 1986), 214ff. Sollors errs, however, in ascribing to Hansen himself sentiments that Hansen attributed to spokesmen for the first generation. For the place of the Augustana Synod in the history of Swedish immigration, see George M. Stephenson, *The Religious Aspects of Swedish Immigration* (Minneapolis, Minn., 1932), chaps. 13, 16, 22–25; for the establishment of the Augustana Historical Society, 379n.

2. Hansen, "Problem of the Third Generation," 15–18.

3. Ibid., 18–21.

4. Ibid., 21–23.

5. This talk, "Who Shall Inherit America?" was not included in the printed proceedings of the 1937 meeting of the National Conference of Social Work, but it appeared in single-space typescript format *Interpreter Releases*, 14, no. 34 (July 6, 1937), 226–33. Moses Rischin first called attention to it in his "Marcus Lee Hansen: America's First Transethnic Historian," in Richard L. Bushman et al., eds., *Uprooted Americans: Essays to Honor Oscar Handlin* (Boston, 1979), 319–47.

6. Marcus Lee Hansen, *The Immigrant in American History*, ed. Arthur M. Schlesinger (Cambridge, Mass., 1940), ix–xi; C. Frederick Hansen, "Marcus Lee Hansen—Historian of Immigration," *Common Ground*, 2 (Summer 1942), 87–94.

7. Margaret Mead, *And Keep Your Powder Dry: An Anthropologist Looks at America* (New York, 1942), chap. 3. Peter Kivisto's mention of Mead in his introductory remarks to the 1987 reprint version of Hansen's Augustana lecture leaves the impression that Mead knew Hansen's work. Rischin's review essay of Stephan Thernstrom, Ann Orlov, and Oscar Handlin, eds., *Harvard Encyclopedia of American Ethnic Groups* (Cambridge, Mass., 1980) notes the divergence between Mead's and Hansen's views on the third generation. See *Journal of American Ethnic History*, 2 (Spring 1983), 74–75.

8. William Carlson Smith, *Americans in the Making: The Natural History of the Assimilation of Immigrants* (New York, 1939), which devotes almost half its space to the second generation, has only one index reference to the third generation. There Smith observes, "Even if members of the third generation may be found using more of the parental practices than some of the second generation they may be much further along in the assimilative process, since these traits have been selected on the basis of deliberation" (350).

9. Francis J. Brown and Joseph S. Roucek, eds., *Our Racial and National Minorities* (New York, 1937), for the citation to Hansen, "The Minor Stocks in the American Population of 1790," which appeared in American Historical Association, *Annual Report, 1931*, see 680. Brown and Roucek, eds., *One America: The History, Contributions, and Present Problems of Our Racial and National Minorities*, rev. ed. (New York, 1946), 471–85 (Koenig essay), 661, 680 (bibliographical citations); 3d ed. (New York, 1952), 505–22 (Koenig essay), 706, 726 (bibliographical citations).

10. Edward N. Saveth, ed., *Understanding the American Past* (Boston, 1954), 472–88.

11. Edward N. Saveth, "The Immigrant in American History," *Commentary*, 2 (August 1946), 180–85; Saveth, *American Historians and European Immigrants,*

1875–1925 (New York, 1948), 217ff. For Saveth's connection with the American Jewish Committee, see *Commentary*, 14 (September 1952), 296.

12. Marcus Lee Hansen, "The Third Generation in America: A Classic Essay in Immigrant History," *Commentary*, 14 (November 1952), 492–500. Nathan Glazer described the background of the essay's republication in a conversation with the author.

13. Hansen, "Third Generation," 492–93.

14. Saveth, *Understanding the American Past*, 473.

15. Nathan Glazer, "Ethnic Groups in America: From National Culture to Ideology," in Morroe Berger, Theodore Abel, and Charles Page, eds., *Freedom and Control in Modern Society* (New York, 1954; 1978), 158–73; the earlier version, entitled "America's Ethnic Pattern," appeared first in *Commentary*, 15 (April 1953), 401–8, and then in *Perspectives USA*, no. 9 (Autumn 1954), 137–52.

16. Will Herberg, "The 'Triple Melting Pot': The Third Generation, from Ethnic to Religious Diversity," *Commentary*, 20 (August 1955), 101–8; Herberg, "America's New Religiousness: A Way of Belonging or the Way of God?" *Commentary*, 20 (September 1955), 240–47; Herberg, *Protestant-Catholic-Jew: An Essay in American Religious Sociology* (Garden City, N.Y., 1955). (A revised edition appeared as an Anchor paperback [Garden City, N.Y., 1960]). For a discussion of this work in the context of Herberg's life, see Harry J. Ausmus, *Will Herberg: From Right to Right* (Chapel Hill, N.C., 1987), chap. 8.

17. The quotation is from Charles F. Marden, *Minorities in American Society* (New York, 1952), 394. For other evidence (besides chap. 3. of *Protestant-Catholic-Jew*), see Alfred McClung Lee, "Sociological Insights into American Culture and Personality," *Journal of Social Issues*, 7, no. 4 (1951), 10–11; and Oscar Handlin, *The American People in the Twentieth Century*, rev. ed. (1954; Boston, 1963), 223.

18. Nathan Glazer and Daniel P. Moynihan, *Beyond the Melting Pot: The Negroes, Puerto Ricans, Jews, Italians, and Irish of New York City* (Cambridge, Mass., 1963), 314–15; Milton M. Gordon, *Assimilation in American Life* (New York, 1964), chap. 7.

19. Nathan Glazer, "Religion without Faith," *New Republic*, 133 (November 4, 1955), 18–20; Glazer, "The Jewish Revival in America: I," *Commentary*, 20 (December 1955), 493–99; Glazer, "The Jewish Revival in America: II, Its Religious Side," *Commentary*, 21 (January 1956), 17–24; Marshall Sklare, review of Herberg, *Protestant-Catholic-Jew*, in *Commentary*, 21 (February 1956), 195–96; Herbert Gans, "American Jewry: Present and Future, Part I: Present," *Commentary*, 21 (May 1956), 422–30; Herbert Gans, "The Future of American Jewry, Part II," *Commentary*, 21 (June 1956), 555–63, esp. 561n. for Hansen; C. B. Sherman, *Jews within American Society: A Study of Ethnic Individuality* (Detroit, 1961), 207–8.

20. *Christian Century*, 73 (May 30, 1956), 662–63.

21. Gustave Weigel, "Religion Is a Good Thing," *America*, 94 (November 5, 1955), 150–54. See also Weigel, review of Herberg, *Protestant-Catholic-Jew*, in *Theological Studies*, 16 (1955), 651–53; Joseph Fitzpatrick, review of Herberg, *Protestant-Catholic-Jew*, in *Thought*, 30 (Winter 1955), 595–600; C. J. Nuesse's review in *Catholic Historical Review*, 42 (July 1956), 214–15.

22. Fitzpatrick, review, 596.

23. See Philip Gleason, *Keeping the Faith: American Catholicism Past and Present* (Notre Dame, Ind., 1987), 181–87.

24. Erich Rosenthal, "Acculturation without Assimilation: The Jewish Community of Chicago, Illinois," *American Journal of Sociology*, 66 (November 1960), 275–88; quotation from 287. For Glazer's and Gans's arguments, see above, n. 19. See also

Herberg, *Protestant-Catholic-Jew* (New York, 1960) 186–90, and the literature cited there, including Marshall Sklare, *Conservative Judaism: An American Religious Movement* (New York, 1955).

25. In an authoritative discussion, Arthur A. Goren states that East European immigrants and their children constituted five-sixths of the Jewish population in 1920. See Goren, "Jews," in Stephan Thernstrom, Ann Orlov, and Oscar Handlin, eds., *Harvard Encyclopedia of American Ethnic Groups* (Cambridge, Mass., 1980), 579.

26. See Nathan Glazer, *American Judaism*, 2d ed. (Chicago, 1972), 3–8; Charles S. Liebman, *The Ambivalent American Jew: Politics, Religion, and Family in American Jewish Life* (Philadelphia, 1976), esp. chaps. 1, 3.

27. In discussing this development, Glazer calls attention to its practical similarity to Mordecai Kaplan's view that Judaism expressed, but did not exhaust, Jewishness as a "civilization." See Nathan Glazer, "The Jewish Revival in America: I," *Commentary*, 20 (December 1955), 499; see also Liebman, *Ambivalent American Jew*, 73–77.

28. Herberg, *Protestant-Catholic-Jew* (1960), 186–87.

29. Nicholas V. Montalto, "The Forgotten Dream: A History of the Intercultural Education Movement, 1924–1941" (Ph.D. diss., University of Minnesota, 1978), 188ff. for discussion of the conference; 200–201 for funding issue. Herberg, *Protestant-Catholic-Jew* (1960), 242–44 discusses the conference but makes no particular mention of Jewish support.

30. Montalto, "Forgotten Dream," 199n., 188, where the subheading for the discussion is "Cementing 'American's Religious Triangle': The AJC and the National Conference of Christians and Jews."

31. Ibid., 185, 186, 204–5. Montalto quotes the phrase about "ethnic separatism" from Naomi W. Cohen, *Not Free to Desist: The American Jewish Committee, 1906–1966* (Philadelphia, 1972), 193.

32. A general work and guide to the literature is David A. Gerber, ed., *Anti-Semitism in American History* (Urbana, Ill., 1986). See also Donald S. Strong, *Organized Anti-Semitism in America: The Rise of Group Prejudice during the Decade 1930–1940* (Washington, D.C., 1941); Charles Herbert Stember et al., *Jews in the Mind of America* (New York, 1966), esp. 110ff., 237–58, 259–72; Cohen, *Not Free to Desist*, chaps. 8–9; Richard Weiss, "Ethnicity and Reform: Minorities and the Ambience of the Depression Years," *Journal of American History*, 66 (December 1979), 571–72, 574–75.

33. Sollors, *Beyond Ethnicity*, 21ff.; and above, chap. 6.

34. Sidney Hook, "The New Failure of Nerve," *Partisan Review*, 10 (January–February, 1943), 2–23; Edward A. Purcell, Jr., *The Crisis of Democratic Theory: Scientific Naturalism and the Problem of Value* (Lexington, Ky., 1973), 203–4, 218ff.; and above, chap. 8.

35. This group has not been studied; for a brief description and citation of relevant documents, see chap. 7.

36. Mark Silk, "Notes on the Judeo-Christian Tradition in America," *American Quarterly*, 36 (Spring 1984), 65–85.

37. Oscar Handlin, "Group Life within the American Pattern," *Commentary*, 8 (November 1949), 411–17; Handlin, *American People*, 223.

|| 10 ||

Immigration, Religion, and Civil Religion

The following essay was prepared for a 1989 conference, jointly sponsored by the American Academy of Arts and Sciences and the Ecole
normale supérieure, on immigration as a factor in United States history
and in French history. Since few scholars are expert in both fields, the
planners of the conference tried to get at the comparative dimensions of
the subject by commissioning papers on the same subtopics, one by a
student of American immigration, the other by a specialist on the French
situation. My topic was religion as a factor in American immigration and
intergroup relations. Upon getting into it, I was somewhat surprised to
discover how little systematic attention the interaction of religion and
immigration has received, despite the considerable literature in both
fields that touches on one aspect or another of the subject. Sketchy as
it is, I hope the following discussion will serve to awaken greater interest
in the general subject, and especially in its educational and civil-religious
aspects. Except for a few minor changes, this essay is reprinted as it
stands in the volume that resulted from the 1989 conference.

Religion played too vast and complex a role in the history of American
immigration for comprehensive treatment here. What follows offers
only the barest outline of two dimensions of the topic. The first part
sketches the way historians have dealt with the issue. My purpose here
is not to provide a full survey of the literature but simply to suggest the
scope of the topic and indicate the principal interpretive approaches
adopted by earlier scholars. The second part ventures into more speculative territory by focusing on education as a locus of interaction between
immigration, religion, and American civil religion.

Although most historical studies of immigration take some note of
religion, relatively few have systematically analyzed its role in the adjustment of immigrants to their new life; until recently, scholars of Amer-

ican religious history were even more neglectful of immigration.[1] For our purposes, most historical treatments can be grouped under two broad headings: those that focus on the positive role of religion in helping immigrants adjust to American life, and those that stress its negative aspects, especially its divisiveness. We will begin with the former.

It says something about the neglect of this subject that not until Robert A. Orsi's recent study of Italian-Americans did any historical work come close to rivaling George M. Stephenson's 1932 volume *The Religious Aspects of Swedish Immigration* as a comprehensive analysis of the place of religion in the life of an American immigrant group.[2] Stephenson provides detailed coverage of religious conditions in the homeland and ecclesiastical developments in the United States between the 1840s and the 1920s. What justifies calling his approach positive, however, is his insistence that the Lutheran church (Augustana Synod) constituted the essential institutional nucleus around which the group life of Swedish immigrants structured itself. The same could be said, *mutatis mutandis*, of most other immigrant groups and, as historians have recently emphasized, of African-Americans as well.[3]

Stephenson did full justice to the bitter doctrinal quarrels and organizational splits that disrupted the religious life of Scandinavian immigrants. In that sense, his work documented the negative, as well as the positive, role of religion. But taken as a whole, Stephenson's study illustrates the theoretical point made earlier by the great sociologist and student of Polish immigration W. I. Thomas, namely, that ethnic institutions such as churches, far from isolating newcomers from American life, actually provide the organizational vehicles that allow them to participate in it.[4]

Besides illustrating this fundamental point about the positive role of religion, Stephenson alluded in his Preface to the similarity between the religious concerns of his subjects and those of the New England Puritans. This effort to integrate the immigrant story with the dominant national tradition was developed more systematically by another historian of Scandinavian background, Marcus Lee Hansen. In an essay entitled "Immigration and Puritanism," Hansen argued that moral rigor (which is what Puritanism primarily connoted in the 1920s and 1930s) was the clergy's natural reaction to the disruption of social norms and community controls brought on by emigration in the case of colonial New Englanders and nineteenth-century immigrants alike.[5] Hansen thus both linked immigrants firmly to the nation's mythic past and used their experience to throw new interpretive light upon it.

Neither Stephenson nor Hansen developed a point implicit in their discussions of religion—that it played a positive role psychologically, as well as institutionally, by providing emotional anchorage for persons undergoing the traumatic shock of dislocation and resettlement in a strange land. The explication of this phenomenon was left to Oscar Handlin, whose book *The Uprooted* (1951) shaped a whole generation's understanding of the immigrant experience. Religion, in his poignant account, was what gave meaning to life in the ancestral village; after migration, it took on even greater significance as the one feature of Old World culture that seemed capable of being transplanted into the New World. But the church of the homeland could not be reconstituted in its old form in the new society, and the effort to do so was inevitably attended by frustration, disappointment, and strife. Even so, the conflicts over religion that erupted among Handlin's urban immigrants (as among Stephenson's Swedes) could be understood in a positive way, for they required the newcomers to reflect on their novel situation and to forge a new kind of self-definition.[6]

Will Herberg likewise stressed the psychological angle in his *Protestant-Catholic-Jew* (1955), a work that undertook to explain how the midcentury "revival of religion" could occur in a society growing ever more secularized. The key to the puzzle was to be sought in the social psychology of an immigrant-derived people. Appealing to what he called "Hansen's law"—what the son wishes to forget the grandson wishes to remember—Herberg argued that third-generation Americans were "returning" to the churches and synagogues as a means of reestablishing contact with their ancestral heritages. Besides constituting a link with the past, religion met the much talked of psychological need for "belonging" by providing an answer to the "aching question" of identity. Who am I?[7]

Herberg thus assigned great social and psychological importance to the interaction between immigration and religion. But as a believing Jew, he was troubled by his findings. Americans, he feared, valued religion for the social and psychological functions it served, not because it offered a message of transcendent intrinsic worth. Protestantism, Catholicism, and Judaism might be hailed as "the three great faiths of democracy," but only because they embodied the "spiritual values" underlying "the American Way of Life," which was the real religion of Americans.[8] This aspect of Herberg's analysis anticipated the discovery in the late 1960s of "civil religion," but he gave much greater prominence to immigration as a factor in its development than any other commentator.

Herberg also popularized the notion of the "triple melting pot." This interpretation—introduced by Ruby Jo Reeves Kennedy in a study of ethnic intermarriages in New Haven, Connecticut—held that the assimilation of immigrants tended to follow broadly religious lines rather than taking place in an undifferentiated fashion.[9] Thus Protestantism, Catholicism, and Judaism constituted three distinct "melting pots," and religion became an important analytical tool for understanding American society at midcentury. Although forgotten in the racial and ethnic upheaval of the sixties and seventies, the assumption that Protestants, Catholics, and Jews—along with blacks—constituted the principal social groupings in the American population is still to be found in two works that attained the status of classics: Glazer and Moynihan's *Beyond the Melting Pot* (1963), and Gordon's *Assimilation in American Life* (1964).[10]

In terms of assigning analytical importance to the religious factor, Herberg's work represents the high point in the literature. But the so-called revival of ethnicity along with the upsurge of interest in social history have since combined to produce an outpouring of scholarship on immigration, ethnicity, and religion. The most recent comprehensive history of American Catholicism, for example, gives unprecedented attention to immigration; and since its publication (in 1985) two other general studies of Catholic immigration have appeared.[11] Although predominantly descriptive, virtually all of the new historical work assumes that "pluralism" is desirable and deprecates "assimilation" implicitly if not explicitly. Much of it also exhibits a more diffuse tendency to treat "religion" as merely an aspect of "ethnicity," that is, as an epiphenomenon or function of something more basic.

At least in part as a reaction to the erosion of religion's status as an independent variable, Timothy L. Smith vigorously reaffirmed its causal potency in an essay entitled "Religion and Ethnicity in America" (1978).[12] He makes three important claims. First, he maintains that religion was the key element in the process by which immigrants who were strangers to each other, and who lacked a common "national" identity, molded themselves into relatively coherent groups, each with its own distinctive sense of peoplehood. It does not stretch categories unduly to think of this as an elaboration of the institutional nucleus function noted earlier.

Second, Smith calls immigration a "theologizing experience" because it intensified "the psychic basis of religious commitment," personalized it by requiring new choices, gave it an ethical slant ("How should we live our new lives?"), and provided resources (e.g., biblical images of hope and redemption) that nourished a forward-looking, progressive outlook on the part of immigrants. This goes much further than Handlin's psychologism, but it too focuses on the personal rather than the institutional dimension of religion. In his third point, which is less fully developed but more of a genuine novelty, Smith draws attention to religious universalism, the "idea of a common humanity [that] stands at the center of all major western religions." By affirming this idea, he suggests, all the "ethnosectarian versions of Jewish and Christian faith in America" contributed to America's "integrative pluralism."

Something of a tour de force, Smith's essay is the most systematically developed and explicitly positive analysis of the interaction between religion and immigration known to me. Taking it as the capstone of that interpretive tradition, we turn now to treatments that focus on the negative dimensions of the interaction. These accounts concern themselves not with the unifying and stabilizing functions of religion but with its divisiveness. Religion can create or exacerbate ill feeling in two ways: within and among immigrant groups themselves; and between immigrants and the host society. The former we have already noted in passing, and there is no room here to discuss the literature in detail; the latter, which falls under the heading of "nativism," requires brief discussion.

Given the salience of nativism as a theme in immigration historiography, it is remarkable that two works published many years ago still dominate the field: Ray Allen Billington's *Protestant Crusade* (1938), a study of the origins of nativism in the antebellum period; and John Higham's *Strangers in the Land* (1955), which covers the period 1860–1925.[13] The former identifies religion—specifically the anti-Catholicism of the Protestant majority—as the central element in American nativism; the latter takes religion into account, but its interpretive scheme is more complex.

An intellectual historian sensitive to the dangers of nationalism, Higham portrayed nativism as an inverse form of nationalism directed against groups that seemed to threaten the well-being of the Republic from within. It varied in intensity according to the degree of confidence or anxiety felt by the cultural majority, and it was guided in its selection of targets by three ideological principles—anti-Catholicism, antiradicalism, and racialism. Religion thus remained central to Higham's analysis, but it was no longer the primary element in nativism.

Although it allowed him to deal fully with anti-Catholicism, Higham's approach was less well suited to an exploration of the anti-Semitic dimension of American nativism. Hence he devoted several later essays to that subject, the most important of which are included in his *Send These To Me: Jews and Other Immigrants in Urban America* (1975).[14] Catholic and Jewish historians also dealt with nativism as it affected the two groups, but the timing of their studies differs. Catholics produced many monographs on nativism in the era when Billington's book appeared, but interest in the topic has slackened in the more recent past.[15] Just the opposite tendency is discernible among Jewish historians: anti-Semitism has become a major focus of scholarly attention only in the past two decades.[16]

After the appearance of *Strangers in the Land*, scholarship on matters related to nativism took a different turn, probably because that book seemed definitive on the subject as traditionally understood. Higham himself signaled the new direction when he pointed out in 1958 that his "ideological" interpretation was but one approach to the problem. Nativism also reflected genuine conflicts—for material advantage, for prestige, and over "real issues of faith"—among different segments of society and had to be seen as part of the "total complex of ethnic tensions in American society." The new task, therefore, was "to analyze the historical composition of American society in ethnic terms."[17]

Higham's prescience in this matter is noted by James Bergquist in a survey of recent work on nativism which provides an admirable review of the new literature. In politics, the "ethnocultural approach" highlighted the importance of religious, linguistic, and other immigrant-related issues in the party battles of the past. Social historians explored the relation of ethnicity and religion to mobility patterns and their accompanying tensions, while labor historians featured the linkages between ethnicity and working-class culture. Historians of education showed how often ethnoreligious factors were at work in conflicts over school reform, and the same applies to other areas of reform as well.[18]

Although this literature has given new prominence to ethnic-religious issues, most historians would probably agree with Higham that the term *nativism* should not be applied "to all or even most of this recent scholarship." *Nativism*, he goes on to say, is "a one-sided word, pinpointing exclusionary impulses expressed in the name of the native population," and its use should be confined to that "traditional meaning."[19] The point is well taken, and Higham might have added that historians still conventionally regard nativism in this sense as an unqualified evil. For despite mounting evidence that ethnoreligious conflicts are complex and may involve legitimate concerns on the part of "nativists," historians still tend almost automatically to side with the "victims." Indeed, this disposition is the most powerful, most widely held, and least critically examined attitude—not to say prejudice—that shapes historical work in the field of immigration and religion.[20]

Broadly as it has been applied, the positive/negative classification does not compass all the works that demand notice even in this schematic overview. A highly relevant work that escapes these (or any other) categories is R. Laurence Moore's *Religious Outsiders and the Making of Americans* (1986). Here Moore pursues a problem he encountered in an earlier study of spiritualism: What constitutes "the mainstream" in American culture and why are certain groups (insiders) considered part of it, while others (outsiders) are not? The immigrant dimension as such is present in only two of the groups Moore examines (Catholics and Jews), but the profoundly "ethnic" question of how group boundaries are established and maintained is central to *Religious Outsiders*.[21]

A series of related essays rather than a systematic historical treatise, Moore's book sparkles with insights but resists easy encapsulation. He argues that the metaphor of the mainstream distorts reality and should be dropped, pointing out again and again that groups regarded as outsiders shared the same values and assumptions as insiders even though they employed the rhetoric of outsiderhood for purposes of boundary maintenance. He also urges historians to look more deeply at the conflicts between these groups because they played so essential a role in forging the religious identities through which men and women invested their lives with significance.

If Moore's message is hard to pin down, that is even more true of the literature on American civil religion; but it demands attention as relevant, particularly to the second part of this essay. The general idea—namely, that religion and politics had somehow blended together imparting a sacred dimension to American ideology and institutions—long antedated the appearance in 1967 of Robert Bellah's famous essay "Civil Religion in America." Why that piece set off such a flood of publications, both popular and academic, is a subject deserving of analysis in its own right.[22] In any case, the notion—elusive at best—had assumed such protean form by 1980 that Bellah himself described it as having lost all conceptual coherence "or at least . . . anything I ever meant by the term."[23]

For Bellah, who can fairly be called a theologian of this form of faith, civil religion is the spiritual bond that unifies Americans and, as it were, sanctifies their common life. This obviously suggests that American civil religion is a kind of superreligion with which immigrant groups professing various "particularistic" faiths must somehow to come to terms. Even though Bellah later conceded that "two different types of civil religion" might be distinguished, "both [were] operative in America" and the unifying function seemed unaffected.[24] But if civil religions continued to multiply, what would that do to national unity? Martin Marty did not address the question when he explained that America really had "Two Kinds of Two Kinds of Civil Religion." Neither did Michael Novak, although he brought immigration decisively into the picture by asserting that there were at least four Protestant, three Jewish, three Irish Catholic, and an unspecified number of other ethnic civil religions.[25] But these formulations unquestionably complicated civil religion's unifying role, and Laurence Moore was unkind enough to suggest that, like the other faiths he studied, civil religion probably "split Americans into separate camps as often as it has brought them together."[26]

The only work known to me that attempts to explain just *how* civil religion promotes national unity by moderating interreligious strife is John Murray Cuddihy's *No Offense* (1977).[27] In what he calls a willful misreading of Bellah's work, Cuddihy converts civil religion into the "religion of civility." He then proceeds to show how the American imperative of civility—showing respect for others; at its blandest, "being nice"—requires the believers in different religious faiths to moderate their public claims to exclusive possession of the truth, extend de facto recognition to others, and thereby implicitly acquiesce in the reduction of their own faith-position to one among many, all of which must abide by the prescriptions of the secular religion of civility. Cuddihy's brilliant analysis not only "operationalizes" civil religion but also explains why the ideal of pluralistic tolerance is emotionally unsatisfying, for civility does not promise genuine solidarity, much less salvation. Mutual forebearance, necessary and admirable though it be, fails to stir the soul.

Cuddihy also contributed to a volume entitled *Uncivil Religion* (1987).[28] Although Bellah is a co-editor and contributor, the book has little to say about civil religion as such. It presents, rather, a useful survey of tensions affecting a wide range of religious groups, and between society at large and "cults," such as the Reverend Sun Myung Moon's Unification church. In his concluding commentary, Bellah focuses on the issue of group boundaries. While rejecting rigid exclusivity, he sees greater danger at present from the "radical individualism" that threatens to dissolve group boundaries entirely, "relativize" all judgments, and undermine "the moral norms that provide the terms for our democratic conversation." Bellah prescribes maintaining "group identities and group boundaries while remaining open to knowledge of and cooperation with others, including those of different faiths." He calls this position "authentically biblical and authentically American."[29] It might even be an authentic expression of American civil religion, although Bellah does not make that claim; but as the long history of controversy over religion, education, and Americanism demonstrates, the reconciliation of conflicting group identities and group boundaries is a perennial problem.

Group identities and group boundaries are inescapably involved in education because its primary purpose is to inculcate in children and young people the knowledge, beliefs, and values of the groups of which they are a part. In the Christian West, this activity was traditionally carried out under religious auspices, suffused with religious assumptions, and oriented toward religious goals. But in the era of modern nationalism that dates from the French Revolution, the traditional arrangement came into conflict with, and was progressively displaced by, state control of education. The new system was promoted by political leaders who perceived the crucial role the schools could play in molding national unity, and whose outlook often had a strongly civil-religious cast. Conflicts over secular (political) versus religious (church-related) control of education were more embittered in Europe, particularly France, than in the United States.[30] But those that occurred here are particularly relevant to our interest because religious diversity arising from immigration was so centrally involved and because civil religion, broadly understood, has been so prominent a theme. Although the discussion must be schematic in the extreme, it will give us a more concrete sense of the issues to look at the school question over time.

Few difficulties arose in the colonial era because formal education at the elementary level, which was religious in inspiration, operated in localized fashion and on a small scale.[31] After independence, there was a gradual shift toward greater reliance on the state, but church-related schooling continued strongly into the early decades of the nineteenth century. Although various schemes of "national education" were floated as early as the 1790s, they resembled the educational projects of revolutionary France too closely to gain much support. Only in the late 1830s did a groundswell of opinion begin to build up in favor of state control of education—which in America meant, of course, control by the states, not the national government. Many factors were at work in this transition, but it could not have occurred at all had it not been perceived as a necessary, *and authentically religious*, modification of church-related schooling.[32]

Horace Mann was the key figure in articulating the religious rationale for the shift.[33] Mann believed fervently in using the powers of the state to elevate the condition of mankind, but his policies as secretary of the Massachusetts Board of Education also reflected his deeply held religious beliefs. A Unitarian, Mann stressed the ethical element in religion: he looked upon Jesus as the exemplar of human perfectibility, the Bible as a treasury of spiritual inspiration, and Christianity as a summons to work for moral improvement in oneself and others. This kind of religion—Mann called it the "religion of heaven"—*belonged* in the schools, for without it they could not effectively carry out their primary task, moral formation. Nor could the task be adequately performed in any but a statewide, publicly supported system of "common schools," in which children of all social and religious backgrounds were brought together and molded into good citizens along lines suggested by Mann's understanding of religion, pedagogy, and civic virtue. Hence Mann opposed more traditional forms of church-related schooling.

His opposition was powerfully reinforced by the repugnance he felt for the content of the religious instruction carried on in such schools. This too reflected his Unitarianism, a religion that developed as a reaction against traditional Calvinism and repudiated its teachings as the worst kind of religious error. Mann shared passionately in this aspect of his faith; he objected vehemently to the inclusion of Calvinist beliefs in any educational program. Such "sectarian" teaching, besides being wrong, was socially divisive; his "religion of heaven," besides being true, brought young people together on a "nonsectarian" basis and formed them into good Christians and good citizens. Hence it served patriotic as well as religious purposes. By midcentury, the dominant cultural majority had swung behind this position, rejecting church-related schools in favor of "common schools" in which moral and civic formation took place in an atmosphere of nondenominational Protestantism.[34]

Mann's emphasis on classroom reading of the Bible—the moral efficacy of which he regarded in almost magical terms—helped immensely in rallying support to his plan and overcoming the resistance of Protestant traditionalists, which was at first considerable. Even more important, however, was the terrific growth of the Catholic population, which affected the public school issue in two ways. On the one hand, the vast increase in Catholic immigration heightened the perceived need for "common schools" to assimilate the newcomers and thereby mitigate the strain on national unity their very presence was thought to entail. On the other hand, Catholic espousal of the church-related plan of education—to say nothing of demands for public funds to support *their* schools—discredited the older system in Protestant eyes and converted all but a few foreign-speaking conservatives (most notably the Missouri Synod Lutherans) into supporters of public schools and "common school religion."[35]

The controversies set off by massive Catholic immigration forged an ideological outlook that assimilated Protestantism to Americanism. This view, which dominated the public mind through the second half of the nineteenth century, may be summarized as follows: 1) It was indeed

possible for public schools to teach those elements of the Christian religion essential to personal morality and civic virtue without transgressing
on the doctrinal territory disputed among the various churches; hence
Catholics had no valid religious grounds for objecting to public school
education. 2) Since the public schools were—as they should be—teaching this kind of religion, the charge of "godlessness" leveled against them
was unfounded. 3) Because such religious education, rooted in the nation's historic Protestant heritage, was an essential constituent of American nationality, Catholics brought their civic loyalty into question by
criticizing and refusing to patronize the public schools. 4) Despite earlier
precedents to the contrary, the kind of tax-supported denominational
schools Catholics demanded were out of the question because they would
frustrate the nation-building mission of public education, encourage sectarian strife, and benefit a church that was basically anti-American in
its inherent structure and in the policies it pursued.[36]

The same controversies that produced this Protestant consensus
convinced Catholics they would have to go it alone with respect to schooling. Hence they built up a vast educational system of their own, financed
entirely from private resources.[37] Three points about it are especially
pertinent to this discussion: the religio-ethnic mix of motivations; the
Catholic view of the public policy issue; and Catholics' understanding of
the relationship between religious education and civic loyalty.

Among non-English-speaking groups such as the Germans and
Poles, the desire to preserve mother tongue as well as religion was a
significant factor in the founding of Catholic schools. Indeed, German
Catholics often contrasted their zeal for parochial schools with the relative
lukewarmness of Irish Catholics. But most Irish Catholics were equally
committed to parochial schools, in part because religion served for these
immigrants as the chief symbol of group identity and focus of ethnic
loyalty.[38] Catholic "Americanizers" often criticized their coreligionists on
this very point: Orestes Brownson protested in the 1850s against using
"the pretext of providing for Catholic education" to preserve what he
called "Irishism"; thirty years later Archbishop John Ireland of Saint Paul
lodged the same basic complaint against German Catholics.[39]

The undeniable significance of linguistic-cultural factors should not,
however, mislead us into dismissing religion as the chief motivation for
the founding of Catholic schools. Such an interpretation, which reflects
the tendency noted earlier to demote religion from the status of an independent variable, reads too much of the present back into the past. As
George F. Theriault showed in a brilliant but neglected study of French-
Canadians in New England, language, religion, and nationality were not

discrete elements in the thinking of nineteenth-century immigrants.[40] Rather, they were intermingled in—or, more precisely, had not yet been differentiated as parts of—a complex cultural whole that also included local and familial traditions. Religion was thus centrally involved in the heritage Catholic immigrants founded schools to preserve; it provided the institutional vehicle for realizing this aim; and as the constituent elements of immigrant heritages were gradually differentiated, religion proved the most enduring.

With respect to the issue of public policy, the Catholics' view derived from their more fundamental conviction that the personal formation essential to true education had to be based on religion in its dogmatic fullness, not on a least-common-denominator moralism (which was actually, as Catholics saw it, a diluted form of Protestantism). The only way the Catholic prescription could be realized in a religiously diverse society was for each religious group to have its own schools; and if the state supported any, it should in justice support all of them equally. Catholic spokesmen, liberals as well as conservatives, advanced this argument from the 1840s through the 1880s. But it was doomed by mid-century because Protestants regarded the common schools as essential to the survival of the Republic. Even maintaining their own schools on a purely voluntary basis branded Catholics as un-American. As Cardinal Gibbons explained to Rome, the school question more than anything else persuaded Americans "that the Catholic Church is opposed by principle to the institutions of the country and that a sincere Catholic cannot be a loyal citizen of the United States."[41]

Catholics of course rejected this view of the relation between education and civic loyalty. They could not deny that their schools were, in a sense, divisive; the criticism of the Americanizers testified to internal disagreement about how severe that drawback was and what could be done to mitigate it. But the dominant opinion among Catholics held that the need for religious schooling outweighed the negative effects of having a system that kept their children apart from other young people. And not even the Americanizers would concede that social divisiveness implied civic disloyalty. On the contrary, Catholics claimed to be as good Americans as anyone else. Their schools taught that love of country, respect for her institutions, and obedience to her laws were moral duties. And those schools themselves had come into being through the free exercise of religion—a right guaranteed by the Constitution. By the time the issue was explicitly formulated as "divisiveness" (around 1950), Catholics were learning to turn it aside by appealing to "pluralism."[42] Neither that term nor *civil religion* was available to them in the nineteenth century. Had they been, Catholics might well have responded that the charge of disloyalty could seem convincing only to people who identified Americanism with the acceptance of civil religion in its public school-Protestant form.

In the twentieth century, this form of civil religion underwent a process of secularization. That, along with the persistence of the Catholic issue and the emergence of Jews as a major factor on the religious/educational scene, requires brief notice.

"Secularization" is, of course, a complex and controversial concept. I use it here in the loose vernacular sense to designate the process by which public education lost most of its nonsectarian-Protestant coloration but retained certain vestiges that merged with elements from other sources to form a fuzzier and more generalized version of public school civil religion associated primarily with unifying Americans on the basis of commonly shared "moral and spiritual values."[43] The continuities in this process are clearly observable in the thinking of John Dewey, the philosopher whose ideas dominated American public education in the first half of the twentieth century.

Dewey abandoned the Protestantism of his New England ancestors but not their moralism and concern for social betterment. In 1908, just as immigration reached its climax, he published an essay entitled "Religion and Our Schools," in which he affirmed that the public schools were "performing an infinitely significant religious work" by taking young people of diverse backgrounds and "assimilating them together on the basis of what is common and public in endeavor and achievement." By teaching both self-respect and respect for others, the schools promoted a social unity that was truly religious in character. While properly eschewing the formalism of traditional religious instruction, which could inhibit the development of "state-consciousness," they were nevertheless providing education genuinely "religious in substance and in promise."[44]

Dewey's revisionist understanding of religious education was, as it were, expanded and generalized in his 1934 book A Common Faith. Here he sought to emancipate "the religious"—by which he meant those dimensions of our experience which elevate, inspire, and unite us with others—from its stultifying identification with "religion"—by which he meant formal religion, the creeds and cults of the organized churches.[45] According to this view of things, the public schools ought definitely to engage in "religious" education; but to teach "religion" would militate directly against the success of "religious" education, rightly understood. The terminology confuses, but a close analogy can be drawn between Dewey's position and that of Horace Mann. Where Mann prescribed "the religion of heaven," Dewey prescribes "the religious"; where Mann rejected "sectarianism," Dewey rejects "religion." With respect to their understanding of the broadly "religious" aims of public education—personal development of the individual meshing with social improvement and national cohesion—there is not just analogy but straightforward continuity between the positions of the two men.

Dewey was not alone in viewing the public schools from a civil-religious perspective. Ellwood P. Cubberly, an educational historian whose remarks on assimilating immigrants are regularly exhibited as a nativistic horror, also observed that the work of the public schools was "to a large degree" religious. Denis Brogan likewise emphasized their religious quality in his well-known delineation of *The American Character* (1944).[46] The wartime crisis, which linked democracy to "our Judeo-Christian heritage," prompted J. Paul Williams, a professor of religion at Mount Holyoke College, to speak of the public school as "a veritable temple for the indoctrination of democracy," which should be taught explicitly "*as religion* [sic]."[47] This kind of talk embarrassed most public school spokespersons, who were strict separationists on the church-state issue, but it was taken seriously by the prominent church historian Sidney E. Mead and other commentators on civil religion. And the programs to "teach about religion" that sprouted in the public schools after the U.S. Supreme Court outlawed prayer and Bible reading were permeated by civil-religious goals such as deepening students' appreciation for national values, promoting intergroup harmony, and contributing to the moral renewal of society.[48]

Since separation of church and state, religious neutrality, and the "secularity" of the schools are fundamental postulates of the whole system of public education, willingness to recognize its religious quality, even in the Deweyan sense, has been rare. Such willingness as exists is important, however, for the testimony it gives to the substratum of religious seriousness with which Americans regard public education, particularly in its function—which is closely related to immigration—of integrating the diverse elements of the population around the values of freedom, equality, and other elements of the national ideology.[49] It is this underlying concern with unity that continued to make the existence of a separate system of Catholic schools problematic—particularly since Catholics were widely regarded by important opinion leaders, both religious and secular, as committed by their religion to principles incompatible with Americanism.[50]

Concern for national unity and doubts about the civic loyalty of Catholics were both involved in the Oregon School Law of 1922 which would have put Catholic schools out of business by requiring all students to attend public schools. In the nativistic atmosphere of the time, several other states were considering similar legislation, but the U.S. Supreme Court struck down the Oregon statute, denying that the state's regulatory authority included the power "to standardize its children by forcing them to accept instruction from public teachers only."[51] Extremely important in itself, the Oregon case gave a hint of what was to come, for it marked the U.S. Supreme Court's entry into a constitutional area that was to become increasingly active after World War II, namely, church-state questions involving the schools.

The issue of aid to parochial schools, which was seen by non-Catholics as part of a Catholic campaign to subvert the principle of church-state separation, figured very prominently in this post–World War II development, but we cannot enter upon its complexities.[52] Two observations will have to suffice. The first is that the U.S. Supreme Court's educational decisions have defined separation more and more stringently, with the result that public funds are available to Catholic schools only for quite marginal types of assistance (except at the level of higher education, where a more flexible interpretation permits public support for nonreligious purposes). The second is that moving this key aspect of the Catholic question to the sphere of constitutional adjudication has helped to contain intergroup friction by bringing it within a framework of settlement that everyone regards as legitimate, disappointing as the outcomes may be to one or another party in any given case.

American Jews, who resemble Catholics in their character as immigrants, take a very different position on matters relating to religion and education. In the nineteenth century, German Jews maintained a few full-time day schools; more recently, Orthodox Jews have established them. But these are exceptions to the general rule. Most American Jews have always patronized the public schools, relying on various types of supplemental education to provide the specifically Jewish content of their children's formation. Besides being strongly committed to secular public schools, Jews have also championed strict separationism on church-state issues. So deeply rooted is this complex of attitudes that even during the "ethnic studies" boom of the 1970s, Jews remained "wary of encouraging the teaching of Jewish studies" in the public schools.[53]

The process by which "Jews transformed themselves from a group which gave primacy to sacred learning into one which gave primacy to secular learning" may be, as Marshall Sklare observes, imperfectly understood, but the congruence between Reform Judaism and the public school ideology, both of which emerged in the mid nineteenth century, goes far to explain their original acceptance of the American system. Reformism envisioned Jews as "fully integrated citizens of the modern secular state, differentiated only by religion," and with all outmoded or discordant features of the Jewish religious tradition trimmed away. In the words of Lloyd P. Gartner, Reform Jews looked upon religiously neutral public schools as "a blessing and a necessity, for they were a microcosm of the society in which Jewish children would find a place as adults. . . . The public school was viewed as the symbol and guarantee of Jewish equality and full opportunity in America."[54]

The commitment to public education intensified with the coming of the East European Jews, who immigrated in massive numbers around the turn of the century. Heavily concentrated in New York City and "overwhelmed," as Gartner says, by "modern secular culture," many East European Jews simply abandoned Judaism, while others reintegrated the religious elements of their tradition with more modern ways of thinking. Theorists of Jewish education were naturally involved in this ferment; several of the most important were in contact with, and influenced by, John Dewey, who had moved to Columbia University in 1904. One such was Mordecai M. Kaplan, and echoes of Dewey's ideas—including the distinction between "the religious" and "religion"—are clearly discernible in the Reconstructionist movement, of which Kaplan was the founder.[55]

Reconstructionism holds that "Jewishness" is broader and more basic than "Judaism," for the former designates a "religious civilization," while the latter refers to the "religion" that has historically given expression to the civilization but that does not exhaust its spiritual potentialities. The Reconstructionist program of integrating the Jewish heritage with the best in the modern world had an obvious affinity with civil religion. "Indeed," writes Charles S. Liebman, "Kaplan's belief that church and state must be separate, but that every civilization must have its own religion to assure social cohesion and unity, makes a civil religion a necessity."[56] Hence it is not surprising that Kaplan collaborated with J. Paul Williams in editing *The Faith of America* (1951), a devotional anthology of "prayers, readings, and songs for the celebration of American holidays," and that his son-in-law and successor, Ira Eisenstein, took satisfaction in noting that the country seemed to be ready for a civil religion in 1976.[57]

Commitment to American civil religion is an equally prominent motif in certain varieties of Jewish "secularism." For our purposes, the key figure here is Horace M. Kallen, formulator of the theory of cultural pluralism, which has become a kind of shibboleth among commentators on education, as well as ethnicity and religion.[58] Kallen's active career spanned more than half a century (he was 92 when he died in 1974) and covered a wide range of topics. A pragmatic philosopher like John Dewey, with whom he was closely acquainted, Kallen shared Dewey's quasi-religious understanding of democracy, his enthusiasm for public education, his opposition to public aid for Catholic schools, and his hostility to Catholic "authoritarianism" in general.

Kallen's views on ethnicity, religion, and American nationality, which were first set forth in strongly antiassimilationist terms (in 1915 and 1924), represented his personal integration of Jewish and American elements. His cultural pluralism originally envisaged American society as a kind of federation of ethnic nationalities; but the concept took on a life of its own and, by World War II, had converged with the kind of assimilationism that stressed the acceptance by all groups of American ideals, especially "tolerance for diversity." When Kallen himself returned to the subject in the 1950s, cultural pluralism had become indistinguishable in his thinking from "the American Idea," which he capitalized and invested with explicitly religious authority. Yet his version of American civil religion was in its own way quite "sectarian." He described it as a distinctive "apprehension of human nature and human relations" which *everyone* ("every sort and condition of Protestant, Catholic, Judaist, Moslem, Buddhist, and every other communion") had to accept and live by in order to be a good American.[59]

Kallen made his sweeping assertion in responding to a Catholic critic who had objected to his elevating the "American Idea" into a "surrogate religion." We should not, of course, make too much of a single episode, but this one is highly symptomatic of the quite different ways Catholics and Jews—the two major immigrant religions in the United States—have understood the relations between religion, ethnicity, and civic loyalty. It is too early to discern what additional differences will come to light as a result of recent immigration that has augmented the strength of religious traditions (Islam, Hinduism, Buddhism, and others) that have not hitherto played a significant role in American developments. For that matter, we are still far from really understanding the interaction between immigration and religion among the groups that did figure prominently in our past. But the little that we know strongly suggests that education is likely to be a flash point of conflict and that "civil religion" needs to be taken into account along with the traditional faiths of both immigrants and host society.

NOTES

Source: Donald Horowitz and Gerard Noiriel, eds., *Immigrants in Two Democracies: French and American Experience* (New York: New York University Press), forthcoming. Reprinted by permission of the publisher.

1. This point is documented for religious historians by Jay P. Dolan, "Immigration and American Christianity: A History of Their Histories," in Henry W. Bowden, ed., *A Century of Church History: The Legacy of Philip Schaff* (Carbondale, Ill., 1988), 119–47.

2. George M. Stephenson, *The Religious Aspects of Swedish Immigration* (Minneapolis, Minn., 1932); Robert A. Orsi, *The Madonna of 115th Street: Faith and Community in Italian Harlem, 1880–1950* (New Haven, Conn., 1985).

3. For Catholics, see Dolores Liptak, *Immigrants and Their Church* (New York, 1989); for Jews, Deborah Dash Moore, *At Home in America: Second Generation New York Jews* (New York, 1981), 124, 129, 131, 137–39, 145; for blacks, Eugene D. Genovese, *Roll, Jordan, Roll: The World the Slaves Made* (New York, 1972), esp. bk. 2; Albert J. Raboteau, *Slave Religion: The "Invisible Institution" in the Antebellum South* (New York, 1978); C. Eric Lincoln and Lawrence Mamaiya, *The Black Church and the African-American Experience* (Durham, N.C., 1990).

4. W. I. Thomas, Robert E. Park, H. A. Miller, *Old World Traits Transplanted* (1921; Montclair, N.J., 1971), chap. 9. (On Thomas's role in the publication of this work, see Donald R. Young's Introduction to the reprint cited.)

5. Stephenson, *Religious Aspects*, vi; Marcus Lee Hansen, *The Immigrant in American History* (1940; New York, 1964), 97–128. For comments on Hansen's essay by a historian of American religion, see John F. Wilson, *Public Religion in American Culture* (Philadelphia, 1979), 98, 101–2; for Hansen more generally, Moses Rischin, "Marcus Lee Hansen: America's First Transethnic Historian," in Richard L. Bushman et al., eds., *Uprooted Americans: Essays to Honor Oscar Handlin* (Boston, 1979), 319–47.

6. Oscar Handlin, *The Uprooted* (Boston, 1951), chap. 5. A book to which Handlin contributed a Foreword interprets religious splits among Scandinavian immigrants in these terms; see Dorothy B. Skardal, *The Divided Heart: Scandinavian Immigrant Experience through Literary Sources* (Lincoln, 1974), 183–85. In a variation of this interpretation, Victor Greene contends that the split between "clericalists" and "nationalists" catalyzed the development of group consciousness among Polish Americans. See Greene, *For God and Country: The Rise of Polish and Lithuanian Ethnic Consciousness in America, 1860–1910* (Madison, Wis., 1975).

7. Will Herberg, *Protestant-Catholic-Jew: An Essay in American Religious Sociology*, rev. ed. (Garden City, N.Y., 1960 [orig. ed. 1955]), esp. chaps. 2–3. For Hansen's law, see above, chap. 9.

8. Ibid., chaps. 5, 11.

9. Ibid., chaps. 2–3; Ruby Jo Reeves Kennedy, "Single or Triple Melting Pot?" *American Journal of Sociology*, 49 (January 1944), 332; Kennedy, "Single or Triple Melting Pot?" ibid., 58 (1952), 56–59; Thomas J. Archdeacon, *Becoming American: An Ethnic History* (New York, 1983), chap. 8, "The Triple Melting Pot and Beyond."

10. Nathan Glazer and Daniel P. Moynihan, *Beyond the Melting Pot* (Cambridge, Mass., 1963), 314–15; Milton M. Gordon *Assimilation in American Life* (New York, 1964), chap. 7. See also Alfred McClung Lee, "Sociological Insights into American Culture and Personality," *Journal of Social Issues*, 7, no. 4 (1951), 10–11; Charles F. Marden, *Minorities in American Society* (New York, 1952), 394; Oscar Handlin, *The American People in the Twentieth Century*, rev. ed. (Boston, 1963 [orig. ed. 1954]), 223.

11. Jay P. Dolan, *The American Catholic Experience: A History from Colonial Times to the Present* (Garden City, N.Y., 1985); James S. Olson, *Catholic Immigrants in America* (Chicago, 1987); Liptak, *Immigrants and Their Church*. See also Randall

M. Miller and Thomas D. Marzik, eds., *Immigrants and Religion in Urban America* (Philadelphia, 1977). The notes to these works provide a guide to the more specialized literature published in the past quarter-century.

12. Timothy L. Smith, "Religion and Ethnicity in America," *American Historical Review*, 83 (December 1978), 1155–85.

13. Ray Allen Billington, *The Protestant Crusade, 1800 to 1860: A Study of the Origins of American Nativism* (New York, 1938); John Higham, *Strangers in the Land: Patterns of American Nativism, 1860–1925* (New Brunswick, N.J., 1955). Two more recent general works are: Thomas J. Curran, *Xenophobia and Immigration, 1820–1930* (Boston, 1975); and David H. Bennett, *The Party of Fear: From Nativist Movement to the New Right in American History* (Chapel Hill, N.C., 1988).

14. John Higham, *Send These to Me: Jews and Other Immigrants in Urban America* (New York, 1975), chaps. 7–9. The December 1986 issue of *American Jewish History* (vol. 76) is devoted to reconsiderations of Higham's work. Particularly interesting for anti-Semitism are Edward S. Shapiro's critique (201–13), and Higham's response (214–26).

15. Many doctoral dissertations published by the Catholic University of America in the 1930s and 1940s dealt with nativism; see also Mary Augustana Ray, *American Opinion of Roman Catholicism in the Eighteenth Century* (New York, 1936). It should be noted, however, that Thomas Curran (see above, n. 13) is a Catholic.

16. See David A. Gerber, ed., *Anti-Semitism in American History* (Urbana, Ill., 1986), esp. 7–13.

17. John Higham, "Another Look at Nativism," *Catholic Historical Review*, 44 (July 1958), 147–58.

18. James Bergquist, "The Concept of Nativism in Historical Study since *Strangers in the Land*," *American Jewish History*, 76 (December 1986), 125–41.

19. Higham, "The Strange Career of *Strangers in the Land*," *American Jewish History*, 76 (December 1986), 224.

20. The only critical discussion of this attitude by a historian of which I am aware is by Otis L. Graham, Jr., "Uses and Misuses of History in the Debate over Immigration Reform," *Public Historian*, 8 (Spring 1986), 41–64.

21. R. Laurence Moore, *Religious Outsiders and the Making of Americans* (New York, 1986). Besides Catholics and Jews, Moore discusses Mormons, Christian Scientists, and various types of Protestant fundamentalists.

22. Robert N. Bellah's original essay, "Civil Religion in America," *Daedalus*, 96 (Winter 1967), 1–21, has been reprinted often. James A. Mathisen, "Twenty Years after Bellah: Whatever Happened to American Civil Religion?" *Sociological Analysis*, 50 (1989), 129–46 provides a convenient listing of publications but does little to explain the phenomenon. Highly relevant, although not about civil religion as such, is Robert T. Handy, *A Christian America: Protestant Hopes and Historical Realities*, 2d ed. (New York, 1989).

23. Robert N. Bellah and Phillip E. Hammond, *Varieties of Civil Religion* (San Francisco, 1980), 1.

24. Robert N. Bellah, "Civil Religion and the American Future," *Religious Education*, 71 (1976), 237.

25. Martin E. Marty, "Two Kinds of Two Kinds of Civil Religion," in Russell E. Richey and Donald G. Jones, eds., *American Civil Religion* (New York, 1971), 139–57; Michael Novak, "America as Religion," *Religious Education*, 71 (1976), 260–67. In the Introduction to their volume, Richey and Jones discuss "Five Meanings of Civil Religion" (14–18).

26. Moore, *Religious Outsiders*, 202.

27. John Murray Cuddihy, *No Offense: Civil Religion and Protestant Taste* (New York, 1977).

28. Robert N. Bellah and Frederick E. Greespahn, eds., *Uncivil Religion: Inter-religious Hostility in America* (New York, 1987).

29. Ibid., 219–32.

30. For a temperate survey of the French experience by an American Catholic historian, see Joseph N. Moody, *French Education since Napoleon* (Syracuse, N.Y., 1978).

31. For a problem that arose in the colonial melting pot of Pennsylvania, see Sally Schwartz, *"A Mixed Multitude": The Struggle for Toleration in Colonial Pennsylvania* (New York, 1987), 185–93. For a general bibliography and commentary, see John W. Lowe, Jr., "Church-State Issues in Education: The Colonial Pattern and the Nineteenth Century to 1870," and Lowe, "Religion and Education: 1870 to the Present," in John F. Wilson, ed., *Church and State in America: A Bibliographical Guide*, 2 vols. (Westport, Conn., 1986–87), 1:297–329, 2:301–37. For a closely related topic, see Maxine S. Seller, "The Education of Immigrants in the United States: An Introduction to the Literature," *Immigration History Newsletter*, 13 (May 1981), 1–8.

32. Lloyd P. Jorgenson, *The State and the Non-Public School, 1825–1925* (Columbia, Mo., 1987), chaps. 1–2; Charles Leslie Glenn, Jr., *The Myth of the Common School* (Amherst, Mass., 1988), chap. 4.

33. My treatment of Mann is based on Glenn, *Myth of the Common School*, esp. 79–82, 158ff.; Robert Michaelsen, *Piety in the Public School* (New York, 1970), 70–79; Raymond B. Culver, *Horace Mann and Religion in the Massachusetts Public Schools* (New Haven, Conn., 1929); and Neil G. McCluskey, *Public Schools and Moral Education: The Influence of Horace Mann, William Torrey Harris, and John Dewey* (New York, 1958), chaps. 2–4.

34. Classical on this point is Timothy L. Smith, "Protestant Schooling and American Nationality, 1800–1850," *Journal of American History*, 53 (March 1967), 679–95; see also Jorgenson, *Non-Public School*, chaps. 3–4.

35. Jorgenson, *Non-Public School*, chap. 5; Glenn, *Myth of the Common School*, chap. 8; see also Francis X. Curran, *The Churches and the Schools: American Protestantism and Popular Elementary Education* (Chicago, 1954); Walter H. Beck, *Lutheran Elementary Schools in the United States* (St. Louis, Mo., 1939); and for early Jewish schools, Lloyd P. Gartner, "Temples of Liberty Unpolluted: American Jews and Public Schools, 1840–1875," in Bertram Wallace Korn, ed., *A Bicentennial Festschrift for Jacob Rader Marcus* (Waltham, Mass., 1976), 157–89.

36. For elaboration, see Philip Gleason, *Keeping the Faith: American Catholicism Past and Present* (Notre Dame, Ind., 1987), 115–35. Jorgenson, *Non-Public School*, chaps. 6–9, is unparalleled for the late nineteenth century.

37. Dolan, *American Catholic Experience*, chap. 10 provides general coverage; James W. Sanders, *The Education of an Urban Minority: Catholics in Chicago, 1833–1965* (New York, 1977) is the best case study; F. Michael Perko, ed., *Enlightening the Next Generation: Catholics and Their Schools, 1830–1980* (New York, 1988) anthologizes recent scholarship.

38. For German Catholic commitment to the parochial school, see Colman J. Barry, *The Catholic Church and German Americans* (Milwaukee, Wis., 1953), esp. 184–200; for the Irish and Italians (who, like the later Hispanic Catholics, showed less interest than the Irish, Germans, Poles, and French Canadians), see Howard R. Weisz, *Irish-American and Italian-American Educational Views and Activities, 1870–1900* (New York, 1976).

39. For Brownson, see Gleason, *Keeping the Faith*, 161; for Ireland, Daniel F.

Reilly, *The School Controversy (1891–1893)* (Washington, D.C., 1943), 256–57; and, more generally, Marvin R. O'Connell's superb biography, *John Ireland and the American Catholic Church* (St. Paul, Minn., 1988).

40. George F. Theriault, "The Franco-Americans in a New England Community: An Experiment in Survival" (Ph.D. diss., Harvard University, 1951), esp. 378–79, 538ff.

41. John Tracy Ellis, *The Life of James Cardinal Gibbons, Archbishop of Baltimore, 1834–1921*, 2 vols. (Milwaukee, Wis., 1952), 1:664–65. See also Gleason, *Keeping the Faith*, 122.

42. For divisiveness and pluralism, see above, chaps. 3, 8.

43. A special commission set up by the National Education Association stated in 1951 that all other educational objectives must be subordinated to developing in children the "moral and spiritual values" central to the American heritage. Cited in Michaelsen, *Piety in the Public School*, 46. My discussion here is much indebted to Michaelsen's chapter 2, "The Public School as 'Established Church'?"

44. John Dewey, "Religion and Our Schools," *Hibbert Journal*, 6 (July 1908), 796–809, as summarized and quoted in Michaelsen, *Piety in the Public School*, 57, 59; see also McCluskey, *Public Schools and Moral Education*, chaps. 8–10.

45. John Dewey, *A Common Faith* (New Haven, Conn., 1934), esp. chap. 1.

46. Elwood P. Cubberly, *Changing Conceptions of Education* (New York, 1909), 68 for religion, 15–16 for Americanization; D. W. Brogan, *The American Character* (New York, 1944), 136–37.

47. J. Paul Williams, *What Americans Believe and How They Worship* (New York, 1952), 371; Williams, "The Schoolmen and Religion," *School and Society*, 70 (August 13, 1949), 97–100; Williams, *The New Education and Religion* (New York, 1945), 159ff., 180ff. See also Mark Silk, "Notes on the Judeo-Christian Tradition in America," *American Quarterly*, 36 (Spring 1984), 65–85; and for war-inspired elevation of democracy to religious status, Herbert Agar et al., *The City of Man: A Declaration of World Democracy* (New York, 1941), 80–85.

48. For Sidney E. Mead, see his *Lively Experiment: The Shaping of Christianity in America* (New York, 1963), 68–71; John F. Wilson, who is skeptical of the public-school-as-civil-religious-church interpretation, reviews the issue in his *Public Religion in American Culture*, 125–30. For teaching-about-religion programs, see Philip Gleason, "Blurring the Line of Separation: Education, Civil Religion, and Teaching about Religion," *Journal of Church and State*, 19 (Autumn 1977), 517–38; Paul J. Will, ed., *Public Education Religion Studies: An Overview* (Chico, Calif., 1981).

49. In this connection, it should be noted that the civil rights movement gained its first great impetus from the Brown v. Board of Education of Topeka decision (1954) in which the U.S. Supreme Court struck down racial segregation *in the schools*.

50. For doubts on this score in the first work of twentieth-century social science to apply the minority concept to American intergroup relations, see Donald Young, *American Minority Peoples: A Study in Racial and Cultural Conflicts in the United States* (New York, 1932), 499–500.

51. Jorgenson, *Non-Public School*, chap. 10; for the Catholic response, see Thomas J. Shelley, "The Oregon School Case and the National Catholic Welfare Conference," *Catholic Historical Review*, 75 (July 1989), 439–57; Fayette Veverke, "The Ambiguity of Catholic Educational Separatism," *Religious Education*, 80 (1985), 64–100.

52. For the post–World War II controversies, see above, chap. 8, and Gleason, "Blurring the Line of Separation," esp. 518–24.

53. See Lloyd P. Gartner, ed., *Jewish Education in the United States: A Docu-*

mentary History (New York, 1969), esp. Gartner's Introduction, which is reprinted with interesting prefatory comments by Marshall Sklare (including the passage quoted in the text about ethnic studies) in Sklare, ed., *American Jews: A Reader* (New York, 1983), 365–92. See also Gartner, "Temples of Liberty"; Moses Rischin, *The Promised City: New York's Jews, 1870–1914* (Cambridge, Mass., 1962), 100–103, 199–200; and Moore, *At Home in America*, chap. 4.

54. Sklare, *American Jews*, 366 for quotation from Sklare; 375 for quotation from Gartner.

55. Gartner quoted from Sklare, *American Jews*, 376; on contacts with Dewey, see Moore, *At Home in America*, 107–9; I. B. Berkson, "Jewish Education—Achievements and Needs," in Oscar I. Janowsky, ed., *The American Jew: A Composite Portrait* (Freeport, N.Y., 1971 [orig. pub. 1942]), pp. 57–59; and Ronald Kronish, "Horace M. Kallen and John Dewey on Cultural Pluralism and Jewish Education," in Milton R. Konvitz, ed., *The Legacy of Horace M. Kallen* (Rutherford, N.J., 1987), 90–107, esp. 91, 103.

56. Charles S. Liebman, "Reconstructionism in American Jewish Life," *American Jewish Year Book 1970*, vol. 71 (New York, 1970), 3–100; quotation from 22.

57. Ira Eisenstein, "Is the U.S. Ready for a Civil Religion?" *Religious Education*, 71 (1976), 227–29. The editors state that the selections in *Faith of America*, which are taken mainly from "American literature and . . . historic documents of permanent spiritual value" and arranged in "the form of a religious service," provide "a religious interpretation to American history and institutions without reference to the specific doctrines of any of the historic religions with which individual Americans may be affiliated." See Mordecai M. Kaplan, J. Paul Williams, and Eugene Kohn, eds., *The Faith of America*, 2d ed. (New York, 1961), xxiv–xxv.

58. Konvitz, *Legacy of Horace Kallen*, contains seven essays on Kallen, all sympathetic; more critical are Werner Sollors, "A Critique of Pure Pluralism," in Sacvan Bercovitch, ed., *Reconstructing American Literary History* (Cambridge, Mass., 1986), 250–79; and above, chaps. 3, 8.

59. Horace M. Kallen, *Cultural Pluralism and the American Idea* (Philadelphia, 1956), esp. 204–5. See also Kallen, "Democracy's True Religion," *Saturday Review of Literature*, 34 (July 28, 1951), 6–7, 29–30; Kallen, *Secularism Is the Will of God* (New York, 1954); Kallen, "Secularism as the Common Religion of a Free Society," *Journal for the Scientific Study of Religion*, 4 (1965), 145–51.

|| 11 ||

"Americanism" in American Catholic Discourse

As was noted in chapter 10, the interaction between religion and immigration has only recently begun to attract the attention of historians. In the field of American Catholic history—to stick to the work I know best—religion was in the past so closely identified with the institutional church and its official leaders that Catholic historians traditionally paid little attention to immigration or "nationality" except when it became a problem disturbing the ecclesiastical scene. This, to be sure, began to change when the vogue of social history turned the attention of younger scholars to ethnicity and other nonecclesiastical dimensions of Catholic group life. But the social historians' tendency to interpret religion as merely an "aspect" of ethnicity leads to its own distortion by undervaluing the importance of religion as an independent variable.

My own view, which goes back to my doctoral work on German-American Catholics, is that ethnicity and religion must both be taken into account and that the interaction between them is not only complex but also shifting and situational—that is, shaped by generational transition and a multitude of contingent historical factors. The following essay was not written to illustrate that belief, but it is impossible to follow the use of *Americanism* in Catholic discourse without observing that it and the related term *Americanization* have been applied both to the very "ethnic" issue of immigrant assimilation and to broader ideological or "religious" questions having to do with the adaptation of Catholic belief and practice to American circumstances. Tracing this semantic history over the long term reveals many shifts in the close interrelationship between the two kinds of issue; but it also shows that over time the religious connotations of "Americanism" became more important and the ethnic less so. Another quite interesting finding brought to light by this survey of usage is that historical study of a particular episode of "Americanism" played a key role in reintroducing the term into Catholic discourse in the mid twentieth century.

The essay that follows synthesizes two articles, both extensively revised in this version. The first, originally presented at a joint session of the American Catholic Historical Association and the American Jewish Historical Association, was published in *Societas* (Autumn 1973). It benefited along the way from discussion at a conference on American religious history organized by Timothy L. Smith of the Johns Hopkins University, to whom I am very much indebted for his longstanding interest, encouragement, and advice. The second and more recent treatment of Americanism was presented at a session entitled "New Directions in American Catholic History" at the March 1990 meeting of the Organization of American Historians. That panel was organized by my colleague at Notre Dame, Jay Dolan, whose friendship and intellectual companionship over two decades have meant a great deal to me. The second paper on Americanism will appear in *U.S. Catholic Historian*. Both it and the earlier published articles contain fuller documentation on certain points than the present essay.

The terms *Americanism* and *Americanization* loom large in the history and historiography of the Roman Catholic church in the United States. Generally speaking, they refer to the relationship of the Catholic church, or of Catholics as a subgroup of the population, to the social, political, and cultural environment of the nation. From their form alone, one would expect to find *Americanism* employed where these relationships are discussed at the level of abstract principle and *Americanization* used where attention is focused on the actual processes of interaction between church and society. This is a good rule of thumb, but there are some complications. For example, historians who talk about "Americanism" often have in mind an intra-Catholic controversy that arose in the 1890s over an alleged heresy known by that name; and "Americanization" may refer either to the assimilation of Catholic immigrants or to changes in the structure or mode of operation of the church as an institution. The evaluative overtones carried by these terms can be either positive or negative, depending on whether the user approves or disapproves the phenomena to which they refer.

The phenomena in question are important not only to understanding the development of American Catholicism but also to understanding the nature and limits of American "diversity." For discussions employing these terms have to do with the compatibility of the Catholic religion with American values and institutions; with the social, cultural, and ideological accommodations the church has had to make to the American environment; and with the interaction of Catholic ethnic groups among themselves, with other elements of the population, and with the institutions of the host society.

These issues are too broad and complex for comprehensive treatment in a short essay, but they lend themselves to the semantic history approach. We can, in other words, follow the same method employed in part 1 of this book, inquiring how the terms *Americanism* and *Americanization* have functioned in the discourse of American Catholics. Such a review will shed useful light on the substantive issues involved and help us identify elements of both continuity and change over a considerable span of time.

According to lexicographers, John Witherspoon, a well known Presbyterian divine and Revolutionary War patriot, introduced the term *Americanism* in 1781 to designate words or usages distinctive to the English language as it was spoken in the United States. As early as 1797, however, Thomas Jefferson referred to "the dictates of reason and pure Americanism," and in 1806 Noah Webster gave as one of the definitions of the word: "a love of America and preference of her interest." The standard *Dictionary of American English on Historical Principles* cites several examples of usage in this sense between 1807 and 1884, but Mitford M. Mathews points out that *Americanism* became associated with Know-Nothingism in the 1850s when it was applied to the principles of the nativist "American Party."[1]

Americanization first appeared in the Know-Nothing era. It is of special interest for us that the earliest example cited by lexical scholars is from a Catholic source, *Brownson's Quarterly Review* for April 1858. Orestes A. Brownson, a convert to Catholicism, wrote in the passage cited, "All the Americanization I insist on is, that our Catholic population shall feel and believe that a man may be a true American and a good Catholic."[2] I have not found earlier use of either term by Catholic writers; that negative finding, coupled with the evidence supplied by the lexicographers, strongly suggests that Catholics did not begin talking about Americanism and Americanization until the 1850s and that they did so then against the background of Know-Nothing nativism.

Since the nativists claimed to stand for Americanism, Catholic immigrants who were the object of their hostility tended to regard such terms as part of the polemic directed against them. Thus the *Irish-American* protested in 1858: "There is no cant more in vogue than that the Irish ought to lose their identity in the American people. Forget your past and become Americanized, is the common cry. It is, nevertheless, a false, foolish, and absurd cry. The great fault is the other way. The

Irish become *Americanized*, in a certain sense, far too thoroughly and too soon." Too rapid adoption of traits like individualism and materialism demoralized the newcomers, according to the *Irish-American*, but preserving the best of their old-country heritage would help immigrants "adopt and love what [was] good and noble" in the new homeland.[3]

Brownson, a Vermont Yankee by birth, did not find this line of argumentation to his liking. Although staunchly Catholic, he was also thoroughly American and could not enter fully into the feeling of his immigrant coreligionists on these matters. He could understand that they felt strong ties to their homelands and that religion and nationality were tightly interwoven in the case of the Irish. But these facts did not excuse immigrant Catholics from trying to understand American ways and endeavoring to accommodate to them as fully as possible. Unfortunately, in Brownson's view, they did not always do this; on the contrary, he was convinced that many Catholic priests and bishops actively disliked "the American people and character." This attitude contributed materially to nativism because it stood in the way of "getting our religion fairly presented to the American mind."[4]

Brownson repudiated nativism insofar as it rested on religious prejudice, but he understood the alarm felt by Americans as they reacted against the threat to national values posed by the flood of immigration. In 1854 he undertook to explain the situation to his fellow Catholics in two articles entitled "Native Americanism" and "The Know Nothings."[5]

The nativists, Brownson conceded, were misguided in their bigotry, but they also gave voice to legitimate national concerns. What their outcry signified—and what Catholics must realize—was that America had a nationality of its own and that Americans would not tolerate the perpetuation of foreign nationalities on their soil. For that reason, the Catholic religion would never prosper here if it were inseparably linked to a foreign nationality. Immigrant Irish Catholics must therefore distinguish their Catholicity from their Irish nationality and learn American ways.

Catholic schools also came in for censure from Brownson, for he perceived that they served, and were intended to serve, ethnic-national as well as religious purposes. He deprecated the hostility with which Catholic leaders regarded the common schools, for he did not think it was always justified on strictly religious grounds. Where real anti-Catholicism made Catholic schools a necessity, he approved their existence but regretted the social separation of Catholic from Protestant youngsters they entailed. Above all, he opposed schools that, "under the pretext of providing for Catholic education . . . train up our children to be foreigners in the land of their birth."[6]

His reflection on these issues persuaded Brownson that one had to distinguish between "the traditions of Catholics" and "Catholic tradition."[7] This perception, I suspect, played a key role in moving him toward the most "liberal" position on religious questions he ever adopted in his career as a Catholic. Alerted by the ethnic issue, Brownson realized that many "traditional" Catholic positions were the product of social custom and historical contingency, rather than being essential to the faith. Hence he urged flexibility in seeking to bring the church into fruitful contact with the modern world. After all, he pointed out, if the universality of the Catholic church were to be made real, it must be at home in all ages as well as in all climes.

Brownson later repented his lapse into liberalism and reverted to a rigid hostility toward the modern world. He did not, to the best of my knowledge, apply the term *Americanism* to the liberal tendency of his thinking between 1854 and 1864, although that was what the word came to mean in Catholic discourse three decades later. In the context of the strictly ethnic-national discussion, however, Brownson alluded to "that Americanism which we have uniformly professed . . . since we became a Catholic."[8] And this kind of Americanism sufficed to bring down upon his head a storm of criticism from immigrant Catholics who equated his position with outright nativism.

Americanize and its variations, unlike *Americanism*, were used freely by Brownson in the 1850s. The passage cited by lexicographers as the first recorded usage of *Americanization* occurred in a dialogue, a literary device Brownson often used to present divergent views on a complex issue. The following exchange between characters called Dieffenbach and Father John furnishes the context of the passage.

> "But you forget, Father John," said Dieffenbach, "that this Catholic body, large as it is, and zealous as it may be, is separated from the American community by difference of national origin, manners, and customs, and to some extent even of language. The Church they support is still regarded as the church of a foreign body in the American community. . . . Your Catholic body does not act on the American body, and you want . . . a larger infusion of the American element. Instead of relying on this foreign body, you should direct all your efforts to the conversion of Americans, who have the sentiment of American nationality, and thus Americanize the Church."
>
> "Undoubtedly," replied Father John, "it is desirable that the Catholic body should be or become American, so far as to avoid

all that is repugnant to a just American national sentiment; but I want the Church Americanized no more than I want her Irishized, Germanized, Englishized, or Gallicized. The Church always suffers from having imposed on her the form of any nationality. . . . The Americanization of the Catholic body does and will go on of itself, as rapidly as is desirable, and all we have to do with it is, to take care that they do not imbibe the notion that to Americanize is necessarily to Protestantize. The transition from one nationality to another is always a dangerous process, and all the Americanization I insist on is, that our Catholic population shall feel and believe that a man may be a true American and a good Catholic.[9]

Thus were the issues associated with Americanization laid out when the term was introduced. The circumstances surrounding its introduction also made clear that these issues had terrific explosive potential.

The explosion came some thirty years later. This time the conflict began in the 1880s over the place of German nationality in American Catholicism; by the late 1890s, the focal point of conflict had shifted to something called "Americanism." Few of the participants recalled the controversy of Brownson's time, but the parallels are striking.[10]

Most pertinently, the words *Americanization* and (in the latter period) *Americanism* figured prominently in the disputes. Secondly, both sets of "Americanizers" deprecated the tendency to identify the Catholic church with imported cultural forms, striving instead to bring her into closer touch with the modern world. Thirdly, both Brownson and the later Americanists, most notably Archbishop John Ireland of Saint Paul, were sanguine about the future of Catholicism in America. They believed the spirit of the American people would dispose them to accept the Catholic faith once it took root in the national culture and expressed itself in indigenous forms. Hence they took a more positive stand than the "conservatives" on Catholics' mixing with non-Catholics; they were more open-minded about the public schools, and they disapproved Catholic schooling that served to perpetuate a foreign language or culture in the United States.

A fourth broad parallel is that both sets of controversies took place against a background of nativism, and the place of foreign nationalities in the American church was basic in both cases. Brownson and the later Americanizers were accused of being nativists themselves, and they were, indeed, tinged with a nationalistic Anglo-Saxonism. They both, however, denied being hostile to the ethnic groups in question, maintaining that they opposed only deliberate efforts to frustrate the natural processes of assimilation.

Finally, Brownson and Archbishop Ireland explained what they meant by Americanization of Catholic immigrants in very similar terms. Brownson was not asking the Irish to forget their homeland, he maintained. However, he did "ask them not to regard this country as the land of their exile, but . . . as their new home, freely chosen, around which they are to cluster the affections of their hearts, and with whose fortunes, not with those of Ireland, are henceforth bound up their own fortunes, and those of their children and their children's children." Thirty-eight years later, Archbishop Ireland told a group of German Catholics that he did not favor "hasty, over-active Americanization"; nor did he demand "the forgetting of the old land, or the setting aside of precious traditions." Rather, he continued:

> What I do mean by Americanization is the filling up of the
> heart with love for America and for her institutions. It is the
> harmonizing of ourselves with our surroundings, so that we will
> be as to the manner born, and not as strangers in a strange
> land, caring but slightly for it, and entitled to receive from it but
> meagre favors. It is the knowing of the language of the land
> and failing in nothing to prove our attachment to our laws, and
> our willingness to adopt, as dutiful citizens, all that is good and
> laudable in its social life and civilization.[11]

There were, of course, differences between the two controversies over Americanization. For one thing, the battles of the 1880s and 1890s lasted longer and constituted a more important chapter in the history of American Catholicism. A chapter, incidentally, that historians have studied intently, while the storm that swirled around Brownson in the 1850s has been largely overlooked by scholars.

The dramatis personae had also changed. Brownson died in 1876, and the Irish, whom he chided for resisting Americanization in the fifties, furnished all the leading Americanizers in the later episode. The role previously played by the Irish was taken over by the Germans, who had not figured at all in the earlier controversy.

Finally, *the* Americanist controversy had a much higher ideological content than the skirmishes of the fifties. Its history is tangled but may be summarized as follows. Difficulties arising in the 1880s between German- and English-speaking Catholics persisted through the next decade, becoming interwoven in the process with liberal-conservative splits across a wide spectrum of other issues—such as whether Catholics could

belong to secret societies, including the Knights of Labor; the theories
of Henry George; the question of parochial versus public schooling; and
the appointment of an apostolic delegate to the United States. These
disputes involved intense politicking in Rome and eventually drew the
attention of European Catholics, both liberals and conservatives, to what
was going on in this country. The Europeans were engaged in their own
quarrels, and both parties attempted to make polemical use of the American example. Especially in France, Catholic progressives pointed to the
American church as leading the way in the reconciliation of Catholicism
with the modern world, while conservatives portrayed "Americanism" as
tantamount to surrendering the faith. By 1899 the quarrel had reached
such a pitch that Pope Leo XIII issued the Apostolic Letter *Testem Benevolentiae*, in which he pronounced unacceptable "the opinions which
some comprise under the head of Americanism."[12]

The basic principle rejected by the pope was that "the Church ought
to adapt herself somewhat to our advanced civilization" and relax "her
ancient rigor," not only with respect to practical matters "but also to the
doctrines in which the *deposit of faith* is contained." From this principle
there flowed several opinions concerning the role of the church in guiding
the religious life of the individual, the importance of the natural as compared to the supernatural virtues, the place of religious orders in the
church, and methods of evangelization—all of which the pope condemned in detail.

But while he condemned "Americanism" so defined, Leo took care
to add that Americanism was unobjectionable if it meant "the characteristic qualities which reflect honor on the people of America . . . or if
it implies the condition of your commonwealth, or the laws and customs
which prevail in them." Archbishop Ireland and his fellow Americanizers
maintained that this was all they understood by *Americanism*, and they
denied holding the opinions condemned by the pope. Their opponents,
however, insisted that the dangerous tendencies singled out in *Testem*
did exist in America and that the papal admonition was necessary and
timely.

The equivocal nature of the term gave rise to disagreements not only
at the time; it also caused difficulties for later historians. Thomas T.
McAvoy, who became the leading authority on the subject in the mid
twentieth century, distinguished three varieties of Americanism: 1) the
civic and political principles on which American society and government
rest; 2) the views of certain progressive Catholics in France which were
tinctured with a theological liberalism regarded at the time as heretical;
and 3) the Americanism that was the shorthand term for the practical

modifications of Catholic life made in response to the pressures of the American environment. But McAvoy conceded that it was difficult to determine "when the word Americanism acquired a religious meaning above its normal political and social meanings."[13]

We can, however, say with some confidence that the controversy moved from a focus on *Americanization* to primary concern with *Americanism*. The former term occurs frequently in the 1880s in disputes over the status of German Catholics and the German language in the American church. When the term *Americanism* appears in this phase of the controversy, the context usually links it closely with matters of language and ethnicity. At least one contemporary traced the origins of that term back to the German issue, arguing that the German Catholics who opposed Ireland's emphasis on Americanization "retorted upon him the name of 'Americanism' as a stigma . . . redolent of 'Liberalism' and all evil things."[14]

The publication in France of a biography of Isaac T. Hecker was a landmark in the controversy and also with respect to the semantics of Americanism. Hecker, a New Yorker born in 1819, was a convert to Catholicism who became a priest and founded the Congregation of St. Paul (popularly known as Paulists), a religious community that Hecker hoped would become the instrument through which America would be converted to the Catholic faith. Hecker's irenic temper and his confidence that Catholicism would thrive as never before in republican America made him an appealing figure to the French Catholic progressives who wished to break away from the tradition of Catholic hostility to the French republic. Hence the appearance in 1897 of a French *Life of Father Hecker*, and the exaggerated publicity accompanying it, intensified the conflict between liberals and conservatives in the French church. The posthumous figure of Hecker became the symbol of Americanism and a polemical storm center. Looking back on the controversy two decades later, the historian Peter Guilday asserted that "it was Paris that coined the much abused word, 'Americanism.' "[15]

A key episode linking Hecker and Americanism was a talk given by Denis J. O'Connell at a congress of Catholic savants in Fribourg, Switzerland. At that time (1897) rector of the North American College in Rome (a residence for American seminarians), O'Connell was a fervent Americanist. His lecture, entitled "A New Idea in the Life of Father Hecker," constituted an important theoretical statement of Americanism which emphasized the tradition of Anglo-American law as contrasted to Roman and canon law. The talk is particularly relevant here because O'Connell stated that this "new idea" was "called by the name of 'Americanism.' " The term, he said, was not merely to be found here and there in the biography of Hecker; rather, "the idea expressed by it shines like a golden thread from the beginning to the end of the volume." It was, he added, a term "that one will not find in any dictionary of Europe, and hardly, I may venture to say, in any dictionary of America—never, I am sure, in that full precise significance that it bore in the mind of the illustrious Founder of the Paulists." Unfortunately, O'Connell thereupon dismissed as unnecessary "the consideration of its etymology or genesis."[16]

Since O'Connell later admitted he had not read the Hecker biography, he can scarcely be considered a reliable authority on what Hecker thought Americanism might be. In view of the word's occurring only once in the original American version of the biography in question, we can safely conclude that its widespread usage in the late 1890s did not trace back to that source.[17] What actually seems to have happened is that the term *Americanization* was employed in a number of disputes about the adjustment of Catholicism to American circumstances; eventually *Americanism* became a label designating the position of one party in those disputes—the "liberals" who favored flexibility and accommodation wherever possible. Vague enough as a political term, it became even more ambiguous when carried over into the realm of religious controversy. With the complications resulting from its use by both friendly and unfriendly Catholic publicists in France, *Americanism* became so diffuse that it could be interpreted to mean almost anything. But the pope condemned one interpretation. And although he exempted another meaning from his censure, the papal letter *Testem Benevolentiae* effectively removed *Americanism* from Catholic discourse for a long time.

While papal disfavor put Americanism under a cloud, other developments around 1900 caused the German Catholics to soft-pedal their resistance to Americanization. They really had no choice because generational transition and other social changes made accommodation imperative. The most revealing incident concerned orders issued by two German bishops in Wisconsin that sermons be preached in English at least once on Sunday. When Polish and French-Canadian Catholics attacked this "Americanizing ukase," a leading German Catholic journalist defended the bishops' actions. Arthur Preuss, who had founded his *Review* to combat the liberals in the 1890s and who then characterized Americanization as a demand for "national apostasy," now warned the critics against making Americanization a "scarecrow." Drawing the same basic distinction as Archbishop Ireland had earlier, Preuss rejected "parforce Americanization" but declared that recognition of the natural processes of assimilation could "prove beneficial." The German Catholics had realized "almost too late," he explained, that the process of assimilation now required concessions to the English language if many of the old German parishes were to survive.[18]

The almost complete cessation of German immigration after 1900, along with emergence of the second generation as the dominant element, had in fact plunged the German-American Catholics into a crisis of assimilation.[19] Although the erosion of ethnic feeling could not be wholly stemmed, the German Catholics' national organization, the Central-Verein, responded to the challenge very creatively. A reorganization brought its structure up to date; a newly developed interest in social reform gave it a mission attuned to the spirit of the Progressive Era; and new leadership guided it to greater visibility on the national Catholic scene than it had ever enjoyed before, especially through its bilingual journal, *Central-Blatt and Social Justice* (est. 1909). The partial acceptance of English, along with the social reform mission, in fact constituted a kind of Americanization, but the Central-Verein's leaders never called it that. They continued to regard the positions taken by the Americanists of the 1890s as mistaken, and it probably never occurred to them that they were in effect Americanizing the structure and outlook of the principal organizational symbol of their ethnoreligious consciousness. But neither did they keep up the anti-Americanizing rhetoric of the past, and as the German Catholics quietly dropped the subject, the word *Americanization* receded from view for several years.

It—and to a lesser extent *Americanism*—reappeared in Catholic discourse in the context of the "Americanization movement" set off by World War I. Against the background of wartime patriotism and suspicion of "hyphenated Americans," Catholics mobilized their energies for participation in the war effort through a new organization, the National Catholic War Council (NCWC). An account of its activities published in 1921 illustrates how Catholics' pride in their wartime service was assimilated to their fundamental commitment to the nation. As a preamble to his story of *American Catholics and the War*, Michael Williams devoted four chapters to the history of Catholicism in the United States. He did not apply the term *Americanism* to Catholic devotion to the nation; nor did he conceive the relationship between church and society as involving a process of adjustment that could be called Americanization. No such adjustment was needed because "the very marrow" of Williams's story was "the blessed harmony that has always existed, and which now exists, and which, please God, shall always exist, between the spirit of the

Catholic Church and the spirit of the United States of America." Thanks to this natural harmony, an "intimate . . . inseparable intermingling" had always subsisted between Catholic and national values, of which the most recent testimony was the Catholic contribution to the war effort and postwar reconstruction.[20]

The only time Williams used the word *Americanization* in the book, he placed quotation marks around it and applied it specifically to the citizenship education program carried on by the NCWC. This program was designed to provide a deeper understanding of American institutions. The NCWC professed itself to be "interested especially in emphasizing the lessons of American patriotism for the benefit of the foreigners within our shores; in pointing out to them . . . the opportunities for happy and useful employment in American industries; in inspiring them with the desire to become American citizens; and in teaching them the lessons of sanitation, better housing, and better living."[21]

Carrying out this program was a major activity of the National Catholic Welfare Conference, which succeeded the National Catholic War Council and continued to be known as the NCWC for nearly a half-century. Much of the NCWC's Americanization work in the twenties featured Italian-Americans, but some attention was also devoted to the Spanish-speaking population of the Southwest. Although the program was prosecuted energetically, its director, John A. Lapp, warned against the abuses that sometimes accompanied Americanization campaigns. In certain unfortunate instances, Lapp wrote, "the terms 'Americanism' and 'Americanization' were found to be . . . mere cloaks for un-American activities" such as reactionary antiunion drives. As a result, not a few people grew distrustful of "the very idea of Americanization itself." Lapp regretted this development, prescribing for its remedy the removal of "the dollar sign" from programs of Americanization. In more positive terms, he asserted that nothing less than "complete social justice should be held as a goal for good citizenship or Americanization."[22] Lapp thus attempted to give Americanization a progressive orientation by associating it with the reformist goals being pursued by his more famous colleague, John A. Ryan, the head of the NCWC's Social Action Department.

Other Catholic observers took note of *Americanization* as a new word that had come into great vogue and was not infrequently applied to highly questionable activities—such as efforts to proselytize among Catholic children by means of Protestant-sponsored recreational programs. At the same time, Catholics boasted that their own religious education work among immigrants was the best kind of Americanization.

Such a claim found little resonance in the larger culture, for most Americans still regarded the Catholic church and its adherents as a foreign presence on the national scene. As restrictionist feeling mounted in the early twenties, the Ku Klux Klan gave powerful expression to the fear of Catholicism that was a perennial feature of American nativism. The emergence of Al Smith as a serious contender for the presidency not only reinforced crude no-popery; it also aroused uneasiness among those less susceptible to bigotry over how fully Catholics were committed to church-state separation. Catholics felt the need to respond to these developments, and by 1923 items protesting the Klan's appropriation of the term *Americanism* began to appear in the *National Catholic Welfare Conference Bulletin* alongside reports of the Americanization work being carried on by the NCWC itself. The following year Frederick J. Kinsman, a former bishop of the Protestant Episcopal church who had embraced Catholicism, published a book entitled *Americanism and Catholicism* dedicated to proving the compatibility of the two.[23]

The weekly magazine *Commonweal*, founded in 1924 as an organ of Catholic liberalism, took up the same task. Although critical of shortcomings in Catholic life and hoping to follow an irenic editorial line, its editors had to spend much of their energy in the early years defending the church against misrepresentation and affirming the Americanism of the Catholic faithful. The 1928 presidential campaign, when it portrayed attacks on Al Smith's religion as betrayals of true Americanism, brought this phase of *Commonweal*'s existence to its climax.[24] After Smith's defeat, Michael Williams, who had resigned from the NCWC in order to found the magazine, wrote a book called *The Shadow of the Pope*, which he said was about religious liberty but which actually focused on the history of anti-Catholicism in America.[25]

The year before Smith ran for president, George N. Shuster, who was managing editor of *Commonweal*, published a book entitled *The Catholic Spirit in America*. Here Shuster restated once again the position Williams had built into his earlier book on the NCWC—and that *Commonweal* and virtually all American Catholic commentators maintained in the twenties—namely, that a natural harmony existed between the Catholic spirit and the American spirit.[26] So perfect was the congruence between religious principles and national values, Shuster argued, that native-born converts to Catholicism "did not attain to the full stature of their Americanism until they joined the Church."[27]

Although Catholics might still have agreed with Shuster after the 1928 election, the eruption of virulent anti-Catholicism which impugned their civic integrity was a severe shock to their morale. To a "bitterly resigned" nun teaching in a parochial school in Chicago, Al Smith's defeat meant that none of the boys in her classroom could aspire to be president. Her telling them that stuck in the memory of a youngster named John Cogley, who was later to serve as an editor of *Commonweal* and who had a hand in writing John F. Kennedy's most famous statement on the church-state issue, his speech before the Houston Ministerial Association. Even after Kennedy's election, Cogley recalled his teacher's remark as the occasion of his "first doubts about the power of prayer, and the power of the American idea as well."[28]

Summarizing the years from World War I to 1928, we should note first that the terms *Americanism* and *Americanization* were widely used by, or in reference to, Catholics. But the context of usage and the connotations of the terms had shifted since the 1890s. Then Catholics were talking largely among themselves about Americanism and Americanization, while their fellow countrymen stood by as interested spectators. The context was an intra-Catholic quarrel, and the terms had reference to socio-religious policy or theological stance. In the 1920s, however, the discussion engaged the whole national community and dealt with political ideology and civic loyalty. At first, Catholics were merely one among the parties to the discussion. But by the middle of the decade, they were the object of discussion as well—it was *their* Americanism, or the lack thereof, that was being talked about. In the first phase, Catholic self-confidence and a sense of national belongingness that grew out of wartime solidarity encouraged the NCWC to throw itself into the work of Americanization. By the end of the decade, Catholics had absorbed the bitter lesson that their own Americanism was still in question.

The passing of the Americanization movement and the freighting of *Americanism* with negative overtones contributed to the relative absence of these terms in Catholic discourse in the 1930s. But the economic depression, the New Deal, and ominous international developments operated more decisively to turn the attention of Catholics to concrete economic and political issues. In these circumstances, the relevance of "papal social teaching" to the American situation became the primary context in which Catholics explored the relationship between their religious principles and their civic commitments. In general, Catholic leaders strongly reaffirmed the consistency between their prescriptions for a Christian social order on the one hand and true Americanism on the other. But Catholics also disagreed among themselves about both terms of this equation. For as David J. O'Brien concluded after a painstaking survey of Catholic social thought in the 1930s, "Americanism, like Catholic social doctrine, turned out to be a magician's hat that produced prepackaged rabbits."[29] On the whole, however, the issues of the New Deal era did not lend themselves very readily to discussion under the categories of "Americanism" or "Americanization." The shifting dynamics were vividly illustrated in the case of John A. Lapp. The former director of the NCWC's Americanization program found himself dealing in the 1930s with such matters as "Christian Principles Applied to the Building Trades."[30]

As we have seen in other contexts, World War II proved once again to be a major watershed in terminological usage. After the war "Americanism" and "Americanization" really came into their own as key concepts, but they reentered Catholic discourse by an unusual route—through historiography. That is, *Americanism* and *Americanization* regained their currency as a result of historical scholarship devoted to the controversies of the late nineteenth century and were primarily associated with the issues that pitted Archbishop Ireland and his friends against the conservatives of that era. But the underlying issue to which the terms referred—how the Catholic church should accommodate itself to American society—still existed in the mid twentieth century; hence the recovery of the terminology of Americanism had definite ideological implications. The stages through which the semantic development in question proceeded can be laid out roughly as follows: the basic historical recovery of Americanism extends from World War II to the late 1950s; then, after a relative lull, a new wave of scholarship from the late 1960s to the present has drawn out the ideological implications of Americanism in much sharper fashion.

A striking feature of the first wave of scholarship on Americanism was that it came after four decades of near total historical silence on the controversies of the nineties. Theodore Maynard, who devoted a chapter to "The American Heresy" in his popular *Story of American Catholicism* (1941), observed that few Catholics had ever heard of such a thing and those who tried to find out more would quickly run into a dead end.[31] All that was soon to change. 1943 saw the appearance of Daniel F. Reilly's important monograph on the "school controversy," and of Thomas T. McAvoy's article "Americanism and Frontier Catholicism," the first of the publications that were to make McAvoy the leading authority on Americanism as such. The July 1945 issue of the *Catholic Historical Review* carried two articles on Americanism, one by McAvoy, the other by the Paulist historian Vincent F. Holden. Six months later the same journal ran the first of a two-part series by John J. Meng on the German "nationality question"; soon thereafter Meng's more comprehensive lectures on the Americanist era appeared in the publication of the U.S. Catholic Historical Society of New York.[32]

Between 1946 and 1958 Americanism completely dominated the relatively small world of American Catholic historical scholarship. Besides articles and unpublished dissertations, more than a dozen books dealt with one aspect or another of the controversial era. Included among these works were John Tracy Ellis's magisterial biography of Cardinal Gibbons; biographies of two other leading Amerizanizers (Archbishop Ireland and Bishop John J. Keane); the memoirs of the Abbé Felix Klein, the only surviving participant in the controversies; McAvoy's *Great Crisis in American Catholic History*, which became the standard account; and Robert D. Cross's *Emergence of Liberal Catholicism in America*, the appearance of which a few months after McAvoy's book marked the climax of the first wave of Americanist historiography.[33]

Cross's work, originally written as a Harvard dissertation, likewise showed that interest in Americanism had expanded beyond "the Catholic ghetto." Further evidence of the same kind could be noted in Will Herberg's *Protestant-Catholic-Jew* (1955), which drew heavily on the work of Ellis, McAvoy, and other Catholic historians. Among Catholic commentators, the writings of Walter Ong and Daniel Callahan indicated that the new historiographical understanding of Americanism had become a common resource of the Catholic intellectual community.[34]

The question that immediately suggests itself about this first wave of Americanist scholarship is why it gushed forth so abundantly after almost a half-century of neglect. Obviously, the generational factor played a role. Except for Klein, the participants in (and historians who could remember) the quarrels of the nineties had passed from the scene, and partisan feeling had subsided. Matters that Peter Guilday, the leading Catholic historian of the interwar years, considered too hot to handle could now be taken up.[35] Nor should we overlook the concidence of the generational shift with the great postwar expansion of graduate education; hence many more workers were entering the field of American Catholic history as the new historiographical focus emerged.

But why did this focus prove so attractive to these younger scholars? The main reason, I believe, was that Americanism seemed strikingly relevant—that is, attractive as a historical subject to a generation of Catholics who were very self-conscious about their own Americanism. Positively, they were affected like everyone else by the upsurge of democratic fervor set off by World War II and especially by the enthusiasm it engendered for "pluralism" and "tolerance for diversity." Negatively, they had to deal with the criticism of Paul Blanshard and other secular liberals who charged the church with being un-American. In these cir-cumstances, Catholic intellectuals, including historians, could hardly avoid thinking about how the church should relate to the national cul-ture.[36]

Most of them supported the broadly liberal policy line that deprecated "separatism," exhorted Catholics to "break out of the ghetto," and en-couraged them to plunge boldly into the mainstream of American life.[37] The congruence between this policy and the views of the Americanists of the 1890s was obvious, and it is no accident that Archbishop Ireland and his friends were the heroes of the new outpouring of historical schol-arship. Whether these historians consciously realized it—much less in-tended it—their work implicitly supported midcentury Catholic liberal-ism by supplying it with a historical precedent. Indeed, it could be plausibly asserted that the historical recovery of Americanism played a significant role in mediating the rapprochement between American Ca-tholicism and modernity which was to take more explicit form in the 1960s.

Not that this first wave of Americanist historians wanted to nudge the church toward a more liberal *theological* position. Consideration of three points will demonstrate that this was definitely not their intention.

First, none of the writings mentioned above made any effort to defend the opinions specified in *Testem Benevolentiae* as erroneous. On the contrary, these opinions were usually referred to as "heresies." Ironically, the only writer to stress the point that Leo XIII had not actually designated them as heretical was the very conservative theologian Joseph Clifford Fenton, and he strongly insisted that they were errors deserving of re-probation. McAvoy was among those who used the term *heresy* more loosely than Fenton approved; but even when he was being more careful about terminology, McAvoy was willing to concede that the positions actually held by the Americanists had heretical potentialities.[38]

Secondly, the historians of the first wave, including McAvoy, de-fended the orthodoxy of the Americanists by denying that they actually held the opinions censured in *Testem*. They often pointed out in this connection that the Americanists were not theologians but active church-men concerned with practical matters of socio-ecclesiastical policy and therefore not sensitive to the remote doctrinal implications of stands they may have taken on this or that concrete issue. In what became known as its "phantom heresy" form, this interpretation held that the heterodox positions condemned by the pope were wrongly imputed to the Ameri-canists by their ultraconservative critics in France who misunderstood, or deliberately distorted, the real views of Hecker, Ireland, and the other Americanists.[39]

The third point supplies even stronger evidence that these historians had no desire to make theological liberals out of their subjects. The issue here concerns the relation of Americanism to Modernism, the "synthesis of all heresies" condemned by Pope Pius X in 1907. Given their general adherence to the phantom heresy interpretation, the Americanist historians naturally dismissed the reality of a connection. But they had to address the issue explicitly because European Catholic commentators assumed that Americanism was the "practical preface" to Modernism. In 1952, McAvoy documented the degree to which this view had become the conventional wisdom in Europe and argued that it was an oversimplification based on inadequate knowledge—a deficiency his *Great Crisis* was designed to correct. And in reviewing McAvoy's book, John Tracy Ellis stressed the point that it should disabuse the Europeans of their erroneous views on the relation of Americanism and Modernism.[40] Thus, only a few years before the Second Vatican Council (1962–65) put the whole issue in a new light, the leading figures in the historical recovery of Americanism strove to distinguish it from theological liberalism.

Although essayists and popularizers noted that Vatican II vindicated the irenic and progressive policies advocated by the Americanists, little new scholarship on the subject appeared while the council was going on and immediately thereafter. The most important new work published during this historiographic lull was James Hennesey's study of the American bishops at the First Council of the Vatican, which took place in 1869–70, well before the Americanist controversies began.[41] While it did not deal with Americanism as such, Hennesey's book (and later essays) had a direct bearing on that topic because he argued that the historical experience of American Catholics had a *theological dimension* in that it set them thinking in ways different from European Catholics about religious liberty and other matters fraught with theological implications. Hennesey was the first American Catholic historian to endow his subject with this kind of theological significance. His innovation complemented the new "historical mindedness" of Catholic theologians and constituted a response from history's side of the disciplinary fence to a much more pronounced opening toward history from theology's side.

The relaxation of disciplinary boundaries had asymmetrical results—historians became only marginally more venturesome in theology, but beginning around 1970, a whole cohort of recently trained specialists in religious studies devoted themselves to historico-theological analysis of Americanism. All this took place under the aegis of the liberalization of Catholic thinking sparked by Vatican II, which legitimized a new way of looking at church/world relations and generally loosened up the church's doctrinal stance. Historians too were soon affected by "postconciliar mentality," and their defensiveness about the orthodoxy of the Americanists abated markedly. By contrast to the historians of the previous epoch, a significant proportion of the new cohort of Americanist scholars did indeed want to move the church toward a more liberal theological posture and approached their study of the past with that mindset.

The post-1970 scholarship is too voluminous to survey in detail, but we should note the general categories into which it falls and cite some illustrative titles. Biographies and other studies of the major figures in the Americanist era constitute one important class. These have added much nuance to our understanding of the period, and some are frankly revisionist in approach.[42]

Other writers have dealt with one or another aspect of Americanism or treated it as part of a larger study. Examples of the former would be Thomas Wangler's studies of the formation of the Americanist faction and the propagandistic techniques it employed; of the latter, Gerald Fogarty's treatment of Americanism as an episode in his book on relations between the American bishops and the Vatican.[43] And of course recent general works on American Catholic history by James Hennesey, Jay Dolan, and David O'Brien all discuss Americanism.[44]

Deserving of separate mention are works devoted to Isaac Hecker. So severely was Hecker's reputation for orthodoxy damaged in the Americanist controversy that biographers steered shy of his later life until after Vatican II. Since 1977, however, at least ten doctoral dissertations on Hecker have been completed, several of which focus directly on his relationship to Americanism. This new work has begun to find its way into print; some of Hecker's own writings have been reprinted, and a new biography is nearing completion.[45]

Another area of new scholarship, and one closely related to our interest in Americanism, deals with Modernism. Indeed, the recovery and reassessment of Modernism is one of the most striking historiographic results of the new mentality legitimized by Vatican II. Modernism in Europe is the main focus of interest, even among American scholars. But to the extent it existed in the United States, Modernism has been brought out of the shadows where earlier Catholic historians were quite content to leave it.[46]

That is not the only way the new historiography of Americanism differs from the old. But before looking into the Modernist issue more closely, let us inquire about two other points of comparison between old and new.

First, are the Americanists still the heroes? Does the new historiography endorse their ideological orientation as strongly as the older works did? In general, yes—but not without qualification. For though the Americanists are still clearly preferred to their more conservative opponents, Archbishop Ireland and company have been chided for their hypernationalism, their lack of sensitivity to immigrant cultures, and their uncritical acceptance of American society. And as more has come to light about their manipulative tactics in controversy, the Americanists have lost some of the luster deriving from their ideological liberalism.

Second, do the more recent writers agree with their predecessors that Americanism was a "phantom heresy"? In general, no—but once again distinctions are in order. Among the relatively few scholars who have addressed the issue directly, a rough consensus exists to this effect: 1) the position espoused by Hecker and the Americanists did have theological content, especially with respect to its ecclesiological and theology-of-history implications; and 2) some of the opinions condemned in *Testem Benevolentiae* were in fact actually held in this country, at least by Hecker and by Bishop John Lancaster Spalding.[47] Those who take this position clearly disagree with the "phantom heresy" interpretation, which, it will be recalled, held that the Americanists didn't really hold the opinions the pope condemned as Americanism. *But*, according to the new view, these opinions ought not be considered heretical; rather, they should be seen as legitimate theological options wrongly rejected by churchmen animated by political motives and constrained by an outdated theology.

Turning now to the question of Modernism—specifically to whether a connection existed between Americanism and Modernism—we have a 180-degree shift between the old and the new Americanist scholarship. Where the older generation of scholars strove to deny a connection, the more recent writers are strongly disposed to affirm a connection.[48] Since relatively little new historical evidence bearing on the question has been brought to light, we can safely conclude that this reversal of judgment derives from a more basic change in theological perspective. In other words, historians are now more receptive to the idea of a linkage because Modernism itself is seen more sympathetically.

To sum up the comparison of old and new Americanist scholarship, we might say that what the former interpreted as social or procedural

liberalism the latter tends to interpret as theological liberalism. That sums
it up for scholarship on the Americanist period as such. But there is also
a new Americanist interpretation much broader in scope. That is, the
same shift in outlook—one that gives "Americanism" a sharper ideological accentuation—is discernible across a broader spectrum of Catholic
historical studies. And quite recently this historically generalized "Americanist" outlook has been raised to an even higher level of abstraction by
writers who deal not with history but with theology or religious studies.
This two-stage expansion of Americanism, as we might call it, can at
present only be glimpsed in its broad outlines.

In historical studies, it is most clearly discernible in work devoted
to early American Catholicism. Here recent scholarship stresses the influence of Enlightenment ideas on the nuclear group of Anglo-American
Catholics, especially John Carroll, the new nation's first Catholic bishop.
Patrick Carey's revisionist work on "lay trusteeism" treats sympathetically
the trustees' argument that "republican" principles should be applied to
church government in the United States. Other manifestations of auroral
liberalism noted approvingly are the cultivation of good relations with
non-Catholics, frequent expressions of attachment to American institutions, a desire on Carroll's part to hold Roman authorities at arm's length,
and his interest in using the vernacular (rather than Latin) in worship.
Jay Dolan goes furthest in speaking of Carroll's "republican blueprint,"
but other authorities agree that an early version of the liberal American
spirit set the tone in the age of John Carroll.[49]

Jay Dolan was also the first to apply the new Americanist perspective
in a comprehensive survey of the whole of U.S. Catholic history. The
interpretive stance adopted in his *American Catholic Experience* (1985)
is quite self-consciously that of post–Vatican II liberalism. The author's
disappointment over Carroll's retreat from an early (largely preepiscopal)
liberalism is obvious, as is his distaste for the "devotional Catholicism"
that swamped the more restrained spirituality of the Anglo-American
nucleus. Dolan interprets Americanism and Modernism as successive
phases of a progressive development that reached its belated culmination
in the Second Vatican Council and the changes it legitimized. He adopts
as his own the "new spirit" of postconciliar American Catholicism and
concludes that "the twenty-first century belongs to it."[50]

Dolan's historically comprehensive liberalism figures in the next
phase of the story, namely, Americanism's being raised to a new level of
abstraction by theologians or specialists in religious studies. The issue
here is how Americanism, as recovered and generalized from systematic

reflection on the historical past, is to be appropriated and applied in the here and now.

The person who has done this most explicitly is Dennis P. McCann, a layman who teaches religious studies at DePaul University in Chicago. His *New Experiment in Democracy* (1987) uses as a springboard the American bishops' recent pastoral letter on the economy. McCann argues that the notion of "justice as participation," which the pastoral espoused in the economic realm, must also be applied to the Catholic church's internal constitution and mode of operation. He links this thesis to Americanism in his first chapter, which is entitled "The Return of the Repressed: Owning Up to the Americanist Heresy." Besides the Americanists of the 1890s, McCann refers approvingly to John Carroll's supposed "republican blueprint," and he credits a group of early nineteenth-century lay trustees with "brilliant insight" into the theological implications of the American revolution.[51]

McCann's book outdoes the Americanists of the past in erecting Americanism into a consciously held principle that is to be understood as normative in religious affairs. But his liberal version of Americanism is not the only ideological variant available. George Weigel, Michael Novak, and Richard John Neuhaus would all agree that Catholicism and Americanism are compatible and should be more purposefully integrated; but as neoconservatives they differ sharply from McCann in the way they understand both elements in the equation.[52] David O'Brien and the "evangelical" Catholics whose stance he has recently identified are critical of Americanism from the left; while Joseph Varacalli and Michael Schwartz call attention to its dangers from the traditionalist, or "restorationist," end of the ideological spectrum.[53] Although it is not yet clear how fully these divergent positions will be developed, we are surely justified in saying that a "new Americanism" has emerged which may well set off a new cycle of liberal-conservative controversies among American Catholics.[54]

What does this review of usage over almost a century and a half suggest by way of conclusions about Catholic Americanism and Americanization? Without pretending to say the final word, it seems to me that the historical record warrants several observations.

First, by way of summary, we note that the salience of the terms has varied over time. They emerged in the 1850s; reached their apex of visibility and importance in the 1890s; reappeared briefly in a very different context in the 1920s; and then made a strong comeback by way of historiography after World War II.

Historically, it is clear that the terms have been used in reference to both ethnic and ideological issues. By *ethnic* is meant issues directly related to the cultural assimilation of Catholic immigrants; by *ideological*, those relating to the Catholic church as a corporate entity and how (or whether) it should adjust its policies and practices to American circumstances. Though they are closely interrelated, the relative importance of these two kinds of issue has changed over time, the former becoming less central, the latter more so. A quick review of the periods of salience listed above will help to clarify this very general statement.

When the terms emerged in the 1850s, *Americanization* referred primarily to the cultural assimilation of Irish Catholic immigrants. But the linkage between the ethnic and the ideological is illustrated by the fact that Brownson's concern over the former prompted him to distinguish "Catholic tradition" from "the traditions of Catholics" and carried him along to a broader kind of theoretical liberalism. In the classic Americanist period at the end of the century, ethnic and ideological issues were intertangled throughout. However, the same dynamic is observable here as well—the so-called nationality controversy came early in the period; lingering ethnic bitterness accentuated later disputes over matters of a more clearly ideological nature (such as the school question); and the whole conflict finally came into focus over a highly abstract form of Americanism that was defined as theologically aberrant.

By the 1920s, ethnic issues were ostensibly central in that Catholics spoke of Americanization only in connection with programs designed to help immigrants assimilate. Yet this usage was very limited in scope, being confined to a bureaucratically inspired program that was quite marginal to Catholic life in general. By comparison with the 1880s and 1890s, questions related to the assimilation of immigrants were of negligible importance from the viewpoint of national Catholic leaders. Nor did these leaders think they had a problem ideologically. On the contrary, they exulted in the fundamental harmony that existed between Catholic and American principles. Hence there was no need for programmatic adjustments or new emphases in teaching such as those suggested by Americanists such as Hecker and Ireland.

The anti-Catholicism that culminated in Al Smith's defeat demonstrated that non-Catholics had very different ideas about the relationship of Catholicism and Americanism. Catholics remained staunchly convinced of their own Americanism, but after World War II a growing number of their publicists and intellectuals strove to articulate a Catholic liberalism that would be true to the church's doctrinal teaching, yet at the same time be critical of rigid and outdated practices and more positively oriented toward American "pluralism." In these circumstances, the Americanism that was restored to Catholic discourse by historians inevitably took on a more decidedly ideological cast. At first the kind of liberalism implicitly endorsed by the historical recovery of Americanism was strictly social and procedural. But after the upheaval set off by Vatican II, Americanism was broadened out to cover shifts in what had hitherto been regarded as established doctrinal teaching as well.

Although quite recessive, the ethnic dimension was not altogether lacking in the earlier phase of post–World War II Americanism since its adherents also espoused a participationist version of pluralism that deprecated "separatism," ethnic or otherwise, and urged Catholics to plunge into "the mainstream of American life." But this latent assimilationism could not survive the transvaluation of values associated with the revival of ethnicity in which Catholics such as Andrew Greeley and Michael Novak played very prominent roles.[55] The result is that Catholic proponents of ideological Americanism would no doubt reject the imputation that their position implies the Americanization of immigrants.

The prominence that these terms have long had in Catholic discourse makes the anomaly just mentioned especially obvious, but the feeling that true Americanism somehow rules out expecting immigrants to become Americanized is not peculiar to Catholics. It is, rather, an example of the conceptual muddle into which Americans have so often been led by the genuine complexities of intergroup relations and the ambiguities of the language we must use in discussing them.

Catholics figure in the overall context of American diversity as the oldest and largest element of the population set apart from the whole by religion. True, religion and ethnicity are closely interwoven. They are, however, distinguishable—especially so in the case of Catholics, whose religion certainly cannot be said to lack definiteness either as a social institution or as a body of beliefs and practices. Because this religion can and does serve as a locus of loyalty and source of motivation, both for individuals and for larger collectivities, the tendency of modern scholarship to deprecate the importance, or even the reality, of religion as an independent variable is seriously misplaced in the case of American Catholics. To be understood in themselves and with respect to their role in American society, Catholics must be studied as a group defined by religious belief as well as—indeed, much more than—by ethnic identity.

What has this contention to do with the foregoing survey of linguistic usage? Simply this. The survey shows that for Catholics, Americanism and Americanization mean more than the cultural assimilation of immigrants.[56] They also point toward beliefs about and disagreements over what it means to be a Catholic and what it means to be an American. In a word, the prominence of these terms in their discourse testifies to the historic—and continuing—exigency for American Catholics of what H. Richard Niebuhr called the problem of "Christ and culture."[57] *Americanism* and *Americanization* are the terms Catholics use when they grapple with perennial questions about how church should relate to world, religion to society, faith to life. The degree to which the terms have been and remain "contested" shows that for American Catholics both of the elements in these polarities make legitimate claims and that neither is to be subsumed into the other. For as long as they remain steadfast in their resolve to do justice to both of these dimensions of reality, Catholics will remain a distinctive element in the kaleidoscope of American diversity.

NOTES

Source: "Coming to Terms with American Catholic History," *Societas,* 3 (Autumn 1973), 283–312; and "The New Americanism in Catholic Historiography," *U.S. Catholic Historian,* forthcoming. Reprinted by permission of the publishers.

1. William A. Craigie and James R. Hulbert, *A Dictionary of American English on Historical Principles,* 4 vols. (Chicago, 1938–44); Mitford M. Mathews, *A Dictionary of Americanisms on Historical Principles,* 2 vols. (Chicago, 1951).

2. Mathews, *Dictionary of Americanisms,* 27; cf. Craigie and Hulbert, *Dictionary of American English,* 1:44–45.

3. Quoted in Robert F. Hueston, *The Catholic Press and Nativism, 1840–1860* (New York, 1976), 308–9 (emphasis in original).

4. Joseph F. Gower and Richard M. Leliaert, eds., *The Brownson-Hecker Correspondence* (Notre Dame, Ind., 1979), 182–83; the best biography is Thomas R. Ryan, *Orestes A. Brownson* (Huntington, Ind., 1976).

5. Orestes A. Brownson, "Native Americanism," *Brownson's Quarterly Review,* 11 (July, 1854), 328–54; Brownson, "The Know-Nothings," ibid., 11 (October 1854), 447–87.

6. Orestes A. Brownson, "Parochial Schools and Education," *Brownson's Quarterly Review,* 16 (July 1859), 324–42; quotation from 331. For a careful study of Brownson's shifting views on education, see James M. McDonnell, *Orestes A. Brownson and Nineteenth-Century Catholic Education* (New York, 1988).

7. Orestes A. Brownson, "The Rights of the Temporal," *Brownson's Quarterly Review,* 17 (October 1860), 464. For detailed treatment of this period of Brownson's life, see Ryan, *Brownson,* 455–612, esp. 597–612 for evaluation of his liberalism.

8. Brownson, "Know Nothings," 486. The New York Catholic magazine the *Metropolitan,* 2 (August 1854), 442 used the word *Americanism* in discussing Brownson's article "Native Americanism."

9. Orestes A. Brownson, "Conversations of Our Club," *Brownson's Quarterly Review,* 15 (April 1858), 189–90.

10. These generalizations are based on the literature discussed later in this essay. For the most recent scholarly overview of the Americanist era, see Gerald P. Fogarty,

The Vatican and the American Hierarchy from 1870 to 1965 (1982; Wilmington, Del., 1985), chaps. 2–7.

11. For Brownson, "Know Nothings," 486; for Ireland, *St. Paul Northwestern Chronicle*, October 26, 1888.

12. The pope's letter is reprinted in Thomas T. McAvoy, *The Great Crisis in American Catholic History, 1895–1900* (Chicago, 1957), 379–91.

13. McAvoy introduced this threefold distinction in his "Americanism and Frontier Catholicism," *Review of Politics*, 5 (July 1943), 276; repeated it, with the comment quoted in the text, in his "Americanism, Fact and Fiction," *Catholic Historical Review*, 31 (July 1945), 134–35; and left it essentially unmodified in his *Great Crisis*, 349.

14. William Barry, " 'Americanism,' True and False," *North American Review*, 169 (July 1899), 42–43.

15. Peter Guilday, "The Church in the United States (1870–1920): A Retrospect of Fifty Years," *Catholic Historical Review*, 6 (January 1921), 544. For the Hecker biography and the controversy in France, see McAvoy, *Great Crisis*, chap. 4.

16. Denis J. O'Connell, "A New Idea in the Life of Father Hecker," is reproduced in Felix Klein, *Americanism: A Phantom Heresy* (Atchison, Kans., 1951), 71–75; Gerald P. Fogarty, *The Vatican and the Americanist Crisis: Denis J. O'Connell, American Agent in Rome, 1885–1903* (Rome, 1974) both reprints it (319–26) and analyzes it (262ff.).

17. For O'Connell's admission, see McAvoy, *Great Crisis*, 174n.; for the single occurrence of *Americanism* in the Hecker biography, see Walter Elliott, *Life of Father Hecker* (New York, 1891), 339.

18. Arthur Preuss, "The Passing of the 'Nationality Question,' " *Review*, 7 (December 6, 1900), 289–90; for "national apostasy," see ibid., 3 (April 23, 1896), 1.

19. These matters are discussed at length in Philip Gleason, *The Conservative Reformers: German-American Catholics and the Social Order* (Notre Dame, Ind., 1968).

20. Michael Williams, *American Catholics and the War: National Catholic War Council, 1917–1921* (New York, 1921); quotations from 69–70, 43. The only time Williams used the word *Americanism* in his historical review (38), it referred to the American cause in the Revolutionary War.

21. Ibid., 339–40.

22. John A. Lapp, "Bogus Propaganda," *National Catholic Welfare Council Bulletin*, 1 (June–July 1920), 9. For Catholic Americanization work, see Richard M. Linkh, *American Catholicism and European Immigrants, 1900–1924* (New York, 1975), chaps. 10–11.

23. Frederick J. Kinsman, *Americanism and Catholicism* (New York, 1924), esp. 57–58, 127–31, for the author's views on the need for immigrant assimilation and the role of the Catholic church in this area.

24. Robert B. Clements, "*The Commonweal*, 1924–1938: The Williams-Shuster Years" (Ph.D. diss., University of Notre Dame, 1972), chap. 4.

25. Michael Williams, *The Shadow of the Pope* (New York, 1932); see also the essay entitled "The Present Position of Catholics in the United States," in Michael Williams, *Catholicism and the Modern Mind* (New York, 1928), 95–128.

26. This view was based on the supposed congruence between the "higher law" basis of American constitutionalism and the natural law teachings of medieval Catholic theologians, particularly the point that political authority derived its legitimacy from the consent of the people.

27. George N. Shuster, *The Catholic Spirit in America* (New York, 1927), 90.

28. John Cogley, "American Catholic Panorama," in Eugene K. Culhane, ed., *American Catholic Horizons* (New York, 1966), 269.

29. David J. O'Brien, *American Catholics and Social Reform: The New Deal Years* (New York, 1968), 220.

30. John A. Lapp, "Christian Principles Applied to the Building Trades," *Proceedings, First National Catholic Social Action Conference* (Milwaukee, Wis., 1938), 288–94.

31. Theodore Maynard, *The Story of American Catholicism* (New York, 1941), chap. 25. The only major works to discuss Americanism before the 1940s were Allen Sinclair Will, *Life of Cardinal Gibbons, Archbishop of Baltimore*, 2 vols. (New York, 1922); and Frederick J. Zwierlein, *The Life and Letters of Bishop McQuaid*, 3 vols. (Rochester, N.Y., 1925–27).

32. For McAvoy's articles, see above, n. 13. The other works mentioned are: Daniel F. Reilly, *The School Controversy (1891–1893)* (Washington, D.C., 1943); Vincent F. Holden, "A Myth in 'L'Americanisme,' " *Catholic Historical Review*, 31 (July 1945), 154–70; John J. Meng, "Cahensylism: The First Stage, 1883–1891," ibid., 31 (January 1946), 389–413; Meng, "Cahensylism: The Second Chapter, 1891–1910," ibid., 32 (October 1946), 302–40; Meng, "Growing Pains in the American Catholic Church, 1880–1908," *Historical Records and Studies*, 36 (1947), 17–67.

33. McAvoy, *Great Crisis*; Klein, *Americanism*; John Tracy Ellis, *The Life of James Cardinal Gibbons*, 2 vols. (Milwaukee, Wis., 1952); James H. Moynihan, *The Life of Archbishop John Ireland* (New York, 1953); Patrick H. Ahern, *The Life of John J. Keane* (Milwaukee, Wis., 1955); Robert D. Cross, *The Emergence of Liberal Catholicism in America* (Cambridge, Mass., 1958). Two other important works were Henry J. Browne, *The Catholic Church and the Knights of Labor* (Washington, D.C., 1949); and Colman J. Barry, *The Catholic Church and German Americans* (Milwaukee, Wis., 1953).

34. Will Herberg, *Protestant-Catholic-Jew: An Essay in American Religious Sociology* (New York, 1955), chap. 7; Walter J. Ong, *Frontiers of American Catholicism* (New York, 1957), 20–23; Ong, *American Catholic Crossroads* (1959; New York, 1962), 25 and chap. 3; Daniel Callahan, *The Mind of the Catholic Layman* (New York, 1963), chap. 3. See also Aaron I. Abell, *American Catholicism and Social Action: A Search for Social Justice, 1865–1950* (Garden City, N.Y., 1960), 24.

35. For Guilday's unwillingness to lift the lid on Americanism, see Philip Gleason, *Keeping the Faith: American Catholicism Past and Present* (Notre Dame, Ind., 1987), 248, n. 11; Lawrence V. McDonnell, "Walter Elliott and the Hecker Tradition in the Americanist Era," *U.S. Catholic Historian*, 3 (1983), 129–30. For other evidence of lingering inhibitions, see the unpaginated "Preface about This Little Book" in Frederick J. Zwierlein, *Letters of Archbishop Corrigan and Bishop McQuaid and Allied Documents* (Rochester, N.Y., 1946).

36. See above, chaps. 3, 8.

37. See the collection entitled *Catholicism in America. A Series of Articles from the Commonweal* (New York, 1954).

38. Joseph Clifford Fenton, "The Teaching of *Testem Benevolentiae*," *American Ecclesiastical Review*, 129 (August 1953), 124–33. McAvoy's threefold differentiation of Americanism (see above at n. 13) tacitly acknowledged the heretical potentialities of the liberals' position.

39. McAvoy's threefold distinction (see above, n. 13) is the most sophisticated version of the view that the Americanists did not hold the reprobated positions. "Phantom heresy" comes from the title of Klein's memoirs. Cardinal Gibbons spoke for the Americanists themselves in writing to Leo XIII: "This doctrine, which I deliberately

call extravagant and absurd, this Americanism as it is called, has nothing in common with the views, aspirations, doctrine and conduct of Americans." Quoted in John Tracy Ellis, *American Catholicism* (Chicago, 1956), 119.

40. Thomas T. McAvoy, "Liberalism, Americanism, Modernism," *Records of the American Catholic Historical Society of Philadelphia*, 63 (December 1952), 225–31; Ellis, review in *Theological Studies*, 19 (1958), 239.

41. James Hennesey, *The First Council of the Vatican: The American Experience* (New York, 1963).

42. Examples are: David F. Sweeney, *The Life of John Lancaster Spalding* (New York, 1965); David P. Killen, "Americanism Revisited: John Spalding and *Testem Benevolentiae*," *Harvard Theological Review*, 66 (October 1973), 413–54; Fogarty, *O'Connell*; R. Emmett Curran, *Michael Augustine Corrigan and the Shaping of Conservative Catholicism in America, 1878–1902* (New York, 1978); Thomas E. Wangler, "Emergence of John J. Keane as a Liberal Catholic and Americanist," *American Ecclesiastical Review*, 166 (September 1972), 457–78; Wangler, "John Ireland and the Origins of Liberal Catholicism in the United States," *Catholic Historical Review*, 56 (January 1971), 617–29; Marvin R. O'Connell, *John Ireland and the American Catholic Church* (St. Paul, Minn., 1988).

43. Thomas E. Wangler, "The Birth of Americanism: 'Westward the Apocalyptic Candlestick,'" *Harvard Theological Review*, 65 (July 1972), 415–36; Wangler, "American Catholic Expansionism: 1886–1894," ibid., 75 (1982), 369–93; Fogarty, *Vatican and American Hierarchy*.

44. James Hennesey, *American Catholics: A History of the Roman Catholic Community in the United States* (New York, 1981), chap. 15; Jay Dolan, *The American Catholic Experience: A History from Colonial Times to the Present* (Garden City, N.Y., 1985), chap. 11; David O'Brien, *Public Catholicism* (New York, 1989), chap. 5. See also O'Brien, *The Renewal of American Catholicism* (New York, 1972); Patrick W. Carey, *American Catholic Religious Thought* (New York, 1987).

45. For guides to this new work, see John Farina, ed., *Hecker Studies: Essays on the Thought of Isaac Hecker* (New York, 1983); and the March/April 1989 issue of *Catholic World*, which is devoted to "Isaac Hecker and the Future of the American Church."

46. The most recent work here is R. Scott Appleby, *Church and Age Unite: The Modernist Impulse in American Catholicism* (Notre Dame, Ind., 1991); more generally, see Ronald Burke, "Catholic Modernism in the Labor of Centuries," *Religious Studies Review*, 7 (October 1981), 291–98.

47. See Margaret Mary Reher, "The Church and the Kingdom of God in America: The Ecclesiology of the Americanists," (Ph.D. diss., Fordham University, 1972); Reher, "Pope Leo XIII and Americanism," *Theological Studies*, 34 (1973), 679–89; Reher, *American Catholic Intellectual Life* (New York, 1989), chap. 4; Killen, "Americanism Revisited."

48. Margaret Mary Reher, "Americanism and Modernism—Continuity or Discontinuity," *U.S. Catholic Historian*, 1 (Summer 1981), 87–103; Christopher J. Kauffman, *Tradition and Transformation in Catholic Culture* (New York, 1988), chap. 7; Dolan, *American Catholic Experience*, 310–11. See also, however, Hennessey, *American Catholics*, 197; Gerald P. Fogarty, *American Catholic Biblical Scholarship* (San Francisco, 1989), 76–77.

49. Joseph P. Chinnici, *Living Stones: The History and Structure of Catholic Spiritual Life in the United States* (New York, 1989), chaps. 1–4; Patrick W. Carey, *People, Priests, and Prelates: Ecclesiastical Democracy and the Tensions of Trusteeism*

(Notre Dame, Ind., 1987); Dolan, *American Catholic Experience*, chap. 4; Reher, *Catholic Intellectual Life*, chap. 1; O'Brien, *Public Catholicism*, chap. 2; Thomas W. Spalding, *The Premier See: A History of the Archdiocese of Baltimore, 1789–1989* (Baltimore, Md., 1989), 17–20 and chaps. 1–2.

50. Dolan, *American Catholic Experience*, esp. chaps. 4, 8, 11, 14; quotation from 454.

51. Dennis P. McCann, *New Experiment in Democracy: The Challenge for American Catholicism* (Kansas City, Mo., 1987), chap. 1 and pp. 163, 165.

52. George Weigel, *Catholicism and the Renewal of American Democracy* (New York, 1987); Michael Novak, *Freedom with Justice: Catholic Social Thought* (San Francisco, 1984); Richard John Neuhaus, *The Catholic Moment* (San Francisco, 1987).

53. O'Brien, *Public Catholicism*, 242–52; Joseph Varacalli, *Toward the Establishment of Liberal Catholicism in America* (Lanham, Md., 1983); and, among a number of similar articles: Varacalli, "The Constitutive Elements of the Idea of an 'American' Catholic Church," *Social Justice Review*, 80 (May–June 1989), 85–91; Michael Schwartz, "The Restorationist Perspective: Catholic Challenge to Secularist America," in Joe Holland and Anne Barsanti, eds., *American and Catholic: The New Debate* (South Orange, N.J., 1988), 71–96.

54. George Weigel and Joseph Varacalli are both explicitly critical of the "new Americanist" orientation in historiography. See Weigel, "Telling the American Catholic Story," *First Things*, 1 (November 1990), 43–49; Varacalli, "Review: The 'Remakers' of American Catholic History," *Faith and Reason*, 16 (Winter 1990), 387–405. For a detached survey of the contending schools of thought, see Avery Dulles, "Catholicism and American Culture: The Uneasy Dialogue," *America*, 162 (January 27, 1990), 54–59.

55. The reversal is strikingly illustrated in the case of Andrew M. Greeley. His popular history of American Catholicism, *The Catholic Experience* (Garden City, N.Y., 1967), heartily endorsed Americanization; his bicentennial article, "Catholicism in America: Two Hundred Years and Counting," *Critic*, 34 (Summer 1976), 14–47, 54–70 was sharply critical of Americanization.

56. I believe, however, that an analogy can be drawn between immigrant assimilation and the challenge confronting the Catholic church after Vatican II. See Gleason, *Keeping the Faith*, chap. 3.

57. H. Richard Niebuhr, *Christ and Culture* (New York, 1951).

Index